FLYBOYS

FLYBOYS

A TRUE STORY OF COURAGE

James Bradley

Little, Brown and Company
Boston New York London

First Edition

Maps by George Ward
Photograph of Chichi Jima by Minoru Ota
Chapter opener illustrations by Grady York appear courtesy of Pearl J. York Diffenderfer
Design by Bernard Klein

The author is grateful for permission to include excerpts from the following previously copyrighted material: Copyright © 1992 *Japan at War: An Oral History* by Haruko Taya Cook and Theodore F. Cook. Reprinted by permission of the New Press. (800) 233-4830. Butow, Robert J.; *Tojo and the Coming of the War.* Copyright © 1961 by Princeton University Press. Reprinted by permission of Princeton University Press. English translation copyright © 1995 by the Pacific Basin Institute. From Frank Gibney, ed., and Beth Cary, trans., *Senso: The Japanese Remember the Pacific War.* Letters to the Editor of *Asahi Shimbun* (Armonk, NY: M.E. Sharpe, 1995), pp. 9, 23, 27, 28, 30, 54, 65, 96, 192. Reprinted with permission. From *The Doolittle Raid: America's Daring First Strike Against Japan* by Carroll V. Glines. Copyright © 1988 by Carroll V. Glines. (Orion Books, 1988; Schiffer Publishing Ltd., 1991.) Reprinted by permission of Carroll V. Glines. From *Hidden Horrors: Japanese War Crimes in World War II* by Toshiyuki Takaka. Copyright © by Westview Press. Reprinted by permission of Westview Press, a member of Perseus Books, L.L.C. From *War Without Mercy* by John Dower, copyright © 1986 by John W. Dower. Used by permission of Pantheon Books, a division of Random House, Inc. From *Embracing Defeat: Japan in the Wake of World War II* by John W. Dower. Copyright © 1999 by John W. Dower. Used by permission of W. W. Norton & Company, Inc. From *Downfall: The End of the Japanese Imperial Empire* by Richard Frank, copyright © 1999 by Richard Frank. Used by permission of Random House, Inc. *Hell in the Pacific: From Pearl Harbor to Hiroshima* by Jonathan Lewis and Ben Steele. (London and Oxford: Channel 4 Books, an imprint of Macmillan Publishers, Ltd., London, 2001.) Used by permission of Macmillan Publishers, Ltd.

Library of Congress Cataloging-in-Publication Data

Bradley, James.
  Flyboys : a true story of courage / James Bradley — 1st ed.
    p. cm.
  Includes bibliographical references and index.
  ISBN 0-316-10584-8
  1. World War, 1939–1945 — Atrocities — Japan — Chichi Island. 2. World War, 1939–1945 — Japan — Chichi Island. 3. World War, 1939–1945 — Prisoners and prisons, Japanese — Biography. 4. Chichi Island (Japan) — History, Military — 20th century. 5. Air pilots, Military — United States — Biography. 6. Prisoners of war — United States — History — 20th century. 7. Prisoners of war — Japan — Chichi Island — History — 20th century. 8. War crime trials — Guam. I. Title.

D804.J3B73 2003
940.54'05'09528 — dc21   2003044725

10 9 8 7 6 5 4 3 2 1

Q-KP

Printed in the United States of America

Dedicated to

Jimmy Dye, Glenn Frazier, Floyd Hall, Marve Mershon,
Warren Earl Vaughn, Dick Woellhof, Grady York,
the Unidentified Airman, and to all Others

Contents

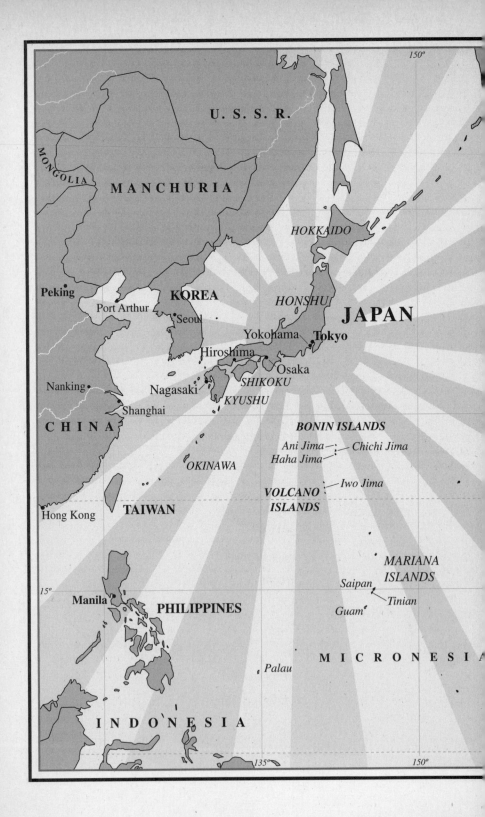

165° 180° 165°

45°

Pacific

| 0 | 500 | Miles | 1000 |

0   500   1000   Kilometers

Scale at Equator

30°

Midway Island

TROPIC OF CANCER

Wake Island

HAWAII

P a c i f i c

15°

O c e a n

MARSHALL
ISLANDS

EQUATOR

165°   180°   165°

Chichi Jima

1. General Yoshio Tachibana's headquarters
   Dick Woellhof, Floyd Hall, Marve Mershon, Jimmy Dye,
   Grady York, and Warren Earl Vaughn were tied up here.

2. Major Yoshitaka Horie's headquarters
   Floyd Hall, Marve Mershon, Jimmy Dye, Grady York, and
   Warren Earl Vaughn were questioned here.

3. 307th Battalion's rifle range
   Dick Woellhof and Grady York were killed here.

4. Warren Earl Vaughn crashed into the water here.

5. Mount Yoake
   Jimmy Dye and Warren Earl Vaughn spent time at the radio station
   here, and Jimmy was killed nearby.

6. Mount Asahi
   The radio station here was George Bush's main target.

7. The cliff from which Iwatake-san observed George Bush
   floating in the water

8. Major Sueo Matoba's cave

9. 307th Battalion headquarters
   General Tachibana and Major Matoba partied here.

10. 308th Battalion headquarters
    Floyd Hall and Marve Mershon were brought ashore here after
    their crash. (Glenn Frazier swam away from Chichi Jima to the
    small island of Ani Jima.) Floyd Hall and Glenn Frazier were later
    killed near here.

11. Omura Cemetery
    Marve Mershon was killed here.

12. Warren Earl Vaughn was killed here.

13. Bill Connell and Dick Woellhof parachuted into the water here.

14. Bill Connell, tied to a tree, saw Dick Woellhof here.

15. George Bush parachuted into the water near here.

16. Floyd Hall, Marve Mershon, and Glenn Frazier crash-landed
    near here.

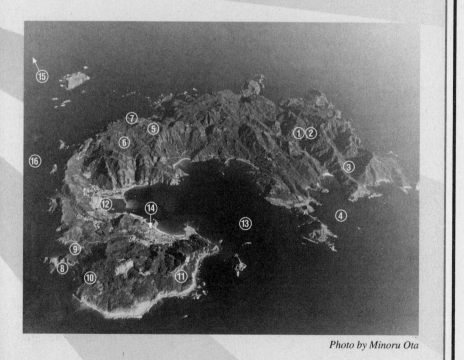

Photo by Minoru Ota

FLYBOYS

Declassified

All these years I had this nagging feeling these guys wanted their story told.

— *Bill Doran*

THE e-mail was from Iris Chang, author of the groundbreaking bestseller *The Rape of Nanking*. Iris and I had developed a professional relationship after the publication of my first book, *Flags of Our Fathers*. In her e-mail, Iris suggested I contact a man named Bill Doran in Iowa. She said Bill had some "interesting" information.

This was in early February 2001. I was hearing many "interesting" war stories at that point. *Flags of Our Fathers* had been published recently. The book was about the six Iwo Jima flagraisers. One of them was my father.

Indeed, scarcely a day passed without someone suggesting a topic for my next book. So I was curious as I touched his Iowa number on my New York telephone keypad.

Bill quickly focused our call on a tall stack of papers on his kitchen table. Within twenty minutes I knew I had to look Bill in the eye and see that stack. I asked if I could catch the first plane out the next day.

"Sure. I'll pick you up at the airport," Bill offered. "Stay at my place. It's just me and Stripe, my hunting dog, here. I have three empty bedrooms. You can sleep in one."

Riding from the Des Moines airport in Bill's truck, I learned that Stripe was the best hunting dog in the world and that his seventy-six-year-old owner was a retired lawyer. Bill and Stripe spent their days hunting and fishing. Soon Bill and I were seated at his Formica-topped kitchen table. Between us was a pile of paper, a bowl of popcorn, and two gin and tonics.

The papers were the transcript of a secret war crimes trial held on Guam in 1946. Fifty-five years earlier, Bill, a recent U.S. Naval Academy graduate, had been ordered to attend the trial as an observer. Bill was instructed to report to the "courtroom," a huge Quonset hut. At the entrance, a Marine guard eyed the twenty-one-year-old. After finding Bill's name on the approved list, he shoved a piece of paper across a table.

"Sign this," the Marine ordered matter-of-factly. Everybody was required to.

Bill read the single-spaced navy document. The legal and binding language informed young Bill that he was never to reveal what he would hear in that steaming Quonset hut / courtroom.

Bill signed the secrecy oath and he signed another copy late that afternoon when he left the trial. He would repeat this process every morning and every afternoon for the trial's duration. And when it was over, Bill returned home to Iowa. He kept silent but could not forget what he had heard.

Then, in 1997, Bill noticed a tiny newspaper item announcing that vast stashes of government documents from 1946 had been declassified. "When I realized the trial was declassified," Bill said, "I thought, Maybe I can do something for these guys now."

As a lawyer, Bill had spent his professional life ferreting out documents. He made some inquiries and dedicated eleven months to following where they led. Then one day, a boxed transcript arrived in the mail from Washington. Bill told Stripe they weren't going hunting that day.

The transcript contained the full proceedings of a trial establishing the fates of eight American airmen — Flyboys — downed in waters in the vicinity of Iwo Jima during World War II. Each was shot down during bombing runs against Chichi Jima, the next island north of Iwo Jima. Iwo Jima was coveted for its airstrips, Chichi Jima for its communications stations. Powerful short- and long-wave receivers and transmitters atop Chichi's Mount Yoake and Mount Asahi were the critical communications link between Imperial Headquarters in Tokyo and Japanese troops in the Pacific. The radio stations had to be destroyed, the U.S. military decided, and the Flyboys had been charged with doing so.

A stack of papers my brother found in my dad's office closet after his death in 1994 had launched me on a quest to find my father's past. Now, on Bill's table, I was looking at the stack of papers that would become the first step in another journey.

On the same day my father and his buddies raised that flag on Iwo Jima, Flyboys were held prisoner just 150 miles away on Chichi Jima. But while everyone knows the famous Iwo Jima photo, no one knew the story of these eight Chichi Jima Flyboys.

Nobody knew for a reason: For over two generations, the truth about their demise was kept secret. The U.S. government decided the facts were so horrible that the families were never told. Over the decades, relatives of the airmen wrote letters and even traveled to Washington, D.C., in search of the truth. Well-meaning bureaucrats turned them away with vague cover stories.

"All those years I had this nagging feeling these guys wanted their story told," Bill said.

Eight mothers had gone to their graves not knowing the fates of their lost sons. Sitting at Bill's table, I suddenly realized that now I knew what the Flyboys' mothers had never learned.

History buffs know that 22,000 Japanese soldiers defended Iwo Jima. Few realize that neighboring Chichi Jima was defended by even more — Japanese troops numbering 25,000. Whereas Iwo had flat areas suitable for assault from the sea, Chichi had a hilly inland and a craggy coast. One Marine who later examined the defenses of both islands told me, "Iwo was hell. Chichi would have been impossible." Land troops — Marines — would neutralize Iwo's threat. But it was up to the Flyboys to take out Chichi.

The U.S. tried to blow up Chichi Jima's communications stations for quite some time. Beginning in June of 1944, eight months before the Iwo Jima invasion, American aircraft carriers surrounded Chichi

Jima. These floating airports catapulted steel-encased Flyboys off their decks into the air. The mission of these young airmen was to fly into the teeth of Chichi Jima's lethal antiaircraft guns, somehow dodge the hot metal aimed at them, and release their loads of bombs onto the reinforced concrete communications cubes atop the island's twin peaks.

The WWII Flyboys were the first to engage in combat aviation in large numbers. In bomber jackets, posing with thumbs up, they epitomized masculine glamour. They were cool, and they knew it, and any earthbound fool had to know it too. Their planes were named after girlfriends and pinups, whose curvy forms or pretty faces sometimes adorned their sides. And inside the cockpit, the Flyboys were lone knights in an age of mass warfare.

In the North Pacific in 1945, the Flyboys flew the original "missions impossible." Climbing into 1940s-era tin cans with bombs strapped below their feet, they hurtled off carrier decks into howling winds or took off from island airfields. Sandwiched between blue expanses of sky and sea, Flyboys would wing toward distant targets, dive into flak shot from huge guns, and drop their lethal payloads. With their hearts in their throats, adrenaline pumping through their veins, the Flyboys then had to dead-reckon their way back to a tiny speck of landing deck or to a distant airfield their often-damaged planes never made it to.

The Flyboys were part of an air war that dwarfed the land war below. In 1945, the endgame in the northern Pacific was the incineration of Japan. This required two layers of bombers in the sky — huge B-29s lumbering high above with their cargo of napalm to burn cities, and smaller, lower-flying carrier-based planes to neutralize threats to the B-29s. My father on Iwo Jima shared the same mission with the Chichi Jima Flyboys: to make the skies safe for the B-29s.

Japanese military experts would later agree that the napalm dropped by these B-29s had more to do with Japan's surrender than the atomic bombs. Certainly, napalm killed more Japanese civilians than died at Hiroshima and Nagasaki combined.

Most of the Chichi Jima Flyboys fought and died during the worst killing month in the history of all warfare — a thirty-day period in February and March of 1945 when the dying in WWII reached its climax. If you look at a graph charting casualties over the four years of the Pacific war, you will see the line jump dramatically beginning with the battle of Iwo Jima and the Flyboys' assaults against mainland Japan. And few realize the U.S. killed more Japanese civilians than Japanese soldiers and sailors. This was war at its most disturbing intensity.

It was a time of obscene casualties, a time when grandparents burned to death in cities aflame, and *kamikaze* sons swooped out of the sky to immolate themselves against American ships. It was the time of the worst battle in the history of the United States Marine Corps, the most decorated month in U.S. history, a valorous and brutish time of all-out slaughter.

By February of 1945, logical, technocratic American military experts had concluded that Japan was beaten. Yet the empire would not surrender. Americans judged the Japanese to be "fanatic" in their willingness to fight with no hope of victory. But Japan was not fighting a logical war. Japan, an island nation, existed in its own moral universe, enclosed in a separate ethical biosphere. Japanese leaders believed that "Japanese spirit" was the key to beating back the barbarians at their door. They fought because they believed they could not lose.

And while America cheered its flyers as its best and brightest, the Japanese had a very different view of those who wreaked havoc from the skies. To them, airmen who dropped napalm on defenseless civilians living in paper houses were the nonhuman devils.

This is a story of war, so it is a story of death. But it is not a story of defeat. I have tracked down the eight Flyboys' brothers and sisters, girlfriends, and aviator buddies who drilled and drank with them. Their relatives and friends gave me photos, letters, and medals. I have scoured yearbooks, logbooks, and little black books to find out who they were and what they mean to us today. I read and reread six thousand pages of trial documents and conducted hundreds of interviews in the U.S. and Japan.

The families and friends of the Flyboys could only tell me so much. Their hometown buddies and relatives had stories of their youth and enlistment. Their military comrades had remembrances from training camp up until they disappeared. But none of them — not even the next of kin or the bunkmates who served in the Pacific with them — knew exactly what happened to these eight on Chichi Jima. It was all a dark hole, an unfathomable secret.

In Japan, some knew, but they had kept their silence. I met Japanese soldiers who knew the Flyboys as prisoners. I heard stories about how they were treated, about their interrogations, about how some of the Flyboys had lived among their captors for weeks. I met soldiers who swapped jokes with them, who slept in the same rooms.

And I ventured to Chichi Jima. Chichi Jima is part of an island chain due south of Tokyo the Japanese call the Ogasawara Islands. On English maps the chain is called the Bonin Islands. The name Bonin is a French cartographer's corruption of the old Japanese word *munin,* which means "no man." These islands were uninhabited for most of Japan's existence. They literally contained "no peoples" or "no mans." So Bonin translates loosely into English as No Mans Land.

I hacked through forest growth in No Mans Land to uncover the last days of the Flyboys. I stood on cliffs with Japanese veterans who pointed to where they saw the Flyboys parachute into the Pacific. I strode where Flyboys had walked. I heard from eyewitnesses who told me much. Others revealed a great deal by refusing to tell me anything.

Eventually, I understood the facts about what happened to Dick, Marve, Glenn, Grady, Jimmy, Floyd, Warren Earl, and the Unknown Airman. I comprehended the "what" of their fates.

But to determine the "why" of their story, I had to embark upon another journey. A trip back in time, back 149 years, to another century. Back to when the first American military men walked in No Mans Land.

CHAPTER TWO

Civilize-ation

When others use violence we must be violent too.

— *Yukichi Fukuzawa, quoted in* Japan: A Modern History

IN the nineteenth century, the United States transformed itself from thirteen tiny colonies hugging the eastern seaboard to a continental giant stretching from sea to shining sea. America accomplished this with a government policy of ethnic cleansing. As ethnobiologist Melvin Gilmore later observed: "The people of the European race in coming into the New World have not really sought to make friends of the native population, or to make adequate use of the plants, or the animals indigenous to this continent, but rather to exterminate everything they found here and to supplant it with plants and animals to which they were accustomed."

Alexis de Tocqueville, the perceptive chronicler of early America, noted that he often heard fine Christian Americans casually discuss the extermination of Indians:

This world here belongs to us, they add. God, in refusing the first inhabitants the capacity to become civilized, has destined them in advance to inevitable destruction. The true owners of this continent are those who know how to take advantage of its riches. Satisfied with this reasoning, the American goes to the church, where he hears a minister of the Gospel repeat to him that men are brothers and that the Eternal Being, who has made them all in the same mould, has imposed on them the duty to help one another.

There was a sense among white European Christians of themselves as civilized and "Others" who were not. The slaughter of these Others brought little hand-wringing — it was, after all, the normal course of things in the nineteenth century, the original era of Darwinian thought. In his book *The Descent of Man,* Charles Darwin predicted, "At some future period, not very distant as measured by centuries, the civilized races will almost certainly exterminate, and replace, the savage races throughout the world." Teddy Roosevelt, who often wrote of the winning of the West, observed, "Of course our whole national history has been one of expansion. . . . That the barbarians recede or are conquered, with the attendant fact that peace follows their retrogression or conquest, is due solely to the power of the mighty civilized races which have not lost the fighting instinct, and which by their expansion are gradually bringing peace into the red wastes where the barbarian peoples of the world hold sway."

Teddy, like so many of his countrymen, found nothing wrong in even the most barbaric American actions. In December of 1864, an audience in a Denver theater applauded wildly as on stage an ordained Methodist minister displayed the results of the latest encounter between the civilized races and the Others. The minister's name was John Chivington — Preacher John. Preacher John was a volunteer in the cavalry. Days earlier, he had led an attacking party to Sand Creek, Colorado, where they had surprised and massacred at least 150 Indian children, women, and old men. The braves had been away hunting.

What elicited the roars of approval from the Denver theater audience was not just Preacher John's tale of "victory" but the grisly evidence. A pile of hacked Indian penises brought laughter. Applause greeted American soldiers who displayed hats over which they had stretched the vaginal skin of Indian women.

None of Denver's civilized residents saw much wrong with this. No one was ever charged with any wrongdoing. The grateful people of Denver made Preacher John a deputy sheriff, a job he held until he died peacefully in his sleep forty-eight years later at the age of seventy-one.

Teddy Roosevelt not only approved of this atrocity, he thought it was one of the single great moments in American history. About the Sand Creek massacre he said, "In spite of certain most objectionable details . . . it was on the whole as righteous and beneficial a deed as ever took place on the frontier."

Almost the entire West was ethnically cleansed of Indians in the same manner, by American soldiers acting on government orders to remove the Red Devils from their land by imprisoning them on reservations or killing them. As Teddy said, "I don't go so far as to think that the only good Indians are dead Indians, but I believe nine out of every ten are, and I shouldn't like to inquire too closely into the case of the tenth."

The extermination and confinement of the Indians won America only part of the continent. Much of the West was held by Mexicans, people whom Senator Thomas Corwin of Ohio called a "half-savage, half-civilized race." Colonel Stephen Austin, who dealt with Mexicans for years, informed his government that "they want nothing but tails to be more brutes than the Apes." Unitarian minister Theodore Parker said that Mexicans were "a wretched people; wretched in their origin, history and character," a race destined, regardless of American policies, to "melt away as the Indians before the white man." American expansionists felt they had a "Manifest Destiny" to bring Christian civilization to Mexican lands. Or, as Walt Whitman, America's greatest poet, put it: "What has miserable, inefficient Mexico — with her superstition, her burlesque upon freedom, her actual tyranny by the few over the many — what has she to do with the great mission of peopling the new world with a noble race? Be it ours, to achieve that mission!"

President James Polk fomented a conflict Americans called "the Mexican War" (later, "the Mexican-American War"). The Mexicans referred to it as "the U.S. invasion." Ulysses S. Grant, later a general and president, fought in the war as a young man and wrote in his memoirs that "we were sent to provoke a fight" and that the war was "one of the most unjust ever waged by a stronger against a weaker nation." Mexico was unprepared for the invasion and after two years of slaughter ceded her vast territories of California, New Mexico, and what is now Nevada, Utah, Colorado, Wyoming, and parts of Arizona in the Treaty of Guadalupe Hidalgo.

On February 2, 1848, just as diplomats from the United States and

Mexico were about to sign the treaty, one of the Mexicans turned to American commissioner Nicholas Trist and remarked, "This must be a proud moment for you; no less proud for you than it is humiliating for us." To this, Commissioner Trist quickly replied, "We are making peace; let that be our only thought." But Trist later wrote to his wife, "Could those Mexicans have seen into my heart at that moment, they would have known that my feeling of shame as an American was far stronger than theirs could be as Mexicans. For though it would not have done for me to say so there, that was a thing for every right-minded American to be ashamed of, and I was ashamed of it, most cordially and intensely ashamed of it."

With new lands on the west coast and excellent new ports as bases, expansionists continued the tradition of gazing westward for opportunity, looking out to America's far west — the Pacific Ocean.

To the Americans of the day, the significance of the Pacific meant first and foremost oil. Generations before black crude was tapped from the earth, whale oil greased the gears of the Industrial Revolution and lit the streets of America. Wildcatters from New England roamed for years over the Pacific, which to them was "a vast field of warm-blooded oil deposits known as sperm whales." Whaling was big business, a major component of the American economy. Herman Melville estimated that by the 1840s the American whaling industry employed 18,000 men aboard 700 ships, reaping a harvest of $7 million annually.

The whaling business was driven by hardy seamen and entrepreneurs who risked fortunes and life and limb on dangerous multiyear voyages over a scarcely charted wilderness. One of these entrepreneurs was Nathaniel Savory, a Massachusetts native who sailed off to the Pacific in 1814 at the age of twenty. Savory spent ten years in and around Hawaii (then known as the Sandwich Islands), which was the main Pacific base for American crews who increasingly turned their attention to the rich whaling grounds near Japan.

Realizing a need for provisioning outposts nearer to Japan, Savory — in true manifest destiny Yankee spirit — looked west from Hawaii for a suitable harbor to found his whaling supply enterprise. Whalers stopping in Hawaii told him of a tiny uninhabited island near Japan with natural springs. So in May of 1830, at the age of thirty-six, Nathaniel Savory sailed west from Pearl Harbor with twenty-two other adventurous men and women on a three-thousand-mile-long trip to seek their futures on the beautiful island of Chichi Jima.

In 1848, Congressman Thomas King of Georgia, chairman of the U.S. House of Representatives' Committee on Naval Affairs, held hearings to discuss how America might span the Pacific. The government was already subsidizing four steamship lines in the Atlantic and the Caribbean. A Yankee line across the Pacific would be a significant boon to American commerce. But while steamships could conquer the Atlantic, the Pacific was far too wide.

The Pacific Ocean is the largest physical feature on the planet. If all the world's landmasses were placed in the Pacific, there would still be room left over for an additional Africa, Canada, United States, and Mexico. The Pacific is two and one half times larger than the Atlantic Ocean, hiding mountain ranges that dwarf the Himalayas.

The most compelling witness to testify before Congressman King's Naval Affairs Committee was the Navy Department's chief oceanographer, Lieutenant Matthew Maury. Lieutenant Maury placed a large globe before the committee's congressmen. Maury bent over his satchel and extracted a long piece of white string. He placed one end of the string on San Francisco. Then he ran the string across the blue expanse to the next landfall, the Hawaiian Islands. Steamships had proven their ability to reach Honolulu, 2,100 miles from San Francisco. But it was the next leg, from Honolulu to Shanghai, at 4,700 miles, that posed the big challenge. Marine engines of the time burned so much coal that if enough were brought along to fuel such a long journey, there would be scant room for any other cargo.

All eyes were fixed on Lieutenant Maury's globe as he ran the white string from Hawaii to Shanghai. The congressmen could see that the string ran through the Bonin Islands — No Mans Land — on its journey to Shanghai. Maury explained that if they established a coal depot there — perhaps on Chichi Jima — the steam trip to Shanghai was possible. Honolulu to Chichi was a distance of 3,200 miles. After coaling there, a steamship could easily make the last leg from Chichi Jima to Shanghai — a distance of 1,500 miles.

The implications of this simple demonstration were staggering, Lieutenant Maury explained to the congressmen. A letter, a person, or a pinch of tea now took eighty days to traverse the British route from

New York to Shanghai, which went across the Atlantic and around Cape Town, a distance of twenty thousand miles. By exploiting the strategic location of Chichi Jima, the U.S. could reduce the journey's length by two thirds. "It is in our power to establish and control the most rapid means of communicating with . . . China," Maury explained to the hushed room. "By establishing the quickest lines of communication to the Orient, the U.S. could break up the [British] channels of commerce [in] the Pacific and turn [these channels] through the U.S." It was clear to the congressmen that Lieutenant Maury was suggesting no less a prize than commercial domination of the Pacific.

There was one catch to the plan, however. No Mans Land lay perilously close to Japan. How would Japan react to America establishing a coaling station on Chichi Jima, so near its mainland? Did Japan consider No Mans Land part of its territory?

Nobody knew.

Japan was a closed book. Western ignorance of Japan was not the fault of the westerners but the design of the Japanese. For two hundred years, Japan had been shut tight. By national law, a Japanese could not leave Japan and no outsider was allowed in. Death sentences were meted out to any who gave foreigners information about the land of the gods. Almost no maps and no books existed in the English-speaking world describing the closed land.

Looking back now, what is amazing about the western lack of knowledge is that Japan was not some New Guinea backwater but arguably the most civilized, most urbanized, most highly organized, most literate and peaceful country in the world. Many historians say that Japan was enjoying the planet's highest standard of living at this time.

A reliable record of Japan's imperial rulers dates back to A.D. 300. Japan's founding fathers finished drafting Japan's constitution by A.D. 604. Around A.D. 1000, Lady Murasaki penned the world's first novel, *The Tale of Genji*.

According to Japan's "Bible," the *Kojiki* — the "Records of Ancient Matters," it was a female, the sun goddess Amaterasu, who created Japan. Amaterasu peopled it through her descendant Jimmu, Japan's first earthly emperor. Jimmu was of the Yamato (Mountain People) clan. As emperor, Jimmu's mission was *Hakko Ichiu,* which translated as "the eight corners of the world under one roof." For the

Japanese, the "world" was their islands and it was the mission of Jimmu's Yamato descendants to unite the islands' peoples under one imperial, holy house.

Christians were mortals born in sin whose belief in God offered them salvation. But the Japanese had god blood flowing through their veins. They had a direct connect to the heavens. The Americans might refer to their land as "blessed *by* God," but the Japanese were living in the "land *of* the gods."

All a Japanese had to do to affirm his belief that his land was blessed above all was open his eyes in the morning. There it was, goddess Amaterasu's sun rising over the Pacific islands, then proceeding over Japan and on to the rest of the world. Japan provided the world with light. (Japan's name for itself — Nippon — expresses this concept with *ni,* meaning "sun," and *pon,* meaning "origin." Thus Japan is the "Land of the Rising Sun.")

Isolated on an island archipelago, with no other peoples or foreign creeds to challenge their beliefs, generations of Japanese intensified the idea of Japan as the chosen land. But the gods could not keep peace within Japan, and for centuries civil wars raged. While the never-seen emperor lay secluded and impotent in his palace, a series of military dictators ruled. Finally, in 1600, the skilled warrior Ieyasu Tokugawa vanquished his enemies, emerged preeminent, and consolidated his control over the country.

Ieyasu Tokugawa was a visionary who dreamed of bringing eternal peace to Japan and establishing the House of Tokugawa to rule for the ages. To accomplish his goals, the shrewd Tokugawa did nothing less than remake the Japanese state and national character.

First, he had himself declared supreme ruler, or shogun, by the emperor. The emperor — who was an invisible nonentity to the ordinary Japanese — reigned from the ancient capital of Kyoto but did not rule. Instead, he was a virtual prisoner of the current military dictator. The shogun perpetuated the myth of imperial rule in exchange for having legitimacy conferred upon him. Tokugawa's title "shogun" is translated as "barbarian-expelling generalissimo." And the current barbarians were the Christians of the West.

The Japanese word for foreigner is *gaizin*. The prefix *gai* means "outside," and *zin* means "person." All foreigners were *gaizin* — "outside people." The term implied not just that *gaizin* were from outside

Japan, but also that they were outside the human race. *Gaizin* weren't just *semi*human but *non*human. This idea is captured by an anonymous account of the landing of a *gaizin* ship on Japanese shores during Tokugawa's time:

> From this ship emerged an unnamable creature, somewhat similar in shape to a human being, but looking rather like a long-nosed goblin. Upon close investigation, it was discovered that this was a being called a "Padre." The length of the nose was the first thing which attracted attention: it was like a conch shell attached by suction to his face. His head was small; on his hands and feet he had long claws, his teeth were longer than the teeth of a horse. What he was could not be understood at all; his voice was like the screech of an owl. One and all rushed out to see him, crowding all the roads.

When Portuguese missionaries had first landed in Japan in 1543, they found the Japanese naturally curious, hospitable, and highly refined. The missionaries were welcomed and their conversion efforts were tolerated. The missionary Saint Francis Xavier remarked, "I know not when to cease in speaking of the Japanese. They are truly the delight of my heart." By the time of Ieyasu Tokugawa's ascension as shogun, Portuguese and Spanish missionaries had made more than 300,000 converts in Japan. But Tokugawa noticed something was very different about this barbarian religion from the West.

Shintoism, the native animist religion of Japan, and Buddhism, which had been imported from India via China, were inclusionary faiths. One could bow before a Shinto shrine one minute and recite a Buddhist sutra the next with no conflict. But the Christian missionaries demanded that a choice be made. Christianity excluded other beliefs. Tokugawa soon became suspicious of a religion whose very First Commandment required loyalty to one jealous, non-Japanese god.

Tokugawa had also heard stories of how other countries had been subjugated after allowing missionaries in. As one Japanese writer observed, "When those barbarians plan to subdue a country they start by opening commerce and watch for a sign of weakness. If an opportunity is presented they will preach their alien religion to captivate the people's hearts. Once the people's allegiance has been shifted, they can be manipulated and nothing can be done to stop it."

Convinced that he could not establish a stable peace if the people's allegiance was to a *gaizin* god, in 1614, Tokugawa ordered all missionaries banished. Japanese Christians were given the choice of treading on a crucifix and renouncing the *gaizin* religion or being crucified themselves. Soon the West became synonymous with Christianity and any contact with *gaizin* was seen as a threat to Japan. The crucifix was a symbol of evil and Christ was referred to as "the devil of Japan." Foreign trade was abolished except through the Dutch, who agreed to be isolated from the Japanese populace and confined to a small prisonlike artificial island in Nagasaki Bay. Only one Dutch ship a year would enter Japan. And the Dutch traders were required to regularly step on a crucifix.

With the *gaizin* gone, Japan became an ideologically sealed archipelago. Shogun Tokugawa created a brilliant plan to bring eternal peace to the land of the gods. He rejiggered Japan's social order, decreeing a strictly hierarchal society with the military class — samurai — on top. Tokugawa ensured that his public servants were noble samurai who led with integrity. Their selfless leadership earned the loyalty of the people. Japanese society came to prize military virtues above all, and the preeminent virtue was strict obedience to the dominant military class. Woe to any mere mortal who did not instantly obey his military masters. "The Tokugawa code was clear: 'Common people who behave unbecomingly to members of the military class . . . may be cut down on the spot.'"

The House of Tokugawa's farsighted reordering of Japanese society resulted in *Taihai,* the "Great Peace" — over two hundred fifty years of Tokugawa family rule and no wars. For two and a half centuries, there was no Japanese army or Japanese navy. There was no need for large-scale military force. Tokugawa's system guaranteed that no external or internal conflicts would occur. It was an extraordinary stretch of absolute peace unmatched by any other nation over a comparable period of time.

The traditional arts for which Japan is now known flourished during the Great Peace. But the Japanese people forfeited all personal liberties in exchange for this unprecedented stability. There were thousands of rules of personal etiquette. "Laws listed two hundred and sixteen varieties of dress for everyone from the lowest serf to the emperor. The size, shape and color of the stitches were specified. What they could buy at the market, the types of houses they were allowed to build, whom they must bow to, the types of dolls children could play with, where a person could travel — laws imposed from on high governed the tiniest details of life in Japan."

Japan became the most regimented society in the world. Life was not about independent action or striking out on one's own, but recognizing one's "proper place" in the flywheel of society. Patterns of thought were firmly established. Proper decorum was more rigorously observed in Japan than in any other country in the world. This allowed a large population to live on cramped islands with little friction, but it also resulted in a people unusually dependent upon known rules of conduct and orders from above.

The Japanese population in 1850, thirty-one million people, was larger than that of the United States, at twenty-three million. Although no one realized it at the time, Tokyo (then called Edo) had become the world's largest and most vibrant city, with a population of over one million. (This at a time when Washington, D.C., had a population of thirty-five thousand, and pigs and chickens roamed the streets.) Japan was the most urbanized country in the world, with almost 7 percent of its population living in cities, compared with 2 percent in Europe. By many measures, Japan had the highest standard of living in the world, with a nationwide system of roads, a national marketing system, and "majestic citadels, many exceeding in size the largest castles built in medieval Europe" that "loomed over the countryside as awesome symbols of their prodigious strength."

In June of 1851, the thirteenth president of the United States met with U.S. Navy officials in the Oval Office to consider American expansion in the Pacific. By now, President Millard Fillmore was well aware of Lieutenant Maury's argument regarding the San Francisco–Honolulu–No Mans Land–Shanghai route. But Fillmore had political concerns. Americans were focused on digesting their recently acquired continental empire. The advantages of Pacific trade were not much of a hot button to a country with most of its citizenry still in the east. San Francisco's total population was under seven hundred people, and the entire Oregon territory held fewer than one thousand Americans.

But ambitious navy officers presented President Fillmore the political cover to establish a steamship route through Japan. It was an official report that would outrage the chattering classes and provide the pretext for the executive branch to project military might directly to No Mans Land and Japan. The report's name was "Documents Relative to the Empire of Japan." It detailed how the Japanese had treated a shipwrecked crew of American whalemen in an "inhumane and barbaric" fashion. A navy captain assured President Fillmore that "the facts of that case are of a character to excite the indignation of the people of the United States." The captain told Fillmore, "The nation stands upon strong vantage ground. We want accommodations for fuel and a depot for our steamers and we have a good cause for a quarrel."

A good cause for a quarrel. Congress had been slow to act on Maury's call for a Pacific steamship line, but when President Fillmore released "Documents Relative to the Empire of Japan," Congress bestirred itself and called for an investigation. Japanese officials had held the whalemen in protective custody, and they had been released to U.S. officials unharmed, but some facts galled the civilized American senators.

The report said Japanese officials had told the imprisoned whalemen that Christ was "the devil of Japan." And when a whaleman asked his jailor for a Christian Bible, "his keeper told him angrily, 'Don't speak of the Bible in Japan — it is not a good book.'" The senators were further outraged that one of the "common prisons" used to confine the whalemen was a former church and that the Americans had been made to "trample on [a brass crucifix] by putting the left foot on the cross and then the right foot."

And besides demeaning the Christian God, the Japanese claimed superiority for gods of their own. An American prisoner had complained of his mistreatment and threatened that the U.S. Navy would come to punish Japan. Upon hearing this, a Japanese official laughed and said that if American ships came, the *kamikaze* "would blow them away by aid of their priests."

Kamikaze means "god" (*kami*) "wind" (*kaze*). The *kamikaze* / god winds were central to Japan's self-conception as a divine, unconquerable land. The *kamikaze* was Japan's protective angel force. In 1274 and again in 1281, Kublai Khan had led his Mongol armies across the Sea of Japan on an amphibious invasion of Japan. Khan's forces were superior and Japan feared it would be conquered. But both attacks were repelled by the *kamikaze* / god winds, in the form of fierce ty-

19

phoons, which sank Mongol vessels and drowned more than 150,000 invaders. These miracle winds, appearing at just the right providential moment, convinced the Japanese that their country enjoyed unique spiritual protection and was thus impervious to foreign attack.

After a whipped-up congressional hearing on the treatment of the whalemen, Fillmore ordered Secretary of State Daniel Webster to dispatch a squadron of warships. Commodore Matthew Perry was appointed commander of this historic presidential mission to bring civilization to Japan. Perry was America's preeminent navy officer, with a tall, commanding presence. His mouth was stern and he had a luxuriant head of hair without a hint of gray despite his fifty-nine years of age. Perry agreed to go along with the cover story that the mission was about the mistreatment of American whalemen and that the "real object of the expedition should be concealed from public view." But once Perry was at sea and "free of Washington and the controversy surrounding steamship lines, he could state his objectives clearly: ports of refuge for whalers might be the ostensible reason for the Japan expedition, but the United States' global rivalry with England and the need to secure ports on a Pacific steamship line were its real raisons d'être." Perry made a beeline to Chichi Jima via the British route to the Orient.

Fifty-eight-year-old Nathaniel Savory must have been amazed when the belching steamship *Susquehanna,* towing the schooner *Saratoga,* sailed into Chichi Jima's harbor on June 15, 1853. Life on Chichi Jima had been a quiet affair for Savory and the thirty-nine other hardy colonists remaining from the original group that had sailed from Pearl Harbor twenty-three years earlier. The colonists had erected thatched-roof cottages and hollowed out logs for canoes; they planted crops and mended the nets used to catch fish and turtles. The weather was fairly constant year round — bright and sunny — with the summer months slightly hotter and more humid. The big event for the islanders was the arrival of whaling ships, which called for fresh water, supplies of fresh turtle and fish, vegetables, fruits, liquor, and occasional sexual services.

Perry beheld a beautiful mini Maui, a tropical slice of green jade in the Pacific. The commodore described Chichi Jima as "high, bold, and rocky, and . . . evidently of volcanic formation. [It is] green with verdure and a full growth of tropical vegetation, which is, here and there, edged with coral reefs." Chichi Jima, just twice the size of New York's Central Park, had "two prominent peaks . . . one which reaches an elevation of a thousand feet, the other eleven hundred. . . . They are clearly seen on entering the harbor."

On the morning of June 16, 1853, Perry and a contingent of sailors rowed ashore. No nation had exerted authority over Chichi Jima, so Perry proceeded to lay his claim. The commodore appointed Nathaniel Savory an agent of the U.S. Navy and formed a governing council with the delighted Savory as chief. On the island where navy Flyboys would later die, this navy commander then anointed Chichi Jima a key Pacific outpost for American power. On behalf of the United States, he purchased fifty acres of land from Savory for a price of fifty dollars, four cattle, five Shanghai sheep, and six goats. This historic transaction was proudly reported in the *Herald Tribune* of New York as representing the "first piece of land bought by Americans in the Pacific."

After a stay of three days, and confident that America now had a firm foothold in the North Pacific, Commodore Perry bid adieu to his new agent Savory and steamed away to continue his journey to mainland Japan.

Two weeks later, on Friday, July 8, 1853, four U.S. Navy ships bristling with civilization and sixty-one state-of-the-art cannon entered Tokyo Bay. Atop their masts flew the American flag, with thirty-one stars on a blue field.

Martians landing in spaceships with gamma-ray guns would not have caused more of an uproar.

Fishermen in the bay were the first to behold the huge, noisy, black-cloud-belching monsters. These men were not even aware of the existence of steam engines and suddenly there they were in front of them — giant dragons puffing smoke! A general alarm spread across the land. Temple bells rang as fleet-footed messengers spread out to warn that "the Black Ships of the Evil Men" had descended on the land of the gods.

The story grew as it spread. The word was that "one hundred thousand devils with white faces" were about to overrun the country. The world's largest city lay defenseless before alien guns. People panicked. Families ran from their homes with their valuables on their backs. Japanese newspaper artists sailed out to make sketches of the strange ships and the *gaizin*. Readers scooped up special editions with pictures of the "hairy barbarians" and their machines. Samurai who had never dressed for warfare worked to scrape rust from their spears. Throngs packed the shrines and temples praying to the gods for deliverance. People trembled and beseeched the gods to once again blow the *gaizin* away with another *kamikaze*.

In the drama that unfolded over the next few days, Commodore Perry played his role masterfully. He remained mysteriously secluded in his cabin like an Oriental potentate, refusing to reveal his august presence to the Japanese negotiators. He rebuffed all entreaties to go away or to retreat to Nagasaki.

Perry's ships, just thirty miles away from the capital, presented an insoluble dilemma for the Tokugawa shogunate. Japanese government dealings with barbarians had previously been small private affairs in Nagasaki, with only a few officials even aware of the *gaizin*'s presence. Now the entire nation knew. Commodore Perry with his steam engines and powerful cannon had more mechanized firepower on his four ships than was possessed by the entire nation of Japan. The shogun could not force the *gaizin* to leave. And if they ignored Perry's requests, would he bombard the capital? Were there more such powerful ships coming after these? Would the Japanese people take matters into their own hands and revolt? Ieyasu Tokugawa's descendant Shogun Ieyashi Tokugawa — the "barbarian-expelling generalissimo" — could not live up to his title.

Finally, after days of negotiating, Japanese authorities agreed to Perry's demand that he be allowed to come ashore to deliver a letter from President Fillmore.

On Thursday, July 14, 1853, two hundred and forty Americans — one hundred Marines, one hundred sailors, and forty musicians — all heavily armed and snappy in their blue-and-white dress uniforms — came ashore on fifteen launches. Commander Franklin Buchanan was the first out of the lead launch, making him the first American military man to set foot on the Japanese mainland.

Debonair Commodore Perry, who realized pageantry would impress his hosts, choreographed a fantastic spectacle. Stiff-backed Marines formed a smart honor guard as the navy band belted out martial tunes. Natty U.S. sailors paraded sprightly behind. When Perry disembarked, ships' cannon boomed and the band struck up "Hail Columbia," the expansionists' favorite tune. Two tall, handsome black Marines flanked Perry and caused a sensation — the Japanese didn't know black men existed. Thousands of civilians craned their necks for a look at the *gaizin.*

For the Americans, it was a trip back in time. The samurai — their hair pulled back in topknots — wore silk dresses and sandals and two dangling swords signifying their rank. Thousands of armor-encased soldier-archers with eight-foot longbows and pikes stood by. It was one of history's most extraordinary encounters. Two highly civilized cultures that viewed the other as uncivilized meeting for the first time.

Commodore Perry and his entourage sauntered into a grand reception hall specially built for the occasion. Unbeknownst to Perry, armed samurai crouched below the false floor in case the barbarians became violent. Perry was the first foreign ambassador received in Japan in two and a half centuries. The Japanese were not taking any chances.

With great ceremony, the commodore turned over a custom-made gold box in which lay President Fillmore's letter to the emperor. Upon receiving it, the Japanese hoped they were now finished with this foreign nuisance and presented Perry with a written response. Perry was taken aback when the last sentence was translated for him as, "Your letter being received, you will now leave."

Commodore Perry interpreted this last blunt line as a diplomatic slap at the United States — the country that had just acquired an independent base of power only six hundred miles due south of Tokyo. The commodore ordered his ships not to sail away but rather to go farther inland, up Tokyo Bay toward the capital. Perhaps, Perry thought, when the Japanese saw four American warships plumbing their channel depths and surveying their shore defenses, it "would produce a decided influence upon [the] government and cause a more favorable consideration of the President's letter."

A Japanese launch was hastily rowed out to confront the Evil Men in their belching Black Ships. A frantic representative of the shogun called out to Commander Buchanan that the Black Ships must turn back. "It's against Japanese law," the official pleaded. From the deck of his mighty steamship, the bemused commander looked down at the nervous official in his small launch. Clearly the Japanese were unschooled in the ways of foreign relations where might determined what was right.

Commander Buchanan called back to the official, "The United States Navy operates under American law wherever we go."

The next day, Commodore Perry did sail away from Japanese waters, promising to return the next year for a response from the emperor. His historic visits would have lasting repercussions in Japan. For almost two decades, controversy swirled regarding the best ways to deal with the dreaded barbarians and the new world that had been thrust upon the land of the gods.

But with the Civil War brewing back home, America lost interest in Pacific steamship lines and seizing territory in the North Pacific. Even Nathaniel Savory's written pleas to the State Department requesting annexation of No Mans Land by the U.S. fell upon deaf ears.

Eight and one half years after Perry's visit, Japan dispatched a warship on a foreign mission of its own. On January 17, 1862, a shocked Nathaniel Savory watched as a ship bristling with cannon, flying the Rising Sun flag, anchored in Chichi Jima's harbor. Diplomats rowed ashore and claimed all of No Mans Land for Japan. Savory tried his best to argue the case that Japan had no right to his little island. But glancing at the armed warship in the harbor, he realized they had the might and therefore possessed the right.

No Mans Land was Japan's first overseas conquest. Isolation and peace were now part of her past.

The Japanese had learned the lesson well.

Through Perry, Japan experienced the outside world primarily as a military threat. And a glance across the Sea of Japan made it obvious there was much to worry about. Once-proud China had been dismembered and was being sucked dry by western merchants who used gunboats to foist opium upon the populace. Farther south, the Dutch had conquered Indonesia; the French ruled Vietnam, Laos, and Cambodia, while the acquisitive British held vast colonies in Hong Kong, Singapore, Malaya, Burma, and India. To its north, Japan saw the marauding Russian bear subjugate all within its path. Across the Pacific, energetic Americans had slaves working their land, were digesting the spoils of their invasion of Mexico, and were continuing the nasty campaign of ethnic cleansing against the native Indians. And on November 15, 1884, German chancellor Otto von Bismarck opened a grand international conference in Berlin to carve up pagan Africa. Not surprisingly, Japanese leaders felt their first priority was to build a strong military. All sectors of society had to serve that goal.

From the Japanese perspective, the distinguishing characteristic of rich countries with strong militaries was that they were religious. They believed in a god and this belief unified western countries from within and justified their forays against unbelievers. But Japan did not have one such god. So one would have to be created.

The new leaders of Japan — samurai who filled the vacuum when the shogunate fell — dusted off the emperor institution and placed it front and center in Japanese national life. They plucked the young emperor from obscurity in Kyoto and installed him in the shogun's former Tokyo palace. He was named Meiji, which means "enlightened rule." A renovated emperor system would serve as a counterpart to western Christianity. Meiji would be the symbol to ideologically unite the nation, though he had little actual power. Former samurai pulled the strings from behind the throne.

On February 11, 1889, Emperor Meiji, dressed in a western-style military uniform, stood before Japanese government officials dressed in their western-style military uniforms, with ladies of the court in western-style dresses, and announced a western-style constitution. But it was western in name only.

In the West, a constitution is written "by the people, for the people" and defines citizens' rights and sets limits on government power. Meiji's constitution was just the opposite, a top-down document. It was a "gift of the emperor," which he "bestowed upon the nation." The emperor was declared "sacred and inviolable," "head of the empire," supreme commander of the armed forces, and superintendent of all the powers of sovereignty. Emperor Meiji was the very source of law and he transcended the constitution. He could issue ordinances in place of laws and appoint and dismiss all officers of the government and even the Imperial Diet, Japan's parliament. The purpose of this constitution was not to place limits on his powers but to ensure that he was above the government, with authority unimpeded by limits. There was no bill of rights, since the Japanese people were not even considered citizens — they were the emperor's subjects, *shinmin*. *Shinmin* meant "people who obediently comply with their orders." Indeed, the motive for establishing a constitution was not to satisfy an intrinsic need of the populace but to show foreign observers Japan was a civilized country with a body of law. It was a response to external rather than internal forces.

To guarantee the primacy of the warrior class, a clause in the constitution allowed a direct connect between the emperor and the military. The heads of the army and navy could bypass the civilian rulers, in effect acting as a second shadow government. The army and navy would report directly to the emperor. This direct connect with the emperor imbued the military with a mystical aura as special servants of the divine.

With almost all of Asia and Africa under western colonial control, Japan sought to emulate the imperialists and exploit its weaker neighbors across the Sea of Japan.

China was a hopeless mess, unable to oust the Europeans and Americans who were, as my former professor John Dower has put it, "slicing the Chinese melon." Korea was backward and was not civilizing quickly along western lines like Japan. "We cannot wait for neighboring countries to become enlightened and unite to make Asia strong," the influential scholar Yukichi Fukuzawa wrote. "We must rather break out of formation and join the civilized countries of the West on the path of progress. We should not give any special treatment to China and Korea but should treat them in the same way as do the Western nations." As a popular Japanese children's song of the era put it:

> There is a Law of Nations
> It is true.
> But when the moment comes, remember
> The Strong Eat up the Weak.

As the Japanese studied the ways of the westerners, they could plainly see that successful nations were rich ones. And it was clear that rich nations got that way by subjugating non-Christian countries, enslaving their peoples and appropriating their resources.

China was Korea's traditional protector and had tried to prevent Japanese encroachment on the peninsula. So Japan focused its *Hakko Ichiu* manifest destiny by targeting China. In traditional samurai fashion, the Japanese army invaded China without a declaration of war, which it later issued on August 1, 1894. In the western tradition, the Japanese press called the conflict "a religious war" fought "between a country that is trying to develop civilization and a country that inhibits the progress of civilization." Newspapers serialized accounts of the fighting and sold out every edition. Woodblock prints depicted Japanese army men in heroic poses, looking suspiciously western with handlebar mustaches, as they gallantly fought the inferior Chinese.

Few thought the small island nation would prevail against the continental giant, but Japan's victories stunned the world. On April 17, 1895, in the Treaty of Shimonoseki, China conceded defeat to its smaller rival. China was forced to cede Taiwan, the Pescadores Islands, and the strategic Liaodong Peninsula in southern Manchuria to Japan. China paid a large indemnity, accepted the full independence of Korea, and accorded the Japanese the same unequal diplomatic and commercial privileges the westerners had extorted.

To the Japanese man in the street, the startling triumph over China swept away the humiliation of the Black Ships and proved that Japan was a great country. The United States, far from condemning Japan for its aggression, initially complimented it for so quickly grasping the West's lesson. As one Japanese writer proudly noted, the West now realized that "civilization is not a monopoly of the white man" and that the Japanese too had "a character suitable for great achievements in the world." Japan was bursting with patriotic pride. It was the only nonwhite member of the civilized imperialist club.

But to the West, that was exactly the problem. The imperialist club was white. Now Japan had turned the natural order upside down. Less than one month after its victory, Tokyo received a surprise message from Russia that "advised" Japan to forgo its territorial gains on the mainland and return the Liaodong Peninsula to China. The Russians stated further that Germany and France concurred with that "friendly counsel."

Japanese leaders could hardly believe it. They had played the imperialist game fair and square. Japan had picked a fight with an uncivilized country, proven its superiority on the battlefield, and received concessions that were its due. Tokyo appealed to the British and the Americans. Surely they would see the unfairness of the Russian demand. But the Anglo-Americans sided with their western counterparts and told Japan not to rock the boat.

27

It was as if the Japanese had won soccer's World Cup only to have it taken away by a biased referee because of the color of their skin. Japan mourned this stab in the back as the "Shame of Liaodong." And when Russia cynically grabbed the Liaodong Peninsula for itself and none of the western powers complained, shame turned to fury.

Proud Japan redoubled its efforts to become a civilized, rich country. Greater taxes were levied to build a stronger military. And to gain the world's respect, Japan's next target would be a western country. The patient rulers of the ancient land where the sun originated would bide their time. Japan would wait until the next century to flex its muscle. Then it would surprise a certain western navy found sleeping in a harbor on an infamous and bloody morning.

CHAPTER THREE

Spirit War

True combat power is arms multiplied by fighting spirit. If one of them is infinitely strong, you will succeed.

— Asahi Shimbun *newspaper, quoted in* Japan at War: An Oral History

THE unsuspecting navy ships lay peaceably in their Pacific harbor that winter morning. A world away, the drowsy sailors' commander in chief had been negotiating with Japanese diplomats. But then, with no advance warning, Japan launched the infamous sneak attack. Deadly torpedoes and bombs came out of nowhere, and soon the harbor was a flaming mess of sunken ships. Screaming sailors swam for their lives through fiery oil-blackened waters.

President Roosevelt admired the sneak attack. "I was thoroughly well pleased with the Japanese victory," the president wrote his son.

Maybe Teddy would have felt differently if the sailors had been Americans. But it was the Russians who were taken by surprise that morning at Port Arthur on February 8, 1904.

Just fifty years earlier, Commodore Perry had forced open a small, pre-industrial hermit island nation with few obvious resources. Now Japan mounted a sophisticated war against a stronger western military power. The Russo-Japanese War became the largest conflict the world had ever seen. The massive land battles with their hundreds of thousands of troops in single clashes dwarfed Gettysburg.

Russia had enormous military resources and was clearly the stronger of the two combatants. But Russia had to move its land and sea forces halfway across the world over a single-track railroad and around the cape of Africa. And the Bear had never faced a stubborn opponent like this before. Japan fought furiously, sacrificing tens of thousands of dead just to capture a hill here, a castle there.

The war's astounding climax was the Battle of Tsushima on May 27, 1905, the largest sea clash in world history. Only two generations earlier, the buttons on the tunics of Perry's soldiers had fascinated the Japanese. Now Japan pounded a shocked western enemy with Japanese-made shells as high-tech Japanese battleships blew them out of the water.

Little Japan's victory over Mother Russia at the Battle of Tsushima shocked people around the world, including the Japanese. It was as if a skinny underdog had whipped the brawny heavyweight champion. But as the jubilant *shinmin* celebrated the improbable victory, the leaders of Japan were conflicted. The Land of the Rising Sun was winning battles, but ultimately it could not win the war. Russia had endless resources and could just keep on coming. And Japan had stretched itself to the limit. By the spring of 1905, more than a hundred thousand Japanese had died. The Japanese army was wobbling, low on supplies, bleeding men, and unable to replenish troops as fast as Russia. The Japanese now lacked the ability to deliver the coup de grâce to the Russians.

The controllers of the Japanese state were canny poker players who knew when it was time to fold their hand. One of them was good friends with President Theodore Roosevelt, who mediated the Portsmouth treaty of August 23, 1905. Russia had to cede the strategic Kwantung Peninsula, Port Arthur, and the southern part of Sakhalin Island to Japan.

With the Portsmouth treaty, the land of the gods was officially on the world map as a civilized nation. In just two generations, Japan had moved from supplicant to victor. Internally, the Russo-Japanese War became to Japan what football is to the University of Notre Dame. Monuments rose throughout the country enshrining the country's boundless pride. The veterans of the war were feted as national heroes.

Japan had become the only nonwhite, non-Christian nation to beat a white western Christian country.

Teddy Roosevelt stood in admiration. At Mukden in February and March, Japanese forces had killed 97,000 Russians in the biggest land battle in the history of modern warfare. At Tsushima, the Japanese navy had lost only 600 sailors, compared to the 6,000 Russian dead. "Neither Trafalgar nor the defeat of the Spanish Armada was as complete and overwhelming," Roosevelt wrote about Tsushima. He considered Japan "the great civilizing force of the entire East." He believed that "all the great masterful races have been fighting races," and Japan had won the fight. "I was pro-Japanese before," Roosevelt wrote, "but . . . I am far stronger pro-Japanese than ever."

To Teddy, Japan had the all-important "race capacity for self-rule" and could now take on the responsibility of a civilized race — to dominate its neighbors. The president told his Japanese friends that he expected them to take their place among the great nations, "with, of course, a paramount interest in what surrounds the Yellow Sea, just as the United States has a paramount interest in what surrounds the Caribbean."

In a White House meeting, Teddy told diplomat Baron Suyematsu that Japan should have a position with Korea "just like we have with Cuba." Four months later, Teddy lunched with two other Japanese diplomats at the White House and reiterated that "Korea should be entirely within Japan's sphere of interest." To Roosevelt, Korea was weak, Japan's Darwinian "natural prey." In January 1905, he told his secretary of state that America would allow Japan to swallow up her frail neighbor. Sensing what was coming, the king of Korea looked to the United States for protection. Instead, Roosevelt ordered the withdrawal of the American legation from Seoul to pave the way for his Japanese friends. Within days, the other western powers also withdrew their ambassadors. "It is like the stampede of rats from a sinking ship," observed an American diplomat. The Japanese army quickly deposed the king and took over Korea in 1905. Soon thousands of Korean nationalists swung from gallows.

Japan marveled at its good fortune. In just two short years, it had defeated a Christian country and become a bona fide member of the imperialist club, with its very own enslaved country to dominate. Japan's victory in the Russo-Japanese War took on mythic proportions in Japanese minds as a key turning point in its history.

But like the brilliant entrepreneur who leaves his business to an untalented son who proceeds to lose the family fortune, Meiji was succeeded by less capable men. Meiji's son, the emperor Taisho, was physically frail and mentally unbalanced. He lingered ineffectually for ten years until his son, twenty-year-old Emperor Hirohito, became regent in his place. (Taisho died in 1926, and Hirohito became emperor at the age of twenty-four.) And no farsighted leaders emerged to guide the Japanese state. Meiji's constitution spiritually intertwined the emperor and the military on a cloud high above civilian control. Now lesser military minds exploited this constitutional weakness and gained control over the government and the institution of the emperor.

In the early years of the twentieth century, Japan's first-generation army underwent a shift to the second generation, which had its own ideas about leadership, strategy, and tactics. Japan's new military leaders were not former samurai. They were commoners who had fought in the front lines of the Russo-Japanese War. These simple men were not strategists and valued the old-style tactics that had brought them glory on the front lines of premodern battles with China and Russia. They quickly forgot that Japan had actually not had the strength to press home victory against Russia. And they did not appreciate the strategic wisdom with which their predecessors had sought Roosevelt's timely mediation.

These new military leaders believed it was *Yamato damashii* (Japanese spirit) that had emboldened Japan to challenge the militarily superior Russian state in the first place and that had led to Japan's victory. They convinced themselves that Japanese spirit was a new secret weapon that would protect Japan, like the *kamikaze* of centuries past. *Yamato damashii* became the mantra of these self-congratulatory "Spirit Warriors" who felt their blood-and-guts style embodied the historic greatness of Japan. Among the many things lost in this formula was the fact that in Russia, Japan had been fighting a brutish, nonmechanized foe. Bravery in hand-to-hand fighting had been important in that war. But combat was changing. While other countries were mechanizing their forces for future technological war, the Spirit Warriors stayed focused on their past, smug that *Yamato damashii,* the spirit of Japan, would always triumph.

The Spirit Warriors rammed through a law that required the navy and army members of the prime minister's cabinet to be active-duty officers. Unable to appoint independent retired officers, the prime minister was forced to choose only from among those controlled by the Spirit Warriors. Whenever the Spirit boys disapproved of a prime minister or his policies, they would simply withdraw the minister, refuse to recommend a new one, and the prime minister's cabinet would collapse. Already above civil authority, the military thus consolidated its control of the civilian sector of the government as well. And because of Emperor Taisho's mental illness, the Spirit Warriors had the opportunity to mold his son.

Hirohito entered the world at the dawn of the new era of Japan's military obsession. He was seventy days old when he was taken from his parents to be raised at the home of an elderly retired admiral to inculcate the proper military values in the emperor-to-be. The Russo-Japanese War was the signature event of Hirohito's childhood. From his youngest years, he saw his grandfather, stately in his military uniform, basking in Japan's new status as a first-rate power. Hirohito was surrounded by military men and socialized to believe that military might was key to Japan's maintaining its place in the world. Like a young Ford heir growing up in Detroit who knows his future will be cars, Hirohito believed he and Japan's military would play a special role in Japan's continuing greatness.

Japanese emperors traditionally grew up isolated and powerless in splendid surroundings in Kyoto, studying ancient Chinese and Japanese texts, composing poetry, and remaining distant from political and military affairs. But Hirohito's education was strictly and narrowly militarized. This was not by choice but by Imperial decree. Emperor Meiji's Imperial Household Regulation Number 17 mandated military training for all members of the Imperial family, even though Meiji himself had not received a military education. Hirohito was enrolled at the age of seven in a school whose principal, appointed by Meiji, was a heroic infantry general of the Russo-Japanese War. The young prince was even made a second lieutenant in the Imperial Japanese Army and an ensign in the Imperial Japanese Navy — at the age of eleven.

Hirohito attended middle school with five other children chosen by the school's principal — a former navy captain. The other students stood at their desks and bowed when the emperor-to-be entered the classroom. Liberal arts were given short shrift, with the emphasis on military subjects. His teachers included an army general, two navy rear admirals, and four active-duty lieutenant generals, all of whom owed their status to the victory over Russia. The gangly teenage Hirohito buckled down to a curriculum of "map exercises, military history; the principles of military leadership, tactics . . . strategy and chess." Outdoor activities consisted of "training in horsemanship and military drills by junior army officers." At noon, the young prince took his classmates' bows and departed to eat separately, accompanied by a military aide. At home, the army "had a trench dug inside the crown prince's compound so that Hirohito could practice firing machine guns." In the evenings, military tutors "played war-strategy games with him."

Summers offered the Boy Soldier little relief. He toured the army and navy academies and General Staff Headquarters, and observed maneuvers at army camps and naval bases across the land. Constantly in the company of older military men who encouraged him to act in a military manner, Hirohito was totally isolated from normal Japanese life. He was not even allowed free access to newspapers until he was seventeen.

"Hirohito was brought up to believe that the entire history of modern Japan centered on his grandfather and the small group of talented officials who had assisted him." Questions regarding the wisdom of challenging a superior power, of what might have happened if Russia hadn't been required to exhaust its fleet by sailing around the world before meeting the Japanese in battle, of possible negative outcomes if bloodied but unconquered Russia had not agreed to negotiations — these were left unasked. Hirohito's instructors instead taught him what they were teaching a new generation of Spirit Warriors in the military academies: the overarching importance of Japanese spirit and the minutia of tactics at the expense of overall strategy. The future emperor's navy teachers taught that battles were won on the high seas by hurling the entire battleship fleet into a "decisive battle" like Tsushima. Japanese army instructors, completely oblivious to the lessons of World War I, taught the future emperor that artillery, tanks, and aircraft were all secondary to brave bayonet charges by the infantry. The future commander in chief learned that "hand-to-hand combat rather than firepower determined victory or defeat in battle."

The future emperor was far from alone in having a martial curriculum. For decades, the army had seen to it that "physical culture, military training in the public schools and 'military spirit education' in general should be encouraged" to produce "good and faithful subjects," willing, as Meiji's "Imperial Rescript on Education" had put it, to "offer yourselves courageously to the State." The military-influenced educational order soon morphed into a chain of mini boot camps that served as a feeder system for the army. In 1923, a great earthquake leveled much of Tokyo and Yokohama. The government, needing to divert funds for rebuilding, temporarily cut back on some army personnel. In a scheme to provide state employment for military personnel, the army insisted that a system of military training in all schools be established and thousands of active-duty army officers be placed in the schools to inculcate "right thinking." "Every facet of the curriculum was permeated with emperor worship and militarism." When first graders opened their *Japanese Reader* to "the first double-page spread, there was a picture of three toy soldiers with the caption 'Advance! Advance! Soldiers move forward!'"

As historian Saburo Ienaga has noted:

War and patriotism were to be stressed in every subject. In ethics the teachers were to discuss "the meaning of the imperial edict declaring war, the imperial edict on the course of the war, the exploits of valiant Japan and our valiant military men, the special behavior expected of children during the war, and the duty of military service." Japanese language classes were to study "the imperial edicts related to the war, articles about the war situation, letters to and from soldiers at the front." Teachers were to show war-related pictures provided by the government to spark discussion. Arithmetic classes were to do "calculations about military matters." The topics for science were "general information about searchlights, wireless communication, land mines and torpedoes, submarines, military dirigibles, Shimose explosives, military carrier pigeons, heavy cannon, mortars, machine guns, the Arisaka cannon, and military sanitation." Physical education would include "character training and war games." Music classes were to reverberate with war songs.

"The emperor was regarded as a god, and therefore we had to obey whatever the emperor said," remembered Masayo Enomoto, a typical 1930s farm-boy student. "We had been taught such things since we were very young. I did believe that he was a god. I was prepared to serve the emperor in any way possible."

The military-minded teachers made it clear to their students what kind of future service they would render to the emperor. One child burst out crying while dissecting frogs at a school in Yamagata prefecture. He got two hard knocks on the side of his head as his teacher shouted, "Why are you crying about one lousy frog? When you grow up you'll have to kill a hundred, two hundred Chinks."

The boot camp atmosphere permeated young students' days. "When you were called into the teachers' room," Hideo Sato recalled, "you had to announce, 'Sixth-grade pupil, third class Sato Hideo has business for Teacher Yamada. May I enter?' The teacher would respond, 'Enter!' It was just like in the army. If we encountered our teacher on our way to school, or on our way home, we had to stand at attention and salute." The army officer–custodians of young Japanese minds had long endured rough corporal punishment in their barracks, and they transplanted the brutal treatment to the schools. "If you averted your face, they declared that you were rebelling against the teachers," Sato remembered. "You got an extra two blows, rather than the just the one you expected. You simply bore up under it, your teeth clenched."

With the emperor, the government, and the civilian populace now under firm control, the Spirit Warriors began to beat the war drums. Soon the cry of *Hakko Ichiu* — "eight corners of the world under one roof" — became the call for further expansion beyond Japan's shores. An editorial in a Yokohama newspaper proclaimed: "Today's Japan should indeed not confine itself to its own small sphere. Neither should it remain in its position in the Orient or continue to occupy the place it holds in the world. This is an age in which Japan bears a global mission. It has become the center, the principal, and the commander and is advancing with the times to lead the entire world."

One Japanese army general wrote, "A tree must have roots, so too must a nation. Britain had such roots. They stretched into Africa, India, Australia, and Canada, giving strength and wealth and power to the mother country. The United States had such roots — nurtured in her own vast territory and in the rich soil of Central and South America. Unless Japan was permitted to extend her roots to the Asian continent and thus escape her 'potted-plant' existence, she would shrivel up and die."

Military service fell upon the most impoverished farm boys. First-born sons, persons of property, bureaucrats, intellectuals, and others received a deferment. Draftees were referred to by their officers as *"issen gorin." Issen gorin* meant "one yen, five rin," the cost of mailing a draft-notice postcard — less than a penny.

When the *issen gorin* arrived at boot camp, they entered a brutal gulag of horrors. Far from a meritocracy, the Japanese army more closely represented a feudal slave system, with two distinct strata. On top were the officers, who demanded to be treated like privileged imperial officials. "The officer class in general had the status and authority of feudal lords. The privates, especially the new recruits, were at the miserable bottom of the pyramid. They had no human rights. They were non-persons."

The officers who ran the gulag styled themselves as samurai in the great Japanese tradition. But these Spirit Warriors were not samurai. They were products of a blinkered training regimen "narrowly focused on military subjects. The result was an officer corps of rigid mentality and limited experience." They assumed the mantle of samurai past only to corrupt Japan's proud Bushido (Way of the Warrior) tradition.

Samurai values represented the best in a man. If a samurai did not live up to his code of honor and brought shame upon himself, his family, or his lord, he would kill himself to atone for his failure. This ceremonial killing was called seppuku, known in the West as hara-kiri. Samurai who lived by such a strict code of honor were seen as trustworthy, selfless, and fearless in battle. But samurai were a very small slice of the general population and the number that actually committed seppuku was tinier still.

Samurai were shrewd strategists and tacticians. Samurai fought to win, to protect their lives and the lives of their compatriots. There was no concept that death in battle was a sound strategy. Mass suicide was never part of Bushido. A true samurai would agree with U.S. Army general George Patton that "no one ever won a war by dying for their country. They won by making the other son-of-a-bitch die for his."

In an effort to make warriors out of the entire male populace, the Spirit Warriors distorted the essence of Bushido and began to peddle a bastardized version that taught a cult of death. This twisted version focused not on the sublime personal standards of honor among samurai, but on the base blood and guts of death.

The Japanese army field regulations of 1912 systematically stated the Spirit Warriors' strategic doctrine for the first time. This document revealed that the pseudo samurai understood and cared little for strategy, instead placing an excessive emphasis on *Yamato damashii*. "The literature is full of phrases about 'the attack spirit,' 'confidence in certain victory,' 'loyalty to the emperor,' 'love of country,' 'absolute sincerity,' and 'sacrifice one's life to the country, absolute obedience to superiors.'"

Fear of death is the most powerful disabler of warriors, so the Spirit boys turned this weakness into a strength by removing the *possibility* of death from their *issen gorin*'s minds. Instead, they taught a cult of death *guaranteeing* soldiers they would die for the emperor, figuring that a soldier who was ready to die transcended fear. This willingness, even eagerness, to die for the emperor would, it was believed, provide a magic multiplier effect that would squash all enemies. Recruits were constantly told their lives were worth nothing compared to the glorious contribution they could make to their country by dying in battle for the emperor.

In the Sino-Japanese and Russo-Japanese Wars, many Japanese troops had surrendered, served as POWs, and later been welcomed back to Japan with open arms. But as the Meiji leaders passed, the new crop of *Yamato damashii* boys decreed that it was absolutely forbidden to withdraw, surrender, or become a prisoner of war. The 1908 army criminal code contained the following provision: "A commander who allows his unit to surrender to the enemy without fighting to the last man or who concedes a strategic area to the enemy shall be punishable by death." The field service code contained an additional injunction: "Do not be taken prisoner alive." To drive the point home, the army helpfully told the story of a Major Kuga, who was captured by the Chinese. Major Kuga had been wounded and was captured while he was unconscious. When he was released, he committed suicide. The commentary instructed the reader, "This act typifies the glorious spirit of the Imperial Army."

The Japanese navy was slightly less brutal than the army, with less need for close-up fighting, but it too glorified death, as can be seen in the words of the mournful Japanese navy anthem, the *"Umi Yukaba"*:

> *Across the sea, corpses floating in the water.*
> *Across the mountains, corpses heaped upon the grass.*
> *We shall die by the side of our lord.*
> *We shall never look back.*

The second component of Japanese spirit valued by the Spirit Warriors was brutality. War is cold and by definition makes killers of those who practice it. But no army in history so systematically instilled hatred in its troops as this version of the Imperial Japanese Army. "Brutality and cruelty were the rule rather than the exception in the Japanese army. It was the last primitive infantry army of modern times." The new army recruit entered a violent asylum where he was pummeled, slapped, kicked, and beaten daily. Shinji Ito remembered his first swimming lesson: "A rope was tied around my body, and . . . I was thrown into the river from a boat. When I lost consciousness from swallowing too much water, I was pulled up. Once I caught my breath, I would be thrown back into the water. My uniform froze."

All militaries have incidents of corporal abuse by officers. But only the IJA actively encouraged regular and vicious abuse of its charges. "For forty-some years I've suffered from ringing in my ears," remembered Katsumi Watanabe. "This is the aftereffect of severe beatings by higher-ranking privates when I was a draftee. It was the norm in the military that new recruits and draftees were beaten for no reason. The members of the military were ignorant and had lost their humanity. They thought that beatings were a form of education."

"Before inflicting punishment," Tsuyoshi Saka recalled, "they always said they were indoctrinating us with the military man's spirit. We were made to form a single line and stand at attention and then ordered to clench our teeth. Then they hit us with their fists. This was better than the occasions when they struck us with the leather straps of their swords or with their leather indoor shoes. At the limit of the human body's endurance, greasy sweat pouring from my forehead, I nearly fainted in agony."

Recruit Shinji Ito's mother and father had sent their son off to the benevolent emperor's army. "During my first year," he recalled, "my head was beaten with green bamboo poles and my face slapped with leather slippers. This changed the shape of my face. I wonder what my parents would have felt had they seen me in this state."

Enomoto-san, the sixth son of a poor rice farmer, remembered that his superiors beat him up every night. "It was like I couldn't sleep without being beaten up at least once," he says. "Once they got tired of slapping you with their hands they used their shoes, which had nails on the soles. They hit you with these hard shoes until your face was all swollen up."

The final component of *Yamato damashii* was absolute, unhesitating, unthinking, blind obedience to orders. The very first article in Meiji's "Imperial Rescript to Soldiers and Sailors" had proclaimed that "loyalty" was the "essential duty" of the soldier and sailor. But young Japanese soldiers were not just being asked to obey orders merely from men of authority, as in other militaries. Japanese officers, with their direct connect to the throne, spoke with divine authority. Recruits were taught "to regard the orders of their superiors as issuing directly from the emperor. This meant that orders were infallible and obedience to them had to be absolute and unconditional." There was no concept of "legal" or "illegal" orders.

"We were educated again and again," Enomoto-san recalled, "that the emperor was a living god. In those days, I totally believed that. During the morning when we lined up we would face toward the east, in the direction of the emperor, and salute. We would pledge that we would do our best that day. We did this every morning." And as the emperor's chosen elite, army officers were also owed unquestioning obedience. "We learned that the senior soldiers were gods," is how Tsuyoshi Saka put it. "When training ended for the day, the recruits fought for the privilege of untying the squad leader's puttees. In the bath they held the soap for the NCOs and washed their backs."

"No one could resist," said Enomoto-san. "Not a single person could resist. Once the officers got tired of beating you, they had the young soldiers face each other for twenty minutes and slap the soldier across from you. So we, the teammates, would slap each other instead of being slapped by an instructor. That was the hardest, because you don't want to hit your teammate too hard, but if you took it easy then your superior would scold you for not being serious. Punishment is something that we took for granted."

"Some forms of punishment degrade human nature," Tsuyoshi Saka reflected. "The senior soldiers looked on, laughing. They justified it by saying we should consider it an act of kindness. This method of inflicting brutal punishment without any cause and destroying our power to think was a way of transforming us into men who would carry out our superiors' orders as a reflex action."

CHAPTER FOUR

The Third Dimension

Japan never declares war before attacking.

— *Billy Mitchell, 1932, quoted in* Mitchell: Pioneer of Air Power

I<small>N</small> the early days of the airplane, few predicted it would ever play a part in warfare. After all, the early models were fragile machines — canvas and wood held together with clothesline and powered by small put-put engines. "At the dawn of World War I, planes were still manu-factured from flimsy wood and easily ripped canvas (aviation giant Boeing, in fact, began life as a timber company). The pilot and pas-senger sat, with goggles, leather helmet, and seat belt, out in the open air, and flew with engines about as powerful as a lawnmower's. The controls were basic and simple: a stabilizer, a stick, a rudder, a throt-tle, and a spark control. You just got in and flew." Navy admirals with their enormous battleships and army generals with their rows and rows of cannon saw little merit in these frail flying machines.

But one visionary saw the future. Billy Mitchell was handsome and articulate, the son of a wealthy United States senator from Milwaukee. In World War I, Mitchell had been a thirty-eight-year-old army colonel in charge of America's air support. In France, he had witnessed the hellish stalemate of trench warfare — enormous armies dug in, unable to advance, murdering one another in the mud. He was the first Amer-ican to fly over an enemy in battle, and his airmen — French, English, and American — provided behind-the-lines intelligence and led key assaults. Billy had led the largest winged armada in history — unmatched until the outbreak of World War II.

Billy had discovered his planes could leap over enemy lines and attack the opponent's "vital centers" — the industries that produced the beans and bullets necessary for modern warfare. "Strategic bombing" — targeting the enemy's manufacturing base to choke off its continuing ability to fight — meant that there was no longer a front line, that the trenches mapped only a subset of a greater battlefield. Extending war to civilian areas where factories were based was not only a radical idea; to many, it was an immoral one. During World War I, warriors had fought warriors on the front lines, while mom back home was not considered a target. But Billy reasoned that once the enemy's industrial capacity was sufficiently reduced, that enemy could not continue to fight. The airplane, Billy believed, would shorten wars and make them more humane. True, bombing plants, rail yards, factories, and communications grids increased the chance of civilian deaths, but Mitchell reasoned that this would actually save lives in comparison to the mindless static warfare that killed millions of soldiers in the trenches. And this would not be a momentary tactical shift. At a time when young sailors were absorbing battleship doctrine at Annapolis and cadets were studying horse charges at West Point, Billy was convinced that airpower had radically changed warfare forever. Warriors accustomed to thinking in two dimensions — land and sea — now had to understand a "Third Dimension" — the air.

Billy's ideas were seen by most as farfetched. Few people had ever driven a car, much less flown. Airplanes were famous for their fragility — just nicking a telegraph wire in flight could mean a flaming death, while on the ground a single lit match or a child with an ax could destroy an entire plane. To the generals and admirals in the early decades of the twentieth century, warfare was about massing the brawny iron might of the industrial revolution. The idea that a fluttering canvas and wood contraption could threaten nations was like believing that sparrows threatened castles. Real men believed in battleships and artillery.

But Billy knew better. After WWI, he returned to the United States preaching his vision of the airplane-dominated future of warfare with the fervor of the converted. A swashbuckling general now, with a chest full of shiny medals, he had glimpsed the future and thought everyone should shift their strategic thinking. Billy wanted everyone to believe his Third-Dimension gospel.

Before World War II, there was no Pentagon, no secretary of defense, no unified voice regarding the American military. Instead, there was a secretary of war, representing the army, and a secretary of the navy, an arrangement reflecting a two-dimensional view of warfare — land and sea — with no overlap. Billy wanted to overhaul the entire American defense structure. First, he lectured, establish a separate Department of the Air Force, coequal with the army and the navy. Second, these three services had to be united under a single command, a Department of Defense.

Billy's suggestions, in light of history, not only made sense but were inevitable. But in Billy's time, this was heresy. He proclaimed, "Just as today we record battles on land and sea, so tomorrow we shall write of battles in the skies." But like all prophets, Billy threatened the status quo and was considered dangerous to entrenched interests.

After all, the dogma of the day held that the navy's battleships guaranteed the nation's defense. Battleships were the product of hundreds of years of evolution, floating behemoths bristling with the strength and power of the industrial revolution. Battleships were the most expensive weapons in the American arsenal, and powerful financial, manufacturing, and political interests had much invested in maintaining their primacy. But articulate and dashing Billy told all that airpower made the battleship just outmoded floating scrap metal. For the cost of one battleship, Billy preached, the nation could purchase a fleet of airplanes that could sink an armada foolish enough to approach our shores. No sea or land power could threaten America if it had control of the Third Dimension.

Not surprisingly, this was heresy to the traditionalists. Mitchell was a convincing speaker with a growing number of acolytes, but he was also an officer in the United States Army, subject to discipline. His superiors ordered him to tone it down. But when opposed, Billy only fought harder to convey his vision of the future. He took his case to the American people, because, as he often said, "Changes in military systems come about only through the pressure of public opinion or disaster in war." He also convinced the navy to put his ideas to a very public test.

The captured German battleship *Ostfriesland* was considered a solid Rock of Gibraltar by the old-line American admirals. She had struck a mine after seeing action in the WWI Battle of Jutland and made it to port despite serious injury. As one officer declared to the *Washington Star:* "She was a wonderful ship, built [to be] as nearly unsinkable as possible. She had four skins to protect her against mines and torpedoes and heavy projectiles. She was also divided into many watertight compartments by bulkheads, so that, no matter how many big holes were made in her hulls, she would still be able to get home."

On July 21, 1921, some three hundred notables, including "Cabinet officers, Senators and Representatives, military attachés of foreign powers, aeronautical and naval experts, and half a hundred newspapermen," waited aboard an observation ship out on the Atlantic Ocean. Most were confident that they were about to witness the defeat of Billy Mitchell and his harebrained ideas about a "Third Dimension." Former Secretary of the Navy Joe Daniels had stated publicly that he would be happy to stand bareheaded on the deck of any ship while Billy tried to sink it from the air. On the eve of the bombing trial, the *New York Times* reported that "naval officers are insisting that the flyers will never sink the *Ostfriesland,*" and one navy officer who was present at the tests said, "General Mitchell was ridiculed, derided and made fun of by the secretary of the navy and by officers of the navy department in high authority."

When the observation ship was in place, Billy dispatched a fleet of his rudimentary Martin bombers from shore. Each carried no more than two thousand pounds of explosives. Mitchell's planes puttered toward their target, in no need to push to their limits of acceleration, a mere ninety-eight miles per hour. At 12:19 P.M. they dropped their first bomb. To conclusively prove the strength of airpower, Billy had ordered his men not to bomb the ship directly but to score near misses on either side of the great battleship, creating a "water hammer" to collapse the "unsinkable vessel." At exactly 12:40 P.M., just twenty-one minutes into the trial, the *Ostfriesland* vanished beneath the surface. "The chins of navy officers watching, dropped," wrote an observer. "Their eyes seemed to be coming out of the ends of their marine glasses. . . . Many seasoned admirals and captains were sobbing audibly at the sight, while others hid their faces behind handkerchiefs." It was the end of an era.

Billy's victory in the Atlantic over the navy made him a national hero, his conclusive demonstration of airpower garnering front-page headlines. The *New York Times* reported, "No fleet afloat is safe if it loses control of the air. Control of the sea is now insufficient. Control of the air is vitally necessary. The impression one got in watching the bombing was that it hardly seemed possible that such a small amount of offensive equipment could damage this powerful monarch of the sea. It is evident to everyone who attended the demonstration that history is being made."

Eight days after sinking the *Ostfriesland,* Billy staged mock air attacks on New York, Philadelphia, and Baltimore to further demonstrate the dominance of airpower. Bold headlines informed readers that their army and navy could not defend them against the airplane. To rub it in, Billy had his flyers hover over the Naval Academy at Annapolis to symbolize the navy's new secondary role in the nation's defense.

Just two weeks after Billy sank the *Ostfriesland,* Senator William Borah of Idaho rose on the floor of the Senate to challenge "the wisdom of completing at a cost of $240,000,000 six great battleships under construction, in view of 'the experiment off the Virginia coast' which demonstrated 'that with sufficient airplane and submarine protection this country was perfectly safe from attack." Senator William King of Utah "declared that 'those tests demonstrated the vulnerability of the battleship,' and introduced a bill providing that three proposed battle cruisers, the Saratoga, Lexington and Constellation be converted into aircraft carriers." Disarmament was the call of the day, and many thoughtful observers had now concluded that investing limited peacetime dollars in Billy's airpower seemed a prudent idea.

Backed into a corner, the battleship school, with hundreds of millions of dollars in battleship contracts at stake, struck back. The army and navy leadership issued a report under the name of the country's great WWI hero General John Pershing concluding that "the battleship is still the backbone of the fleet and the bulwark of the nation's sea defense." Mitchell blithely responded with a report in which he said that if he mobilized all his airplanes, he could obliterate the entire Atlantic fleet. But while the public was with him, behind the scenes his position was being deliberately eroded.

When Billy was married on October 11, 1923, his superiors used the occasion to ship him off on a "honeymoon" inspection tour of Hawaii, the Philippines, China, India, and Japan, hoping the fever for airpower would die out in his absence. But when Billy returned nine months later, he had even more ammunition for his call for an air force and unified command. He told Congress, "When I was in the Hawaiian Islands relations between the army and the navy were such that the commanding general of the army and the commanding admiral of the navy would not even go to the same social functions together. I have never seen anything like it." A divided command in Hawaii was the equivalent of no defense at all, and he warned that Hawaii was in grave danger of air attack by Japan and that "in making estimates of Japanese air power, care must be taken that it is not underestimated." "They can fly, are going to fly, and may end up by developing the greatest air power in the world," Mitchell declared. He also told Congress, "I think if we plunged into war tomorrow, it would take us at least two years to get on a par with . . . Japan."

Billy Mitchell saw clearly that a war with Japan for control of Asia was inevitable. He warned of "aerial attacks by the enemy against Hawaii and the Philippines. The object of these operations would be for Japan to possess herself of all the southern approaches to Asia and the initial successes, as things stand now, would probably be with the Japanese." When asked to give his opinion as to why airpower was stillborn in the U.S., with little funding or interest coming from the navy or army, he replied: "Conservatism. . . . You see, the army and the navy are the oldest institutions we have. They place everything on precedent. You can't do that in the air business. You have got to look ahead."

Billy's testimony outraged the War Department. Headlines blared, "Foes May Force General Mitchell Out." One congressman denounced the "determined effort" to subject Mitchell, "America's only fighting flying general of the world war and one of the outstanding figures in world aeronautics, to humiliation, demotion and discipline."

To silence the rising chorus of support for what was now called "Mitchellism," Secretary of War John Weeks scheduled public tests to prove that antiaircraft fire would protect the country from air attack. Billy had long derided the effectiveness of antiaircraft fire, comparing the difficulty of hitting airplanes with guns with "knocking a butterfly out of the air with water from a garden hose."

Once again army, navy, congressional, and media observers assembled for the tests.

Under the supervision of General Mitchell, three planes, each towing at a comparatively low speed a target about 10 feet in length and 4 in diameter, flew at fixed altitudes while three-inch guns on the ground tried to hit them, and kept missing again and again. . . . During the tests, the coast artillery fired 39 shots at the aerial targets. Not a single hit was scored. Two planes then descended with their targets to within 1,000 feet and less. Machine guns opened fire from the ground, expending thousands of rounds. When the two targets were later examined, it was found that one was in perfect condition. The other one, which the ordnance experts thought would be riddled to shreds, bore the mark of a single bullet hole.

The next day, a *New York Times* headline blared, "Air Targets Defy Secretary Weeks' Gunners," and the article proclaimed, "These maneuvers, planned . . . to prove that anti-aircraft defenses are adequate against enemy airplanes, proved the exact opposite." The *Brooklyn Eagle,* in an editorial entitled "The Proof That Fizzled," remarked, "Everything came out as General Mitchell predicted and the exact opposite of what [Secretary of War Weeks] tried to prove. The nation wants no report from the War College that fortresses and anti-aircraft devices remain the 'backbone' of coast defense."

Rather than face facts, the War Department demoted Mitchell and exiled him to "a mosquito post in Texas," as Will Rogers put it. The military expected him to resign, but Billy proclaimed, "I have not even begun to fight" and that he would "jar the bureaucrats out of their swivel chairs." He published incendiary articles with titles like "Why Have Treaties about Battleships When Airplanes Can Destroy Them?" He further hammered away at the inevitability of conflict with Japan and declared that a Pacific war would not be won on the surface of the sea but above it with airplanes and below it with submarines.

Then, after a series of bungles by the military that resulted in the deaths of some of his airmen, Billy released a statement charging:

These accidents are the direct results of incompetency, criminal negligence and almost treasonable administration of the national defense by the war and navy departments.

All aviation policies, schemes and systems are dictated by the non-flying officers of the army and navy who know practically nothing about it. The lives of the airmen are being used merely as pawns in their hands.

The great Congress of the United States, that makes laws for the organization and use of our air, land and water forces, is treated by these two departments as if it were an organization created for their benefit. . . . Officers and agents sent by the war and navy departments to Congress have almost always given incomplete, misleading or false information about aeronautics, which either they knew to be false when given or was the result of such gross ignorance of the question that they should not be allowed to appear before a legislative body.

The airmen themselves are bluffed and bulldozed so that they dare not tell the truth in the majority of cases, knowing full well that if they do, they will be deprived of their future career, sent to the most out of the way places to prevent their telling the truth, and deprived of any chance for advancement unless they subscribe to the dictates of their non-flying bureaucratic superiors. These either distort facts, or openly tell falsehoods about aviation to the people and to the Congress.

The broadside stunned Washington; no officer in the history of the United States had ever criticized his command to this extent. As Mitchell later told the *Cleveland Press:* "I considered it my duty to tell what I knew, although it meant sure disciplinary action and probably court-martial. All these things were well understood by me. In fact, I showed the paper I had prepared on the subject to our military judge advocate before I issued it, and he told me that I would certainly be tried for it."

Billy was right. President Calvin Coolidge himself ordered Billy's court-martial, declaring, "Any organization of men in the military service bent on inflaming the public mind for the purpose of forcing government action through the pressure of public opinion is an exceedingly dangerous undertaking and precedent." Billy responded by complaining that the indictment avoided the main issue of what the country should do about airpower: "The truth or untruth of my accusations against the bureaucrats is not permitted to become a part of the court-martial proceedings. I am just going to be tried for daring to remind the conservatives that there is something new under the sun, that there is a great new modern branch of the service, aircraft, which is being ignored in the administration of national defense."

Billy's trial was a media circus. It stands today as the longest court-martial in the history of the United States. Witness after witness supported Billy's views, but it didn't matter — he was being tried for challenging the president and his military-contractor friends. To lessen the public relations blow, Coolidge released a report compiled by a blue-ribbon committee chosen to support the battleship school of the navy. The report was a whitewash that concluded that the battleship was supreme and "there was no ground for anticipating the development of aviation 'to a point which would constitute a direct menace to the United States,'" that "the next war may well start in the air, but in all probability, it will wind up, as the last one did, in the mud," and that "wars against high-spirited people never will be ended by sudden attacks upon important nerve centers such as manufacturing plants, depots, lighting and power plants and railway centers. The last war taught us that man cannot make a machine stronger than the spirit of man."

Predictably, Mitchell was found guilty of insubordination and sentenced "to be suspended from rank, command, and duty, with forfeiture of all pay and allowances for five years." Yet even after his court-martial, Billy would not give up the fight. A compelling orator, he spoke at Carnegie Hall and across the nation, and he wrote many magazine and newspaper articles warning that the United States was unprepared for war. He warned of Japanese plans "to seize Alaska, Hawaii and the Philippines." In April of 1926, fifteen years prior to Pearl Harbor, Billy predicted that Japan would initiate war in the Pacific "with an aerial attack against the United States involving the dispatch of two huge disguised aircraft carriers to American shores in a surprise move while negotiations would be going on behind diplomats' doors." A keen student of history, Billy warned of surprise, saying in 1932, "Japan never declares war before attacking."

Years later, Flyboys beating back Japan in the Pacific must have reflected upon how America could have prevented the shock of December 7 if their prophet's warnings had been heeded. The military experts who compiled the 1946 "United States Strategic Bombing Survey" agreed with Billy. In the chapter headed "Hindsight," they wrote:

> [America] underestimated the predominant role that air power was to play [in the Pacific war] and allocated to it too small a share of even the inadequate resources then available to the Army and Navy. At the outbreak of the Pacific war our deficiency was particularly great in modern land-based fighters and in carriers. One thousand planes . . . dispersed on some 50 airfields, would have seriously impeded the original Japanese advance if knowledge of their existence had not entirely dissuaded the Japanese from making the attempt.

Divided command at Pearl Harbor, reliance on outdated battleships, and lack of American airpower tempted the Japanese warlords and gave them what Billy had predicted, "the greatest military surprise in history." The *Washington Post*'s Raymond Clapper later summarized the findings of the president's Pearl Harbor commission: "The Army thought the Navy was patrolling. The Navy thought the Army had its detection service operating. Neither bothered to check with the other — or maybe they were not on speaking terms. . . . The two services were totally uncoordinated, and neither knew what the other was doing — or in this case, not doing. And the air force, so supremely important in the new warfare, apparently was regarded by both as a minor auxiliary."

To his dying day, Billy prophesied, "Our most dangerous enemy is Japan and our planes should be designed to attack Japan," and that "history and destiny unmistakably point to the next contest being for the possession of the Pacific. Whenever the Japanese see a decadent military power near them, they pounce on it if they have anything to gain. The Japanese consider us a decadent military power. They consider that on account of the riches we possess, the easy existence we have led and the false theories that have grown up among us as to national defense, in a little while we will be as easy to attack as a large jellyfish."

In the 1930s, bills were introduced in Congress to reverse Billy's court-martial and clear his name. But on January 28, 1936, the House Military Affairs Committee voted against reinstating Billy. His court-martial would stand. That same day, Billy entered Doctors' Hospital in New York, never to come out alive. The Flyboy prophet died there at the age of fifty-seven on February 19, 1936, a broken man. One of his last utterances was to fellow airman Homer Berry: "The American people will regret the day I was crucified by politics and bureaucracy."

CHAPTER FIVE

The Rape of China

Japan is expanding, and what country in its expansion has ever failed to be trying to its neighbors? Ask the American Indian or the Mexican how excruciatingly trying the young United States used to be once upon a time.

— *Foreign Minister Yosuke Matsuoka,*
quoted in Tojo and the Coming of the War

IN 1933, a motion picture featuring an army general was a hit across Japan. He delivered an emotional *Hakko Ichiu* / manifest destiny speech. Superimposed upon the screen was a map of Japan and Manchuria with the words "New World Order" glowing. China, Siberia, India, and the South Pacific formed the outer edges. The sound track boomed, "Can we expect the waves of the Pacific of tomorrow to be as calm as they are today? It is the holy mission of Japan to establish peace in the Orient. . . . The day will come when we will make the whole world look up to our national virtues."

The Spirit Warriors constantly bombarded the Japanese public with the message that Japan was gradually being encircled by *gaizin* who might pounce at any moment. Countless speeches, articles, and movies depicted tiny Japan overshadowed by the westerners in China; the Americans hovering in Alaska, Hawaii, Wake, Guam, and the Philippines; the British in Hong Kong, Malaya, Singapore, Australia, and throughout the Indian subcontinent; the French and the Dutch to the south and the menacing Russians to the north. The army's message was that it was the duty of each and every child of the gods to rise up and break the ring before it closed. "Japan's holy mission beckoned: defend the imperial way and build a paradise in Asia!"

And of course Japan needed more "living space." One military writer proclaimed: "It is well known that Japan's overpopulation grows more serious every year. Where should we find an outlet for these millions?"

Most Japanese were never aware that the Japanese army had provoked China until after Japan's surrender in 1945. The army controlled the media and constantly put forth the case that Japan was "implementing Japan's historic mission to expand on the continent, to secure the peace of East Asia, and to save its 600,000,000 from 'imperialistic oppression'" by the rapacious western conquerors.

Ignorance combined with arrogance was common in the Spirit Warriors' government. In 1937, when major hostilities with China broke out, General Hajime Sugiyama advised the emperor that his sacred army would vanquish China "in about three months." He predicted, "We'll send large forces, smash them in a hurry and get the whole thing over with quickly." Another general boasted, "China may squirm and struggle but it will not slow down the Japanese army. Three or four divisions and a few river gunboats will be quite enough to handle the Chinese bandits."

This "three-month war" continued for eight years. This time China was no longer the prostrate power it had been in the 1800s. In 1911, Dr. Sun Yat-sen — modern China's George Washington — had overthrown the corrupt Ching dynasty and founded the Republic of China. After his death, one of his generals, the ruthless Chiang Kai-shek, seized control, defeated local warlords, and ruled some of the country from Nanking. Chiang commanded immense armies and had Anglo-American financial and technical support in his fight against the Japanese invaders. England and America did not want to lose their trading rights in China.

In addition to Chiang, Japan also faced the twentieth century's greatest guerrilla leader, the wily Mao Tse-tung, who himself controlled part of China, commanded large forces, and enjoyed the support of the peasants.

With Chiang's forces, the Japanese faced a traditional army of uniformed soldiers carrying out traditional operations. But Japanese army strategists had no appreciation for the strength of Mao's brilliant guerrilla tactics. Whereas the Japanese army pursued a ruthless policy of slaughter known as the "Three Alls" ("Kill All, Loot All, Burn All"), Mao insisted on decorous "rules" when dealing with the Chinese peasants:

All actions are subject to command.
Do not steal from the people.
Be neither selfish nor unjust.
Replace the door when you leave the house.
Roll up the bedding on which you have slept.
Be courteous.
Be honest in your transactions.
Return what you borrow.
Replace what you break.
Do not bathe in the presence of women.
Do not without authority search those you arrest.

The Spirit Warriors soon became frustrated with the "unfair" tactics of the guerrillas in their midst. "Massacres of civilians were routine," one soldier later recalled. "They cooperated with the enemy, sheltered them in their houses, gave them information. We viewed them as the enemy. During combat, all villagers went into hiding. We pilfered anything useful from their houses or, in winter, burned them for firewood. If anyone was found wandering about, we captured and killed them. Spies! This was war."

Countries avoid a declaration of war so they may claim "the laws and customs of war did not apply and need not be observed." Japan never declared war on China. Instead, the fighting was euphemized as an "incident." Chinese troops were not "soldiers," but "bandits." One of the customs of war Japan was able to flout in this "incident" against "bandits" was acknowledgment that captured Chinese soldiers were prisoners of war. A 1933 army infantry textbook assured IJA officers that when they took prisoners, "if you kill them there will be no repercussions." In a 1937 directive, the army vice chief stated: "In the present situation, in order to wage total war in China, the empire will neither apply, nor act in accordance with, all the concrete articles of the Treaty Concerning the Laws and Customs of Land Warfare and Other Treaties Concerning the Laws and Regulations of Belligerency." The same directive ordered "staff officers in China to stop using the term 'prisoner of war.'" As Pulitzer Prize–winning historian Herb Bix pointed out, Hirohito himself "supported the policy of withholding a declaration of war against China and ratified and personally endorsed the decision to remove the constraints of international law on the treatment of Chinese prisoners of war." Thus Chinese soldiers taken in battle were "denied the status of prisoners of war upon the same pretext and many of them were massacred, tortured, or drafted into Japanese labor camps."

When young Shozo Tominaga arrived in China as a new Japanese army lieutenant, he was introduced to the twenty soldiers he was to lead. He was shocked by what he saw.

Tominaga was a gentle and studious boy. He had made his parents proud by graduating from prestigious Tokyo Imperial University — in Japan the equivalent of Harvard and Oxford rolled into one. Tominaga had planned for a peaceful civilian career but was drafted and soon found himself in China as a lieutenant in the emperor's army. Fresh out of officers' school, he had never seen battle. Decades later, he remembered what made his skin crawl that day.

"I'll never forget meeting them," Tominaga recalled. "When I looked at the men of my platoon I was stunned — they had evil eyes. They weren't human eyes, but the eyes of leopards or tigers. They'd experienced many battles and I was completely green. I'd seen nothing. How could I give these guys orders, or even look into those faces? I lost all my confidence. Among the men were new conscripts, two-year men, and three-year men. The longer the men had been at the front, the more evil their eyes appeared."

For five days, Tominaga and twenty-one other newly minted officers toured past battlefields where they could examine "the physical features, trying to apply our book knowledge to geography real war had touched." Then it was time to acquire a little fighting spirit, Japanese army style.

A dehumanized enemy is easy to kill, and Japanese soldiers were instructed that they were not dealing with humans at all but *kichiku,* or "devils." The idea of treating the Chinese as beasts was not informal scuttlebutt but a command from officers whose directives had to be considered orders of the emperor. Tominaga recalled:

The next-to-last day of the exercise, Second Lieutenant Tanaka took us to the detention center. Pointing at the people in a room, all Chinese, he announced, "These are the raw materials for your trial of courage." We were astonished at how thin and emaciated they looked. Tanaka told us, "They haven't been fed for several days, and so they'll be ready for their part in tomorrow's plan." He said that it was to be a test to see if we were qualified to be platoon leaders. He said we wouldn't be qualified if we couldn't chop off a head.

On the final day, we were taken out to the site of our trial. Twenty-four prisoners were squatting there with their hands tied behind their backs. They were blindfolded. A big hole had been dug — ten meters long, two meters wide, and more than three meters deep. The regimental commander, the battalion commanders, and the company commanders all took the seats arranged for them. Second Lieutenant Tanaka bowed to the regimental commander and reported, "We shall now begin." He ordered a soldier on fatigue duty to haul one of the prisoners to the edge of the pit; the prisoner was kicked when he resisted. The soldier finally dragged him over and forced him to his knees. Tanaka turned toward us and looked into each of our faces in turn. "Heads should be cut off like this," he said, unsheathing his army sword. He scooped water from a bucket with a dipper, and then poured it over both sides of the blade. Swishing off the water, he raised his sword in a long arc. Standing behind the prisoner, Tanaka steadied himself, legs spread apart, and cut off the man's head with a shout, "Yo!" The head flew more than a meter away. Blood spurted up in two fountains from the body and sprayed into the hole.

The scene was so appalling that I felt I couldn't breathe. All the candidate officers stiffened. Second Lieutenant Tanaka designated the person on the right end of our line to go next. I was fourth. When my turn came, the only thought I had was "Don't do anything unseemly!" I didn't want to disgrace myself. I bowed to the regimental commander and stepped forward. Contrary to my expectations, my feet firmly met the ground. One thin, worn-out prisoner was at the edge of the pit, blindfolded. I unsheathed my sword, a gift from my brother-in-law, wet it down as the lieutenant had demonstrated, and stood behind the man. The prisoner didn't move. He kept his head lowered. Perhaps he was resigned to his fate. I was tense, thinking I couldn't afford to fail. I took a deep breath and recovered my composure. I steadied myself, holding the sword at a point above my right shoulder, and swung down. The head flew away and the body tumbled down, spouting blood. The air reeked from all that blood. I washed blood off the blade, then wiped it with the paper provided. Fat stuck to it and wouldn't come off.

At that moment, I felt something change inside me. I don't know how to put it, but I gained strength somewhere in my gut. Until that day I had been overwhelmed by the sharp eyes of my men when I called the roll each night. That night I realized I was not self-conscious at all in front of them. I didn't even find their eyes evil anymore. I felt I was looking down on them. Later, when the National Defense Women's Association welcomed us in Manchuria, they mentioned to me that they had never seen men with such evil eyes. I no longer even noticed.

Soon Lieutenant Tominaga was imparting his newly acquired Japanese spirit to recently arrived conscripts. Officers like him wore swords, but the ordinary soldiers used bayonets to prove they were worthy to perform their "divine mission" in China.

"As the last stage of their training, we made them bayonet a living human," Tominaga said. "When I was a company commander, this was used as a finishing touch to training for the men and a trial of courage for the officers. Prisoners were blindfolded and tied to poles. The soldiers dashed forward to bayonet their target at the shout of 'Charge!' Some stopped on their way. We kicked them and made them do it. After that, a man could do anything easily."

Years later, Masato Kawana remembered his test of courage with live Chinese prisoners: "The prisoners were blindfolded and tied to the post. A circle was drawn in red chalk around the area of the heart on their grimy clothes. As the bayonet training began, the instructor bellowed out, 'Ready? The red circle is where the heart is. That's the one place you're prohibited to stab. Understand?' I thought that the instructor had marked the area to make it easier for the new recruits to stab the heart. But that was my misunderstanding. It was to make the prisoners last as long as possible."

"We made them like this," Tominaga concluded. "Good sons, good daddies, good elder brothers at home were brought to the front to kill each other. Human beings turned into murdering demons. Everyone became a demon within three months. Men were able to fight coura-geously only when their human characteristics were suppressed. So we believed. It was a natural extension of our training back in Japan. This was the Emperor's Army."

Armies travel on their stomachs. Military professionals realize that the care and feeding of the troops is an essential part of warfare. Securing and moving vast stores of foodstuff requires enormous resources. The Spirit Warriors, with their "three-month war" mentality, never both-ered mobilizing these resources. So they solved their supply problem with a euphemism — "local supply."

Newspaper reporter Tatsuzo Asai remembers with disgust the staff officers who "hardly ever went out to the front themselves," who "just sat with their legs apart, looking tough, engaging in desktop strategiz-ing in Tokyo." "They'd land thousands of men somewhere," Asai said, "but there'd be no supplies coming from the rear. 'Use local supply,' they'd order them. The local people would be growing barely enough to feed themselves, and here would come thousands of Japanese to take away what the natives had."

"Food had to be supplied locally," Enomoto-san remembered. "We were entitled to take what we needed. We could help ourselves. When we went into a village, the first thing we'd do is to look for food."

"When we went searching for food, we found women hiding," said soldier Shiro Azuma. "We thought, 'Oh, they look tasty.' So we raped them. But every single time a woman was raped, the soldiers would kill her. Any villagers who had not run off by nightfall would be mur-dered — to ensure no one could report where the invaders slept." To-minaga remembered, "Most of us thought then that murdering, raping, and setting fire to villages were unavoidable acts in war, nothing par-ticularly wrong." After all their indoctrination, this was not surprising.

One hundred thousand Americans would die in the Pacific war, while Japan would suffer about 2.5 million military and civilian casu-alties fighting the U.S. and China. No one will ever know for sure, but estimates are that nearly 30 million Chinese died in the Rape of China. They died in military operations, for being guerrillas, for possessing some food, for being in the way, for being a girl, or just because a bored Japanese soldier wanted to have some fun. Entertainment in-cluded rape, dousing people with gasoline and lighting a match, forcing sons to rape mothers, shoving sticks of dynamite up girls' vaginas to blow them up, cutting fetuses out of pregnant wombs, and chopping off countless heads.

"I went into a village and saw a girl about fourteen or fifteen years old," Enomoto-san told me years later. "I approached her, and her father appeared. I wanted to rape her. I thought, Well, if he were her father he probably wouldn't be very happy if I was raping his daughter, so I shot him. I killed him. She started crying and she was shaking. She knew what was going to happen to her. I just raped her and then I killed her. It just took one thrust of the bayonet and then she fell over."

When I asked the aged Enomoto-san how he felt about rape back then, he answered, "I was young so it felt all right. Also I felt some satisfaction as a soldier." When I asked him if he remembered the expression on the girl's face as he raped her, Enomoto-san said, "I wasn't looking at her. As soon as I finished, I killed her. That was that." Any guilt at the time? "Absolutely none."

Ni Nianke remembered an especially horrific incident that happened when he was a scared ten-year-old boy living in Niyong village, Guhuang province in China. Japanese soldiers had spent the day ransacking his village. That evening he hid in fear with his mother. In the distance he heard a local boy, Li Taidong, scream for a half hour and then stop. The German shepherd dogs accompanying the Japanese soldiers had barked as Li screamed and they continued to bark for thirty more minutes after his cries ceased. The next day, Ni and his mother ventured out to see what had happened and encountered a gruesome sight: Li's nearly fleshless skeleton hung from a tree. "Strips of meat that had clearly been torn at by dogs lay on the ground below." It was obvious that "Li had been strung up naked and that the soldiers had sliced off his flesh to feed to the dogs."

Japanese army soldier Genzo Honma remembered that the Chinese devils were useful for all sorts of experiments: "To test the power of hand grenades, the officers would go and grab a nearby man and thrust one against his stomach, after pulling the pin. As the man writhed in protest, the grenade would fall to the ground and explode — just seven seconds after the pin was pulled. The man's legs would scatter like clouds and disappear like mist; only his torso remained on the ground."

"I personally severed more than forty heads," Shintaro Uno remembered. "Today, I no longer remember each of them well. It might sound extreme, but I can almost say that if more than two weeks went by without my taking a head, I didn't feel right. Physically, I needed to be refreshed. I would go to the stockade and bring someone out, one who looked as if he wouldn't live long. I'd do it on the riverbank, by the regimental headquarters, or by the side of the road. I'd order the one I planned to kill to dig a hole, then cut him down and cover him over."

Back home, the press reported the exciting competition between Lieutenant "M" and Lieutenant "N" to see who would be the first to sever one hundred heads. On November 30, 1937, the newspaper *Tokyo Nichinichi Shimbun* featured the headline:

CONTEST TO CUT DOWN A HUNDRED!
TWO SECOND LIEUTENANTS ALREADY UP TO EIGHTY

The December 6 headline kept the home front abreast of the contest:

IT'S 89-78 IN THE "CONTEST TO CUT DOWN A HUNDRED"
A CLOSE RACE, HOW HEROIC!

And finally, on December 13:

CONTEST TO CUT DOWN A HUNDRED GOES OVER THE
TOP, M-106, N-105
PAIR PLANS TO EXTEND CONTEST

The Japanese soldiers who saw no value in Chinese lives were aware that their officers placed little value on theirs. The soldiers in the field were constantly reminded that they were only worthless *issen gorin*. Yoshio Nakamura winced as he recalled brutal marches lugging a heavy machine gun across China. "If we were lax in our care, the devil sergeant would slap our faces and scold us, saying, 'I can replace you draftees with a single red card, but I can't immediately replace a light machine gun. It's a valuable weapon.'"

The resources dedicated to medical care of wounded soldiers are an excellent measure of a country's attitude toward its boys in the field. Evacuation of the wounded is always a burden for any military. The

Spirit Warriors simplified the problem. "We evacuated only the ones able to walk," Tominaga said, "and only as many as we could. The rest of the injured were expected to kill themselves."

The Spirit Warriors did show some concern about their soldiers raping Chinese women. Not out of any concern for the women-beasts, but because rape might spread disease among the troops. An army medical report warned that "a soldier suffering from venereal disease required an average of 86 days' hospitalization; thus the spread of such a disease would weaken the strength of the Army considerably." Eventually, to reduce the incidence of happenstance rapes with the potential for spreading disease, the Spirit Warriors devised a system of organized and regulated mass rape. The euphemism for the victims of this crime was *jugun ianfu,* or "military comfort women." These comfort women were "recruited" to serve in military "comfort stations." Health officials monitored these comfort stations so the soldiers could express their "natural desires" in a relatively safe manner.

"Recruitment" of comfort women meant kidnapping Korean and Chinese girls. Virgins twelve to fifteen years old were best, since they would be disease free. These girls were simply plucked off streets and playgrounds and shipped by train, truck, or ship to where they were forced to render their service. The new girls, completely unaware of what was in store for them, would be ushered into a room and one by one raped as the others shrieked and cowered. High-ranking officers got the first chance. Once the officers were satisfied, the dazed girls were confined to the nearby comfort station.

Wherever troops were stationed, they were raping young sex slaves. The army estimated that "20,000 comfort women were required for every 700,000 Japanese soldiers, or 1 woman for every 35 soldiers." Each young sex slave had to "service" at least forty and up to seventy soldiers a day. The girls got one day off a month — the day the doctors examined them for disease. Army documents referred to the terrified high school–age girls as "military supplies." Perhaps 200,000 girls were dragged into this nightmare sex-slavery gulag; less than 10 percent survived.

The soldiers were required to use condoms to prevent infection. In one year alone, "32.1 million condoms were sent to units stationed outside Japan." Frank Gibney, an American intelligence officer who later debriefed Japanese POWs, remembered finding a packet of condoms issued by the Japanese army to its soldiers. "On the wrapping of each," he recalled, "was a picture of a Japanese soldier charging with the bayonet. The caption below read simply *Totsugeki* — 'Charge!'"

During the Rape of China, every imaginable depravity occurred. Enomoto-san told me years later:

We ran out of food. We only had these withered seed potatoes. We soaked shoes in water and ate the leather. We could find water, but little food.

We came to an empty village. All the villagers had fled because they were afraid. There was just one woman left in this village. She could speak Japanese. She told me her parents told her to flee. But she told them, "The Japanese people aren't such bad people."

This was the enemy zone. And I hadn't been to a comfort station for three months. So when I saw a woman, the first thing that came to my mind was to rape her. I had no hesitation.

She resisted. But her resistance didn't affect me. I didn't listen to her. I didn't look at her face. I raped her. Then I killed her.

I stabbed her. On television, you see a lot of blood flow out, but that's not the reality. I've cut people with swords, and you're not covered with blood. It doesn't splash like you see in movies. If you cut the neck, you see a bit of blood, but it's not like the films. I don't know how many people I've killed, but I've never experienced anything like that. When I killed that woman, I wasn't covered with blood. There was just a little blood flowing out from her heart.

After I killed her, I thought of eating her. I was thinking of how to feed my soldiers.

I didn't need much force. It went very smoothly. I used a sharp Chinese kitchen knife. It only took me about ten minutes. I didn't cut the bones. I just cut where there was a lot of meat — mainly the thighs, bottom, and shoulder. When I cut her up into meat, there wasn't that much blood.

I took her meat back and gave it to one of my soldiers to cook. If you cut it up into slices, you can't recognize what sort of meat it is. He didn't ask where the meat came from. I told them this was a special distribution of food.

We had a barbecue and we ate her meat. There were only a few slices per soldier. There were sixty people in my company. They were happy to have this meat. They said it tasted very good.

CHAPTER SIX

The ABCD Encirclement

Our candid idea at the time was that the Americans, being merchants, would not continue for long with an unprofitable war.

— *Colonel Masanobu Tsuji, quoted in* Hell in the Pacific

ON Tuesday, September 21, 1937, Japanese airplanes bombed the capital of China, Nanking. Over the next few days, the front-page *New York Times* headlines reflected the West's horror:

U.S. SHARP NOTE TO JAPAN "OBJECTS"
TO NANKING RAIDS
ATTACKS TERMED ILLEGAL

20 CHINESE CITIES BOMBED; 2,000 CASUALTIES
CIVILIANS VICTIMS

BRITAIN EXPRESSES "HORROR" OF BOMBINGS, TALKS
BOYCOTT
LONDON IN PROTEST
ENVOY CITES SLAUGHTER OF NONCOMBATANTS

The accompanying articles denounced Japan's "campaign of death and terror." Britain "called the attention of Japan officially to the fact that no nation has a right in law or in morality to bomb crowded cities from the air and so make war indiscriminately upon noncombatants and combatants alike." For its part, the U.S. State Department dispatched a stiff note to Japan, stating, "This Government holds the view that any general bombing of an extensive area wherein there resides a large populace engaged in peaceful pursuits is unwarranted and contrary to principles of law and of humanity." Secretary of State Cordell Hull condemned the bombing with these torrid words: "When the methods used in the conduct of these hostilities take the form of ruthless bombing of unfortified localities with the resultant slaughter of civilian populations, and in particular of women and children, public opinion in the US regards such methods as barbarous. Such acts are in violation of the most elementary principles of those standards of humane conduct which have been developed as an essential part of modern civilization."

President Franklin D. Roosevelt expressed the shock of "every civilized man and woman": "The ruthless bombing from the air of civilians in unfortified centers of population during the course of the hostilities which have raged in various quarters of the earth during the past few years, which has resulted in the maiming and in the death of thousands of defenseless men, women and children, has sickened the hearts of every civilized man and woman, and has profoundly shocked the conscience of humanity."

In floor debate, senators said the Japanese had committed a "crime against humanity" and were pursuing methods "reminiscent of the cruelties perpetrated by primitive and barbarous nations upon inoffensive people." A resolution was quickly passed denouncing the "inhuman bombing of civilian populations."

Soon the entire world, in the form of the League of Nations, had condemned Japan. In a resolution, the League declared that "taking into urgent consideration the question of aerial bombardment by Japanese aircraft of open towns in China, [the League] expresses its profound distress at the loss of life caused to innocent civilians, including great numbers of women and children, as a result of such bombardments, and declares that no excuse can be made for such acts, which have aroused horror and indignation throughout the world, and solemnly condemns them."

Japan's reaction was to continue bombing. And why not? The same issues of the *New York Times* discussing the West's hand-wringing also revealed that Tokyo was facing all bark and no bite. "What the United States would do if the protest should go unheeded was not revealed," the *Times* pointed out. As for the British, "At the moment it is inconceivable that Britain will do more officially than deliver moral protests. Her eyes are firmly fixed on Europe and neither her people nor her government wishes to become embroiled in the Far East." Intervention was not in the cards. Coincidentally, the American Legion was holding its annual convention in New York. Under the headline "Legion Leaders Draft Program to Keep the Country Out of War," the *Times* reported, "While New York took a holiday yesterday to enjoy the spectacle of the American Legion parade, the veterans' brain-trusters, in hotel rooms far from the rattle of drums and the blare of trumpets, met in little groups to evolve a program to keep the United States out of war and safeguard the democracy they fought to save twenty years ago." During the preceding April, German planes had shocked the world by bombing and machine-gunning civilians going to market in the historic Basque town of Guernica. Picasso later immortalized the slaughter, but at the time no western power had stepped in. In fact, that same month, one million American college students had shut down campuses across the country in the fourth annual "peace strike" as they recited the American version of the Oxford antiwar oath: "I refuse to support the Government of the United States in any war it may conduct."

The Japanese agreed that the U.S. didn't need to conduct war — because through countless slaughters, America had already cobbled together a vast country rich in resources. Now, as proud *Hakko Ichiu* Spirit Warriors tried to secure additional land and resources for their tiny island country, they resented western carping. Japan felt like a boy who got to the dinner table late only to be told by the gorged adults not to eat so much. League delegate Yosuke Matsuoka admitted that Japan had been "exceedingly annoying" to China. "And what country in its expansion has ever failed to be trying to its neighbors? Ask the American Indian or the Mexican how excruciatingly trying the young United States used to be once upon a time."

Japan was only trying to escape her "potted-plant" existence and yet, as an exasperated Japanese army general complained, "the U.S., a country two and one-half times as large as Japan proper, with a population density of only 31 per square mile to Japan's 400, was cruelly endeavoring to sever Japan's roots in order to pursue more fully her own grandiose designs. Why should the U.S., Britain and other powers which had had every opportunity to advance their own vital interests now cry, 'Thief!' if Japan even so much as looked at a neighboring territory?"

To the Japanese, the depth of the western Christians' hypocrisy was breathtaking. Japan was taming her own Wild West as the Americans had theirs: by bringing the light of civilization through divine war against a barbaric enemy. Indeed, even as America criticized Japan, the United States was proudly memorializing the chief ethnic cleansers of its West. As if to mock the defeated natives, Americans were honoring Christian expansion with a memorial carved out of Indian tribal lands. This was Mount Rushmore — a grand tableau honoring white supremacy in the midst of Indian sacred territory, the Black Hills.

The bronze tablet at its base referred to Mount Rushmore as a "pulpit of stone" and proclaimed that the pioneers represented a "new era of civilization brought forth upon this continent." The Indian holy lands were called "vast wilderness territories," as if real humans had not been present before the whites arrived. A history of repeated massacres of Indians to steal their lands was sanitized, as the tablet claimed the land was "acquired by treaties . . . where progressive, adventurous Americans spread civilization and Christianity."

It was a staggering falsehood. In 1868, the U.S. government had judged the Black Hills to be worthless, so they decided this was one place the Indians could live in peace forever. The Treaty of 1868 solemnly promised, "No white person or persons shall be permitted to settle upon or occupy any portion of the territory, or without the consent of the Indians to pass through the same." But within four years, white miners seeking gold were violating the treaty. Rather than enforce the law, the United States sent the army into the Black Hills to make a reconnaissance. This was an armed invasion, and the secretary of war warned of trouble "unless something is done to obtain possession of that section for the white miners who have been strongly attracted there by reports of rich deposits of the precious metal." Soon the Indians who had been ceded the Black Hills "forever" became "hostile Indians" to the U.S. government and were ordered off their land and into reservations.

In 1876, the federal government told the army to assume control of the Black Hills and to treat all the Indians there as prisoners of war. What, the Indians asked, about the treaty? It was, the government responded, null and void because the Indians had gone to war against the U.S. This was news to the Indians, and Spotted Tail, a Sioux chief, accused the government of broken promises and false words. "This war did not spring up here in our land; this war was brought upon us by the children of the Great Father who came to take our land from us without price, and who, in our land, do a great many evil things. . . . This war has come from robbery — from the stealing of our land."

Teddy Roosevelt disagreed. "The conquest and settlement by the whites of the Indian lands was necessary to the greatness of the race and to the well-being of civilized mankind," he said. "Such conquests are commonly undertaken by . . . a masterful people, still in its raw barbarian prime, which finds itself face to face with the weaker and wholly alien race which holds a coveted prize in its feeble grasp."

The four presidents depicted on Mount Rushmore had all supported the ethnic cleansing of the Indian. George Washington referred to Indians as "wolves," Thomas Jefferson had devised the plan to push them over the Rockies, Abraham Lincoln personally took up arms against Indians in Illinois, and Teddy Roosevelt was the top apologist for the rampage. Even the name Mount Rushmore was an affront. Charles Rushmore, a New York lawyer grubbing for mining rights, had put his own name on the sacred hill.

The Japanese knew the earth of America was soaked with Indian blood, the continent haunted by the ghosts of tribes who had been pushed, kicked, raped, and slaughtered. Indeed, the European immigrants had cleansed the continent of Native Americans so efficiently that soon there was no more civilizing left to do. American expansionists then looked to America's far west, the Pacific. As Teddy Roosevelt's political mentor New York senator Orville Platt stated, "It is to the oceans that our children must look as we once looked to the boundless west."

As vice president under William McKinley, then as president in his own right, Teddy Roosevelt had relished the chance to bring Christian civilization to America's first major colonial possession in the Pacific, the Philippines. "Not one competent witness who has actually known the facts believes the Filipinos capable of self-government at the present," Roosevelt said. He found it unthinkable to "abandon the Philippines to their own tribes." To him, the Filipino freedom fighters were "a syndicate of Chinese half-breeds," and to grant them self-government "would be like granting self-government to an Apache reservation under some local chief."

Christian intellectuals saw nothing wrong with "helping" Filipinos by denying them freedom. The *Literary Digest* polled 192 editors of Christian publications and found only three who recommended independence for the Philippines. "Has it ever occurred to you that Jesus was the most imperial of the imperialists?" asked the *Missionary Record.*

Just three decades before Enomoto-san was taught that the Chinese were beasts, American veterans of the Indian wars sailed off to the Philippines. "We had been taught . . . that the Filipinos were savages no better than our Indians," an American officer said. When Senator Joseph Burton of Kansas defended the slaughter of Filipinos on the Senate floor as "entirely within the regulations of civilized warfare" by citing earlier massacres of Indians as a precedent, "no one even bothered to respond."

America would cause the deaths of more than 250,000 Filipinos — men, women, and children — from the beginning of the hostilities on February 4, 1899, to July 4, 1902, when President Roosevelt declared the Philippines "pacified." That is pretty serious killing. America fought WWII over a period of fifty-six months with approximately 400,000 casualties on all fronts. So Hitler and Tojo combined, with all their mechanized weaponry, killed about the same per month — 7,000 — as the American "civilizers" did in the Philippines.

The Filipino uprising against their former Spanish masters had been a guerrilla operation, a popular insurgency supported by the civilian population. The brutality of the Spanish response had been one of the American rationales for kicking Spain out in the first place. Now America replaced the oppressor and adopted the same methods — widespread torture, concentration camps, the killing of disarmed prisoners and helpless civilians — but with a ruthlessness that surpassed even that of the Spanish. The majority of Filipinos killed by the American soldiers were civilians. An army circular attempted to assuage any guilt by rationalizing that "it is an inevitable consequence of war that the innocent must generally suffer with the guilty," and since all natives were treacherous, it was impossible to recognize "the actively bad from only the passively so."

One American army captain wrote of "one of the prettiest little towns we have passed through" — the people there "desire peace and are friendly to Los Americanos. When we came along this road, the natives that had remained stood along the side of the road, took off their hats, touched their foreheads with their hands. 'Buenos Dias, Senors' (means good morning)." The good American boys then proceeded to slaughter the residents and ransack the town.

Anthony Michea of the Third Artillery wrote, "We bombarded a place called Malabon, and then we went in and killed every native we met, men, women and children." Another soldier described the fun of killing innocent civilians: "This shooting human beings is a 'hot game,' and beats rabbit hunting all to pieces. We charged them and such a slaughter you never saw. We killed them like rabbits; hundreds, yes thousands of them. Everyone was crazy."

"I want no prisoners," one American general ordered. "I wish you to kill and burn, the more you kill and burn the better it will please me." An officer asked for clarification, "to know the limit of age to respect." The general replied in writing to kill all those above "ten years of age."

Corporal Richard O'Brien wrote home about "The Beast of La Nog," a Captain Fred McDonald who ravished a village by that name. "O'Brien described how his company had gunned down civilians waving white flags because McDonald had ordered 'take no prisoners.' Only a beautiful mestizo mother was spared to be repeatedly raped by McDonald and several officers and then turned over to the men for their pleasure."

Americans back home knew what was happening in the Philippines. Private Joseph Sladen wrote home about a helpless group of enemy fighters his company trapped in the middle of a stream: "'From then on the fun was fast and furious,' as dead Filipinos piled up 'thicker than buffalo chips,' Sladen recorded. Several western lads informed their dads that 'picking off niggers in the water' was 'more fun

69

than a turkey shoot.'" A soldier from Kingston, New York, wrote his parents a letter that was soon published nationally about the massacre of a thousand civilians in the town of Titatia: "I am probably growing hard-hearted, for I am in my glory when I can sight my gun on some dark skin and pull the trigger. Tell all my inquiring friends that I am doing everything I can for Old Glory and for America I love so well." Letters appeared in American newspapers about American boys "routinely firing on Filipinos carrying white flags." Soldiers were "ordered to take no prisoners and to kill the wounded." American soldiers had no qualms about obeying orders to kill POWs. Private Fred Hinchman complained about some newly arrived Yankee soldiers "with about fifty prisoners, who had been taken before they learned how not to take them."

Killing Filipino POWs was official American policy. Commanders were told that whenever an American soldier was "murdered," the commander was to "by lot select a POW — preferably one from the village in which the assassination took place — and execute him." Officers set the example. "Colonel Funston not only ordered the regiment to take no prisoners, but he bragged to reporters that he had personally strung up thirty-five civilians suspected of being insurrectos. Major Edwin Glenn did not even deny the charge that he made forty-seven prisoners kneel and 'repent of their sins' before ordering them bayoneted and clubbed to death."

For those unfortunates who made it alive into American hands, widespread torture was the rule. Harvard-educated First Lieutenant Grover Flint later recalled for a Senate panel the routine torture of Filipino combatants and civilians — thirty here, forty there. Lieutenant Flint described the "water cure," the standard U.S. Army torture:

> A man is thrown down on his back and three or four men sit or stand on his arms and legs and hold him down, and either a gun barrel or a rifle or a carbine barrel or a stick as big as a belaying pin . . . is simply thrust into his jaws and his jaws are thrust back, and, if possible, a wood log or stone is put under . . . his neck, so he can be held firmly.

Senator Julius Caesar Burrows of Michigan interrupted to ask, "His jaws are forced open, you say? How do you mean, crosswise?"

70

Lieutenant Flint: Yes, sir, as a gag. In the case of very old men I have seen their teeth fall out — I mean when it was done a little roughly. He is simply held down, and then water is poured into his face, down his throat and nose from a jar, and that is kept up until the man gives some sign of giving in or becoming unconscious, and when he becomes unconscious he is simply rolled aside and he is allowed to come to. . . . Well, I know that in a great many cases, in almost every case, the men have been a little roughly handled; they were rolled aside rudely, so that water was expelled. A man suffers tremendously; there is no doubt about that. His suffering must be that of a man who is drowning, but he cannot drown.

President Theodore Roosevelt excused his army's atrocities in the Philippines and hailed "the bravery of American soldiers" who fought "for the triumph of civilization over the black chaos of savagery and barbarism." To Roosevelt, the extermination of hundreds of thousands of noncombatant civilians and defenseless POWs in the Philippines represented "the most glorious war in the nation's history."

When Japanese military men asked themselves how the Christians could be so hypocritical about Japan doing exactly what they had done, there was one clear answer: racism. Off and on for years, the United States Congress had threatened discriminatory immigration bills against yellow Japanese. In October 1906, a year after the Portsmouth treaty, the San Francisco school board had ordered all Japanese children to attend the Oriental school in Chinatown. The Japanese government winced at this "act of discrimination carrying with it a stigma and odium which it is impossible to overlook." Later, Congress overwhelmingly approved an immigration bill denying visas to Japanese and other Asians.

To Japanese military men, the League of Nations could as well be called the "League of Christian Anti-Japanese Nations." Japan had sided with the Allies in WWI, sat at the reparations table at the Paris Peace Conference as the only non-Western power, and been awarded German islands in the Pacific. But Japan feared that "the West intended to use the League of Nations to perpetuate the ascendancy of the white race. 'Our real fear [wrote delegate Prince Fumimaro Konoe] is that the League of Nations might let the powerful nations dom-

71

inate the weak nations economically, and condemn the late-coming nations to remain forever subordinate to the advanced nations.'"

Indeed, when the League passed a resolution calling for self-determination for countries and the end of colonialism, the United States slipped in a clause exempting itself. Freedom was a nice concept, but in the real world, Washington preferred its Monroe Doctrine lock on power in the Americas. So why should Japan, the only civilized power in Asia, not have similar rights in its backyard?

Japan was so convinced of *gaizin* prejudice that it requested a racial equality clause be added to the League's covenant. "The proposal was a blandly worded declaration that member nations would not discriminate against one another on the basis of race or nationality and would try 'as much as possible to grant de jure equality' to foreign subjects living in their territory." Not one western country voted for the clause.

The final straw came in 1931, when the westerners in the League decided to investigate Japan's "aggression" in China without mentioning how they had happened upon their own colonies. Delegate Yosuke Matsuoka, who had studied at the University of Oregon, rose to defend Japan in a classic *Hakko Ichiu* speech: "China lacked a legitimate government that could maintain law and order; it was weak and 'backward,' a country 'in an appalling condition of disintegration and distress' where 'tens of millions of people have lost their lives as a result of internecine warfare, tyranny, banditry, famine and flood.' Japan, in contrast, was 'a great civilizing nation' that 'has been and always will be the mainstay of peace, order and progress in the Far East.' In a region that was hopelessly disorganized, Matsuoka argued, Japan had made Manchuria into an island of stability and prosperity." But the speech fell on deaf ears. The League members who were "helping" their subjugated colonists around the globe voted unanimously against Japan, which cast the only vote in its own favor. Matsuoka and the entire Japanese delegation walked out of the League for good.

How could the Christian imperialists have the gall to tell Japan it wasn't supposed to be involved in countries next door when the westerners had come from across the globe to subjugate Asian nations? The United States had taken the Philippines and Hawaii by bayonet. Washington was constantly invading countries in the Caribbean and Central and South America. If America was sincere about freedom, it could divest its colonial holdings. Japan knew the money it paid for Indonesian oil and Vietnamese rubber went directly to the Dutch and French treasuries in Europe. Laotians who challenged French rule ended up hanging from ropes. The Europeans had exploited Africa without pause or mercy. Where were the calls for independence for the colonies of the Christians?

In July 1939, the United States announced that it was ending its twenty-seven-year-old commercial treaty with Japan. Japan's hated enemy Chiang Kai-shek had convinced FDR to apply economic sanctions against Japan to try and force it into a negotiated settlement with China. "According to an opinion poll, 75 per cent of the American public agreed" with this provocative anti-Japanese action.

Hitler invaded Poland on September 1, 1939, and one month later, in October of 1939, Roosevelt ordered a large part of the American fleet to Pearl Harbor. From the Japanese point of view, this was an extremely threatening move. There were no free countries on the Pacific rim to protect, only American, British, French, and Dutch colonies.

In June of 1940, Germany overran France. Japan pressured the new French government to cut off supplies flowing into China through its colony French Indochina, and persuaded the beleaguered British — who had no other choice — to stop supplies to China from their colony in Burma. America, on the other hand, banned the export of aviation gasoline, lubricating oil, and scrap iron to Japan.

To Japan, it was all very suspicious. America aided China and the white colonial powers of Asia just enough to keep Japan's troops bogged down, while the Yankees simultaneously rearmed and negotiated in a desultory manner. Now it looked as though the mighty U.S.A. wanted to choke Japan with economic sanctions. The Tokyo press spoke of the "ABCD encirclement." The abbreviation referred to the "American-British-Chinese-Dutch" mob that was trying to squeeze the life out of Japan.

Seeking friends in a hostile world, Japan allied with Italy and Germany in the Tripartite Pact. And if Americans didn't like it, Prime Minister Fumimaro Konoe announced where they could stick it: "If the United States does not understand the positions of Japan, Germany, and Italy, and regards our pact as a provocative action directed against it, and if it constantly adopts a confrontational attitude, then the three countries will fight resolutely."

Later that month, Secretary of State Cordell Hull, who had spent years "lecturing the Japanese about the 'principles of good behavior,'" handed Japan's ambassador a list of demands for normalized relations. "Known as Hull's Four Principles, they included respect for the territorial integrity of other nations, noninterference in the internal affairs of other countries, the maintenance of equal commercial opportunity for all and no alteration to the status quo except through peaceful means."

The Japanese must have wondered if Secretary Hull was a comedian and if this was a joke. Western militaries had subdued countries all across Asia and Africa, and now the secretary expected Japan to play by different rules.

But it was no joke, and Roosevelt upped the ante with audacious displays of American power and Anglo-American-Dutch unity. He ordered American naval officers to "participate openly in staff conversations at Singapore with high-ranking British, Dutch, Australian, New Zealand, and Indian officers in April." The American president also sent a message to Emperor Hirohito describing Japanese troops in Indochina as creating a "deep and far-reaching emergency" that threatened the Philippines, the East Indies, Malaya, and Thailand, and peaceful relations with the United States. Roosevelt proposed that the Japanese "dispel the dark clouds" in Asia. But Tokyo only saw dark clouds drifting from the West.

In July 1940, Japan occupied French Indochina in an attempt to encircle China, cut off her lifeline, and end the conflict on Japan's terms. "When the Japanese army moved to occupy southern Indochina, despite American warnings, the [Japanese] government had already calculated that the only way to break the stalemate in China was to risk a war with the whole world."

The U.S. reacted in August by dispatching the largest fleet of U.S. warplanes — more than four hundred from the growing fleet FDR was now building in the shadow of threats from Germany and Japan — to America's colony the Philippines. FDR also promoted Manila-based General Douglas MacArthur as commander in chief of all U.S. military forces in the Far East.

Shortly thereafter, FDR froze all Japanese assets in the United States, ended all trade with Japan, and cut the flow of precious oil. The other white colonizers, Britain and Holland, followed suit. Japan's oil reserves would last only twenty months. Without a source of oil, Japan would be paralyzed, as helpless as a beached whale.

Japan tried to negotiate. If the U.S. would only cut off aid to China and allow Japan access to oil, the emperor's divine peace would rule throughout Asia. All would be well.

The United States countered: Get out of China and we'll sell you oil.

Get out of China! How about Roosevelt withdrawing from California and returning it to Mexico? Or France granting independence to Algeria or Churchill listening to Gandhi's pleas for Indian control of India? FDR had earlier "predicted that Americans would question continued relations with Tokyo 'if the Japanese government were to fail to speak as civilized twentieth-century human beings.'" Civilized? Just months before, the French had razed villages in the Mekong Delta, arrested eight thousand people, including old women and children, run wires through their palms and heels to chain them together, and transported them by barges for days as they roasted under a tropical sun. Was that the civilized behavior Mr. Roosevelt was referring to? Any visitor to the United States could see the "Whites Only" signs, the black bodies swinging from the lynching trees, the dusty Indian reservations where America warehoused its conquered. The United States Congress had enacted fourteen separate discriminatory immigration laws to keep Chinese out of the U.S. — and FDR lectured Japan on how to treat them "fairly." Civilized?

The coming confrontation was a chance for Hirohito to emulate Grandpa Meiji's great military triumph. But when he asked, no one would promise Meiji's forty-year-old grandson that Japan could win a war against the United States. The Spirit Warriors just puffed up their chests, saying Japan must strike while the iron was hot.

The Keystone cops quality of the deliberations leading up to war is illustrated by an exchange between the godly commander in chief and his army and navy heads — General Hajime Sugiyama and Admiral Nagano — in imperial conference on September 5, 1941. Hirohito inquired how long it would take to "dispose of the matter," meaning war with the United States. General Sugiyama responded that "the operations in the South would take about three months. The Emperor broke in at once, tersely observing that as war minister in 1937, Sugiyama had said the China Incident would be over in about a month. That had been four years ago and the fighting was still in progress."

General Sugiyama explained that while China was a vast hinterland, the Pacific was composed of islands, so the problem was not the same. Hirohito responded with incredulity, "If you call the Chinese hinterland vast, would you not describe the Pacific as even more immense? With what confidence do you say 'three months'?"

In other top councils that would have been the end for this general. But Sugiyama just hung his head and maintained his role as the emperor's top army adviser, "perhaps because putting anyone on the spot was considered a rather drastic thing to do."

In early November, Hirohito reviewed the Pearl Harbor attack plan and heard the military pitch its grand strategy for the Pacific war. It was here that the god-emperor, the Boy Soldier trained for war, could have revealed the Spirit Warriors' utter lack of coherent strategy and paucity of planning. They presented him with a "first stage offensive" — the knockout punch at Pearl Harbor and the invasion of Malaya, Singapore, Indonesia, and the Philippines. But there were no follow-up plans, just a "hypothesis" that Japan would later answer enemy responses with brilliant counterthrusts. No one mentioned estimates of potential losses, numbers describing Japan's financial ability to support a war, definitions of adequate supply, manpower requirements, or raw material calculations. How exactly was Japan going to defeat an industrial behemoth like the United States? The U.S. annually produced twelve times the steel, five times the number of ships, one hundred and five times the number of automobiles, and five and a half times the amount of electricity that Japan did.

But to the Spirit Warriors this was just nit-picking. The United States had material strength but lacked the most important virtue. Any Spirit Warrior knew victory was the result of material strength multiplied by spiritual strength. *Yamato damashii* would be the secret ingredient to break the ring of the ABCD encirclement. Japanese leaders reasoned that Yankee culture was soft and that the average American was too selfish to support a long war in a distant place. Colonel Masanobu Tsuji, one of Japan's top war strategists, later said, "Our candid ideas at the time were that the Americans, being merchants, would not continue for long with an unprofitable war, whereas we . . . could carry on a protracted war."

* * *

In November of 1941, U.S. Naval Intelligence detected the first faint signals indicating Japan was about to strike. They were detected by a pipe-smoking man dressed in slippers and a red smoking jacket in a windowless basement room at Pearl Harbor. He was Joseph Rochefort, chief of the navy's Combat Intelligence Unit. The signals emanated from radio transmission stations on Chichi Jima. When Commodore Perry had first beheld Chichi Jima, he had seen two peaks on the tiny island. Now the Imperial Japanese Navy had built reinforced concrete radio buildings on those same mounts.

On November 8, Rochefort compiled the information gleaned from Chichi Jima's transmitters into a "Communication Intelligence Summary" and wired it to Washington. The Chichi Jima signals described a "two-prong" attack, one going east from Japan, the other south.

On November 27, 1941, the U.S. chief of naval operations wired an urgent dispatch to all Pacific stations:

THIS DISPATCH IS TO BE CONSIDERED A WAR WARNING
NEGOTIATIONS WITH JAPAN LOOKING TOWARD
STABILIZATION OF
CONDITIONS IN THE PACIFIC HAVE CEASED AND AN
AGGRESSIVE MOVE
BY JAPAN IS EXPECTED WITHIN THE NEXT FEW DAYS

Americans would always "Remember Pearl Harbor." But the attack against Hawaii was a sideshow meant to cripple America's ability to blunt Japan's all-important thrust to "the South." The opening salvo of the Pacific war occurred one hour and twenty minutes before the strike at Pearl Harbor, when General Hirofumi Yamashita landed his 20,000 troops on the east coast of Malaya. Britain's 88,000 troops vastly outnumbered the Japanese, but the Brits lacked *Yamato damashii* and soon surrendered to the better-motivated sons of the gods.

In his declaration of war, Prime Minister Hideki Tojo said the conflict was the fault of "the United States and England for supporting and encouraging the Chinese in disturbing the peace of East Asia, in pursuit of their inordinate ambition to dominate the Orient." Tojo said the "Emperor's profound hope is that peace be maintained," but the *gaizin* showed "not the least spirit of conciliation," so "Our Empire, for its existence and self-defense, has no other recourse but to appeal to arms and to crush every obstacle in the path." *Yamato damashii* would defeat the American "merchants."

When Japanese leaders referred to Americans as "merchants" they were thinking of one particular Dutchman in the White House. But Tojo and the emperor had miscalculated. In Franklin Roosevelt they were tangling with a man who had had his life devastated by polio and then willed himself into becoming president of the United States. This was a man who had led his citizens through the dark days of the Depression with a smile that radiated confidence from his soul. This Dutchman feared nothing — not even fear itself.

After Japan attacked America, President Roosevelt thought deeply about how best to respond. He evaluated the plans of his military advisers, but they weren't imaginative enough for him. Then he hit upon an idea no military man could have conceived of, because it was presumed to be impossible. When FDR first told his advisers, they were dumbfounded. But since Japanese experts also considered such a concept impossible, they would be taken by surprise when America finally manifested the Dutchman's idea.

The idea involved the Flyboys.

CHAPTER SEVEN

Flyboys

*We were all teenagers or barely into our twenties, totally naive to
the ways of the world. Our patriotic goal was to get even for Pearl
Harbor. All forty-eight states were united. Aviators would be
needed to defeat Japan. We were the Flyboys. . . .*

— *Pilot Lou Grab, quoted in* George Bush: His World War II Years

THE original Pearl Harbor Day found George H. W. Bush walking
across the campus of Phillips Academy in Andover, Massachusetts,
his boarding school. George was seventeen years, six months old,
president of his senior class, a BMOC — big man on campus. He was
also captain of the baseball and soccer teams, a playing manager of the
basketball team, treasurer of the student council, deputy housemaster,
and a member of other boards, societies, and teams.

George's family was wealthy and well connected. If any young man
in the United States "had it made," he did. His father, Prescott Bush,
was managing partner of Brown Brothers Harriman, the nation's
largest private bank. Young George had already been accepted at Yale.
He was a thirteenth cousin, twice removed, of the future Queen Elizabeth. The prestigious Walker Cup, for international golfing competition, was named after his grandfather. With Yale on the horizon, with
solid wealth backing him and important contacts willing to smooth his
way in the world, George was on track to a golden future.

On that walk across campus, someone shouted the shocking news of the surprise Japanese attack and George decided then and there to chuck his privileges. He later admitted, "I didn't fully comprehend world affairs," but he remembered distinctly having "the typical American reaction that we had better do something about this."

Recalled George, "There wasn't any doubt which branch of the service I'd join. My thoughts turned immediately to naval aviation."

Halfway across the country, another future Flyboy — Floyd Ewing Hall — leading a very different life than George Bush's, marched off to his Sedalia, Missouri, hometown post office to sign up to fight. Floyd was twenty-one years old, skinny, with brown hair and eyes. Floyd had graduated from Sedalia's Smith-Cotton High School on May 18, 1939. He followed his dad — a welder — into employ at the Missouri Pacific Railroad yards, Sedalia's largest employer with seven thousand workers. Sedalia was a railroad town: The Missouri-Kansas-Texas Railroad and the Missouri Pacific Railroad had repair shops there. Sedalia, roughly in the center of Missouri, was a city of twenty thousand people, with a skating rink, a pool hall, a bowling alley, and a few bars. Floyd's brother James Hall remembered there were two seasons in Sedalia: "We had winter and summer — cold and hot."

Vivian Dalton Long remembered Floyd as "a good boy, clean and wholesome-minded." Floyd grew up across the street from Vivian and played pinochle with her. "Sedalia," recalled Long, "was a friendly, wonderful place to live. You could walk safely late at night. That was years ago, when neighbors sat on each other's porches and visited."

Floyd was typical of the hardworking American kids spawned by the Depression. "Floyd didn't play sports," remembered his brother, "because he didn't have time." Floyd's first official job was as a soda jerk in the malt shop in the Tullis-Hall Dairy. It was a popular spot in the small city. "You'd go out there on a hot summer day," James said, "and you'd see everybody you knew licking an ice-cream cone." Floyd's friend Elwood McKinney remembered, "After the big shots left, Floyd would give me all the ice cream I could eat. He was a good guy."

A hard worker, Floyd had some change to throw around. "I used to polish his shoes for a nickel," Floyd's sister, Margie Hall, remembered. "I'd make those shoes shine. I worked so hard on them. I thought I was rich."

One day Floyd's father blew his stack over his son's spending habits. Floyd had pooled his money with that of his buddy Howard Herring and bought a used convertible Model T. His father thought they had been entirely too extravagant. He focused his anger not on his son but on the man who had sold Floyd the car. "Dad," remembered James Hall, "went down to the dealer and bawled him out for charging so much. He thought they held him up. The car cost thirty-five dollars."

Floyd loved the car, often brushing the snow off the frozen seats in the winter to drive it to school. No one realized it at the time, but America would soon benefit from the many young Floyd Halls who had fallen in love with their automobiles. America would fight a highly mechanized war in World War II, and airplanes — the key to that mechanized war — were the most sophisticated machines of all. "For the Allied air forces it was a priceless advantage that Western economies were firmly in the era of the internal combustion machine." World War II military aircraft would be complex, expensive, and of vital importance. These warplanes would require many tinkerers to serve as pilots, air crews, and maintenance workers. Floyd working under the hood of his thirty-five-dollar investment or a farm kid fixing the family tractor would later help America win the air war. Japan, by contrast, was much less mechanized, exposing many fewer of its young men to machinery. "It was a bad omen when on March 23, 1939, the original Zero prototype was disassembled, loaded into ox-carts, and moved over poor roads to the large naval air base at Kagami-gahara prior to its initial flight."

"We enlisted the day after Pearl Harbor," Floyd's friend Willard Chewning recalled. "We were called up a week later on December six-teenth. We boarded a train to Saint Louis together. There were different recruiters for each service, and we just got in line for the navy." Floyd's brother said, "There wasn't anything my folks could say. Floyd was twenty-one; he was an adult." On the line "Reason for Enlistment," Floyd wrote, "Serve Country."

In Saint Louis, the navy examiners noted that Floyd Hall stood all of five feet seven inches tall and weighed 128 pounds. Just old enough to vote, the young man from Missouri was now one of thousands of American boys who were off to win the war.

It was hardly surprising that boys in the early 1940s wanted to fly. Most of the Flyboys who flew off aircraft carriers in the northern Pacific in 1944 and 1945 were born in the early 1920s and grew up in the golden age of the airplane. In an era when the original "horsepower" was still making its transformation to the mechanical variation, airplanes and the airmen who flew them were impossibly exciting for impressionable young American boys. They read war stories in the pulps about World War I pilots like the Red Baron and Eddie Rickenbacker. One of the only scientific studies on the subject of bravery, *The Anatomy of Courage,* predicted in the 1920s that "future adventurous young men who sought glory in war would tend to seek it as pilots."

The most famous man in America — arguably the most famous man of the twentieth century — was an aviator named Charles Lindbergh. As a distracted college student, Lindbergh was forever changed by his first ride in an airplane. Remembering it later, he said he felt as though he had lost "all conscious connection with the past," that he lived "only in the moment in this strange, unmortal space, crowded with beauty, pierced with danger."

Flying was the next new thing and had a Wild West thrill about it. Even though he had only eight hours of flying time behind him and had never soloed, Lindbergh didn't have to show a pilot's license when he purchased his first airplane. "They didn't ask to see my license," Lindbergh explained, "because you didn't have to have a license to fly an airplane in 1923."

Lindbergh became a barnstormer, dropping into towns to give exhibitions and sight-seeing flights. He and his fellow travelers would perform "death-defying stunts upon arrival to lure the customers and again upon leaving so they felt they had received their money's worth." About risking his life, Lindbergh decided, "If I could fly for ten years before I was killed in a crash, it would be a worthwhile trade for an ordinary lifetime."

On May 20, 1927, Lindbergh readied his *Spirit of St. Louis* airplane at Roosevelt Field on Long Island for his solo cross-Atlantic flight. The editor of *Aero-Digest* asked if the five sandwiches the young man had packed were enough. "If I get to Paris," Lindbergh said, "I won't need any more, and if I don't get to Paris, I won't need any more, either." His mother told the press, "Tomorrow, Saturday, a holiday for me, will be either the happiest day in my whole life, or the saddest." As the world went to sleep that night with Charles Lindbergh somewhere over the Atlantic, "modern man realized nobody had ever subjected himself to so extreme a test of human courage and capability as Lindbergh. Not even Columbus sailed alone."

When Lindbergh circled an airfield outside Paris thirty-three and one half hours later, he was astounded to see 150,000 people waiting for him. The huge *New York Times* banner headline blared, "LINDBERGH DOES IT!" and his incredible feat filled the first five pages of the newspaper. President Coolidge dispatched a navy transport to bring Lindbergh and his plane home. When the new world celebrity docked at Manhattan's Pier A, there were 300,000 people waiting. New York City's offices, schools, and the financial exchanges closed for "Lindbergh Day." Four million people lined his ticker tape parade. Coverage of his reception consumed the first sixteen pages of the next day's *New York Times.*

Lindbergh's autobiography was a blockbuster bestseller. His story appeared in textbooks, and schoolkids wrote essays in praise of Lucky Lindy's bravery. When he toured the country, an estimated thirty million spectators — one quarter of the nation — turned out. A new magazine called *Time* tried to boost sales with a "Man of the Year" edition at the end of 1927. The honoree was Charles Lindbergh.

"I was seven years old when Lindbergh flew the ocean," remembered Flyboy Ed Baumann of the Bronx, "and he was my hero. He was the 'Lone Eagle.' Even at that age I could recognize that Lindbergh did what no one else would do."

Bruce Hayes of Brooklyn knew he wanted to fly long before WWII came along. As a boy he cut pictures of airplanes out of newspapers. He told me he still has the scrapbook in which he pasted them. "I was five years old when Lindbergh's cruiser threw its hook at the New York pier. His plane was on the ship. That was the beginning of my love affair with flying."

Some fell in love from afar. Young Charlie Brown from Kingwood, West Virginia, saw airplanes only in newspapers and movie reels, but that was enough to convince him to enlist in the navy's flying program in August of 1942.

Airmen were the coolest of the cool. Archie Clapp, who later flew in the Pacific, told me, "I grew up in Miami and my girlfriend's father was an Eastern Airlines pilot. He was the hero of the neighborhood."

Boys across the country constructed model airplanes and dreamed of their future in the Third Dimension. "I was one of those kids who built model airplanes," Ed Baumann told me. "I sent in ten cents to join the Junior Birdmen of America, an organization of model builders. I still have the card."

"My brother and I," recalled Flyboy George Heilsberg of Jersey City, "used to make model airplanes and sell them for ten cents each. We studied all the books about them. I knew more about recognition than trained sailors. We loved airplanes."

The sketches of airplanes that grace the first page of each chapter in this book are the handiwork of Grady York, who grew up at 1058 Dyal Street in Jacksonville, Florida. Why and how Grady first became interested in planes no one remembers. But when he enlisted on February 6, 1943, he listed only one item on the line for "Leisure-Time Activities." He wrote, "Scale-model airplanes."

Grady York certainly did not look like he had the physical wherewithal to help win a war. On enlistment day, he stood only five feet four inches tall and weighed just 106 pounds. But World War II was the first conflict that truly prized combatants of small size like Grady. War in the Third Dimension required gunners and radiomen who could scrunch up in tight, confined spaces behind the pilot. Grady fit the bill.

"He was a nice-looking fella," his sister Pearl York Diffenderfer told me. "He always wore nice clothes. He had pictures of himself with different blondes who knew him." Photos of Grady show an attractive youth with smooth olive skin, curly black hair, and a face handsome yet innocent, with a glowing smile. Maybe it was his air of vulnerability that attracted the girls. His cousin Betty Huckleberry admitted, "I had a crush on him. I thought the world of Grady." Sister Pearl said even the family cat "loved him and would follow him wherever he went."

Grady and Pearl's father was a carpenter, and the family was poor. Entertainment was a tire hung from the backyard tree. Sometimes Dad would come home with a truckload of sawdust for the kids to jump in. "We ate a lot of beans and spaghetti," Pearl remembered. "Steak once in a great while. Candy just wasn't around. I was seven years old before I had bubble gum. I remember it clearly because it was the first time."

Perhaps it is not so surprising that a young boy in Grady's circumstances would dream of soaring.

*   *   *

A verse from the song "Home on the Range" sums up the innocence of the small-town America that produced many of the boys who went off to World War II:

> *Where seldom is heard a discouraging word,*
> *And the skies are not cloudy all day.*

Glenn Frazier literally had a home on the range. Glenn grew up in Athol, Kansas, just six miles from the cabin where Dr. Brewster Higley penned "Home on the Range," which later became the Kansas state song. Glenn was a redheaded, freckled, innocent, open-faced farm boy who might never have left Kansas if he hadn't felt the need to help his country. When he signed up at the age of seventeen years and six months, he wrote just one word on the form that asked his reason for enlisting. That word was "War."

Glenn grew up in a small-town America more connected to the nineteenth century than the twentieth. Radio was just uniting the country, and most homes still did not have telephones or indoor plumbing. "Athol was named after the wife of the railroad superintendent," Glenn's cousin Eugene Frazier told me. "The most population it ever had was four hundred. When the railroad left, it went down to two hundred."

"Glenn's grandfather had been a pioneer," Eugene said. "He had a big farm that he and Glenn's dad worked. Glenn lived out in the country next to that farm." Eugene recalled working with Glenn to harvest the wheat and rye that grew on their grandfather's farm. "We brought our own lunch and got paid twenty-five cents a day. That was big money for eight and nine year olds."

Life in Athol was quiet. "We mashed a lot of pennies when the train would go by," Eugene recalled. "We tried to figure out how to get rich by compressing sand into diamonds. Back then, even sand, anything, was valuable to us. That was when a penny would buy an adult hand of jelly beans."

If not for the war, Glenn probably would have been happy home on the range all his life — or at least in Kansas City, where his parents had moved while he was in high school. His favorite class was metal work, and on his enlistment form, he cited "hunting and fishing" as avocations. During high school he worked on a construction crew erecting prefabricated houses, a job that he probably would have stuck with if not for Pearl Harbor.

One month after high school graduation, Glenn went in for his navy physical. There, navy doctors certified that this five-foot-one-inch, 110-pound specimen of American boyhood could fight for Uncle Sam.

When George Bush told his father that he wanted to sign up for naval aviation and postpone plans to attend Yale, Prescott was supportive, but hesitantly so. Parents across the country were torn between patriotic urges and the knowledge that their boys were, well, just boys.

Secretary of War Henry Stimson was the commencement speaker at George's high school graduation ceremony. "Secretary Stimson," George remembered, "told us the war would be a long one and even though America needed fighting men, we'd serve our country better by getting more education before getting into uniform. After the ceremony, in a crowded hallway outside the auditorium, my father had one last question about my future plans. Dad was an imposing presence, six feet four, with deep-set blue gray eyes and a resonant voice.

"'George,' he said, 'did the secretary say anything to change your mind?'

"'No, sir,' I replied. 'I'm going in.'"

His father nodded and shook his hand.

Years later, I asked former President Bush why he hadn't taken Secretary Stimson's advice. He answered, "By then it was too late. I wanted to fight. It was just something I wanted to do."

George enlisted on his eighteenth birthday, June 12, 1942. "I was a scared, nervous kid," he recalled. He was ordered to report for training in North Carolina two months later. Prescott Bush saw his son off at New York's Penn Station. President Bush later told me, "My dad probably wanted me to stay home. I think I was the youngest guy on the train." George's dad never tried to dissuade his son. But as they said their good-byes on the train platform, his father's feelings were obvious. George remembered, "It was the first time I had ever seen my dad cry."

Some boys didn't have dads to consult. When he enlisted at the age of seventeen in July of 1942, Dick Woellhof of Clay Center, Kansas, could barely remember his father, who had been dead for nine years. He had died on July 26, 1932 — Dick's eighth birthday.

Dick's mother, Laura, worked six days a week to support her three children. Dick was the youngest, Lawrence a year older, and Lucille the oldest. After she was widowed, Laura Woellhof had studied cosmetology and opened a beauty parlor. The family home was the upstairs apartment.

Jane Lassiter lived across the alley from the Woellhofs and remembered Clay Center as "a small town of three thousand churchgoing people. The town had two movie houses (the Rex and Star) and a postage-sized dance floor at the Gingham Apron Restaurant, where we would try some steps to the music of the time.

"Dick was shy," Lassiter recalled, "and he didn't dance much."

Rugged and handsome Dick Woellhof lettered in three sports — football, basketball, and track — for the Clay Center Tigers. In the yearbook, the legend under his photo says, "Many know him, many like him." He had an after-school job pumping gas at a service station, but most of all he was devoted to his family.

"Dick was a family boy," his aunt Ruah Sterrett told me. "He loved his mother, his brother, and his sister. His mother would proudly tell me, 'Dick cleaned house today. He did all the laundry.'"

The little money energetic Dick earned came home to help feed the family. "He was raised by his mother, who had to work hard," Dick's friend John Anderson told me. "There wasn't much income."

"Mom was gone six days a week doing hair," Dick's brother, Lawrence, recalled. "When my sister graduated from high school, we two brothers were alone. I learned how to cook green beans in a can."

The great plains where Dick grew up were canopied by a sweeping arc of sky, and while many looked down, to the earth, for their future, some looked up. In Dick's last year of high school, he told his mother he wanted to enlist in the navy to fly. Laura Woellhof confided to her sister that she was beside herself about the decision to sign Dick's papers. "It made it harder that there was no husband to help her," Ruah Sterrett told me years later. "She had to make the decision herself. Many times she said, 'Dick's so young. I hate to see him go. But that's all he wants to do. He's too young' — I heard her say that many times."

Of course, seventeen-year-old boys don't consider themselves "too young" for anything, not even war. At that age, boys feel indestructible, ready for any challenge. And Dick was big and strong, six feet tall and 169 pounds. Almost every night, he assured his mother that he was ready to fight. "It was the only thing on his mind," Aunt Ruah recalled. "He wanted to go."

Laura Woellhof finally relented and signed her boy over to the United States Navy during the July Fourth weekend. Dick took the papers down to the recruiting office bright and early on Monday, July 6, 1942. Laura phoned Ruah to tell her of her decision. Laura was in her forties and had already lost a husband. The war was not going well for the Allies at that point. Laura was realistic and she knew that what Dick wanted to do was dangerous.

But danger never crossed Dick's mind. To him war was just a glorious adventure. Aunt Ruah recalled young Dick's boyish delight when his mother relented: "Laura said when she signed the papers, Dick hugged her, smiled, and said, 'Mother, you've made this the happiest day of my life!'"

The reasons American youths signed on to become Flyboys were as varied as the boys themselves. Some wanted to be part of an elite flying fraternity. "I decided to go the navy way," was how Carlton Schmidt of Corfu, New York, remembered his motivations as a nineteen-year-old. "Their standards were higher than the army, it was more difficult to get in, so I thought I would be with a good group of guys."

"I figured that the navy air corps was the toughest to get into," Philip Begin of Massachusetts recalled. "Army air corps would have been next if I failed with the navy."

"I became infatuated with the navy growing up in Seattle," Flyboy Bill Connell told me. "In the 1930s, Seattle hosted the navy's Fleet Week, and the Pacific fleet would anchor in Puget Sound. We kids would get on the barges and visit the ships. When I graduated from high school in June of 1942, I saw an edition of *Flying* magazine that covered naval aviation. There was a picture of flying boats in Pensacola. I thought, Wouldn't that be neat!"

Some enlisted without giving it too much thought. "I enlisted on December eleventh," Jesse Naul said. "I had never been in an airplane, but it looked like a good way to go to war."

"I was drunk," Dwain Robertson told me of the day he enlisted. He and his brother were hitting the college bars in Spokane, Washington. "We walked by a big poster that said, 'BE A NAVY FLYER!' My brother said, 'That's for you! You can be an officer. It's better than being in the infantry.' I said, 'I have never been in an airplane!' 'Let's go speak to the recruiter,' he said."

Leland Holdren also made up his mind over drinks. "My buddy and I were having a beer one day and we both said we got our draft notices," Holdren remembered. "We both thought we should be pilots. The navy recruiting office was across the street and the army office was three blocks away. So we went into the navy and came back for another beer."

"My grandparents had a farm," Chuck Galbreath of Chanute, Kansas, remembered. "A buck rake is a wooden machine twelve to fifteen feet wide. It's horse drawn and scoops hay with its prongs. I used to sit out there watching those horses' asses from behind, and a plane would fly overhead. I thought they had better working conditions and made more money. In my second year of engineering school, I saw a full-page ad in the *Saturday Evening Post*. It was an ensign with his hands on a navy plane's propeller, saying, 'You too can earn your Wings of Gold.' That did it for me."

Other future Flyboys enlisted as sailors and later were trained to be airmen riding behind the pilot. Robert Akerblom of Brockton, Massachusetts, told me, "I volunteered for the navy. It's war, I figured, you have to go. This way I could have my choice. Sailing the high seas, get on the bow of the ship — that would be cool."

Some enlisted to fly in order to avoid combat on the ground. "I went in thinking, I better enlist before they draft me," recalled Al Lindstrom of San Francisco. "I enlisted in the navy for flight training. I didn't want to be a grunt."

A. M. Smith from North Carolina was in the Marine Corps ROTC. "While [I was] training one summer," he remembered, "some fighter aircraft came over and simulated strafing. I saw that and thought they had a better deal than me on the ground. So I joined up to fly."

Jacob Cohen of Indianapolis was only fifteen when the flying bug bit him. "I was in the Board of Trade building in Chicago, looking through a periscope. There were planes landing on old coal-converted carriers in Lake Michigan. When I saw those planes landing, then that's all I wanted to do."

Ed Rafferty of Kansas City remembered as a seventeen-year-old in 1942, "I thought navy pilots were next to God." He signed up.

For many young men of the Depression era — Dick Woellhof and Grady York come to mind — "the military world where decent food, adequate clothing, and some pocket cash were universal represented a step up the economic ladder." Harold Wegener of Higginsville, Missouri, became a Flyboy when a friend told him of the rewards. "I had a buddy who said, 'Let's join the navy. Let's become pilots. You can make two hundred dollars a month!' That was a fantastic amount of money. I thought, Two hundred bucks, that's for me."

Others saw enlistment as a chance to get a grip on their lives. Marve Mershon from Los Angeles listed "To learn a trade" as his reason to enlist two months after graduation from L.A.'s Poly High School. Marve had been a Cub Scout and part-time packinghouse meat cutter and parking lot attendant. But the amusement center "the Pike" — a kind of permanent outdoor carnival — was just down the street from Marve's home. Soon the fun-loving big-city boy was having too much fun for his young age.

"Paul the landlord's son was a wild kid," Marve's friend Dick Terry told me. "He might have had an adverse effect on Marve. I heard there was marijuana involved, which I cannot confirm. But I heard stories that Paul led Marve down that road."

Marve's brother, Hoyt, was concerned. Marve had already had brushes with the law — his driver's license had been suspended twice for a period of thirty days each time. Hoyt had enlisted in the army in September of 1940 — long before war clouds gathered. He had learned to value military discipline and thought his younger brother could use a dose.

Susan Mershon, Hoyt's daughter, told me, "There's a family story that my dad talked Marve into going into the navy." Another daughter of Hoyt's, Carol, said, "Yes, I was told by my grandmother that Hoyt talked Marve into going into the service."

Marve followed his brother's advice and enlisted in the navy on July 28, 1943. He stood five feet nine inches tall, weighed 129 pounds, and wore glasses over his blue eyes. Hoyt would be proud when the navy straightened out Marve's life. It never crossed Hoyt's mind that his younger brother might not return home alive.

*   *   *

Flying in airplanes was dangerous in the early 1940s. Engines could spit flames or stall in midair, and navigation was primitive. As a result, serving their country thousands of feet above the earth's surface attracted the adventurous. Warren Earl Vaughn of Childress, Texas, was certainly always ready to try something new.

"Warren Earl was a daredevil," his best high school buddy, Harold Waters, told me. "He liked living life close to the edge. I imagined he would make a good fighter pilot, just the way he lived."

His name was never just Warren, as I learned when I spoke with his cousin Ethelyn Goodner. "How do you say his name?" I asked her. "Warren Earl," she answered. "All of it."

Childress in the 1930s was a dusty West Texas town where mules hauled the farmers' wheat and cotton. "In the 1930s we were poor," Warren Earl's cousin Ralph Sides said. "We didn't travel around for even ten miles."

Warren Earl's father had left his mother, Evi, when Warren Earl was a baby. Evi raised Warren Earl alone. Evi gave Warren Earl his orientation in life, passed on her religious beliefs, taught him right from wrong. There grew a special bond between Evi and her only son. "Evi worshiped him," another relative, Billye Winder, told me. "And Warren Earl worshiped his mother."

Warren Earl was strikingly attractive, with olive skin, black hair, and high cheekbones. Cousin Madeline Riley explained that he was part Cherokee Indian. "The story is," Riley said, "in the early 1800s, some white settlers found an orphaned Cherokee baby, raised him, and he married into our family. Warren Earl's grandfather looked Indian, but of his ten children, only Evi inherited the Cherokee traits of dark skin and high cheekbones, and she passed those on to her son." Ralph Sides remembered his cousin as "very tall, very dark, and very handsome."

The girls certainly noticed his looks. "He was not a virgin when he got out of high school," his buddy Harold Waters remembered decades later. "He was quite the ladies' man. A place was no problem. We would drive a mile out of town and be a mile from anybody. We'd do it in a car. Of course we used condoms. If you got a girl pregnant, then you were going to marry her. No ifs, ands, or buts about it."

I told Harold Waters that I was surprised that high schoolers were so sexually active back in the 1930s. He thought for a moment and then said, "Oh, we did it as often as they do now. Only back then we didn't talk about it as much."

What Harold remembered most about Warren Earl was his fun-loving, daredevil nature. "We drove out into the country to a salt hole. No one knows how deep it is. It was cold, neither I nor anyone else would go in. I thought there were buggers in it or I might be swept away. But Warren Earl jumped right in.

"Then on the way home," Harold continued, "Warren Earl played chicken with a Greyhound bus. He scared the fire out of me when he nearly sideswiped that bus. He was always the one who took chances. It was just his personality, how he approached life.

"Warren Earl was very friendly and outgoing," he added. "He was very positive about everything. He was the kind of guy you liked to be around. He made things happen."

Warren Earl's pranks were kid stuff and never hurt anyone. He could talk Harold and himself into a school play for free, avoiding the expensive ten-cent admission charge. Once he found where they stored the popcorn machine and popcorn that was sold at basketball games. Harold Waters remembered, "Warren Earl said, 'I'll fix the door so it won't lock and we'll have popcorn.' We did this a few times. We'd stuff ourselves and then be on our way."

Harold and Warren Earl were such close buddies that once Harold found himself guilty by association. "One day Mr. McClure, our principal, called me to his office and said, 'You're going to get a paddling.' 'What for?' I asked. 'I caught Warren Earl smoking in the pass between the school and the basketball court, and I'm sure you were somewhere around him,' Mr. McClure said. I hadn't been with him that time, but they assumed that if he was somewhere, I was too. Warren Earl got a kick out of that."

Warren Earl earned his spending money with jobs at the Childress ice plant and the Helpy Selfy grocery. At home, he was a dutiful son who listened to his mother and helped around the house. But when Evi was gone, he was a typical American boy. "Evi went to the doctor in Amarillo by train," Harold told me. "She had some wine in the cabinet; her doctor told her to drink a little every day. We drank too much, so Warren Earl used some food coloring to fill it back up."

There were other things Evi never learned. Harold Waters again: "When his mom would leave, she'd lock the car. She didn't know it, but Warren Earl secretly made extra keys to the car and the garage. He would unhook the odometer and we'd drive around trying to impress the girls. When we'd bring it back he'd sprinkle dust on it to make it look like it hadn't moved. There was plenty of dust around Childress."

The girl Warren Earl wanted to impress most was pretty Jo Evelyn Michie. Jo Evelyn's younger sister Jerry remembers handsome Warren Earl picking her up for dates while they were both in high school. "They were going very steady," Jerry Michie said. "They talked about marriage."

But marriage would have to wait until Warren Earl established himself. After he graduated from Childress High in 1941, he entered Southwest Texas State University and took a job repairing airplane parts at the U.S. naval air station in Corpus Christi. But with the war still raging, Warren Earl thought it was time to enlist as an airman for the United States Marines. Perhaps he felt as Wesley Todd from Milwaukee did: "It sounded like being a Marine pilot was one of the toughest things you could do. I wanted to be somebody, so I went for it." Warren Earl signed up on September 1, 1943 — nineteen days before his twenty-first birthday.

"We were sad when he went into the service," Billye Winder said, "but he wouldn't let us be sad for long. Warren Earl was always pulling a joke, making us laugh."

"My last memory of Warren," remembered Madeline Riley, "is of a fit young man, so very handsome in his Marine uniform, filled with excitement and mentally bracing himself for the dangerous missions ahead. Our whole family was very proud of him." As she told me this, her voice trailed off. After a few moments she said wistfully, "I can tell you one thing for certain: Warren Earl Vaughn was as good-looking a man as I've ever seen."

After the war, many Japanese would claim they were beaten by American material superiority. It is true that the United States was able to toss more metal into the battle than Japan. But it is also true that America beat Japan when it came to having large numbers of educated boys who were handy with a monkey wrench — boys like Floyd, Dick, and Warren Earl who were determined to make the war come to the conclusion their mothers desired. These impossibly young boys who would win the war had little stubble on their chins but plenty of American steel in their hearts.

That same year Warren Earl signed up, another handsome but even younger American boy was itching to fly. Jimmy Dye of Mount Ephraim, New Jersey, hadn't even graduated yet, but he wanted to be the first in his high school class to fly. "Jimmy was a risk taker," his chum Dave Kershaw explained to me many years later. "He would run around and tell everyone he was going to be the first at something. Typical kid bragging. But he would always follow through. Later he would come back and tell you that he did it."

Jimmy Dye's high school portrait reveals a smiling version of James Dean — an open face, slicked-back blond hair, and a toothy smile. "Jimmy was a very nice dresser," his neighbor Cass Cain recalls. "He always had nice clothes and was well put together. To tell you the truth, I had a real crush on Jimmy."

Mount Ephraim was a town of fifteen hundred "near Camden and just seven miles from Philly." Dave Kershaw remembered it as "a country town with streets of just dirt. There were no outside influences. And unlike Andy Griffith's Mayberry, we didn't even have a town drunk.

"In the wintertime," Dave told me, "we young boys would rush outside with ashes from the coal heaters when we'd see a car stuck in the mud in front of their house. We would put the ash under their tires so they'd get traction as we pushed them out. We'd rush to the stuck car because we got a tip when we got them out.

"In those days," he explained, "we went to Sunday school in the morning and then church in the afternoon and evening. Sunday was a day of worship, of doing God's will. There was no drinking ever, but also no cards, no movies, no makeup on girls, no vices. We were taught there was good and evil; we sang hymns like 'The Old Rugged Cross.' *National Geographic* magazine was the worst influence our parents had to worry about."

Mount Ephraim was small but offered big opportunities for a daring country boy who always wanted to be first. "There was this creek outside of town," Dave told me. "You had to walk through the woods, cars couldn't get there, and it was very isolated. The creek carried over-flow sewage from another town. It had a green scum on it, and there was a sign that read, 'CONDEMNED. NO SWIMMING. TYPHOID FEVER.' We just tore the sign down. The water was filthy, about five feet deep. We'd go out there on Palm Sunday. The water was ice-cold, and there could have been dangerous debris under the surface. Jimmy would dare everyone to dive. Then he would go first. He was a risk taker, and you could depend upon him to try something first."

Another time, Jimmy was the first to ride his bike across a narrow wooden construction plank suspended over a deep ditch. "His bike toppled over," Dave said, "and he landed headfirst. He was groggy and didn't know where he was when we pulled him out."

Once Jimmy and a group of his buddies decided it would be a kick to "break in" to the office of a moving and storage company. "We didn't want to steal or vandalize, just experience the thrill of being where we weren't supposed to be," Dave said. "We were in and out of there in ten minutes, more scared of our parents than the police. And I remember who was the first to climb in through the window — Jimmy."

In his 1943 high school yearbook, Jimmy's classmates named him "Class Flirt . . . who seems to believe in 'lovin' and leavin' them.'" But Ethyl Jones dated Jimmy and remembered a tamer boy than the year-book implies. "We never even kissed," she said. Bernice Mawhiney re-called that Jimmy would "sit on my porch analyzing the girls he was trying to date. I remember he was in love with a cheerleader and she had no interest in him."

Jimmy was a good son and brother. Ronnie Dye was six years younger than his brother Jimmy. "Our mother," Ronnie recalled, "would say to him, 'You don't have to take him along; he's your kid brother.' But Jimmy didn't mind and he would take me with his friends to the high school football games.

"Jimmy always had a scheme," Ronnie remembered. "He would buy candy bars at the drugstore, three for ten cents. Then he would sell them back in the neighborhood for five cents each. He had a paper route, he ushered at a movie house, and he delivered telegrams for the post office before school. He made all his own spending money. He was very energetic, and Mom and Dad were real proud of him."

Ronnie told me that once Jimmy won a ticket to the Army-Navy football game by selling magazine subscriptions. But Jimmy wasn't one to sit back and enjoy the game. "Once there, he sold programs," Ronnie said. "He came home with money and a piece of the goalpost."

The Mount Ephraim Chamber of Commerce recognized Jimmy's spunk with an award that read: "To the BOY of the Graduating Class who ranks highest in Preparation for Business based on Scholarship, Personality and Character."

The yearbook that celebrated Jimmy as a chamber awardee, Class Flirt, a contributor to the school paper (the *Parrot*), and an actor in the school play (*You Can't Take It With You*) was infused with a patriotic military theme. On page 56 was a "GREETINGS TO THE CLASS OF 1943" from the Parent-Teacher Association. The second paragraph of the greeting read, "Yours is the privilege of serving your country in her hour of need, of repaying the gifts your country has given you. It is something to be able to say: 'When my country was in danger, I helped defend it!'"

Jimmy wanted to be the first in his class to say those words. And he wanted to soar. It already seemed clear that airplanes would win this war: Even the cover of Jimmy's yearbook was dominated by a huge *V* for victory, set in front of billowing clouds, with a single airplane trailing a plume of exhaust racing across it.

"He had a yearning to fly," Dave Kershaw said. "In wood shop we made black wooden airplane models for the military, for their identification classes." Whittling and painting airplanes day after day gave Jimmy an idea. After he convinced his parents to sign his enlistment papers, Jimmy uncharacteristically did not show up at school.

"They took roll and he didn't answer," Kershaw remembered. "Jimmy just disappeared."

Seventeen-year-old James Dye — all five foot six inches and 120 pounds of him — enlisted in Philadelphia on February 17, 1943. And exactly two years later to the day, it would happen again.

Jimmy just disappeared.

Many Americans had viewed United States involvement in World War I as a mistake. Through the 1920s and 1930s, a majority wanted little spent on military preparedness and no further involvements overseas. America was a deeply isolationist country. On five separate occasions in the 1930s, the United States Congress had enacted formal neutrality laws to keep the country out of war.

When Adolf Hitler heard of the Japanese attack on Pearl Harbor, he slapped his hands together in glee and exclaimed, "Now it is impossible to lose the war. We now have an ally, Japan, who has never been vanquished in three thousand years."

Germany and Japan were threatening the world with massive land armies. But Hitler and Hirohito had never taken the measure of the man in the White House. A former assistant secretary of the navy, Franklin D. Roosevelt had his own ideas about the shape and size of the military juggernaut he would wield.

FDR's military experts told him that only huge American ground forces could meet the threat. But Roosevelt turned aside their requests to conscript tens of millions of Americans to fight a traditional war. The Dutchman would have no part in the mass WWI-type carnage of American boys on European or Asian killing fields. Billy Mitchell was gone, but Roosevelt remembered his words. Now, as Japan and Germany invested in yesterday, FDR invested in tomorrow. He slashed his military planners' dreams of a vast 35-million-man force by more than half. He shrunk the dollars available for battle in the first and second dimensions and put his money on the third.

When the commander in chief called for the production of four thousand airplanes per month, his advisers wondered if he meant *per year.* After all, the U.S. had produced only eight hundred airplanes just two years earlier. FDR was quick to correct them. The contours of Franklin Roosevelt's war would be determined by the Flyboys.

CHAPTER EIGHT

Doing the Impossible

If there's any of you who don't want to go, just tell me. Because the chances of you making it back are pretty slim.

— *Jimmy Doolittle, quoted in the* Los Angeles Times

ON December 21, 1941, just two weeks almost to the hour after Pearl Harbor, President Roosevelt welcomed his military brain trust into his private study on the second floor of the White House. FDR's "Big Three" consisted of General George Marshall, the starchy army chief of staff; General Henry "Hap" Arnold, the genial chief of staff of the army air forces; and Admiral Ernest King, the imperious chief of naval operations. These masters of the land, air, and sea were prepared to request troops and equipment. They came armed with maps and statistics. There were challenges everywhere for an America that had been caught off guard with the sixteenth largest military in the world, behind Portugal, Sweden, Switzerland, and Romania.

But Roosevelt was not interested in the myriad details, not just yet. His finger on America's pulse, FDR knew the nation he led desperately needed a morale boost. Caught unawares at Pearl Harbor, with its back against the wall from Wake Island to the Philippines, America had endured a daily drumbeat of disheartening news. That had to change.

Roosevelt asked his advisers to "out–Pearl Harbor" the enemy and send American Flyboys to bomb Japan. Marshall, King, and Arnold had given no thought to the possibility. There was no reason to even consider the question. They knew it was impossible.

The U.S., like Japan, had two basic types of aircraft in its arsenal: land-based and carrier planes. Carrier planes were relatively small and light, so they could take off and land on short aircraft carrier runways. Their size made them useful as fighter planes and small bombers, but they could not match the bomb loads of their larger cousins. Bigger, heavier, and able to travel farther, land-based planes required longer airstrips to get lift. Also, if a heavy land bomber attempted to land on an aircraft carrier, it would crash through the wooden landing deck.

Small carrier planes had much less range than their larger land-based cousins. Japan's Pearl Harbor strike force had gotten away unscathed because of surprise. With Japan now on the alert, Yankee aircraft carriers would be detected and destroyed if they dared approach the Land of the Rising Sun. And while U.S. land-based planes could reach Japan from airfields in Far Eastern Russia, Joseph Stalin — fighting for his survival on his European border — had kept the USSR neutral in the fight with Japan and refused his American ally permission to originate from Russian territory. The coastal areas of China were all in Japanese hands.

But FDR insisted that a way be found to bomb the empire. The president demanded a visible home run to invigorate his people. He knew that Prime Minister Tojo had intoned in his declaration of war, "The key to victory lies in a 'faith in victory.'" Americans were shaken and needed a shot of faith.

Over the next few weeks, whenever he met with his military brain trust, Roosevelt argued that bombing Tokyo would be the perfect "tit" for the humiliating "tat" suffered at Pearl Harbor. But how could it be done? Nobody knew.

Then one day, an assistant to Admiral King was examining the outline of a carrier deck that had been painted on a Norfolk, Virginia, airstrip. Navy fliers used it to practice carrier landings and takeoffs. Just then a squadron of "Billys" — twin-engined B-25 Mitchell army land-based bombers — flew overhead, and the navy officer noticed their shadows race along the carrier deck shape. It suddenly occurred to him: What if long-range army bombers *could* take off from an aircraft carrier? All military experts — Japanese and American — had simply assumed they could not, that the Billys were too big (50 feet long, with a 67-foot wingspan) and heavy (14 tons) to launch from an aircraft carrier. But if they could, this imaginative long-range punch combining land-based bombers with an aircraft carrier would catch the Japanese with their guard down.

Such a complicated and dangerous mission called for a combat leader who was an inspiring commander, a methodical thinker who could anticipate and solve myriad problems, a scientific mind who could weigh the odds, and a strong personality who could bull his way through the layers of somnolent bureaucracy. Only one person came to mind. He was none other than the Babe Ruth of Flyboys, the irrepressible Jimmy Doolittle.

At the age of forty-five, America's preeminent Flyboy was as old as flying itself. Jimmy had "won nearly every aviation trophy there was." A fearless daredevil, a crowd-pleasing barnstormer, Jimmy had been generating headlines and thrilling world audiences with his aeronautical aerobatics for twenty years. Jimmy regularly set and then broke international racing records. He had been the first to fly coast to coast in less than twenty-four hours and then first to do it in less than twelve. Kids who followed sports heroes like boxers Gene Tunney and Jack Dempsey or baseball players like Ty Cobb also followed Flyboy Jimmy's exploits.

Jimmy was a short, muscular fireplug of a man with a confident grin above his cleft chin. His nose was a little crooked from having been broken on his road to becoming a boxing champion. He was just five feet four inches tall and never weighed more than 145 pounds, but he was a giant who reached the clouds, a king of the sky. Once Jimmy was at a party in Argentina, where he was in an air show. After a few too many tequilas, he was demonstrating handstands on a high balcony when the balcony gave way and Jimmy broke both his ankles. He still flew the next day. His doctors protested, but Jimmy strapped his aching cast-encased feet onto the rudders. "Even in casts, however, the work his feet had to do in piloting made him almost black out a number of times from the pain." Jimmy looked at the bright side — since his feet were strapped in and he couldn't get out in case of a crash, he could leave his bulky parachute behind.

Jimmy was a military and commercial test pilot before wind tunnels enabled aeronautical engineers to predict how much an airplane could withstand before disintegrating. That meant he found out personally, by pushing himself and his flying machines to the limits of near destruction. He crashed on numerous occasions and parachuted three times to save himself. But it was not all spectacular feats of risk taking. Jimmy was the first to be awarded a Ph.D. in aeronautical science from the Massachusetts Institute of Technology and was the brains behind the development of the high-octane gasoline that powers all planes today.

Once Jimmy was on board FDR's secret plan, a group of army Flyboys training in Oregon was given the opportunity to volunteer for a "dangerous mission that would require you to be outside of the United States for a few months." All 140 signed up.

In February of 1942, still unaware of their eventual mission, the Flyboys transferred to Eglin Air Force Base in Florida for training. Taking off on extremely short runways at bare minimum airspeed was the exact opposite of how they had previously flown. Their training had always been on long runways, and they had been taught to have plenty of airspeed before lifting off. Abruptly pulling up a heavy bomber with the tail almost dragging on the ground was unnatural to them, a harrowing experience. "We practiced, over and over, ramming the engines at full power," said copilot Jack Sims, "taking off at sixty-five miles per hour in a five-hundred-foot run. It could be done, as long as an engine didn't skip a beat."

On March 3, 1942, the Flyboys were ordered to assemble to meet their commander. Until now they had never even heard his name; his identity was top secret. In the large conference room the air was abuzz with the usual hanging-around talk when suddenly a door opened and in walked the great little man himself. There was a stunned silence. "Doolittle is my name," he announced. His audience knew exactly who he was. It was as if Frank Sinatra had walked into a college band practice and said they would be accompanying him.

"We're in for something really big," whispered twenty-five-year-old navigator Mac McClure to the men standing near him. "Of course he was a legend," bombardier Herb Macia recalled. "Even then I would not have hesitated to call him America's greatest aviator. One thing was clear: This mission was very important if he was involved in it." Davey Jones recalled, "It didn't take but two minutes, and you were under his spell. We were ready for anything."

Then and on a number of occasions over the next forty-five days,

Jimmy reminded his young volunteers that this vital mission would be dangerous: "If anyone wants to drop out, he can. No questions asked." Not one Flyboy ever accepted his kind offer.

The sailing of a mighty aircraft carrier force is a major event. But when Doolittle's Raiders and the sailors of the USS *Hornet* task force sailed under the Golden Gate Bridge headed for Tokyo, they still only knew they were headed for somewhere "outside the U.S." When the ships were safely out into the Pacific, the loudspeakers boomed: "The target of this task force is Tokyo. The army is going to bomb Japan, and we're going to get them as close to the enemy as we can. This is a chance for all of us to give the Japs a dose of their own medicine."

Cheers filled the air. "They told us over the loudspeaker and when they said it, it was like you were at a football game and somebody has just kicked a goal in the last second," Bob Bourgeois remembered. "People went wild. I rejoiced just like everyone else. I was glad to see somebody was going to retaliate for Pearl Harbor." Mac McClure said, "The sailors I saw were jumping up and down like small children."

The key to the mission was the innovative idea of combining an aircraft carrier with the Billys. Japan assumed itself safe from air threats because land-based U.S. Army aircraft couldn't reach the homeland from Hawaii or Midway. And if the U.S. Navy was foolish enough to move an aircraft carrier within effective striking range of Japan, the American force would be obliterated. No one in Japan imagined that heavy land bombers could lift off from carrier decks — even some on the USS *Hornet* had their doubts.

The plan was simple. The *Hornet* would sail within four to five hundred miles of Japan and the sixteen Billys would launch in the afternoon. The *Hornet* would then skedaddle back toward Pearl Harbor as the raiders dropped their bombs over the cities of Japan at sunset. Then they would fly on to China (the bombers were too heavy to land on the *Hornet*), where homing beacons would guide them safely to an airfield in Chuchow, beyond Japanese control.

As the *Hornet* headed for history, Jimmy and his boys must have wondered if the *kamikaze* threat was more reality than myth. Dark clouds enveloped the task force as a typhoon-force wind buffeted the ships. Howling winds and sheeting sea spray had deckhands crawling across the deck on all fours to keep from being washed overboard.

Then disaster struck early on the morning of April 18, 1942. Unknown to the Americans, the Japanese had stationed a string of fifty radio-equipped "picket boats" 650 miles out in the Pacific. These civilian-manned boats formed their early-warning surveillance network. Two Japanese ships observed the American fleet and radioed a warning to Tokyo.

Even though the picket boats were full of civilian men, women, and children, U.S. destroyers were ordered to sink them. "That I will never forget or feel good about, until the day I die," recalled sailor Rod Steiger. "I watched, I wasn't shooting, but I watched as the 40 millimeters hit them, and the women screaming and the children running around and the men, until they were sunk. . . . They are shooting at these defenseless people, and inside of your mind you think what the hell happened to the Ten Commandments? You know what I mean? We're not supposed to do this to one another."

"They know we're here," the *Hornet*'s captain told Jimmy. It was time to roll.

Takeoff now, eight sailing hours and two hundred miles short of the intended launch point, suddenly transformed a dangerous mission into a suicidal one. With the element of surprise lost, it was a good bet Jimmy and his boys would be shredded by opposing fighter planes. And even if they survived Tokyo's antiaircraft guns, the extra fuel expended to get that far ruled out reaching the do-or-die Chinese airfields. When Ross Greening realized he would launch hundreds of miles early, "Cold chills were running up and down my spine. . . . I don't think there was a man leaving who really believed he would complete the flight safely."

"Doolittle called us all on the deck," Sess Sessler remembered, "and said: 'If there's any of you who don't want to go, just tell me. Because the chances of you making it back are pretty slim.' And nobody batted an eye."

"I assumed quite early in the game that we would not survive the mission," remembered Herb Macia. "First of all I thought if the Japanese had been tipped off that we were coming, and if they had the defense they were supposed to, and if we were going to strike right in the middle of the day, then we were going to encounter a swarm of fighters coming out after us. Second, if we got to the targets and got out, we could not make it past midpoint in the China Sea, we were going to have to ditch our planes in a Japanese-controlled area. I thought the only thing short of being destroyed over the target area would be to end up as a prisoner of war."

In addition to the distance, there was the weather. "The *Hornet* navigation room passed out the latest weather information on Japan and China, which included more bad news: The Doolittle men would face a twenty-four-knot headwind all the way to Honshu." The wind would be blowing against their noses from carrier takeoff to China.

"Now hear this! Now hear this!" The Klaxon horn sounded. "Army pilots, man your planes."

Navy crew and army pilots slipped, slid, and crawled across the heaving, drenched deck to the planes. The *Hornet* was being tossed about in thirty-foot swells, rocking and rolling up and down and from side to side. Gale-force winds made it difficult to stand on deck. The blowing *kaze* tore off the tops of the huge waves and flung heavy salt spray across the ships, soaking the shivering crew.

"This was zero weather conditions. . . . Zero! That means you can't see across the table," recalled Bob Bourgeois. "Have you ever seen a thirty-foot sea? I never had. It's seventy feet from the water to the top of the ship. And the bow of the ship was going down and picking up water and throwing it over the deck. I have never been in worse weather in my life. The rain! Oh, the rain! I've been in a bunch of hurricanes right here in Louisiana. And they were tame compared to this thing."

As if rain squalls, gale-force winds, and thirty-foot waves weren't enough, the Flyboys were forced to take off by speeding down the deck directly into the trough of a huge wave. The *Hornet* was bobbing up and down like a cork. The trick was to time the launch so that the Billys reached the end of the deck as the carrier peaked in its upward movement. Each pilot would get the go signal as the front of the ship tilted into the churning foam. Then he would speed down the deck, seemingly headed into the bowels of a howling sea.

As Jimmy prepared to launch, John Ford, the Oscar-winning director of *Stagecoach* and *The Grapes of Wrath,* captured the moment on film. The confident Dutchman back in the White House planned to delight movie audiences with the trophy film footage.

"I knew hundreds of eyes were on me," Jimmy remembered, "especially those of the B-25 crews who were to follow. If I didn't get off successfully, I'm sure many thought they wouldn't be able to make it either."

Sailor Alvin Kernan wondered: "Could the heavy planes with a bomb load of two thousand pounds get to Japan and then make it to the nearest safe landing point in China? Even before that, could such heavy planes designed for long landing strips get off a short carrier deck? Sailors, like stockbrokers, work everything out by betting, and there was soon heavy money down on both sides: Would they make it, would they not? . . . I put down ten dollars at even money that less than half of them would get off."

Jimmy Doolittle would later be awarded the Medal of Honor by Franklin Roosevelt and a knighthood by the king of England. All American presidents up to and including President Bush in 1989 would shower him with all the honors the country can bestow, including the Presidential Medal of Freedom. Great universities from New York to Alaska would grant him honorary degrees, and nine nations would bestow their highest honors. But at this moment, Jimmy was just a lone Flyboy whose mission was to do the impossible.

Jimmy's roaring engines pulled at his brakes "like circus elephants against their chains." The signalman watching the pitch of the carrier signaled "Now!" The king of the air began his roll. "A navy pilot shouted to anyone within earshot: 'He won't make it! He can't make it!'" But as Jimmy's navigator, Hank Potter, later recalled, "We were particularly confident since we had the best pilot in the Air Force flying with us."

"We watched him like hawks," pilot Ted Lawson remembered. And the boys on deck saw America's premier Flyboy take off with yards to spare. As the *Los Angeles Times* later blared in a headline, "DOOLITTLE DID IT!"

"The entire convoy shouted in a surge of relief, a cheer so loud and throaty and ecstatic that the crewmen could even hear it above the roar of their props." Harry Johnson, though, remembered different feelings: "I doubt if one man expected to return alive. I felt so badly about what I thought was certain death that I could not say good-bye to anyone — just a thumbs-up as each took off."

Jimmy circled around behind the carrier and roared above the flight deck as members of the crew pumped their fists in the air and shouted themselves hoarse. Next stop, Tokyo.

Following Jimmy's lead, the other Flyboys wrestled their fifteen Billys up. Now that they had mastered their dangerous takeoff, they flew for hours just above the angry waves as they contemplated the wiles of the wind. The *kaze* blew steadily against their noses and then alternately buffeted them from each side. The winds slowed the Raiders down, consumed their fuel, and messed with their follow-the-leader flight plan.

As they had feared, their gas gauges confirmed they were on a suicide mission. "We were over six hundred miles [away from Japan] when we launched, so it was pretty obvious that it wasn't going to fit," said pilot Davey Jones. "At the time we just accepted the fact that we weren't going to have enough juice to get to our destinations in China. Putting it in real terms to yourself, that was just a statement and knowledge, and you did your best anyway. It didn't really enter your mind. To me that's the only thing that distinguishes this trip from the thousand other sorties that were flown during the war. We knew when we started that it wasn't going to fit."

The opposing winds meant the Raiders would have to ditch in the cold ocean. This willingness of American boys to risk their lives for their country was not what the Boy Soldier in Tokyo had expected. Rather than stay home in their shells like cowed "merchants," these Americans had as much "fighting spirit" as the Japanese. But they didn't call it that. The Flyboys called it "balls."

When Jimmy made landfall over the Chiba peninsula north of Tokyo, picnickers waved and smiled, believing they were witnessing Japanese maneuvers. Jimmy skimmed the treetops and rooftops and headed for Tokyo. Earlier, aboard the *Hornet,* a pilot had asked him what they should do in case of trouble. "Each pilot is in command of his own plane when we leave the carrier," Jimmy had answered. "He is responsible for the decision he makes for his own plane and his own crew. If you're separated, each one of you will have to decide for yourself what you will do. Personally, I know exactly what I'm going to do."

The room was silent. Doolittle didn't go any further, so a Flyboy asked, "Sir, what will you do?"

"I don't intend to be taken prisoner," he had answered. "If my plane is crippled beyond any possibility of fighting or escaping, I'm going to bail my crew out and then drive it, full throttle, into any target I can find where the crash will do the most damage. I'm forty-five years old and have lived a full life. Most of you are in your twenties and if I were you, I'm not sure I would make the same decision. In the final analysis, it's up to each pilot and, in turn, each man to decide what he will do."

For Japanese on the ground there seemed little to worry about. "It looks real, doesn't it?" said a businessman waiting at a Tokyo railway platform to a fellow passenger as he watched a Billy grazing the treetops. "Just like a foreign aircraft bursting through Japanese air defenses. I guess the Imperial forces want to impress the people that they are fully prepared."

At 12:30 P.M., Jimmy pulled up to twelve hundred feet over Tokyo and released four incendiaries — magnesium firebombs — in rapid succession. Then, as he later wrote, "I dropped down to rooftop level again and slid over the western outskirts of the city into low haze and smoke, then turned south and out to sea." Immediately, he ran into a small black cloud of exploding antiaircraft fire.

"They're missing us by a mile, Paul," Jimmy said to his gunner, Paul Leonard, just as a shell burst, this one close enough to splatter the fuselage. "Colonel," Leonard said, "that was no mile."

"Our fondest wish had come true," remembered Tokyo-based British attaché Frank Moysey. "I saw a black cloud of smoke belch suddenly from behind a hill to the northwest. I ran into a building and climbed to the roof; it was a beautiful sight. There, surging up from Tokyo's heavy industrial district, were six enormous columns of smoke, dense and black. While we watched the smoke increase and spread with the wind, a big twin-engined bomber suddenly roared across the sky a half-mile away." A Japanese woman who worked at the British embassy complained to Moysey, "It is so unfair that you should bomb us. Our houses are only made of wood, while yours are of stone."

Jimmy's raiders dropped their bombs in the Tokyo-Yokohama megalopolis, which included a number of industrial cities like Kawasaki. The Japanese did not zone their urban areas, so military-industrial plants existed side by side with residential neighborhoods. Civilian casualties were inevitable. Just four years earlier, when Japan bombed civilians in China, the United States president, State Department, Congress, media, and the vast majority of the American populace considered the bombing of civilian centers "barbarous." But now the shoe was on the other foot.

Katsuzo Yoshida heard the roar of low-flying planes and looked up just in time to see an incendiary fall on Okasaki Hospital. "The building exploded in flames and smoke. Yoshida helped the orderlies and neighborhood volunteers move the patients out of harm's way, flabbergasted at the Americans' barbaric act."

Schoolboy Kikujiro Suzuki was playing with school chums on the playground of Waseda Middle School when a Flyboy's incendiary bomb struck and killed one of his buddies.

Shinmin ran for their lives as fire rained from the sky. Their faces registered shock and horror. Both Pearl Harbor and the Doolittle Raid were surprise attacks, but the Japanese had targeted a military installation. Now the Americans bombed and strafed hospital patients, children, women, farmers, and fishermen. "We sighted several small fishing craft about five miles offshore, so I machine-gunned them with the .30 caliber in the nose," gunner Bill Birch said. "The tracers put me on target, and I raked the length of the deck from stern to bow."

Gunner Jake DeShazer revealed how easily the thin moral veneer regarding the killing of civilians can be overcome in the heat of battle. "I had read in the newspapers one time about a German aviator shooting at French people," he remembered, "and I thought it was a mean thing to do. I made up my mind while on the *Hornet* that I would not shoot at civilians. But after they shot at us, I changed my mind."

As the Flyboys fled Japan in their desperate attempt to land in China, the headwind that had bedeviled them earlier continued to slow them down. This was no surprise: American intelligence had earlier warned Jimmy that the winds always blew from west to east over the China Sea at this time of year. Jimmy's navigator informed him that "we would run out of gas about 135 miles from the Chinese coast," Doolittle later recalled. "We began to make preparations for ditching. I saw sharks basking in the water below and didn't think ditching among them would be very appealing."

But then the remarkable happened: The gods changed their minds — the *kami* switched sides. The headwind that had condemned the eighty Flyboys changed unexpectedly into a savior tailwind. Even hard-nosed Jimmy remembered the sudden switch as divine intervention: "Fortunately, the Lord was with us. What had been a headwind slowly turned into a tailwind of about 25 miles per hour and eased our minds about ditching."

Later, Jimmy and his boys realized the gods had actually shepherded their mission from the beginning. The storms that had lashed the *Hornet* had also provided cloud cover that rendered the carrier force invisible to Japanese search planes. And the clouds and squalls had also served as a benevolent screen for the task force as it made its way to Japan. Indeed, the *kaze* had dispersed the Billys and forced them to arrive over Japan at different points, which turned out to be the perfect "strategy" to thwart the antiaircraft gunners, who could not anticipate the direction from which the next plane would come. It was as if Japan's divine protectors no longer wished to shield the marauding Spirit Warriors who had betrayed Bushido's true spirit.

At the time, of course, the Flyboys knew none of this, and simply flew on into the darkness and rain. "We tried to contact the field at Chuchow on 4495 kilocycles," Jimmy remembered. "No answer. This meant that the chance of any of us getting to the destination safely was just about nil." With no homing beacons and inaccurate maps, Jimmy could only fly until his fuel tanks were nearly empty and then bail out into the blackness. Falling from 8,000 feet over enemy territory in the liquid darkness, he and his crew would just have to wait for the earth to slam up below their feet. "It was impossible to see anything below, so all I could do was wait until I hit the ground," Jimmy recalled. "My concern as I floated down was about my ankles, which had been broken in South America in 1926. Anticipating a sudden encounter with the ground, I bent my knees to take the shock."

But it was as if Billy Mitchell, looking down from on high, had decided to cushion his fellow Flyboy's fall and at the same time play a practical joke. Jimmy Doolittle landed softly in a heap of Chinese night soil, human manure. At 9:30 P.M. on April 18, 1942, after thirteen hours in the air, America's Flyboy-hero of the moment found himself neck-deep in a pile of shit.

The Doolittle Raid, like the attack on Pearl Harbor, had a profound impact on the conduct of the Pacific war. The Japanese itemized the actual damage as fifty dead, 252 wounded, ninety buildings damaged or destroyed, including the Japanese Diesel Manufacturing Company, the Japanese Steel Corporation's Factory Number One, the Mitsubishi Heavy Industrial Corporation, the Communication Ministry's transformer station, the National Hemp and Dressing Company, the Yokohama Manufacturing Company warehouse, the Nagoya Aircraft Factory, an army arsenal, a naval laboratory, an airfield, an ammunitions dump, nine electric power buildings, six gas tanks, a garment factory, a food storage warehouse, a gas company, two miscellaneous factories, six wards of the Nagoya Second Temporary Army Hospital, six elementary or secondary schools, and innumerable nonmilitary residences.

All the Doolittle Raiders escaped Japan's airspace without a scratch.

Although Japan could easily repair the slight physical damage, the psychological shock remained. One Tokyo resident wrote, "The bombing of Tokyo and several other cities has brought about a tremendous change in the attitude of our people toward the war. Now things are different. The bombs have dropped here on our homes. It does not seem any more that there is such a great difference between the battle front and the home front." Another who experienced the raid remembered, "My people had always placed emphasis on spiritual strength and the medieval belief that Japan would never be attacked. As children we had been taught to believe what the emperor and his advisors told us. It was a severe psychological shock to even the most ardent believer when it was officially announced that we had been attacked. We finally began to realize that all we were told was not true — that the government had lied when it said we were invulnerable. We then began to doubt that we were also invincible."

Japanese belief in their invincibility had been rudely shaken, but "the feat lifted the morale of Americans as nothing else had during five months of bitter defeats. It seemed a promise that America was now going on the attack and had avenged the raid on Pearl Harbor." On April 21, President Roosevelt called a press conference in the Oval Office. With reporters gathered around his desk, FDR confirmed the bare outline of the raid as reported by Japanese sources. But when asked where the Billys had originated, the Dutchman smiled broadly and announced that the American planes had attacked "from our new base in

Shangri-La" — a witty reference to the fictional Himalayan land depicted in James Hilton's novel *Lost Horizon.*

FDR's lighthearted answer delighted Americans and confounded the Japanese. "The Shangri-La remark added the exact psychological note that the nation had been wanting to hear. It proved that the United States could strike back. The boast that Premier Hideki Tojo had made that 'Japan has never lost a war in all the 2,600 years of her glorious history' was going to be destroyed."

Americans were not told that their Flyboys had killed civilians. The strafing of innocent schoolchildren, the intentional murder of innocent farmers and fishermen, and the shocking bombing of hospitals were not mentioned in the American press.

A day before FDR's press conference, Emperor Hirohito signed an order for his army in China "to destroy the air bases from which the enemy might conduct air raids on the Japanese homeland. The captured areas will be occupied for a period estimated at approximately one month. Air fields, military installations, and important lines of communication would be totally destroyed . . . the Commander-in-Chief of the China Expeditionary army will begin the operation as soon as possible."

The Spirit Warriors followed their emperor's orders to a T. To wreak revenge, more than 100,000 Japanese soldiers in 53 battalions drove 200 miles into East China, murdering everyone and burning all villages over an area of 20,000 square miles. Rape and pillage became the order of the day. Soldiers chopped off so many heads that their arms grew weak. For three gruesome months, Chinese men were machine-gunned, the women raped and skewered, and children were thrown down wells. Houses, temples, and shops were reduced to ash.

When the Doolittle crew members parachuted into East China, many Chinese civilians and guerrillas gave them food and shelter. In gratitude, the Flyboys had given their new friends trinkets. "Little did the Doolittle men realize," a Belgian missionary later recalled, "that those same little gifts, which they gave their rescuers in grateful acknowledgment of their hospitality — the parachutes, gloves, nickels, and dimes — would, a few weeks later, become the telltale evidence of their presence and lead to the torture and death of their friends."

When Japanese troops discovered a farmer who had helped the Doolittle flight surgeon, "soldiers wrapped him in a blanket, soaked it in kerosene, and forced his wife to set her husband on fire." One Chinese man told the *New York Times,* "From some of the villagers who had managed to escape death we heard stories far too brutal and savage to relate. Just one charge was not heard — cannibalism. But outside of that, take your choice and you can't miss the savage nature of the Japanese army."

Chiang Kai-shek later cabled Roosevelt about the revenge Japanese forces wrought on his people. "After they had been caught unawares by the falling of American bombs on Tokyo, Japanese troops attacked the coastal areas of China where many of the American flyers had landed. These Japanese troops slaughtered every man, woman and child in those areas — let me repeat — these Japanese troops slaughtered every man, woman and child in those areas." Chiang did not exaggerate. In describing the campaign of retaliation in his memoirs, an American general later wrote, "A quarter million Chinese soldiers and civilians were killed in the three-month campaign."

Two hundred and fifty thousand Chinese dead in *three months.* In *six years* of combat during WWII, France lost 108,000 civilians, Belgium 101,000, the Netherlands 242,000. This Japanese retaliatory operation, invisible to the world at the time, would take more lives than the later atomic bombings at Hiroshima and Nagasaki combined.

But it didn't end there. Japan was so outraged by the Doolittle Raid that it unleashed biological warfare. In 1935, the Japanese army had established the infamous Unit 731, an insidious biological research center where Japanese doctors experimented on Chinese civilians. "It was a testing ground for bacterial warfare, using captured human beings as living guinea pigs to be infected with bubonic plague, pneumonia, epidemic hemorrhagic fever, typhoid, and syphilis." Hiroshi Matsumoto remembered how Chinese prisoners were injected with pathogens and their bodies were used as disease "incubators." "After five to six months," Matsumoto recalled, "these people produced the bacteria within their bodies so we were after their blood. The blood was removed by an incision in the groin vein. Every last drop was collected, with the person still — just — alive: The accompanying soldier, or the civilian war worker, stood on the chest and pressed down on the ribs, or jumped with all his weight, rather. He repeated it several times. The ribs were probably broken. I could hear them break.

This way, the very last drop of blood was collected. This is what actually happened."

In retaliation for the Doolittle Raid, the Japanese sprayed cholera, typhoid, and bubonic plague across East China, making Japan the only combatant of WWII to use biological warfare. The total number of casualties has never been determined, but the effects can be imputed from a chilling episode. "One report stated that during one assault, a last-minute change in the wind led to the death of seventeen hundred Japanese soldiers and the injury of ten thousand more."

Not all the victims were Chinese. Eight of the Doolittle Raiders were captured by Japanese troops in China. Dean Hallmark, Bill Farrow, Harold Spatz, Chase Nielson, George Barr, Bob Hite, Jacob DeShazer, and Bob Meder would be the first of many to learn what the enemy thought of Flyboys.

"According to the Geneva Convention, all I can tell you is my name, rank and serial number," Chase Nielson told his Japanese interrogator. The interrogator responded, "What's the Geneva Convention? We're fighting a war. Don't you know that? We're making our rules as we go." Then the interrogator put his finger right up to Chase's face and said, "I'll tell you something else. I can kill you this afternoon and no one will ever know who did it."

It is true that a Japanese representative had been one of the forty-seven signatories to the International Convention Relative to the Treatment of Prisoners of War signed on July 27, 1929, in Geneva. But Japan never ratified the convention because of opposition back home. The convention condoned surrender by soldiers facing hopeless odds. Their names were to be taken and their relatives were to be told they were alive and well. But of course such rules ran counter to what the brutes running Japan's military deemed proper. Surrender was not compatible with *Yamato damashii:* A young *issen gorin* had to fight to the death. "Even were he taken prisoner after being wounded and unable to move or unconscious, he could never again hold up his head in Japan. He and his family would be disgraced forever." Historian Ikuhiko Hata summarized the view of the Spirit Warriors: "At the heart of the matter lay their belief that their own troops on being taken prisoner should forfeit all human rights. Inevitably this attitude was applied with equal vigor towards enemy POWs."

Hirohito had made it clear that Japan would not respect international agreements. This was in contrast to past war declarations. At the start of the first Sino-Japanese War in 1894, Emperor Meiji had stated: "We command that our subjects make every effort in the performance of their official duties to ensure that international law is not transgressed." Meiji's later declaration of war against Russia had included a similar injunction. Officers were treated especially well. As one scholar has noted, "During the war 79,367 Russians were taken prisoner. They were detained in 29 POW camps throughout Japan and were well treated. Russian officers at the Kanazawa camp were even taken to an inn for entertainment. The Hague Convention was later to stipulate that POWs should be paid a salary equivalent to that of soldiers of the same rank in the forces of the country that was holding them. During the Russo-Japanese War, the Russian prisoners were paid double the amount paid to Japanese soldiers. After the war ended, all of the POWs were safely returned to Russia." And Japan's WWI declaration against Germany had said, "We also command all our competent authorities to make every effort in pursuance of their respective duties to attain the national objectives within the bounds of international law."

But after Meiji, the Spirit Warriors ignored international conventions. Hirohito's rescript declaring war against America stated, "The entire nation with a united will shall mobilize its total strength so that nothing will miscarry in the attainment of our war aims." A call for compliance with international law was intentionally omitted. Japan's first director of the POW Information Bureau said, "In the war with Russia, we gave them excellent treatment in order to gain recognition as a civilized country. Today such a need no longer applies."

To the Japanese soldier, who was under orders to kill himself rather than surrender, an enemy POW had no honor. After all, he had surrendered alive when the honorable thing would have been to commit suicide. The emperor's soldiers were astonished when captured American GIs requested that their families be notified through the Red Cross. The Japanese wondered what kind of lowlifes could raise their hands above their heads and then allow their parents to learn of their humiliation.

Glen Berry of Drinkman, Oklahoma, was twenty-six years old when he endured the horrors of the Bataan Death March. Years later

Berry told me, "The Japanese soldiers told us they would take their own lives rather than surrender. So they thought we were just trash."

Another Bataan survivor, Lester Tenney, described what happened to one such piece of trash:

> At one point on the march, we were ordered to double time, or run, and try to keep up with a fresh group of guards. As we passed a group of Japanese soldiers, our guards ordered us to stop. When we looked over to where the group of soldiers were, we saw an American soldier kneeling in front of a Japanese officer. The officer had his samurai sword out of a scabbard. . . . Up went the blade, then with a great artistry and a loud "Banzai," the officer brought the blade down. We heard a dull thud, and the American was decapitated. The Japanese officer then kicked the body of the American soldier over into the field, and all of the Japanese soldiers laughed merrily and walked away.

Japanese soldiers mistreated and killed Allied prisoners as a matter of course. And they expected such treatment if they ever fell into Allied hands. Kiyofumi Kojima, finding himself hopelessly surrounded by American troops in the Philippines, was one of the few Japanese soldiers in WWII to surrender. In camp, the Americans fed him some tinned provisions. When he finished eating, a U.S. soldier approached, holding out a shovel. Kojima remembers:

> He told me to dig a hole. I turned pale. When Japanese soldiers captured enemies, they always had them dig a hole, made them kneel down, and chopped their heads off. I looked around desperately for some place to run, but all I saw was a wall of iron, so I resigned myself to my fate. I stood up shakily and started to dig. I had no strength left and the soil was as hard as a rock. My hole was very shallow. I thought, this will never be big enough for me. But the soldier took away the shovel and simply threw [in] the can I'd been eating from, and ordering me to collect the rest from the others and bury them, too. I guess I looked stunned, so he added that it was a sanitation measure.

In the eyes of their captors, Doolittle Raider Chase Nielson and his fellow Flyboys had forfeited their honor. When he and his buddies wouldn't talk, the torture began.

"The first thing they did," Nielson recalled, "was to put pencils between my fingers, squeezing my hands and forcing the pencils up and down causing the skin to break." One guard would crush the Americans' hands as hard as he could while another yanked the pencils back and forth, popping out the knuckles.

Later, Nielson was hung up on a wall with his hands handcuffed behind him. Kempetei (secret police) officer Shintaro Uno recalled using this technique on Chinese prisoners: "The most excruciating torture is to tie their hands behind their back with a string and then hang them from a wall by that cord. All their weight is borne by their shoulders. It works better than beheading or strangling. If you use this method, ninety percent of them talk." Hanging from the wall, Nielson found the pain shooting through his entire body so severe that he passed out within minutes. But he and his fellow Flyboys still wouldn't talk.

The Kempetei were not finished. "The guard then brought in a large bamboo pole about three inches in diameter," Nielson remembered. "This was placed directly behind my knees. I was then made to squat on the floor in this position like a kneel. One guard had hold of each of my arms, one other guard then placed his foot on my thigh and would jump up and down causing severe pain in my knees. . . . I felt that my joints were coming apart, but after about five minutes of that my knees were so numb I couldn't feel anything else."

And, of course, there was the torture used by American soldiers in Teddy Roosevelt's imperial actions in the Philippines. "I was given what they call the water cure," Nielson remembered. "I was put on my back on the floor with my arms and legs stretched out, one guard holding each limb. A towel was wrapped around my face and water was poured on. They poured water on this towel until I was almost unconscious from strangulation, then they would let up until I'd get my breath, then they'd start all over again. I felt more or less like I was drowning, just gasping between life and death."

Radio Tokyo beamed taunts aimed at the American merchants who had dared to dispatch Flyboys to Rising Sun land: "Two can play at the same game of bombing. You know, you raid us and we raid you. It's all part of the war. . . . And by the way, don't forget, America, [you can be] sure that every flier that comes here has a special pass to hell. Rest assured, it's strictly a one-way ticket."

Now Japan and America were even. Both had scored surprise air attacks. Pearl Harbor and the Doolittle Raid were the two events that most determined the tenor and approach of the entire Pacific war from that point forward. Both sides were now Others to each other, eager to issue those one-way tickets to hell.

CHAPTER NINE

Airpower

The Japanese had failed fully to appreciate the strategic revolution brought about by the increased capabilities of air power.

— *"U.S. Strategic Bombing Survey Report," 1946*

As American citizens delighted in Roosevelt's Shangri-La remarks about the Doolittle Raid, their military braced for Japan's response. Dwight Eisenhower, then deputy chief of staff for the Pacific and Far East, asked his intelligence arm for their assessment. They told him this loss of face by the Japanese would certainly mean they would retaliate forcefully. Ike was warned that "Seattle, Portland, San Francisco, Los Angeles, and San Diego would become a string of Pearl Harbors. Radio stations across California were ordered off the air so their signals couldn't be used as targets by vengeful enemy bombers, and San Francisco's bridges were shut down. The army, theorizing that Japan would immediately send planes to drop poison, shipped six hundred thousand gas masks to the Western Defense Command."

The Doolittle Raid also dramatically shaped Japan's overall strategy in the Pacific. The Spirit Warriors considered themselves first and foremost protectors of the emperor, in the tradition of the "barbarian-expelling generalissimo" shogun. Now *gaizin* airplanes had flown directly over the royal family, enraging and humiliating military officers.

In their shame, the Warriors would overreach and employ a strategy that would reverse the course of the entire war.

At the time of the raid, the Japanese army and navy were locked in a bitter debate about how best to follow up their initial successes. The army wanted to consolidate their considerable territorial gains, but the navy wanted to finish off the job begun at Pearl Harbor and eliminate the American Pacific fleet once and for all. Admiral Isoroku Yamamoto, commander of Japan's combined fleet, had been preaching the need for a "decisive battle" at Midway Island — an American atoll eleven hundred miles due west of Oahu in the mid-Pacific — where he would finish off the Americans just as the Russians had been destroyed at Tsushima. Yamamoto argued that Jimmy's planes could only have been delivered by a carrier sailing near Midway. By occupying Midway, he could prevent any future air raids against Tokyo.

Politically, Japanese control of Midway would threaten Hawaii with invasion and provide a valuable bargaining chip to force America to negotiate a settlement. Militarily, attacking Midway could draw the U.S. Navy into a battle it was guaranteed to lose, dwarfed by Japan's vastly superior naval power.

Faced with the threat of further aerial assaults on the Son of Heaven, the army accepted Yamamoto's strategy. Midway would be taken and America's Pacific fleet would be destroyed. The faint prospect of victory Yamamoto had only dreamed of before seemed to lie only one battle away.

Yamamoto dispatched nearly two hundred ships amid pomp and ceremony on May 27, the thirty-seventh anniversary of the Battle of Tsushima. The first faint hints of the Japanese plan were detected by that pipe-smoking man in the red smoking jacket and slippers at Pearl Harbor — Joseph Rochefort, still chief of the Combat Intelligence Unit. The Japanese naval code was so complex that Rochefort and his men could only read about 15 percent of all the intercepts. Still, 15 percent was better than nothing. After the Doolittle Raid, one term was frequently picked up: "AF." Over many sleepless nights Rochefort wondered, what — or where — was "AF"?

Rochefort had a shrewd hunch. He guessed that "AF" was Midway Island, and in early May he baited a trap. He had the small Marine garrison on Midway radio in the clear that they were running low on fresh water. Two days later, Rochefort detected a coded Japanese message

119

that "AF" was running out of fresh water. Bingo! Midway, he concluded, was the next target for the Japanese navy. Rochefort's discovery would prove to be the single most potent intelligence success of the Pacific war.

On June 4, 1942, Japanese carrier planes from the naval force tangled with an attacking squadron of low-flying U.S. Navy carrier planes. Unbeknownst to the Japanese, an additional squadron of high-flying U.S. dive-bombers followed behind. The Japanese Zeroes were down low at deck level fighting off the first wave, so the second wave found the skies clear for an attack. The gods were with the Americans once again.

"All the way down there wasn't a gun turned on me, nobody saw me coming," remembered pilot Dick Best. "I pulled up and saw the first hit. . . . There was a solid column of smoke from bow to stern, at least 200 feet high above her. . . . It must have been an inferno below deck. . . . A carrier under destruction. I can see it in my mind right now, the most impressive sight of the day." In just five minutes the U.S. dive-bombers mortally wounded three Japanese carriers; they sank a fourth the next day. At Midway, Flyboys sunk four of the six carriers that just six months earlier had attacked Pearl Harbor.

Yamamoto's gamble was a bust, and Japan had lost the "decisive battle." Before Midway, Japan had six large fleet-class carriers to America's three. With the loss of four aircraft carriers, damage to six other ships, and the loss of more than three hundred Japanese planes and their most experienced pilots, the Japanese navy was crippled. Five minutes of applied American airpower had turned the tide of the Pacific war. As historian David Kennedy has noted, "In the two years following Midway, Japanese shipyards managed to splash only six additional fleet carriers. The United States in the same period added seventeen, along with ten medium carriers and eighty-six escort carriers. Such numbers, to be repeated in myriad categories of war materiel, spelled certain doom for Japan, though it was still a long and harrowing distance in the future."

But there were costs. During the Battle of Midway, Japanese sailors plucked three Flyboys from the water. Two were weighted down with chains and thrown overboard. The third was hacked to death with a fire ax.

*   *   *

On August 28, 1942, the eight Flyboys who had been captured after the Doolittle Raid were brought to a courthouse to stand "trial" for their "crimes." "They announced, in Japanese, our so-called sentence," Bob Hite said. "We didn't really know what it was. The interpreter said, 'They asked me not to tell you.' With that, they dismissed us."

On October 14, twenty-eight-year-old Dean Hallmark of Robert Lee, Texas; twenty-three-year-old Bill Farrow of Darlington, South Carolina; and twenty-one-year-old Harold Spatz of Lebo, Kansas, were told they had been found guilty of war crimes and would be executed the next day. The boys could not believe their ears.

Unbeknownst to them, Japan had passed the Enemy Airmen's Act on August 13, 1942. This ex post facto law held that anyone who bombed or strafed nonmilitary targets would be sentenced to death. All eight Flyboys had received the death sentence, but the emperor in his "benevolence" had commuted the sentences of the other five to life imprisonment. Those spared were not to be treated as ordinary prisoners of war but as guilty of war crimes. "As war criminals," an army message stated, "their treatment shall not be that accorded ordinary prisoners of war [and] even in the event of an exchange of war prisoners they may not be repatriated to the United States forces." So now it was official Spirit Warrior policy that Flyboys be killed.

Japanese army jailers gave Dean, Bill, and Harold pens and paper to write their last letters home.

Dean, too weak to even stand, wrote to his mom in Dallas: "I hardly know what to say. They have just told me that I am liable to execution. I can hardly believe it. . . . I am a prisoner of war and I thought I would be taken care of until the end of the war. . . . I did everything that the Japanese have asked me to do and tried to cooperate with them because I knew that my part in the war was over."

Bill wrote his widowed mother back in Darlington: "Don't let this get you down. Just remember that God will make everything right, and that I will see you again in the hereafter." In a separate letter to his fiancé, Farrow wrote, "You are, to me, the only girl that would have meant the completion of my life" and thanked her "for bringing to my life a deep, rich love for a fine girl." He added, "Please write and comfort Mom, because she will need you — she loves you, and thinks you are a fine girl."

Harold wrote his widowed father, "If I have inherited anything since I became of age, I will give it to you, and Dad, I want you to know that I love you and may God bless you. I want you to know that I died fighting for my country like a soldier."

After the war these letters were found in Japanese military files. The prison officials never mailed them.

On the morning of October 15, 1942, the three condemned Flyboys were handcuffed and driven to Shanghai's Public Cemetery Number One. Overnight, carpenters had constructed three wooden crosses, which were now embedded twenty feet apart from one another in the newly-mown grass.

Prison warden Tatsuta approached the three. "I told them that Christ was born and died on the cross and you on your part must die on the cross, but when you are executed — when you die on the cross you will be honored as gods, and I told them to pray and they made a sign which resembled the sign of the cross and they prayed. I told them, 'You will soon be bound to the crosses and when this is done it is a fact that it is a form that man's faith and cross shall be united. Therefore, have faith.' Then they smiled and said they understood very well. Then I asked them if they had any more to say and they said they had nothing more to say. That was all that was said."

Bill, Dean, and Harold were led to the crosses and made to kneel with their backs against the wood. Guards removed the handcuffs and tied the boys' wrists to the crosspieces. Their faces were covered with white cloth. The guards marked black Xs on the cloths to designate the middle of their foreheads.

The firing squad stood twenty feet away, next to a Shinto altar where incense burned. "Attention!" the commander barked. "Face the target!"

Three shots rang out. Three Flyboys' heads jerked backward. Blood spouted, soaking their white blindfolds red.

Four days later, Japan broadcast, in English, that "the cruel, inhuman and beastlike American pilots who . . . dropped incendiaries and bombs on non-military hospitals, schools and private houses and even dive-strafed playing schoolchildren, were captured and court-martialed and severely punished according to military law." The reports noted the names of the three men but did not mention the form of their punishment.

Up to that point in the Pacific war, the Japanese had maintained much of their earlier advantage. At the end of 1941, the Japanese had captured Wake Island, the westernmost American base in the Pacific. An American counterattack in February 1942 in the Marshall and Gilbert Islands had dented Yamamoto's forces. American Flyboys had fought fierce battles in an attempt to take Rabaul in New Guinea, which the Japanese were transforming into their largest air and naval base, but to little avail. And in the Battle of the Coral Sea in May 1942 (the first pure carrier-against-carrier battle), the Japanese had sustained heavy damage to two of their fleet carriers but had tactically advanced against the Allies.

Back home, more navy Flyboys trained for war in the vast Pacific. These airmen would go to war sitting down. As warriors they were prized not for their brawn but for their brains. Throngs of fighting men were trained not to develop calluses but to master syllabi. Navigation, dead reckoning, map reading, code recognition, and myriad mechanical challenges faced these Flyboys.

After Pearl Harbor the navy had quickly assembled a vast network of training fields and requisitioned university campuses. Training facilities had to be spread out across the country. Airfields themselves didn't take up much room, and the Flyboys' living quarters were the same size as those of first- and second-dimension warriors, but once airborne, Flyboys needed wide-open spaces to do their thing.

The dogfighting fighters needed miles of empty Texas sky; the dive-bombers roamed over rugged California mountains, searching empty valleys for practice targets painted on the ground, driving bombs toward bull's-eyes; the torpedo bombers winged over the Gulf of Mexico's blue green sheen to hit practice rafts or machine-gun target sleeves towed behind training planes. Inside all these aircraft, machine-gunners swiveled in turrets, knees to their chins, as radiomen below them tapped Mr. Morse's code.

Their status was high, and the girls were attracted to them. But there was another side to the coin. It was apparent early on, when a friend would burn to death in a crash, his charred body a smoking heap in a potato field. It was obvious when buddies would lose sight of the horizon on a night flight and plow into the ocean. Even on the ground, chums lost arms, backing into invisible twirling propellers. They wouldn't discuss it much, but they knew. The Flyboys understood that while they were lethal, their business was too.

On the frigid winter morning of November 21, 1942, eighteen-year-old aviation cadet George Bush lifted off a tarmac in Minnesota and flew a small trainer plane by himself for the first time. "It is hard for non-pilots to understand the joy of a first solo flight," Bush later commented. "All of us who soloed thought we were ten feet tall."

Bush was at the controls of a Stearman N2S, an open-cockpit biplane nicknamed "the Yellow Peril." It was called that, Archie Clapp recalled, because "other people better look out — we new pilots were perilous. That's why it was painted bright yellow." Many a Stearman had gone down during training, and cadets sometimes called the plane "the Washing Machine" because so many trainees washed out after being unable to handle it. But the Stearman was sturdy and safe, and so it was the trainer of choice, even though the open cockpit and Minnesota winters didn't go together well — except, perhaps for Bush. He loved the roar of cold air gusting through the plane's struts, which reminded him of being back in Maine, on a boat, when he was a kid and war was something in the history books.

"Your first solo is like when your dad tells you you can have the family car for the first time," Bill Connell from Seattle told me. Solos only came after weeks of training in the air and on the ground. Each step was a first. Jesse Naul was an instructor before he shipped out to the Pacific. "I put them in the plane and then would 'feel them through,'" he said. "The trainer planes had duplicate controls for the student pilot and the teacher. The student would place his hand on the stick and his feet on the pedals. He could feel what I was doing as I took off and landed. When it was his turn, he would 'follow through' and copy my actions. Of course, my hands and feet stayed on the controls to make sure he was doing the right things."

"I didn't have the vaguest idea when I went in," George Bush later recalled about learning to fly. "But I wanted to be a pilot. I went to ground school, passed tests on navigation, learned how the engine works. Then you get in the plane and you are under the trainer's leadership. He tells you what to do. Push the pedal this much, turn this way. You are following his instructions completely. Then it's a seat-of-the-pants thing. You get a feel for altitude, what's safe and what's not.

You go through the fundamental maneuvers — stalling, et cetera. I liked it. The feeling of flying is like nothing else in the world."

"When your instructor was satisfied you were not going to kill yourself, he'd let you solo," said Archie Clapp. "Then you alternate. Your instructor would show you something new. Then he'd be on the ground watching you do it. Slow rolls, loops, how to recover from a spin. You'd make the plane do everything it could do."

"After the pilot has soloed, experience is the best teacher," explained navy flying instructor Robert Banta. "Experience makes the pilot. The best pilots had the most experience. We'd give them plenty of time in the air."

"It's like driving a car," Leland Holdren said. "But you are moving in three dimensions rather than two. With a car you can only go left or right. With a plane you can go up and down also." For some, even that comparison only went so far. "I had never driven a car," recalled John Leboeuf, who hailed from Michigan's rural Upper Peninsula. "In fact, I logged over four hundred flying hours before I learned to drive a car."

Air combat was still relatively new, much more of an art than a science, but the Flyboys were taught a series of offensive and defensive maneuvers. Some seemed relatively simple — like a loop over, or a barrel roll, which was an aerobatic corkscrew that could be used to shake a tailing enemy — and others were much more complicated. A chandelle was a climbing turn that resulted in a 180-degree change of direction and that also often resulted in deadly spins. An Immelmann combined a half loop and a half roll and allowed a pilot to both gain altitude over and turn toward an enemy, but if it was not executed perfectly, the plane would stall, leaving it powerless and in perfect position for enemy machine guns. Pilots were taught which moves were best against specific enemy fighters. The Japanese Mitsubishi Zero, for example, was phenomenally maneuverable and could, at the beginning of the war, at least, outclimb Allied planes. At speeds below 250 miles per hour, its ability to dart and turn and gyrate was incredible and intimidating. But American Flyboys gradually discovered that the Zero's wing, which was light, with a shape that created high lift, hindered the Zero's ability to dive. And at speeds above 300 miles per hour, Japanese pilots had trouble controlling their planes. As long as the Americans could keep the dogfight at higher altitudes (which presented increased dive-attack opportunities, as opposed to lower altitudes, which encouraged fast-climb strategies) and higher speeds, they had a distinct advantage. The Zero also had a design quirk that meant it rolled faster to the left than to the right. Flyboys learned attack maneuvers and formations that took advantage of weaknesses like these, and as the war progressed, they would eventually smash their less experienced and less well informed Japanese counterparts.

The navy Flyboys-in-training were constantly tested and evaluated through every step of the syllabus to make sure they had the "right stuff." If they didn't master a maneuver, they were promptly replaced. "A lot of people don't have the natural coordination to be a pilot," Tex Ellison, who instructed George Bush, told me. "We'd watch them and wash out those who shouldn't be at the controls."

These novice pilots had to understand mechanics and physics. "It's all about the wings and the propeller," Flyboy Charlie Brown explained to me. "The wing is flat on the bottom and the top is curved. The air has to fly over a greater surface on the top, which creates lift and keeps the plane in the air. The propeller is angled so it bites into the air and actually pulls the plane forward. So you have lift from the shape of the wings and motion from the turning of the propeller." These were facts of life and death to the pilots: Without enough speed there would be insufficient lift, but too much speed at the wrong angle could be disastrous.

The toughest skill to master, Charlie Brown recalled, was landing. "When you come in, you reduce your power so you are not moving as fast through the air. The air is not giving you as much lift, so you gradually descend. Each plane has a stalling speed at which it drops. You want to be going just a little faster than stalling speed. But when you are just about on the runway, you pull back on the stick, which raises the nose of the airplane and causes it to stall and you've made a successful landing."

All pilots make landings, but navy pilots had to make the most dangerous ones. To a pilot, an aircraft carrier is a tiny landing strip that is not only sailing away from him but might also be bobbing six to fifteen feet up and down as well as rolling side to side. And getting on deck was just part of it. Cables were strung across the carrier decks. The landing plane had to drop its tail hook and snag a cable to arrest its forward progress. As Charlie Brown described it, "You crash-land on the deck and hope you catch a wire." Harold Wegener told me, "They've instrumented pilots nowadays and found their heart rate is faster landing on a carrier than when they are in combat."

"How do you land on an aircraft carrier?" I asked George Bush. He answered with a knowing smile, "Very carefully . . ." The key was the pilot's confidence in the landing signal officer, the LSO. The LSO was an experienced pilot who directed pilots coming in for a landing by signaling with his paddles. These signaling paddles were like cut-off tennis rackets with strips of colored fabric stretched across the face. (The strips allowed the LSO to wave the paddles about and not worry about catching the strong winds that blew across the deck of the air-craft carrier.) "You depend on the LSO totally," George Bush said. "You're too high, you're too slow, he will signal. It is the landing sig-nal officer who gives you the 'cut signal' to land. You place yourself totally in his hands." Charlie Brown remarked, "The LSO gives you a cut sign or a wave off. The cut sign means you can land. The wave off means you give it full throttle and circle around to try again. Once he gives you the cut sign, you don't touch the throttle again or you'll get court-martialed."

Fighter pilot Lowell Bernard told me about practicing night land-ings on a carrier. "Day landings are bad enough," Lowell said. "But landing in the pitch-dark, with no lights whatsoever, was the most ter-rifying thing I ever did." Harold Wegener remembered a particularly frightening night landing: "There were no stars, no horizon, no lights, and you couldn't see the water. We were flying on instruments alone. Two planes went into the water. When I got out of my plane I was soaking wet. Pure terror and sweat."

Pilots were the quarterbacks of this third-dimensional war, but there were others on the team. It took the skills of highly trained radiomen, radar operators, ground mechanics, machine-gunners, and bombardiers all working together to turn the airplane into a true fighting machine.

There were two main types of carrier pilots. "The big decision," Archie Clapp told me, "was whether you were going to be a fighter pi-lot or a bomber pilot." Fighter planes were sleek and fast; bombers were bigger and heavier, allowing them to carry larger payloads. But both types of carrier planes were smaller than their land-based cousins.

Fighter pilots like Warren Earl Vaughn flew fast single-seat airplanes, and their main job was to fight off opposing enemy fighters. In his final months before shipping out to the Pacific, he was trained by hot-dogging Marine veterans at Mojave Air Base in California.

Warren Earl flew the Vought F4U-1A — better known as the Corsair. Fast (speeds in excess of 400 miles per hour) and with excellent maneuverability, the Corsair was good-sized (more than 33 feet long, with a wingspan of 41 feet) and tough. It bristled with six .50-caliber machine guns and included several armored plates that added to the plane's 14,000-pound weight but helped in a dogfight. (Just as the Spirit Warriors abandoned troops once in the field, they usually chose not to armor Japanese planes, leaving them lighter and more maneuverable at slow speeds but subject to immediate destruction if hit squarely.)

Once they learned how to conquer the Corsair's dangerous spin characteristics, Flyboys came to love the plane. "Smoother than riding in a boat on the water," was how Archie Clapp remembered it. "Like an automobile." Unlike the bombers, this was not a plane for the small. "The Corsair," Archie recalled, "was built for a six-foot-four-inch test pilot, so it was roomy. Small guys needed padding." Pilots sat in a Plexiglas bubble with an armor plate behind them. There were three rearview mirrors, and pilots had to constantly check all of them, as well as the view out the cockpit. The Corsair had an extralong nose that made looking downward difficult, especially when approaching a carrier. "On a carrier landing," Archie explained, "you couldn't see anything except from the side, so you were flying in a constant turn to see the LSO." But as scary as that was, it was even scarier to be a Japanese pilot when a group of Corsairs came screaming in. The Japanese would eventually nickname the Corsair "Whistling Death" for the sound it made when diving and for the damage it wreaked.

"We spent four months at Mojave," recalled Wesley Todd, who flew with Warren Earl Vaughn. "We all figured we were overtrained and we should get overseas. We were eager and ready to go."

"We practiced air tactics," Archie Clapp remembered. "Bombing, rocket work, you'd just keep working at it. We were called 'fighter pilots,' but it would have been more accurate to call us 'fighter-bomber pilots.' We fired air-to-ground rockets off our wings and practiced glide-bombing." Glide-bombing is exactly what the name sounds like — instead of diving down to a target, a plane glides over the target to release its ordnance.

"When you get into maneuvers," Archie recalled, "we wore G-suits." The Corsair pilots wore form-fitted pants that had air bladders in the pelvic area and all down the leg. The bladders, Clapp explained, would squeeze to "cut off blood below to keep the blood up in your upper body so you didn't faint. It was spring-loaded and calibrated to respond to the G-forces. The more Gs, the more it would let the air in the bladders to squeeze more."

After a day's work, the social scene in wartime California offered handsome pilots like Warren Earl some pretty choices. "The bachelors were having a ball," Archie remembered. "We were their knights who were going to protect them. It was common to go into a bar and have everything paid for." Warren Earl and his buddies would go to Hollywood on liberty. These dashing Marine officers with their gold aviator's wings pinned on their smart uniforms attracted the attention of the local blondes and brunettes. "It was pretty easy pickings," Flyboy John McManus remembered years later. "Bill Lynch was the smartest about it. Bill would never go to the bars — he'd go to the church socials. He met more beautiful girls there than we did."

Warren Earl spent a few weekends with some lovelies at Big Bear Lake, California. When I interviewed Wesley Todd, he well remembered the lakeside-cabin scene. "Gals from Hollywood would come up and meet us there," he said. "They'd take off from their jobs; it was a big group-type of thing."

I told Todd, "Warren Earl had a girlfriend up there." To which he laughingly replied, "Yeah, everybody did."

One day, back at Mojave, Warren Earl was feeling his oats and decided to imitate a hotdogging trick he had seen one of the veterans pull. A plane should be well off the tarmac before a pilot retracts its wheels. But Warren Earl had seen a vet demonstrate his confidence by retracting the wheels in conjunction with his plane's initial lift. He decided to give it a try.

"It's a stupid thing to do," Archie Clapp explained to me. "You can't beat the odds in that maneuver. There's something called 'ground effect.' There's greater lift closer to the ground than there is a few feet up. So you might have enough ground speed to lift off a bit, but there are too many variables, like wind currents and air pressure, that could cause you to drop down again."

So why would Warren Earl attempt a dangerous maneuver that didn't make sense? "A fighter pilot has to be a little crazy anyway," Archie answered. "So he thinks it's cool."

"Warren Earl tried it," John McManus remembered, "and his prop chewed into the ground."

Warren Earl's service record described the aftermath of the bent propeller and resulting fire from which he fled for his life: "Received first and second degree burns on hand and neck and flesh burns to face as the result of an aviation accident while on authorized flight." The hotdogging Cherokee Texan spent three days in sick bay licking his wounds. "He was dark anyway," Wesley Todd recalled. "But now his face was even darker, more Indian looking."

John McManus chuckled as he remembered. "In his Texas drawl," he said, "Warren Earl told his commander, 'I couldn't hep it.'"

Most navy carrier planes were bombers and carried pilot plus crew. This called for a slightly more conservative approach to their job. "Usually the fighter pilots are the most aggressive," Flyboy Al Lindstrom told me. "Bombers are a little less reckless; they have crew in the back." There were two types of bombers, a dive-bombing plane that carried pilot and one crew and a torpedo-bombing plane that carried pilot and two crew.

"Dive-bombers carry a bomb," Lindstrom explained. "At twelve thousand to fourteen thousand feet, you dive and drop your bomb on a target. You're going sixty degrees down and you release the bomb at three thousand feet and pull out. You might dive lower. The lower you dive, the more accurate you are.

"Once you commit to your dive," he continued, "the antiaircraft gunners know exactly where you'll be. Once you start down, there is a straight line between you and the target. You end up in a cone of their antiaircraft fire."

Torpedo bombers were designed to fly low over the ocean and launch torpedoes against enemy ships. But by 1944, Japanese shipping had been decimated, so the torpedo planes were now used as glide-bombers.

Dick Woellhof had become a gunner in an SB2C dive-bomber. The

SB2C — better known as the Helldiver — had two cockpits for a pilot and a gunner. The Helldiver's wingspan was almost fifty feet, but the wings could be folded when the plane was in transit aboard ship. The pilot had two wing-mounted cannon and Gunner Dick had two .30-caliber machine guns to guard the plane from attacks. Unlike some other planes, the dive-bombers required the gunner to pull his Plexiglas canopy back to shoot his gun. Only his goggles and leather helmet protected him from the enemy's exploding shells. But Dick depended on his luck and his belief that "the other guy will get it, not me."

The Pacific war was a battle for the Third Dimension, as Billy Mitchell had predicted. Japan had spent vast sums supporting millions of first-dimension troops in China and building the world's greatest second-dimension battleships, but FDR's bet on the Third Dimension paid off. The Japanese established impregnable fortresses on islands like Rabaul and Truk that they thought would secure the South Pacific. But America leap-frogged its way to victory. With their aircraft carriers, the navy projected airpower to soften up islands for the Marines to capture. These islands would then serve as airfields for Flyboys to attack the next islands on the way to Tokyo. Indeed, the first titanic land battle between Japan and the U.S. at Guadalcanal was fought over who would control the strategic airfield there. The Battle of the Coral Sea and the brutal fighting in Papua, New Guinea, were over who would control the airfield at Port Moresby, which held the key to control of Australia. From Bougainville to Okinawa, the value of the islands wrested from Japanese control was in their use as airfields to launch Flyboys. Marines would capture the Mariana Islands to serve as bases for U.S. Army Air Corps B-29 bombers to hit Japan. And Marines would die on Iwo Jima to clear the skies for the Marianas-based Flyboys.

Thanks to the Flyboys, during the six-month-long battle over Guadalcanal that began in August of 1942, the Japanese lost 892 planes and 1,882 pilots. Airpower was crucial to the ground war too. While writing this book, I received an e-mail from a Pacific vet who wrote, "The Marines were abandoned by the Navy on Guadalcanal, with no supplies. They fought on for months. How did they win? The answer is they were supplied by air." It was true. Only airplanes could supply the beleaguered Marines on Guadalcanal, as the Japanese controlled the seas. No less a navy man than Admiral William "Bull"

Halsey declared, "Without the aid of SCAT [the South Pacific Combat Air Transport Command, a sky-based supply squad created by a group of former airline pilots who served in the Marine Corps reserve] some of our most important victories would not have been possible." The Marines dubbed SCAT "the Flying Boxcars." Food, medical supplies, and ammunition were all flown in, and the wounded were flown out. At a time when LaGuardia and Chicago airports serviced just over 100 flights a day, SCAT was running 72. "In one six-month period alone, SCAT moved 43,626,495 pounds of cargo plus 235,596 passengers carried in 34,834 trips." In one typical instance, pilot Skip Kimball "alighted from his plane in the midst of artillery shelling. From a slit trench off the runway, he and his crew witnessed hand-to-hand fighting at the end of the strip. When the Marines 'had the situation well in hand' Kimball loaded his casualties aboard and took off."

A few decades earlier, it would have been impossible to create a supply network like the one the Americans established in the Pacific, where ports and even cities were few. The Flyboys had come along and changed the rules. But the Japanese still drew upon the old playbook. Where they saw islands as fortresses defended by a vast saltwater moat, the Americans saw them as springboards. The span of ocean that in the past had slowed troop movement and supplies was irrelevant to anyone who took to the skies. The imperial command saw the Pacific as a dispersed constellation of strongholds. But the Americans were connecting the dots, and as they did, an already gruesome war took an even bloodier turn.

CHAPTER TEN

Yellow Devils, White Devils

We hold his examples of atrocity screaming to the heavens while we cover up our own and condone them as just retribution for his acts. We claim to be fighting for civilization, but the more I see of this war in the Pacific the less right I think we have to claim to be civilized. In fact, I am not sure that our record in this respect stands so very much higher than the Japanese.

— *Charles Lindbergh,* The Wartime Journals of Charles H. Lindbergh

AMERICA did not learn the fates of the executed Doolittle Raiders until April of 1943, one year after the raid. FDR was "profoundly shocked" and issued a State Department warning threatening "officers of the Japanese Government" with punishment for "uncivilized and inhuman acts" and "acts of criminal barbarity" that were "in violation of the rules of warfare accepted and practiced by civilized nations."

On April 21, 1943, Roosevelt announced in a radio broadcast, "It is with a feeling of the deepest horror, which I know will be shared by all civilized peoples, that I have to announce the barbarous execution by the Japanese Government of some of the members of this country's armed forces who fell into Japanese hands as an incident of warfare."

Two days later, a *New York Times* headline reinforced the inhuman quality of the Japanese action:

JAPAN'S BARBAROUS ACT HAS NO PARALLEL IN WAR: TOKYO STANDS ALONE AS A CRUEL CAPTOR IN DEFIANCE OF GENEVA CONVENTION

Rage swept the country. FDR predicted that Japan's "barbarous" actions "will make the American people more determined than ever to blot out the shameless militarism of Japan." General Hap Arnold sent a message to all his Flyboys saying that "inhuman warlords" had gone beyond "human decency" and that they must be "utterly destroyed." Secretary of State Cordell Hull declared that there would be no negotiation with a country that executed prisoners of war. America would now settle for nothing less than "unconditional surrender" from Japan.

The *New York Times* contacted Chase Nielson's mother, who said, "I wonder if, and hope and pray, that it is propaganda. I don't see how anyone who professes to be of the human race can be so cruel and inhuman." Mrs. John Meder of Lakewood, Ohio, mother of another Raider, commented, "The Japanese just can't be so heartless and inhuman as all that. They just couldn't resort to such vile and insane acts with our boys."

But to the mothers of the children and hospital patients killed in Japan, it was the American Flyboys who were inhuman and heartless.

Killing does not come naturally or easily to humans. Except for the small percentage of psychopaths in a population, most people find it nearly impossible to kill a fellow human being. A process of dehumanization must take place to get large numbers of soldiers to kill other people.

The physical dissimilarities between Americans and Japanese were obvious. And culturally, it was as if the two nations were from different planets. The United States was a new country, an ever-changing dynamo filling out the immense North American landmass like a boy growing into a new suit. Japan was a small ancient land settled in its ways, with a god-king and a semifeudal social structure.

Some of the differences were more trivial. For example, the two countries didn't even agree what year it was. Americans thought Japan bombed Pearl Harbor in 1941. But the Japanese dated the attack as Showa 16. "Showa" referred to Emperor Hirohito, and Pearl Harbor occurred in the sixteenth year of his reign. (Even today the front pages of Japan's daily newspapers express the date in terms of the current emperor's reign.) Likewise, the two countries couldn't agree on how to write someone's name. John Smith in the U.S. was "Smith John" in Japan.

There were other distinctions. In greeting, an American made eye contact and shook hands; a Japanese averted his gaze and bowed. An American sat on a chair to eat with metal tableware; a Japanese sat on the floor and used wooden chopsticks. In the U.S., soup was the first course; in Japan it was the last. Pasta in the West had a sauce poured over it; in Japan the pasta was dipped into a sauce.

The list was almost endless. An American counted on her fingers by displaying a closed fist and then raising each finger as she counted, "One, two, three." A Japanese would hold up her hand with extended fingers and bring them closed to her palm as she counted "One, two, three." An American washed in the bathtub. But the Japanese considered it disgusting to sit in water in which one's body dirt was floating. A Japanese scrubbed down outside the tub and entered it only when she was clean. When an American read a book, she started from the "front" of the book, read left to right horizontally across each page, and turned the pages from right to left. In Japan, the reader started at the "back" of the book, read vertically down each page from top to bottom, going from right to left, and turned the pages from left to right. And on and on.

In the 1930s and 1940s, there were almost no *gaizin* in Japan. And outside of a few pockets in California, there were few Japanese on the U.S. mainland. So each side knew only caricatures of the other, not the real thing. Americans were devils with green blood and tails. Japanese wore thick glasses and had buckteeth. By the time they laid eyes on each other, they had been culturally programmed to view each other as repulsive.

Ernie Pyle was by far the most widely read World War II journalist. His column appeared in seven hundred newspapers every week around the world. Pyle spent most of his war career in Europe but transferred to the Pacific theater in 1944. He introduced the Japanese enemy to his millions of readers this way: "In Europe we felt that our enemies, horrible and deadly as they were, were still people. But out here I soon gathered that the Japanese were looked upon as something subhuman and repulsive, the way some people feel about cockroaches or mice." When he saw Japanese prisoners for the first time, he told his readers, "They were wrestling and laughing and talking just like normal human beings. And yet they gave me the creeps, and I wanted a mental bath after looking at them."

Ashihei Hino was Japan's Ernie Pyle. He called Americans "people whose arrogant nation once tried to unlawfully treat our motherland with contempt." He described American POWs on Bataan this way: "I feel like I am watching filthy water running from the sewage of a nation which derives from impure origins and has lost its pride of race. Japanese soldiers look particularly beautiful, and I feel exceedingly proud of being Japanese."

To the Japanese people, who prided themselves on being genetically "pure," uncontaminated by immigration, Americans were mongrelized devils. Posters in classrooms exhorted students to "kill the American animal." A popular Japanese magazine spoke of "the breath and body odor of the beast . . . the American enemy, driven by its ambition to conquer the world." This "savage . . . barbaric tribe of Americans are devils in human skin" with as much worth "as a foreign ear of corn."

"We had no knowledge of how America was founded. What races made up America. Nothing," said Terumichi Kiyama, who later became a Shinto priest. "We just had the expression 'Kichiku Bei-Ei' — American-English Devils. We saw them as lower animals. These terms were widespread in Japan."

"When you encounter the enemy after landing, think of yourself as an avenger come at last face to face with your father's murderer," wrote Colonel Masanobu Tsuji, who masterminded Japanese planning for the invasion of Malaya. "Here is the man whose death will lighten your heart of its burden of brooding anger. If you fail to destroy him utterly you can never rest in peace."

"The people were easily flattered by a sense of superiority," remembered Masoa Kumai, seventeen years old in 1941.

War leaders always incite their people before they begin a war. Hitler used the propaganda of racial superiority to incite the German people. In Japan the people were incited by the claim that the oracle of the Founder of the Empire had pronounced Japan to be a divine land — the crown of the world — with an unbroken line of emperors. Because of its superiority, the Japanese race could participate in these imperial achievements. Both the German and Japanese people were flattered by this sense of superiority, and it made them lose their sense of justice. It caused them to feel that invasion of other countries and annihilation of other races was justified.

Like Commodore Perry, who knew little about the Japanese except that they were uncivilized Others, most Americans who had never seen a Japanese knew exactly what to think of them. "The most popular float in a day-long victory parade in New York in mid-1942 was titled 'Tokyo: We Are Coming,' and depicted bombs falling on a frantic pack of yellow rats." When an innocent kid asked an older Marine in the 1943 Hollywood film *Guadalcanal Diary* how he felt about killing Japanese people, the Marine responded, "They ain't people." Propaganda reinforced this sensibility. As a veteran of the Pacific fighting wrote, "The Japanese made a perfect enemy. They had so many characteristics that an American Marine could hate. Physically, they were small, a strange color, and, by some standards, unattractive. . . . Marines did not consider that they were killing men. They were wiping out dirty animals." Author Studs Terkel remembered the Japanese portrayed as "subhuman, different and slanty-eyed." Their cultural homogeneity was exploited to make them nameless and the same, like a hill of ants. Terkel remembered that in cartoons, "the Germans were ridiculed, Hitler especially, and Mussolini with his jutting jaw, but in the Japanese case it was tribal, it was collective . . . you know: the grin, the slanty eyes, the glasses, the Jap, or the Nip." A Marine Corps film shot on Tarawa depicted Japanese defenders as "living, snarling rats." The Japanese were routinely presented in print, speech, and cartoons as animals, and popular songs like "We're Gonna Have to Slap the Dirty Little Jap" also encouraged a less-than-human view of the Japanese.

Japanese were considered such despicable Others that most Americans applauded when Franklin Roosevelt ordered American citizens of Japanese ancestry interned in 1942. The general in charge of internment was asked in a congressional hearing to justify the action. The nation understood his reasoning when he answered that Americans of Italian and German ancestry could be trusted, but "a Jap is a Jap — it makes no difference whether he is an American citizen or not." A year later, congressmen asked him why law-abiding Japanese Americans could not now be released. The general answered, "A Jap's a Jap . . . we will be worried about [them] until they are wiped off the face of the map."

The Spirit Warriors had hoped that the Pearl Harbor attack would dishearten the American merchants. But the opposite was true: Pearl Harbor gave America a sense of moral ferocity no government propaganda could come close to matching. American rage bordered on the genocidal. Signs appeared in store windows proclaiming "Open Season on Japs." (Amid the World War II memorabilia on display in my hometown library in Antigo, Wisconsin, I recently found a "Jap-Hunting License.") Admiral Halsey vowed that by the end of the war, Japanese would be spoken only in hell. The admiral's slogan became "Kill Japs, kill Japs, kill more Japs."

American soldiers who had little enthusiasm for killing other western Christians often jumped at the chance to kill Japanese. One U.S. army infantry regiment "was asked 'How would you feel about killing a German soldier?' Just 7 percent gave the answer 'I would really like to' from a list of possible answers. When the word Japanese was inserted into the question, the percentage really wanting to kill the soldier jumped to 44 percent."

Marine George Petio recalled the instructions broadcast by loudspeaker to men in the first assault waves attacking Peleliu: "When we came aboard the LSTs [landing ship tanks] there was a message come through from our colonel, and the word was that we were to take no prisoners." American soldiers were not *shinmin*/subjects of a god-king, forced to obey all orders. They were citizens of a democracy. They were taught that there *was* such a thing as an illegal order. But few protested orders to kill Japanese prisoners.

Marine Eugene Sledge was removing a bayonet from a dead Japanese on Peleliu when he noticed another Marine nearby:

> He wasn't in our mortar section but had happened by and wanted to get in on the spoils. He came up to me dragging what I assumed to be a corpse. But the Japanese wasn't dead. He had been wounded severely in the back

and couldn't move his arms; otherwise he would have resisted to his last breath.

The Japanese's mouth glowed with huge gold-crowned teeth, and his captor wanted them. He put the point of his kabar on the base of a tooth and hit the handle with the palm of his hand. Because the Japanese was kicking his feet and thrashing about, the knifepoint glanced off the tooth and sank deeply into the victim's mouth. The Marine cursed him and with a slash cut his cheeks open to each ear. He put his foot on the sufferer's lower jaw and tried again. Blood poured out of the soldier's mouth. He made a gurgling noise and thrashed wildly. I shouted, "Put the man out of his misery." All I got for an answer was a cussing out. Another Marine ran up, put a bullet in the enemy soldier's brain, and ended his agony. The scavenger grumbled and continued extracting his prizes undisturbed.

During the war, a picture of a pretty blonde appeared in an issue of *Life* magazine. She was seated at a table writing a letter, paper in front of her. Pen to her lips, she gazed at an ornament on her desk as if for inspiration. The ornament was a Japanese skull. The caption read, "Arizona war worker writes her Navy boyfriend a thank-you note for the Japanese skull he sent her." Later in the war, President Roosevelt announced that he had refused to accept a letter opener made of the bone of a Japanese. It's hard to believe this gruesome trophy hunting would have been tolerated if the skulls and bones were German or Italian.

Soldier Dennis Warner recalled standing near a group of Japanese prisoners with upstretched hands. A general ordered the defenseless POWs shot. "But sir, they are wounded and want to surrender," a colonel protested. "You heard me, Colonel," the general replied. "I want no prisoners. Shoot them all."

Army private Nelson Peery recalled that in New Guinea, "We all saw the brutality and in some instances just plain savagery against Japanese soldiers who were trying to surrender, or who had surrendered, who were shot or clubbed. They were pretty brutally treated."

Parachuting Japanese pilots were routinely shot out of the sky. "A few Japs parachuted when they were hit," a young seaman wrote in his diary late in 1943. "But a few sailors and Marines on the 20mm opened up on the ones in the chutes and when they hit the water they were nothing but a piece of meat cut to ribbons."

In January 1943, Commander Dudley Walker Morton, a Naval Academy graduate and commander of the submarine *Wahoo,* sank a Japanese transport ship off New Guinea. He then surfaced and ordered his men to shoot the helpless survivors in the water with deck guns. For over an hour, American submariners killed hundreds, perhaps thousands, of Japanese boys who could not defend themselves. "One of the officers on the Wahoo, recalling the occasion, spoke of the commander's 'overwhelming biological hatred of the enemy.'" Many were repulsed by this cold-blooded murder, but Commander Morton's superiors tacitly condoned the action by awarding him a Navy Cross. General MacArthur awarded him a Distinguished Cross. The navy even named a ship in his honor.

On March 4, 1943, after the three-day Battle of the Bismarck Sea, allied Flyboys strafed Japanese survivors in their rafts. A U.S. major reported, "It was rather a sloppy job and some of the boys got sick. But that is something you have to learn. The enemy is out to kill you and you are out to kill the enemy. You can't be sporting in war." One might expect Geneva convention–honoring Americans to hide cockpit film footage of the machine-gunning of terrified Japanese boys in their life rafts. Instead it was proudly shown in movie theaters in the United States. Civilized American audiences munched their popcorn and loudly applauded this war crime. As chunks of Japanese flesh flew into the air, the commentator intoned:

> . . . the fun begins . . . The lads will do a great shooting-up job on ships and barges crammed with Jap soldiers seeking escape. . . . There's trouble brewing for Tojo today, all right. . . . The Nips have had this coming to them for a long, long time. There they are! Those American bomber boys certainly know their stuff. Let 'em have it, buddy! This is it, boys, give her the gun. Here we go! . . . The convoy carried fifteen thousand Jap troops. . . . There's plenty of them left in barges and lifeboats dotted over the sea. There's a boat! Tiny speck, center screen . . . Miss! One tiny boat on a wide sea isn't so easy to hit! Bull's-eye! And more Japs meet their ancestors. The show's over, boys.

When U.S. prisoners were killed, it was "murder in flagrant disregard of the Geneva Conventions." But when Americans murdered Others, "they had it coming to them."

*　　*　　*

The battle for the island of Attu in the Aleutians illustrated yet another great divide between America and Japan. In May of 1943, after two weeks of fighting, only eight hundred Japanese troops remained. These troops had no ammunition left, and there was nothing they could do militarily. Troops of any other nation would have surrendered. On the night of May 29, 1943, the surviving troops were ordered to attack. Fewer than thirty survived.

To Americans, what happened on Attu was inexplicable. *Time*'s war correspondent Robert Sherrod wrote: "The results of the Jap fanaticism stagger the imagination. The very violence of the scene is incomprehensible to the western mind. Here groups of men . . . met their self-imposed obligation to die rather than accept capture, by blowing themselves to bits. . . . The ordinary, unreasoning Jap is ignorant. Perhaps he is human. Nothing on Attu indicates it."

In Japan, however, the fact that the battle was lost and Japanese boys were needlessly sacrificed didn't matter to the heartless Spirit Warriors. What was important was that Japanese troops had demonstrated *Yamato damashii* by not surrendering. The Warriors presented Attu as heroic, and *shinmin* were reminded that Japanese spirit, like the ancient *kamikaze,* would somehow vanquish the American devils. The desk generals in Tokyo even invented a euphemism to glorify the army's defeats. Losing battles and having everyone slaughtered wasn't something to worry about. It was something to be proud of, for it demonstrated *"gyokusai."*

In the Japanese language, the term *gyokusai* consists of two ideograms. One means "jewel" and the other "smashed." The meaning came from a classic Chinese tale about a morally superior man who, rather than compromise his principles, destroyed his precious possessions. So now dead Japanese boys were admirable "smashed jewels" as the Spirit Warriors converted their military defeats into moral victories.

After all, the dead *shinmin* would become military gods to be revered through the ages. What better way to go than to be remembered as loyal to the emperor?

Far too many Japanese boys would be forced to become *gyokusai* because their Tokyo superiors lacked a realistic strategy. Instead, Japanese generals just scattered their *issen gorin* willy-nilly throughout the Pacific with little hope either of supporting them in battle or evacuating them in defeat. For example, the Spirit boys dispatched more than 150,000 Japanese soldiers to New Guinea, but when they realized they could not support forces there, the army generals simply abandoned them. Sergeant Masatsugu Ogawa's unit landed on New Guinea with seven thousand men. "Only sixty-seven survived," he recalled. He and countless others desperately roamed the difficult terrain of New Guinea "like an army of mud dolls" as "the dead bodies became road markers." When a Kempetei officer on the side of the road asked where his buddy was, Ogawa replied that he had fallen behind. "Why didn't you kill him, then?" the Kempetei officer demanded. "You can't get out of these mountains if you wait for stragglers. It's all right to kill them. One or two of you doesn't mean anything."

Tamotsu Ogawa was a medic in the South Pacific. He later described himself as being "young and simpleminded. I really believed it my duty to serve as a Japanese soldier — one of His Majesty's children." But he soon learned that the emperor's compassion did not extend to the wounded. As esteemed historian Sabura Ienaga has written, "The wounded were an impediment to military operations because attempts to save them often resulted in more casualties or diverted manpower. A battlefield morality of 'not becoming a burden to others' prevailed. The wounded were forced to kill themselves or they were shot, depending on circumstances. Hardened combat veterans used to say, 'On the battlefield ruthlessness is sometimes a virtue.'"

Medical officers in most armies are there to save lives. But in the shattered-jewel army, they were to end them. As Tamotsu Ogawa recalled:

> I became a murderer. I killed men who didn't resist, couldn't resist. I killed men who only sought medicine, comrades I was supposed to help. Naturally the fucking officers didn't do it themselves. They left it to the orderlies. We did it under orders from the company commander, then covered the bodies with coconut palm leaves and left them there.
>
> I think to myself: I deserve a death sentence. I didn't kill just one or two. Only war allows this — these torments I have to bear until I die. My war will continue until that moment. I'm alive. What a pity I can't do anything but weep. I know tears don't erase my sin.

A captured Japanese officer observed American doctors tending to the broken bodies of wounded Japanese soldiers. He expressed surprise at the resources being expended upon these men, who were too badly injured to fight again. "What would you do with these men?" a Marine officer asked him. "We'd give each a grenade," was his answer. "And if they didn't use it, we'd cut their jugular vein."

Incredibly, Allied bullets accounted for only one third of all Japanese troop fatalities in the Pacific war. The Spirit Warriors' lack of strategy and planning accounted for most deaths. Indeed, when the Americans island-hopped toward Tokyo they simply bypassed these pitiful abandoned troops, leaving them to "wither on the vine," in the U.S. phrase. "On Jaluit, Mili, Wotje and Nauru, the Japanese tried to stay alive by farming and fishing. More than one-third died of sickness and starvation. On Wolwei, a force of over 7,000 men numbered fewer than 2,000 by the war's end. One bypassed island, Manus, was even used for training. Raw [Japanese] troops would be sent there to be toughened up, by practicing on the Japanese stragglers living in central and eastern parts of the island."

The "fanatic" Japanese willingness to die astonished Americans. On Guadalcanal, Marine commander Alexander Vandergrift wrote: "I have never heard or read of this kind of fighting. These people refuse to surrender. The wounded wait until men come up to examine them . . . and blow themselves and the other fellow to pieces with a hand grenade."

On the fetid and swampy New Guinea coast, a contingent of waterlogged Japanese boys fought on in horrible conditions, knowing they were trapped and would die. Hopelessness filled the air as buddies died from Allied artillery barrages. They could not bury their own dead in the swamps. Soon there were piles of swollen corpses. The searing equatorial sun roasted the corpses until they rotted and burst. Billions of maggots oozed out of dead mouths and nostrils. The stench was overpowering. "We wondered," said an Allied combat reporter, "how the live Japs had borne it until we discovered they were wearing gas masks as protection against their own dead."

Soon the Spirit Warriors were racking up a number of *gyokusai* "victories," which the Americans considered Japanese defeats. On Attu, 2,350 Japanese soldiers fought to the end and just 29 became prisoners of war, a fatality rate of 98.8 percent. In November of 1943 at Tarawa, 99.7 percent of the imperial navy's force of 2,571 men stood in front of the Marines' bullets rather than surrender; only eight Japanese were captured alive. On Makin, the next island over from Tarawa, one out of more than three hundred survived the battle. "At the Marshalls in February 1944, on Roi-Namur the Japanese lost 3,472 and only 51 were captured, a fatality rate of 98.5 percent. At Kwajalein, the Japanese garrison lost 4,938, with only 79 taken prisoner, a fatality rate of 98.4 percent."

The debacles at Makin and Tarawa opened the central Pacific up to American advances. Rational military minds might have advised broaching peace talks. Yet chief Spirit Warrior Tojo told the Diet on December 27, 1943, "The real war is starting now."

But even Tojo didn't know how bad the situation really was. Communication within the euphemism-ridden, spiritually motivated military establishment was — predictably — poor. The navy "conducted no post-mortem analysis on the influence its Midway losses might have on future operations" and never bothered to tell the army about the debacle. Only Hirohito was informed, and he kept the truth to himself. Thus, even the prime minister of Japan was unaware of his country's disaster at Midway. And when General Sugiyama informed Hirohito that everything in the South Pacific was in peril, the Boy Sailor petulantly cried, "Isn't there someplace where we can strike the United States? When and where on earth are you [people] ever going to put up a good fight? And when are you ever going to fight a decisive battle?" Of course, the public was not told of the useless waste of Japanese boys.

Saipan, an island fifteen hundred miles from Tokyo, was the "crown jewel" among the islands Germany had ceded to Japan as a result of WWI. The Japanese government had steadily developed Saipan until its civilian population reached a prewar peak of 29,000. Tojo declared it to be a "bastion of the Pacific." For the Americans, Saipan and the other Mariana Islands were needed as bases for the B-29s to bomb Japan.

The Spirit Warriors never imagined the war would come so close to home and, until it was reinforced in February of 1944, only a light garrison guarded Saipan. After the reinforcement, approximately forty thousand naval and army forces defended the island. There were also approximately twenty thousand Japanese civilians. But the defenders of Saipan never had a chance against the overwhelming power America threw at them, and the Spirit Warriors in Tokyo knew it. Realizing its soldiers and civilians were hopelessly trapped, military leaders decided that everyone — soldiers and civilians alike — should die. The "Imperial General Headquarters Army Section Confidential War Diary" for June 24, 1944, contains the following entry: "The Saipan defense force should carry out *gyokusai*. It is not possible to conduct the hoped-for direction of the battle. The only thing left is to wait for the enemy to abandon their will to fight because of the '*Gyokusai* of the One Hundred Million.'"

"*Gyokusai* of the One Hundred Million" referred to the shattered-jewel death of the entire population of Japan. So now the Spirit boys were signaling that more than just combatants should offer their lives in Spirit War. They were ready to shatter every Japanese man-, woman-, and child-jewel on earth as part of their impossible dream.

Back on Saipan, the Japanese commanders — Vice Admiral Chuichi Nagumo (who led the attack against Pearl Harbor) and Generals Yoshitsugu Saito and Keiji Igeta — met on July 5, 1944, to consider the *gyokusai* order from Tokyo. They ordered a final assault by all the troops, then the three commanders killed themselves. How the suicides of leaders would help the war effort was left unexplained — real samurai didn't kill themselves *before* battle. Perhaps they believed that their departed spirits would protect the Japanese soldiers, sailors, and civilians they abandoned to their fate. General Igeta's final radio message demonstrated more practical logic: "There can be no victory without control of the air. I strongly hope [you] will increase aircraft production." Over the next few weeks, American Marines crushed Japanese resistance on Saipan.

The final "banzai charge" of the three thousand Japanese survivors came three weeks after the Americans first waded ashore. Reporters from the *New York Times* described the onrushing, suicidal Japanese soldiers "like crowds swarming onto a field after a football game. Some were armed only with bayonets lashed to bamboo sticks, some were unarmed, but all were screaming '*Banzai!*' and '*Shichisei Hokoku!*' ["Seven Lives for the Fatherland!"]." One Marine exclaimed, "These Japs just kept coming and coming and didn't stop. It didn't make any difference if you shot one, five more would take his place."

Americans had grown accustomed to suicidal banzai charges on the part of the Japanese military, but what they witnessed on the northern part of the island shocked even battle-hardened Marines. The civilians on Saipan had been told the Marines were *kichiku* who would torture, rape, and kill them in monstrous ways (flattening their bodies under the tracks of tanks, for example). The alternative to ignominious death was glorious *gyokusai*. At Marpi Point, a beautiful cliff jutting out into the Pacific with a two-hundred-foot drop to jagged coral and surf below, Japanese civilians jumped into the sea rather than surrender. Marines watched dumbfounded as mothers tossed babies off the cliff and then jumped to their own deaths.

Some civilians had surrendered, so the Marines brought in loudspeaker equipment and had the Japanese prisoners broadcast appeals to those on the cliff: "Surrender! Don't jump. We were given food, water and safety. You won't be harmed. Surrender!"

Still they jumped.

Weeks later, reporter Robert Sherrod described what his *Time* editors termed "the gruesome deeds, incomprehensible to the occidental mind, which followed the U.S. victory." The article, which became one of the most read of the war, was entitled "The Nature of the Enemy." "During mopping-up operations a detachment of Marines on amphibious tractors saw seven Japanese offshore on a coral reef and drove out to get them. As the amphtracks approached, six of the Japs knelt down on the reef. Then the seventh, apparently an officer, drew a sword and began methodically to hack at the necks of his men. Four heads had rolled into the sea before the Marines closed in. Then the officer, sword in had, charged the amphtracks. He and the remaining two Japs were mowed down."

Suicidal behavior by the Japanese military was by now an old story. But it was the tales of civilian deaths that galvanized American readers. Sherrod recalled encountering a Marine near Marpi Point who had an incredible story to tell:

"You wouldn't believe it unless you saw it," he said. "Yesterday and the day before there were hundreds of Jap civilians — men, women, and children — up here on this cliff. In the most routine way they would jump off the cliff, or climb down and wade into the sea. I saw a father throw his three children off, and then jump down himself. Those coral pockets down there under the cliff are full of Jap suicides.

He paused and pointed. "Look," he said, "there's one getting ready to drown himself now." Down below, a young Japanese, no more than 15, paced back and forth across the rocks. He swung his arms, as if getting ready to dive; then he sat down at the edge and let the water play over his feet. Finally he eased himself slowly into the water.

"There he goes," the Marine shouted.

A strong wave had washed up to the shore, and the boy floated out with it. At first, he lay on the water, face down, without moving. Then, apparently, a last, desperate instinct to live gripped him and he flailed his arms, thrashing the foam. It was too late. Just as suddenly, it was all over: the air-filled seat of his knee-length black trousers bobbed on the water for ten minutes. Then he disappeared.

Sherrod walked to the edge of the cliff and saw seven bodies bobbing in the surf. "This is nothing," the Marine said. "Half a mile down, on the west side, you can see hundreds of them." Later Sherrod checked with the officer of a minesweeper who reported, "Down there, the sea is so congested with floating bodies we can't avoid running them down." He described men, women, and children — entire families who had jumped into the crashing surf. Fathers had slit their children's throats and tossed their bodies over the cliff. Three women had meticulously brushed their hair and adjusted their clothes before they jumped. One family had bathed, donned fresh clothes, and then held grenades to their stomachs to blow their insides out. One woman had drowned herself as she was giving birth; the fetus stuck halfway out of her lifeless, floating corpse. One Japanese family — father, mother, and three children — walked to the edge of the cliff and hesitated. Sherrod observed a Japanese sniper who "drilled the man from behind, dropping him into the sea. The second bullet hit the woman. The sniper would have shot the children, but a Japanese woman ran across and carried them out of range." And the Japanese gunman had been more than willing to die under the rules he was playing by. "The sniper walked defiantly out of his cave, and crumpled under a hundred Marine bullets."

"What did all this self-destruction mean?" Sherrod asked. His speculative answer must have sent shivers down the spines of all Americans with boys in the Pacific war: "Saipan is the first invaded Jap territory populated with more than a handful of civilians. Do the suicides of Saipan mean that the whole Japanese race will choose death before surrender?"

The fall of Saipan was not just another island defeat in the continuing series of Japanese defeats. The Japanese people had been told that Saipan was in the "inner ring" of Japan's defenses, an "invincible" outpost that assured the safety of the Land of the Rising Sun. Now this shield for Japan had been conquered in just three weeks. American B-29s would soon be in easy striking distance of the Japanese mainland. Tojo's government fell on the news.

On July 18, Imperial General Headquarters issued an "acknowledgment" that Japanese forces on Saipan had made a "last attack" on July 7, and added that some troops had fought on until as late as July 16 before they finally "attained heroic death." A second paragraph described the fate of the civilians: "It appears that the remaining civilian Japanese on Saipan island always cooperated with the military, and those who were able to fight participated bravely in combat and shared the fate of officers and soldiers."

The next day, newspaper headlines told the tale:

ALL MEMBERS OF OUR FORCES ON SAIPAN MEET HEROIC
DEATH
REMAINING JAPANESE CIVILIANS APPEAR TO SHARE FATE

Similar stories of desperate German, English, Soviet, or American civilian women leaping off cliffs with babes in arms would have given pause to citizens of those countries. Hitler was a target of an assassination attempt by his inner circle for much less. But incredibly, the Spirit boys translated and proudly reprinted Sherrod's *Time* article, changing its title to the more glorious "Prefer Death to Surrender." The *Asahi Shimbun* newspaper ran a large block-character headline proclaiming:

THE HEROIC LAST MOMENTS OF OUR FELLOW
COUNTRYMEN ON SAIPAN

Members of the 1853 Perry Expedition on Chichi Jima.
(From Matthew C. Perry, *Narrative of the Expedition of an American Squadron to the China Seas and Japan Performed in the Years 1852, 1853, and 1854, Under the Command of Commodore M. C. Perry, United States Navy, by Order of the Government of the United States.* Compiled by Francis L. Hawks. New York: D. Appleton and Company, 1857.)

Commodore Matthew Perry meeting Japanese officials at Yokohama.
(From Perry, *Narrative of the Expedition of an American Squadron to the China Seas and Japan Performed in the Years 1852, 1853, and 1854.*)

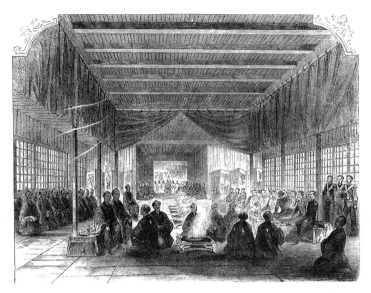

Commodore Perry meeting officials at Uraga.
(From Perry, *Narrative of the Expedition of an American Squadron to the China Seas and Japan Performed in the Years 1852, 1853, and 1854.*)

"Kill Every One Over Ten"—New York *Evening Journal,* May 5, 1902.
American policy in the Philippines was to "Kill everyone over ten years of age."
(© New York Public Library, Art Resource, NY)

Billy Mitchell (standing) at his 1925 court-martial.
(National Archives)

Emperor Hirohito
(National Archives)

A Spirit Warrior chopping off Chinese heads. "I was taught that Chinese are beasts," said one Japanese soldier.

The Japanese army bayoneted live Chinese prisoners in "tests of courage."

Airplanes were the most expensive weapons of World War II. The sale of war bonds raised money for the war. (National Archives)

Jimmy Doolittle lifts off from the *Hornet*, Tokyo bound, on April 18, 1942. "The entire convoy shouted in a surge of relief" as Jimmy demonstrated that a heavy army bomber could take off from an aircraft carrier. (National Archives)

General Henry "Hap" Arnold and Brigadier General James H. "Jimmy"
Doolittle
(National Archives)

TBF Avengers in clouds
(National Archives)

Carrier planes of
the Pacific war
(Courtesy of Torpedo
Squadron 82)

A carrier landing. One Flyboy
said, "You crash-land on the
deck and hope you catch a
wire."
(National Archives)

Australian sergeant Leonard Siffleet being beheaded by Yasuno Chikao in New Guinea on October 24, 1943, in a photo found on the body of a dead Japanese soldier. This photo was widely circulated during the war. (Australian War Memorial Negative Number 101099)

Entitled "Louseous Japanicas," this drawing appeared in the Marine Corps magazine *Leatherneck* just before General Curtis LeMay's devastating fire war on the Japanese mainland. The caption noted, "The breeding grounds around the Tokyo area must be completely annihilated." (Sgt. Fred Lasswell, *Leatherneck* magazine, March 1945)

The Yellow Peril with a white woman. Submitted to a "This Is the Enemy" contest in 1942, this was exhibited at New York's Museum of Modern Art and reprinted in *Life*.

The militarist FDR in Japanese eyes, published in Japan in January 1943.
(Yoshizo Wada, courtesy of Kazuo Wada)

Jimmy Dye, 1944
(Courtesy of J. Ronald Dye)

Jimmy Dye holding A. J. Rykwicz. Leonard Manchuck on left; Pat
Gallagher on right. Virginia Beach, Virginia, June 1944.
(Courtesy of Torpedo Squadron 82)

COURIER-POST, CAMDEN. SAT., NOV. 3, 1945

JAMES W. DYE

PARENTS STILL HOPE SAILOR DYE IS ALIVE

Missing 8 Months in Pacific, Was Seen to Parachute on Island

With little information to go on, the families could only hope. (Courtesy of J. Ronald Dye)

Glenn Frazier on a date, November 1944. (Courtesy of Lyle Leo Comstock)

Floyd Hall as a soda jerk at the Tullis-Hall Dairy, Sedalia, Missouri, in the 1930s.
(Courtesy of James E. Hall)

The "Palace of the Pacific" in Astoria, Oregon, where Floyd Hall spent many nights.
(Courtesy of Bill Hazlehurst)

Floyd Hall with a date, 1944. A friend recalled, "He would only go out with blondes. And for Floyd, there were plenty of blondes." (Courtesy of James E. Hall)

Floyd Hall with a cake commemorating him as the pilot who made the 3,000th landing aboard the USS *Randolph* on February 13, 1945. (Courtesy of James E. Hall)

Marve Mershon, 1944
(Courtesy of Susan
Mershon Brockert)

Marve Mershon (left) and his older
brother, Hoyt Mershon, at the Pike
Bar, Long Beach, California, 1944.
(Courtesy of Susan Mershon Brockert)

Dick Woellhof, 1930s
(Courtesy of Lawrence
Woellhof)

"You've made this the happiest day of my life!" seventeen-year-old Dick Woellhof exclaimed to his mother when she signed his enlistment papers on July 4, 1942.
(Courtesy of Lawrence Woellhof)

Grady York, 1944. "We were just kids in those days," said a fellow Flyboy.
(Courtesy of Pearl J. "York" Diffenderfer)

Grady York in 1944. He signed his letters to his mama, "Pray for me."
(Courtesy of Pearl J. "York" Diffenderfer)

WESTERN UNION

CLASS OF SERVICE
This is a full-rate Telegram or Cablegram unless its deferred character is indicated by a suitable symbol above or preceding the address.

A. N. WILLIAMS
PRESIDENT

SYMBOLS
DL=Day Letter
NL=Night Letter
LC=Deferred Cable
NLT=Cable Night Letter
Ship Radiogram

The filing time shown in the date line on telegrams and day letters is STANDARD TIME at point of origin. Time of receipt is STANDARD TIME at point of destination.

JNU 541 69 GOVT=NR WASHINGTON DC 7 458P

MR AND MRS GRADY ALVAH YORK SR=

=1058 DYAL ST

=THE NAVY DEPARTMENT DEEPLY REGRETS TO INFORM YOU THAT
YOUR SON GRADY ALVAH YORK JR AVIUTION ORDNANCEMAN THIRD CLASS
USN IS MISSING FOLLOWING ACTION WHILE IN THE SERVICE OF HIS
COUNTRY. THE DEPARTMENT APPRECIATES YOUR GREAT ANXIETY BUT
DETAILS NOT NOW AVAILABLE AND DELAY INRECEIPT THEREOF MUST
NECESSARILY BE EXPECTED. TO PREVENT POSSIBLE AID TO OUR ENEMIES
PLEASE DO NOT DIVULGE THE NAME OF HIS SHIP OR STATION=

VICE ADMIRAL RANDALL JACOBS CHIEF OF NAVAL PERSONNEL

The Grady York M.I.A. telegram
(Courtesy of Pearl J. "York" Diffenderfer)

Warren Earl Vaughn and his mother,
Evi. A relative said, "Evi worshiped
him. And Warren Earl worshiped
his mother."
(Courtesy of Billye Winder
and Ann Crockett)

Warren Earl Vaughn at
the controls, 1944
(Courtesy of Billye Winder
and Ann Crockett)

SUBLIMELY WOMEN TOO COMMIT SUICIDE ON ROCKS IN FRONT OF THE GREAT SUN FLAG
PATRIOTIC ESSENCE ASTOUNDS THE WORLD

Sherrod's article followed, and the accompanying commentary read, "It has been reported that noncombatants, women, and children have chosen death rather than to be captured alive and shamed by the devil-like American forces. The world has been astounded by the strength of the fighting spirit and patriotism of the entire people of Japan." The next day, August 20, the *Mainichi Shimbun* proclaimed that Japanese women

CHANGED INTO THEIR BEST APPAREL, PRAYED TO THE IMPERIAL PALACE, SUBLIMELY COMMIT SUICIDE IN FRONT OF THE AMERICAN DEVILS
SACRIFICE THEMSELVES FOR THE NATIONAL EXIGENCY TOGETHER WITH THE BRAVE MEN

The Japanese "translation" of Sherrod's article omitted references to Japanese soldiers "drilling" civilians and any mention of the fact that many civilians on Saipan had surrendered.

Not all Japanese believed the propaganda of the Spirit Warriors. Kiyoshi Kiyosawa, a foreign policy expert and critic of the war, noted in his secret diary that the civilian deaths at Marpi Point represented "feudalism — the influence of ancient warriors — in the time of the airplane, a great admiration for hara-kiri!" Yet neither Kiyosawa nor any other leading figures publicly criticized the government. If they had done so, torture and death would have been their fate.

For the Americans, Marpi Point meant there was no difference between a Japanese civilian and a Japanese military combatant. Both were prepared to continue to the end. And it was clear that even though Japan was beaten — Midway had demolished most of Japan's sea and airpower two years before — it was necessary to bring the fight to the Japanese people in their own homes. At a meeting on July 14, General Marshall explained, "As a result of recent operations in the Pacific it was now clear to the United States Chiefs of Staff that, in order to finish the war with the Japanese quickly, it will be necessary to invade the industrial heart of Japan."

*   *   *

Their war was lost after the fall of Saipan, and if Japan's leaders had heeded the writing on the wall, the majority of its eventual war dead would have been saved. Instead, the Spirit Warriors had set their country up for disaster. Now Americans would tread on their soil, the U.S. Navy would choke their nation with a blockade, and B-29s would burn their cities down. Almost all the half million Japanese civilian casualties of the war and perhaps over half of the more than two million military deaths occurred in the last year of the war. Hirohito and his advisers knew that Hitler's Germany was in its final death throes and that America would soon swing more resources from Europe to the Pacific. But confronted with the certain knowledge that the "American devils" were closing in on Japan, the Boy Soldier still dreamed of Grandpa's glory. On June 17, he admonished Vice Chief of Staff Admiral Shimada, "Rise to the challenge; make a tremendous effort; achieve a splendid victory like at the time of the Japan Sea Naval battle [in the Russo-Japanese War]."

The sole power to stop the war was now in Japan's hands. America had to fight as long as its enemy did. Indeed, U.S. troops in the Pacific theater adopted the adage "Golden Gate in '48," expecting the war to continue another horrible four years. How to defeat an enemy that could not, would not admit defeat?

Marine captain Justice Chambers witnessed the suicides at Marpi Point. He suggested a solution: "To win the war and get it over with, just kill off many of the other side, make it terrible, and the war will stop."

And that is how America beat Japan. The war eventually did stop. But first it got terrible.

CHAPTER ELEVEN

To the Pacific

Never in the field of human conflict was so much owed by so many to so few.

— *Winston Churchill, August 20, 1940, referring to airmen fighting the Battle of Britain*

Aмerican troops did not invade Europe in vast numbers until D-Day at Normandy on June 6, 1944, two and a half years after Pearl Harbor. American Marines did not step on Japanese home soil until three years after Pearl Harbor, on February 19, 1945 — D-Day at Iwo Jima. But just months after Pearl Harbor, the Doolittle Raid shocked Japan, and on August 17, 1942, Flyboy Paul Tibbets, who would later drop the atom bomb on Hiroshima, had led a squadron of exactly one dozen bombers from their base in southern England across the English Channel to bomb a railroad switching yard in Rouen, France. Jimmy Doolittle and Paul Tibbets had initiated the type of war America would fight from 1942 into the next century. For two years, the United States and England sent their Flyboys to bomb and burn out Hitler's ability to wage war. Only after the Flyboys had gained almost complete control of the Third Dimension were American ground troops inserted into the conflict on the European mainland. And for those two years, Adolf Hitler, a man enamored with two-dimensional WWI ideas, had found his vast army useless against U.S. and U.K. forces that refused to engage him in the main ring. Instead, like a swarm of bees disrupting a picnic the führer had to deal with pesky Flyboys who chipped away at his ability to wage war.

In the Pacific, FDR employed Billy Mitchell's ideas to devastating effect. Because of superior intelligence and by seizing airfields, the U.S. sank massive Japanese ships — battleships, carriers, transports packed with troops, and supply ships stuffed with rice. Flyboys at the battles of the Coral Sea, Midway, and Guadalcanal had stymied Japan's advance, seized the strategic offensive for the United States, and placed Japan on the defensive. Gaining control of the Third Dimension, U.S. carrier planes continually tore at Japan's protective shroud.

Hundreds of thousands of Japanese ground troops were now stranded on remote Pacific islands. With no control of the air, Japan was unable to supply these troops or evacuate them. Many starved, others lived on boiled grass and leaves, and some ate one another to survive.

There grew a special hatred for Flyboys in the hearts of these Japanese ground troops. Their rifles might be clean and loaded, their boots and buttons shiny, but they could only shake their fists in anger at the Americans who bombed and strafed them from the air.

"We'll get them! They'll pay for this!" former Japanese soldier Harumichi Nogi remembered thinking. Nogi had been trapped on an island in the Philippines. "Every day those [American planes] would come and run wild, doing what they wanted. All our plans had been destroyed. We could offer no resistance. We were enraged and frustrated. When you lose your own fighting capability and can only suffer under their attacks, you become vengeful yourself."

And when Nogi finally came face-to-face with a trio of captured American pilots, he knew what to do.

"They were very pale," Nogi remembered of the three Flyboys before him in 1944. "You have been sentenced to death," Nogi told them. The Flyboys epitomized America's rational and technological approach to war and highlighted the futility of Spirit War. "Their presence," Nogi said, "was undeniable evidence that Japanese forces were collapsing.

"The only choice for Japan," Nogi thought at the time, was "total annihilation or victory. If we go on losing like this, we'll never return home alive. Will I be questioned on my responsibility? Not likely. We'll all be dead. If we win, there's nothing to worry about because it was ordered from above.

"Holding my sword, I made them kneel down," Nogi remembered.

One, two, then three Flyboys' heads rolled onto the blood-slicked grass.

Japanese hatred of the Flyboys intensified as the American military juggernaut drew closer to the empire. With the fall of Saipan, the next step for the American military boot was Iwo Jima, next to No Mans Land. These islands were Japanese home soil — part of the sacred realm. In 1944, Japan evacuated about seven thousand civilians from No Mans Land to Japan as crack Japanese troops from China took up positions on Iwo Jima and Chichi Jima. The emperor himself chose General Tadamichi Kuribiyashi, a member of a distinguished samurai family that had served the royal house for generations, to command Iwo Jima and protect its vital airfields.

Chichi Jima's value was as a communications relay station for messages to and from Tokyo's Pacific theater. The U.S. Navy wanted to disable the radio stations atop Mounts Yoake and Asahi before the planned invasion of Peleliu. Those stations had been intercepting U.S. military radio transmissions and warning Tokyo and Japanese-held Pacific islands of American plans. Chichi Jima was seen as so crucial that as Yoshi Urazaki of the Tokyo Air Defense remembered, "Japanese anti-aircraft gunners were transferred from the Akasaka Palace of Emperor Hirohito" to defend the radio stations. The hilly island was just five miles by three, about double the size of New York's Central Park. Those hills held concealed defensive cannon and antiaircraft guns shielded by thick concrete. It was the job of these expert antiaircraft gunners to shoot down any Flyboy who invaded Chichi Jima's airspace.

General Yoshio Tachibana, a grizzled veteran of the vicious fighting in China, was chosen to command the defense of Chichi Jima. Tachibana was a big brutal army man who beat his troops into submission by day and drank himself into a stupor at night. He relished the scorched-earth policies he had witnessed in China; he was one who loved to "Kill All, Loot All, Burn All." To him, the Chinese and Americans were both *kichiku*, and if he got his hands on any Flyboys, he would treat them as he had his prisoners in China.

* * *

Floyd Hall had enlisted in the regular navy and after boot camp had found himself aboard ship as a mess cook. But Floyd was ambitious. "Somewhere along the line," fellow pilot Bill Hazlehurst remembered, "Floyd got it into his head that he wanted to be a navy pilot. He studied, took a test, and was accepted into the program. Floyd was above and beyond; he was smart. He wasn't a typical grunt; he had aspirations to be something better. I know he felt he achieved a great deal by being accepted as an aviator. He was proud."

Floyd made the usual Flyboy training pit stops — Corpus Christi, Texas; Fort Lauderdale, Florida; Pensacola, Florida; Glenview, Illinois; and San Diego, California, among them. In the spring of 1944, Floyd was practicing bombing runs with gunner Glenn Frazier and radioman Marve Mershon. Their squadron was stationed in Astoria, Oregon. Astoria was not chosen for its good weather. One pilot remembered, "During the time we were there the coast was almost always blanketed by a shroud of wet, gray, low-hanging clouds. Typically we would immediately become enveloped in the thick, wet gloom. It wasn't long before we became very good instrument flyers."

Floyd was flying a TBM Avenger, a "torpedo plane." But he would launch no torpedoes in later combat out in the Pacific. With the decimation of Japanese shipping, planes originally designed to go in low and launch torpedoes were now being used mostly as glide-bombers.

The Avengers, 40 feet long and 54 feet wide, were big and heavy (the heaviest plane flown from an aircraft carrier), which meant they were stable in the air — more stable than Dick Woellhof's Helldiver, for example. They had a range of over 1,000 miles and could climb to 30,000 feet if need be. They were relatively comfortable too. "The TBM had a spacious cockpit," Jesse Naul recalled. "We had armrests; you could sit comfortably for hours strapped in." Noise was a problem, and the Flyboys dealt with it by wearing foam ear cups under their helmets.

Glide-bombers would fly in formations of four planes known as "divisions"; groups of two planes were called "sections." When it was time to engage the enemy or commence a bombing run, formations could and often would break into smaller units, but usually Flyboys continued to work as teams even when separated. This was in stark contrast to the Japanese pilots, who split apart from one another in battle without any attempt at coordination or team strategy. The results for the Japanese, not surprisingly, were poor and only got worse as the war went on.

Glide-bombing — like dive-bombing — was an art, requiring a pilot to dive at a near perfect angle. Too steep a dive and a plane could become inverted. A glide at the wrong angle could result in missing the target. And when pulling up, pilots had to be careful not to panic and pull back too hard on their sticks or their planes might stall.

The Avenger was a devastating weapon when used correctly. Training was crucial.

"A torpedo plane can't go into a steep dive like a dive-bomber," Bill Hazlehurst explained. "This was glide-bombing. We'd circle the target at one thousand feet, lose enough power to go down, glide in to two hundred feet, sight the target, release the bomb, and get out of there." George Bush, Floyd Hall, and all the other torpedo pilots spent much of their time practicing glide-bombing runs. "We would bomb uninhabited spits of sand off the coast of Oregon," Hazlehurst told me. "The skipper would be circling up above, observing our runs and scoring our hits."

The intensive training caused intense friendships to be formed.

"Floyd was a great person to know," Bill Hazlehurst said. "He had a great sense of humor and a big smile. In any squadron there are certain members who pal together. Joe White, Floyd Hall, and I were close friends. We became inseparable."

Astoria had been a little fishing village until the navy moved in. "On weeknights, Floyd, Joe, and I would go to a nightclub in Astoria called Amato's Palace of the Pacific," Bill recalled. "It wasn't much of a palace, but it was where we'd play poker, drink beer, and chase women."

Snapshots of Floyd Hall confirm Bill's memory that "he was a good-looking man with light brown hair and a fair complexion. . . . Floyd was a ladies' man," he said. Fellow pilot Leland Holdren agreed: "The girls liked Floyd. He was the one who got the date." But Floyd yearned for more female action than backwater Astoria could offer. On their weekends off, Floyd, Joe, and Bill would grab some condoms and thumb a ride to Portland, about a two-hour drive away. In Portland, they would rent three hotel rooms and then head off for the chase. In their officer's uniforms, the three cut attractive figures.

"We were a rarity in Portland," Bill said. "Not many navy personnel came through there. The gals would come running to us."

For more than six months, Floyd Hall, the small-town-Missouri boy, partied in Oregon. "I remember Floyd was involved with many different girls," Bill said. "It was a fun life. We had many hellacious weekends in Portland." Handsome Floyd caught the eye of so many young women that soon he got picky. "He would only go out with blondes," Bill remembered. "And for Floyd, there were plenty of those."

Although he took full advantage of his time off, Floyd was always there on the flight line in the morning. Greeting him, ready to fly, were Glenn Frazier and Marve Mershon. Glenn and Marve were opposites in personality who worked seamlessly together.

Glenn was the machine-gunner who rode in the Avenger's top turret. Once and always a Kansas farm boy, he was sturdy and quiet. "Glenn was a gentle person," fellow crewman Charles Chadwell said. "A quiet red-haired guy doing his duty" is how parachute-rigger Mike Dake described Glenn six decades later.

Gunner Glenn was teamed with radioman Marve, who rode below him. Marve, the outgoing dark-haired city slicker from Los Angeles, enjoyed the spotlight. "Let me do the talking," his buddy Robert Martin remembered Marve saying when they'd enter a store to cut a deal. "Marve was ahead of his time," Mike Dake remembered. "He would streak his hair with different colors. We called him 'Hollywood' because he seemed to want attention."

"Those two were as different as can be," Dake continued. "Glenn Frazier was very conservative and Marve Mershon very liberal. But they got along and did their jobs."

Radioman Jimmy Dye and gunner Grady York were also paired and flew in Ensign Bob King's Avenger. Ralph Sengewalt trained with them. "Jimmy and Grady were extreme opposites," Ralph remembered. "Grady was very quiet; he kept to himself. He would never, ever say a cuss word." Fast-talking East Coaster Jimmy Dye was a different story. "Jimmy was an outgoing people person," Ralph said. "He would start talking and never stop."

Glenn, Grady, Marve, and Jimmy had all enlisted in the navy and gone through regular navy boot camps in Maryland, Florida, Idaho, and California. Their initial training was the same as that of sailors.

"Navy boot camp was rough," gunner Lyle Comstock recalled. "For twelve weeks I never left the base; I didn't even have an ID card for ten weeks. We just drilled and trained. We tied knots, learned about ships and discipline and how to do things the navy way, with towels folded seams in."

Discipline was tight, but there was none of the internal violence of the Japanese military. "Doing double time for too much noise was as violent as it got," Vince Carnazza recalled.

In boot camp, "we were informed we had responsibilities *and* rights," Vince explained. "We learned what the navy expected of us, what an infringement was, what the punishment could be. But we were also taught that we as individuals had rights and were informed clearly that we had recourse if we felt we weren't treated properly."

Another big difference between the two countries' training systems was the attitude toward leadership. "We'd have a lecture and they'd set up a fictitious situation," Vince said. "We learned how to interact with people who weren't doing what they should be doing and how to efficiently get something done if you had to take over." The Japanese military bred frightened followers with the idea that strength flowed from a terrorized organization ready to respond obediently to edicts from on high. Later, in the Pacific, Japanese troops often found themselves at a loss when their officers were killed, but American boys were able to step up into vacant leadership positions and continue the fight.

The navy administered batteries of tests to its recruits, searching for the best and brightest. "Most of the people who went into aviation were in the top ten percent of the grading system," Vince recalled. Six decades after the war, Rowdy Dow from Massachusetts clearly remembered the difficulty of the test. Rowdy was a regular sailor and wanted to be a gunner. "I used to study the gunner's book all the time," he told me. "I can still feel it in my pocket." Finally, the day for Rowdy's test came. "They held a bolt up in the air and asked, 'What is this?' It was an obscure bolt from the inside of the plane's interrupter, the thing that keeps the bullets from hitting the propeller. Everyone flunked that one and went back to study more."

"I was in the top three percent of those tested," Vince Carnazza told me. "They said I could have whatever I wanted. I was young and I had seen the movies and I wanted to avenge our losses. I volunteered to be an aerial gunner." Vince, Rowdy, and the other gunners were all small enough to fit into the cramped spaces of torpedo bombers. "The turret is about a thirty-inch round ball, like a tennis ball," said Rowdy. "A Plexiglas dome goes around the turret and there is a gun sticking out. The seat is small and your back is crushed against the wall. One hand is on the stick, which rotates the turret to where you want to shoot. Your other hand is on the gun trigger." As gunner Robert Overbaugh explained it, "The whole turret swivels; it rotates on a round track. Your knees are up under your chin, and the turret goes around in a circle."

While the pilot faced forward, the gunner faced backward, becoming the pilot's "rearview" eyes. "Turret gunners," said gunner L. E. Brinson, "are always looking where we've been instead of where we're going."

Gunners Glenn Frazier and Grady York trained for over a year and a half to master their discipline. After boot camp, they were sent to aviation ordnance school, where the learning was fast paced and intense. "We'd have a different subject every week," Lyle Comstock recalled. "The first week was tools, wrenches and screwdrivers. We moved on to small arms, then to machine guns. We had to know the name of every part of that gun and then fieldstrip it. They would blindfold us and we would have to take a machine gun apart and put it back together in a minute."

Rowdy remembered, "We stayed with those guns until we knew them like a toothbrush."

After graduating from ordnance school, Grady and Glenn went on to gunnery school — Grady in Jacksonville, Florida, and Glenn in Purcell, Oklahoma. "There we started shooting skeet," Lyle Comstock said. The turrets were mounted on the ground. "We learned how to shoot a gun, how to sight, how to increase accuracy."

The next stop for Glenn and Grady was Fort Lauderdale, Florida, since "that's where the airplanes were," Comstock said. "One airplane would tow a target, a sleeve," he explained. "Each gunner would dip his ammunition in different color paint. Later we could examine the sleeve and see who got a hit. Out of two hundred rounds of ammo, you'd be extremely lucky to get ten hits. With all the movement and speed, you'd have only three seconds to see the sleeve and shoot."

Flying two hundred miles an hour and trying to hit targets in the Third Dimension took a lot of practice. Rowdy Dow had been an instructor at a ground shooting range when he volunteered to be an aviation gunner. He skipped gunnery school and had never fired from a plane when he reported to his flight squadron. "I told the captain I needed some training, but he just said, 'Go up there, press the trigger, and shoot the target,'" Rowdy said. "So I went up and shot my own plane's tail off. We had to make an emergency landing with ambulances waiting. It was a real calamity.

"The captain walked up to me and with a nice smile said, 'You did right; you warned me. This is my fault.'

"That was beautiful for an officer to stoop down to an enlisted man," Rowdy said.

These gunners who were training to shoot Japanese airplanes out of the sky were boys doing a man's job. Grady York and Glenn Frazier were eighteen years old during much of their training. Fellow gunner Joe Bonn remembered, "Grady looked like he was sixteen years old." Grady and Glenn were not alone. Ken Meredith told me, "We were just kids in those days."

Grady manned a machine gun during the day, but during his time off he kept to himself and preferred to write letters and sketch airplanes. "Grady would very seldom go on liberty with us," Ken Meredith remembered. "He was a self-contained person who was very bright." Vince Carnazza recalled that "Grady was a good Christian boy. He would never, ever swear. 'Skillyboo' was the worst word I ever heard him use." Ralph Sengewalt remembered, "Grady didn't cuss and he didn't want others to cuss. We kidded him about it, but we had a lot of respect for him."

Grady's letters home revealed a sensitive, artistic boy proud to be serving his country but also homesick. From boot camp he wrote a letter to "Dear Mama" and said, "Boy, I sure am lonesome. It's been such a long time since I've been home." Grady had been away from his mama for sixty days.

If Grady was not one to drink with the boys, he still paid a lot of attention to the girls. I found flirty notes from Misses Jean Sharp and Ruth Paterson among his letters. In Grady's little black book, I found the names of only one male, three relatives, and twenty-four girls.

In a letter written on November 25, 1943, Grady admitted to his mother how dangerous it was to fly airplanes in World War II. "There's been lots of excitement around here lately," Grady wrote. "A boy got chopped to death by a propeller one morning and two planes ran together that night and killed two more. The next day a pilot went down in the swamps and killed himself. He was in the flight right next to me. I knew him — I guess it was just their time to go."

But Grady believed his Lord would keep him safe. In a November 29, 1943, letter to his mother, he wrote, "Some boys the other night tried to get me to go into a bar with them. They said your Mother isn't here. And I said to myself if you're a Christian you are one anywhere and anytime. That sounded kinda funny. It seemed like if you didn't see me it would be alright. But I know a lot better than that." On December 28, he wrote, "All the boys or most of them went out Christmas Eve night and got drunk. I guess they think that's the way they should celebrate the Lord's birthday. My radioman stayed out all night in a whiskey joint and came right on and went up with us."

The radioman Grady referred to in his letter was probably someone just like the irrepressible Jimmy Dye or streetwise Marve Mershon, neither of whom thought anything of carousing all night and flying all day. Radiomen in an Avenger operated from a cramped space under the gunner. The space was only slightly larger than the gunner's turret. "The radioman's compartment underneath the turret is compact, but not as cramped as the turret," remembered Ralph Sengewalt. "When the bomb bay doors opened below, you could see the whole world."

Radiomen had a .30-caliber gun they could shoot out the back of the plane, so they also went through gunnery practice. But their main focus was, not surprisingly, on becoming expert on the radios. "First we had to learn all the code," radioman Bill Smith of Atlanta told me. "B is 'da dit dit dit' and C is 'da dit da dit' and so on. I'll bet you didn't know that trains whistle the Morse code at railroad crossings. They whistle the letter Q, for here comes the queen, or train. The queen is coming, da da dit da."

"We studied how to use our receivers, navigational aids, semaphore, our beacon," Bill continued. "We were trained about something new called radar and the Doppler effect, how it operates by sending out a pulse and having it bounce back."

"We spent twenty-two weeks at radio school," radioman Joe Hudson of Shreveport said. "It takes a while to learn that code."

The study was hard and serious, but the students weren't. "Looking back now," said Vince Carnazza, "we were so young, just high school kids. Jimmy was always coming up from behind me, grabbing my arms. We would wrestle like two teddy bears. We were just young guys testing each other in a playful manner."

As their long period of training wound down, the realization that they would soon be off to war set in. Leaving home had been a jolt for these young boys, but now they would be leaving their homeland, and it sobered them. The young Flyboys' thoughts of home intensified in the fall of 1944.

Before he shipped out, Warren Earl Vaughn summoned the love of his life to visit him one last time out at Mojave. "It must have been quite a chore for Warren Earl's mother to make that trip all the way from Texas," Archie Clapp told me. "The trains were full of troops, and that would have been a long, tiring drive over those two-lane highways."

"Evi was so proud that Warren Earl was serving in the war," Warren Earl's cousin Madeline Riley said. "I remember her telling us how excited she was to see him fly. She said, 'And here he handled that big plane all by himself.'"

On his last leave home in Jacksonville, Grady York decided to lavish his time and money on a pretty girl. "Grady insisted on taking me to the beauty shop," his sister Pearl Diffenderfer remembered. This was a surprising and rare treat for his baby sister, something he didn't have to do. "It was the City Beauty Shop," she said. "It was the old-time way of putting perms in hair. They had these long rods on wires that hung down and they'd wrap your hair around them and turn on the electricity and perm it. It took a while, but Grady waited. I just knew he would never leave me."

At about the same time, far up the East Coast, Jimmy Dye and his parents discussed his wish for his last night in Mount Ephraim, New Jersey. On an earlier home leave, Jimmy's friend Les had introduced him to cheerleader Gloria Nields, who was a year younger than Jimmy. There was electricity between the two and they fell into sweet teenage puppy love. Fifty-eight years later, Gloria Nields told me of their youthful affair:

I only knew Jimmy a short time, but I was very infatuated. He was my childhood sweetheart.

The moment we met I was breathless. It was like I was coming up for air. There was chemistry. I was naive and he was too. I was seventeen. Jimmy was in a uniform, ready to defend his country. There was something about him. His personality and his beautiful blue eyes. They just held you. It was extremely romantic for me.

We both fell like a ton of bricks. I thought he was the one for me and he felt the same. Our relationship was short but intense. We were in love.

I can remember a girlfriend of mine who saw us together said, "I've never seen you like this!" I was so taken with him.

Before his last night home, Jimmy's mother phoned to ask if I could come over because Jimmy was leaving soon. We didn't have a telephone, so she called the neighbors. I was never allowed to date anyone more than three times in a row, so I was surprised when my parents said yes.

Jimmy's father picked me up in his car and took me to their house. Jimmy took my coat as I entered. He put it on a bed and then he kissed me. I will never forget. He was my first love.

We sat in the living room with his parents. They sat in chairs; we sat on the couch. At one point he lay down and put his head in my lap. I was timid, but I allowed it. He closed his eyes; I could feel that he felt good I was there. He was so affectionate. I touched his wavy hair.

All along, Jimmy's parents kept watch. Fast-talking Jimmy was now old enough to fight and die for his country. But on the last date of his life, he was too young to be alone with a girl.

Across the country, Floyd Hall and his squadron buddies were finishing up their training in Los Alamitos, California, where they had been transferred from Astoria. After so many "hellacious weekends" in Portland, the three musketeers — Floyd, Joe White, and Bill Hazlehurst — had become inseparable. Then, about six weeks before they were about to ship out, Joe and Bill realized that Floyd wasn't around in the evenings anymore. Where was Floyd? Joe and Bill wondered.

"One afternoon we were talking on the flight line," Bill recalled. "'Where you keeping yourself?' we asked Floyd.

"He told us he was living with a girl," Bill continued. "I remember him telling us about the groceries he was going to buy for her and how she'd cook for him. Floyd was a true hell-raiser, and it struck Joe and me as very weird. He was domesticated! He was a different person. This was a complete turnabout that we didn't understand."

"Hell, Floyd, why stick with one when you can have ten girls a week?" Joe asked.

"We kept kidding him about it, and he got exasperated," Bill said. "Finally, Floyd turned to Joe and me and said, 'I don't think I'm going to come out of this alive and I want to enjoy some things and I'm going to do them now.'

"It never occurred to Joe and me that we weren't coming back, so we scoffed at this. He said it with a smile, but he was very serious. 'What are you saying?' we asked him. He elaborated that he had this gal and he was going to enjoy the relationship because it was his last chance."

Years later, I asked Hazlehurst if he had any idea what brought on Floyd's sudden change of heart. "I have no idea," he answered. "About that time Bill Colbert, a senior pilot, flew right into the Salton Sea on a night practice and was lost. But we lost pilots all the time, and I can't say that was it. All I remember is Floyd repeating, 'I'm going to take every opportunity to enjoy myself because I don't think I'm coming back.'"

By the fall of 1944, George Bush was out in the Pacific flying Avengers off the USS *San Jacinto,* and Dick Woellhof was flying the gunner's position in dive-bombers off the USS *Yorktown.* In September of 1944, Warren Earl Vaughn sailed on the USS *Ticonderoga* for further training flying Corsairs over Hawaii. Aboard the USS *Bennington,* Jimmy Dye and Grady York sailed from the East Coast through the Panama Canal to Pearl Harbor. Floyd Hall, Glenn Frazier, and Marve Mershon sailed out under San Francisco's Golden Gate Bridge aboard the USS *Randolph.*

Now in control of the Third Dimension, the United States was able to sail these behemoths out to the Pacific killing fields with relative impunity. The Flyboys played poker, ate steaks, and watched movies on ships that symbolized America's awesome power in the Pacific. With the Japanese fleet severely diminished and Japanese air strength shredded, sailors and Flyboys on American ships had little to be concerned about.

In contrast, without control of the air, the Spirit Warriors were not even safe in their home waters. With the fall of Saipan, there was no hope of regaining the offensive. By the summer of 1944, the Japanese high command had concluded that even if they could not win the war outright, they might force America to negotiate a peace. They reasoned that the American public would not tolerate a long war with growing casualties, so they ordered attrition warfare: fighting that would slow the Americans down and inflict maximum losses. This tactic would capitalize on two great strengths of the Japanese troops — their ability to dig in and their ability to endure the most god-awful shelling from the sea and bombing from the air.

Imperial General Headquarters issued orders calling for "endurance engagement" through the use of "*fukkaku* positions," honeycombed subterranean defensive positions. No longer would Japanese soldiers mount banzai charges; now they were ordered to fight from heavily fortified underground tunnels and caves.

In July of 1944, the Japanese army dispatched a convoy of soldiers to No Mans Land. Nobuaki Iwatake was one of those soldiers, a reluctant combatant with an unusual background. Iwatake-san was born an American citizen in Maui, Hawaii, of Japanese immigrant parents. In 1940, his father died in a fishing accident and relatives in Hiroshima sent for him, promising him the education his mother could no longer afford. After graduating from high school in Maui in June of 1941, he sailed to Japan.

"The U.S. Customs officer in Hawaii said, 'Don't go to Japan, there's going to be a war between us,'" Iwatake-san remembered. "I explained that I had to go because of the death of my father. He understood, but he had tears in his eyes."

Iwatake-san was drafted by the army while studying at Meiji University. "Basic training was very harsh," he recalled. "The older soldiers beat you any time they wanted. There was inspection every night. They'd spot a speck of dust on your shoes and you'd get beaten up. They'd whack you across the face so hard you'd fall over. Some would be bleeding through the nose. The officers would say, 'We want to put *Yamato damashii* into you so you'll be good soldiers.'"

Nobuaki Iwatake boarded the *Nissho Maru* for the trip to No Mans Land. The islands of No Mans Land were the equivalent of America's Florida Keys, stepping-stones to the mainland. If Japan could not protect even these islands, it had no hope of projecting power out into the Pacific. Along the way, the convoy zigzagged to avoid submarines. One night, Iwatake-san heard explosions. American submarines roamed at will just off the coast of Japan, and the next morning he could see that the largest ship in the convoy was gone. The next night another was sunk. "Even as subs sunk our ships near the mainland," Iwatake-san said, "the high command was lying to the people about great victories."

Then it was Iwatake's turn. "A torpedo hit our ship," he remembered. "There was panic. I jumped and got away so I wouldn't get sucked under. I saw the ship crack in two and pull many soldiers down with it."

The survivors were picked up by a smaller freighter, which was now overloaded with troops. The salt-encrusted, shaken boys couldn't find shade, and the summer sun beat down mercilessly. There was no water. "One guy drank his own urine," Iwatake-san recalled. "Another said he drank seawater, which was much worse."

The next day, someone screamed, "Torpedo!" The troops could see the white wake, but the captain swerved the ship and avoided the missile. "I'll always remember the sound that rose up when we saw that torpedo," Iwatake-san said. "It was a wailing sound of people facing certain death."

A rainstorm brought some relief as the troops lay on the deck with their mouths open. Landing on Chichi Jima, Iwatake was assigned to a work party to dig tunnels and caves. The Americans would eventually come, he was told. Iwatake now had to help save Japan with a hammer and chisel.

As the great U.S. carriers sailed farther from home, the reality of coming battles weighed on the Flyboys' minds. Previously hypothetical, imagined danger now became a real possibility. The Spirit Warriors might not be able to mount an offensive, but their determination to fight to the last man meant they were still a lethal enemy. And the Flyboys knew it. "We were told," Bill Hazlehurst said, "that if we were captured by the Japanese, we could expect to be tortured to give them some intelligence."

As Jimmy Dye sailed to his destiny aboard the USS *Bennington*, his ebullient optimism deserted him. Jimmy had come to the same conclusion as Floyd Hall: that he wasn't coming back. As if to inoculate them from the coming pain, Jimmy wrote his "Dearest Folks" to assure them they had been wonderful parents:

> You and Dad never held me back. You gave me everything I ever wanted. I can think of nothing that I ever wished for and didn't get.
>
> My home wasn't just a home it was a place where I could come and bring my friends knowing it was clean and nice and that my friends would be welcomed and treated the way I wanted them to be. Yet at the same time it was a home were we could have fun and act up without feeling like you were in a china shop like some homes are. I guess I was lucky to have such a family and I really don't know how I rated it.

Jimmy referred to Gloria Nields, who had held his head so tenderly on the couch, as "The Girl" and concluded that "Fate" would "keep us apart." While he never came out and wrote explicitly, "I'm not coming back," it's hard to come to any other conclusion about his meaning. "I know that if you ever receive this it will be the toughest time of your lives," he told his parents. They should know, he said, that it was his decision to enlist. "I went in doing what I wanted to do."

"I'm not afraid to go because I know someday we'll be together again," Jimmy continued, telling his parents to be strong: "God be with you and protect you. Keep your chins up. Remember whenever things went wrong Mom and Dad you always said, 'We'll make it somehow' and we always did, this isn't much different." In his final paragraph he wrote, "Goodbye for now. The Lord bless and keep you. We'll be together again someday."

It is very unusual for young men going into combat to think they will die. There's a famous story of three Marines being briefed before battle. Their captain says, "Two out of every three of you will not make it." Each of the three glances at the others and thinks, "Those poor sons-of-bitches."

I have interviewed hundreds of Pacific veterans in the course of writing two books. I never heard a survivor say, "I thought I wouldn't make it." And I never heard a survivor say about another survivor, "He told me he wouldn't make it." In my research, I found only four who said they weren't coming back. Iwo Jima flagraisers Mike Strank and Harlon Block, and Flyboys Floyd Hall and Jimmy Dye told those close to them, "This is it." Four announced they would die. Four were correct.

Jimmy never told Gloria Nields of his belief, and she continued to pen regular letters to him and sleep with his photograph. It was a formal close-up of him in his navy uniform that highlighted Jimmy's blue-eyed, all-American good looks. Gloria had the eight-by-ten photo framed. For Christmas she mailed Jimmy a white scarf. "It was pretty and I could afford it," she said. "I thought of it as a personal gift; I liked the idea of him wearing my scarf around his neck."

Grady York was on the same ship as Jimmy Dye and he also wrote letters home. Grady knew censors read his mail, so he couldn't say much, but he wrote repeatedly of how much he missed home with heart-tugging lines like, "I don't see how you could be any lonelier than I am." In one letter, festooned with a realistic rendition of three airplanes, he asked his mother, "Do you think I'll ever make a good artist? If I had some paints and brushes I would paint you a good picture."

As the ship took him closer to combat, Grady spent his time quietly drawing pictures of fighters and bombers soaring gracefully through the sky. But his sketches belied the reality that these sleek machines were instruments of death and destruction, instruments of war that to the Japanese symbolized their growing impotence in the face of American airpower.

As Grady drew and thought of his mom, in Japan, newsreels described the islands of No Mans Land as "a suitable place to slaughter the American devils." Another magazine declared that as more of the American devils "are sent to hell, the cleaner the world will be."

Nineteen-year-old Flyboy Grady York never wrote about his fears of confronting an enemy that considered him an inhuman Other. But the last words of the last letter Grady ever wrote were these: "Pray for me."

CHAPTER TWELVE

Carrier War

Your brain tells you not to get into the airplane; you'll die a nasty death. But our brain also told us that we had to do something for our country.

— *Rowdy Dow*

THE aircraft carriers taking the Flyboys to war were the equivalent of floating American towns. Boys on board could visit the doctor or climb into a barber's chair. They could read the ship's daily newspaper over their breakfast coffee, then check out a book at the library or shop at the general store. The sailors had regular work schedules, attended church services, ate hamburgers, played basketball, soaped up in hot showers, watched movies, slept in clean bunks, and wore regularly laundered uniforms.

For much of their time on the carriers, it didn't seem as if they were in a war at all. The Pacific conflict was being waged over the largest battlefield in the history of warfare, and the sprawling carrier fleet was often spread out over such a wide expanse that some of the sister ships were beyond the horizon. Because of the distances involved, many days were spent just sailing. American combatants sailing from West Coast ports traveled the equivalent distance of New York to Los Angeles — and back — just to get to Pacific battlefields. Ernie Pyle was astonished to realize that fighters in the western Pacific islands were brought back to Pearl Harbor rest camps, "the equivalent of sending an Anzio beachhead fighter all the way back to Kansas City for his two weeks."

The vast distances involved were just one of the factors that made the carrier war unusual. The European conflict had its aerial component, but it was a more traditional contest of mud, cold, and close combat. But WWII in the Pacific was a war in which pilots took their meals at linen-covered tables, then flew off to sudden, flaming deaths, a war in which airplanes brought misery to millions behind the lines but in which the airmen rarely saw their enemy.

The airmen were considered the most important passengers on the carriers. They provided the fleet with both its offensive thrust and its defensive protection. The massive battleships hurtling shells against one another as in past wars had been replaced by carriers waging a new kind of long-range warfare by flinging their airplanes out to engage in battle. And the carriers, which were vulnerable to attack from the air, depended upon their planes to protect the vital airspace above them.

"We didn't have duties aboard the ship," said radioman George Flashner. "We didn't have anything to do other than fly. And we would fly only three to four hours any given day; and we didn't fly every day. We didn't really feel a part of the ship's crew. We were attached to the ship rather than being part of crew."

In recognition of their cutting-edge potency, the navy assigned the pilots the largest and most comfortable accommodations on its ships. "I preferred being on a carrier to being land based," said pilot Walter Stonebraker. "Aboard an aircraft carrier you have beautiful air-conditioned quarters. The rooms were small, but they were neat and orderly. You had a desk. The food was excellent. Two-day laundry service. You could get a haircut. Friends of mine on islands lived in a tent, standing in lines in the mud to eat off tin plates. On the ships it was first-class living. Linen on the tables, nice tableware, like a five-star hotel. Another thing about carrier duty: Everything is immaculately clean. The airplanes were so clean; there was no opportunity for them to get dirty."

The gunners and radiomen were enlisted men and slept in quarters separate from those of the pilots. "We called the officers' quarters 'God's Country,'" remembered George Flashner. The navy enforced a strict wall of separation between the enlisted men and the officers.

Fraternization was discouraged, and they led separate lives aboard ship. "Even when we went ashore," Flashner recalled, "there were two gangplanks — one for the enlisted men and one for the officers. But there wasn't any antagonism; that's just the way it was."

The one place on the carrier where the all the airmen — officers and enlisted — came together was the "ready room." "The ready room was the flight crews' home away from home. It served as office, classroom, movie theater, and living room. The walls were covered with bulletin boards, charts, maps, posters, and briefing guides." The ready room was "control central," where airmen gathered to receive assignments, get debriefed after a strike, and just hang out. "We read books, horsed around, played cards, dominoes, checkers, looked after our clothes, relaxed, and did anything we felt like," said Vince Carnazza. "The ready room was open twenty-four hours a day," Flashner added. "The officers sat in front; we sat in the back. We didn't interface with them or even play cards with them." Bill Hazlehurst explained, "Even though we shared the ready room with the enlisted men, there was a clear hierarchy. We were officers; we were pilots."

"The ready room was very comfortable," said Vince. "Each one of us had an easy chair, like the kind you get today only not as fluffy. Each chair had a little locker under the seat and there was a dressing room in back with lockers for our flight suits, parachute harness, pistol, and survival knife." The Flyboys got to know their clubhouse well. "In the ready room," Rowdy Dow remembered, "we would talk and talk and talk. We'd be there all day long talking. What *did* we talk about so much? I wonder about that sometimes."

"We also had a little kitchen off the ready room," said radioman Ralph Sengewalt. "We could get food any time we wanted. The men who didn't fly always had things ready for those coming off a flight. There were sandwiches, coffee, milk, juice." "For our main snack," said Vince, "we would take canned corn beef and mix it real well with pickles and make it into meat loaf, then put it on a plate. We had this with sandwiches or sea ration crackers."

But that was just ready-room cuisine. The enlisted men took their three main meals in the mess hall. "We ate dehydrated eggs with tomato sauce," Vince remembered. "Lots of Spam with shredded pineapple, tomato, and cabbage. We ate boiled beef, sliced beef, fresh or dehydrated mashed potatoes, canned vegetables, and a chili made from hamburger meat and ground-up bologna."

"The thing that got me," George Flashner recalled, "is that there was never any red jam, just marmalade. I always wondered if that marmalade manufacturer had paid someone off for that monopoly."

"While we were under attack," remembered Vince, "they would close the mess. 'Secure the mess hall' is how we said it. They would set up urns, blue enamel coffee pots, with two gallons of pea or vegetable soup. Those coffee pots were suspended on a cord, so when the ship swayed, the pots swayed with it.

"As soon as we were under attack, we'd rush up onto the flight deck," Vince continued. "Five or ten times during each attack, we were told, 'Clear the flight deck!' So we would jump down into the cat works, then come back up again. So there would always be several hundred of us on the flight deck who weren't supposed to be there. We couldn't resist. We would be cheering gunners. When they hit an airplane, a huge cheer would go up from all of us. We were average American kids; we loved football, baseball — this was another big game."

When it was time to go on a strike, the airmen gave their full attention to the air combat intelligence officer. "The ACI would give you the knowledge you needed to do your job," Rowdy Dow said. "The ACI is a smart guy who tells you what the target is, where it is, how to find it, what the target buildings are being used for, what kind of opposition to expect, and what to do if you have to bail out."

"When a group would come back from a strike," said Ralph Sengewalt, "they'd have stories to tell and everybody listened intently. They all took an interest in what you saw, what had happened out there. After all, they were going out next." And there was a ritual for returning pilots. "Immediately after a strike," Ralph recalled, "we went down to sick bay and we got a two-ounce shot of whiskey to calm our nerves." Hearts pumped wildly even after safe returns.

The flight deck of an aircraft carrier was an incredibly dangerous place. There were whirling propellers ready to slice off arms, volatile jet fuel that could burst into flames, and bombs ready to explode. Movements on the flight deck had to be choreographed with balletlike precision. "Operations on an aircraft carrier is the most amazing display of teamwork I have seen in my life," said pilot Porter Golden. "The work schedule on a carrier is four to five times more hectic than land based. Everyone has to perform exactly on schedule. And it continues twenty-four hours a day."

The slightest mistake invited catastrophe. A loose bolt could cause a plane to malfunction on takeoff and explode into a ball of flames. A pilot off by a few feet on landing would crumple his plane against the carrier and sink to the bottom of the ocean. Planes landing amid bombs and bullets made for potentially lethal situations. The possibility of disaster was ever present, and quick thinking was required to avert it. Crewman Sparky Frazer remembered watching in horror as a torpedo plane landed and a live bomb dropped out of its bomb bay onto the carrier deck. As Sparky stood frozen with fright, a deckhand named Buglione "slid forward like a slide into second base in a baseball game, flat on his stomach. When he got there he had the arming / disarming wrench off his belt and had it on the percussion cap in nothing flat. He buttoned the fuse off — never got up — lying flat on his stomach, took the thing and threw it backhand. It hit the flight deck once, splashed into the water — bam, it went off, all in less than ten seconds." Sparky concluded, "If he hadn't been there, I wouldn't be telling this."

Indeed, the tiniest mental mistake could cause mayhem. In March of 1945, a pilot took off from the USS *Randolph* but almost immediately declared an emergency because he was losing oil pressure. He was directed to land on the USS *Yorktown,* which was ready to receive aircraft. The pilot had turned his guns on and had an extra tank of gas, a "belly tank," attached below his plane. In his excitement, he forgot to turn his guns off and jettison the belly tank before landing.

The landing was successful, but when his tail hook caught the arresting wire, his plane stopped and the belly tank ripped off and kept going forward. The tank full of aviation fuel slid through the churning propeller. The fuel erupted in flame and the carrier deck was ablaze.

Deckhands moved swiftly to control the fire but were machine-gunned in the attempt. "The pilot instinctively pulled back on the control stick upon landing, squeezing the gun trigger on the control. The machine gun sprayed the flight deck and ship's superstructure with

.50-caliber bullets." A badly burned pilot and seven bullet-riddled sailors were rushed to the sick bay.

George Bush remembered seeing a pilot's leg slide down the landing deck and come to rest in front of him. The torpedo plane's tail hook had failed to catch the arresting wire and the plane had hit a metal barrier. The severed leg was "quivering and separated from the body. The poor guy got cut in half. We young fellows were standing there stunned when this big chief petty officer came along, yelling to the crew, 'All right, clean this mess up,' and everybody snapped back."

Everything had to work just so. Archie Clapp told me how he watched a buddy die: "One guy ran out of fuel and went down just in front of the ship," he said. " He was trying to open the canopy but couldn't get it open. We knew him for a year and we just watched him drown."

And, of course, life off the carrier was even more dangerous.

"One time we had two hundred planes in the air from a few carriers and the visibility turned to zero," recalled gunner Robert Akerblom. "You can't see your hand and you don't know what you're going to hit and when. Jesus, guys died up there in collisions. That's spooky — you can't see your hand — that's hazardous duty."

Navigation was a seat-of-the-pants proposition because the Flyboys had few of the communication and navigational aids we now take for granted. Flying over the trackless Pacific Ocean presented special challenges. Many pilots simply vanished when they got lost, ran out of fuel, or crashed due to antiaircraft damage. Many survivors had harrowing stories to tell.

Pilot George Menard's plane was fatally damaged by antiaircraft fire over Japan on February 17, 1945. He knew he couldn't make it back to his carrier. His radio was out, but a fellow pilot, using hand signals, told him the American destroyer below would pick Menard up if he bailed out now.

However, when Menard opened the canopy, it flew off into the air and an attached cable stretched across his chest, pinning him to his seat. Now Menard controlled his gyrating plane with his knees as he wondered how he was going to get out alive. He managed to get his knife out and started to scrape the cable. "One strand would break," Menard remembered, "then another, and then, finally, all the strands started popping, and the whole cable broke loose. All this took a life-time of five minutes."

Finally, he bailed out, but his Mae West life vest accidentally inflated in midair. Now he could not get his fingers under his chest straps to undo his parachute harness. When Menard hit the water, the wind caught his chute. He found himself skimming across the ocean like a missile, with his head battering through the waves. "I thought, well, if I time my breathing and get in sync with the troughs and the waves, I might last long enough for the tin can to pick me up," he remembered. "I did that as long as I could, and then my timing, my breathing, got out of sync with the waves, and the last thing I remember was I was looking up at the surface of the water about four or five feet above me, and I had to take a breath. I took a breath, and it was just like a rheostat turning the lights out. It was the way I went out."

By the time crewmen on the USS *Taussig* were able to snag his chute and yank him aboard, Menard was technically dead. His face and fingertips were blue, and his breathing had stopped. He miraculously responded to mouth-to-mouth resuscitation and lived to fly another day.

On April 8, 1945, pilot Jay Finley of the USS *Randolph* was shot down over water near Okinawa. Dazed, he bailed out. When he regained consciousness, he found himself fifteen feet under water. "I am glad my head was up and feet down because if it had been the other way around I would have been going straight for the bottom." Finley struggled to inflate his survival raft and fell asleep curled up in five inches of cold water. "The next morning when I opened my eyes and lifted the edge of the poncho, I looked straight out horizontally and saw water. I looked a little higher and saw water, and then I looked a little higher and saw more water. What a scare! I was in the bottom of a trough, and the waves were about twenty feet high. I had been going up and down on those waves and had not even felt them."

Finley spent five days huddled in his raft, cold water sloshing around while he was tossed by the waves. He was flipped over five times. "During these five days it was raining, cold, and there was no sunshine." Finally, crewmen in a plane noticed the reflection of his signaling mirror and brought him back to the ship. After one hundred twenty hours of freezing torment, wondering whether he would live or die, he was asked if he still wanted to fly.

Flyboy Jay Finley did not hesitate with his answer: "Sure, why not?"

Pilot Howard Sankey remarked to me once, "I think many heroes are made because they have to fight their way out of a hole." Marine pilot Phil Vonville found himself in a deep hole after a strike over Japan.

Phil's nightmare began as he regained consciousness nine thousand feet over the Pacific with his plane headed straight down. "I always thought I was indestructible and that nothing could happen to me," he told me. "Then in a blink of an eye a shell hit me." The shell blew Phil's right kneecap off, and a piece of shrapnel embedded in his right temple.

"There was a chunk of metal sticking out of my head," Phil told me. "Blood was oozing down my face, I had a hell of a headache, my leg hurt like crazy, there was blood everywhere, my airplane had a big hole in it, but all I could think was 'sharks.' That scared me more than anything."

In a desperate attempt to stay airborne, Vonville jettisoned his ammunition to lighten his plane. "My right foot was in a pool of my own blood," he remembered. "I was going into shock from loss of blood. I took my belt off my coveralls, wrapped it around my thigh as a tourniquet. I put the end of the belt in my mouth and stuck a knife in the belt to hold it. All the while I'm flying an airplane."

"I called the ship," Phil said. "They said 'Ditch.' I'm thinking sharks. I said, 'Negative!'"

With his fuel gauge on empty, he rode the water for lift. "There's a slight breeze just above the water because of the wave action," he explained. That breeze was enough: His engine quit just as he coaxed his plane over the back of the USS *Bennington* ("They said I cleared it by only six feet"), where he made a belly landing and immediately lost consciousness.

As if the rigors of flying and the fear of being eaten by sharks weren't enough, there was always the terrifying thought of being shot down and falling into enemy hands.

"Our skipper said fight them until they kill you," pilot Jacob Cohen remembered. "You don't want to see what they do if you're captured."

"You have to figure that when you're strafing people, they get pretty pissed," said Howard Sankey. "We thought if we were captured we'd get shot. We didn't think our chances were too great."

"I remember thinking I'd keep one round of my thirty-eight for myself if I went down," said gunner Bob Stasdak. Added pilot Wesley Todd, "We used to kid about it. We'd talk in a falsetto voice about being shot down; maybe they cut your balls off."

I once asked dive-bomber Alfred Smith, "Did you have any close calls?" He answered, "Son, any day you fly is a close call."

"Four hours in the air is like working eight hours on the ground," said George Heilsberg. "You don't get a second chance; there are no mistakes. I went from a hundred and fifty-five pounds to a hundred and twenty-five. You're under a lot of pressure."

"The scariest thing is the flak," said gunner William Raker. "When they're shooting *ack ack* and the flak is all around, that's when you're really scared. I saw planes near us just get blown up. That's scary. You shook a little bit. When you crawled out of that plane, your knees were shaking."

Some Flyboys told me that because of their youth, they did not experience fear. "I was never scared," said Joe Bonn. "I never thought anything would happen to me. When you're young, everything's an adventure."

"It's a funny thing," added Ralph Sengewalt, "but when you're young, you're not afraid of anything. You think you will come out OK, even though you know that everybody won't. Even seeing flak — when you're eighteen, it's exciting versus scary."

But perhaps fear absent in the moment came out later in dreams. "You didn't have emotions until afterward," said Marine pilot David Andre. "After a close one, you'd be controlled. But I remember breaking out in a sweat at night after thinking about it." Gunner William Hale said, "The actual fright wouldn't happen until you were back. That night you'd get the shakes and you'd have interrupted sleep. You couldn't get to sleep or you'd doze and wake up with thoughts of what you went through and apprehension about going through it all over again the next day. You kept it to yourself; you were aware the others were going through the same thing."

"Our flight leader," remembered George Flashner, "would say to us in the ready room, 'Anybody who's not scared of going on this flight, raise your hand.' Nobody raised their hand. He said, 'Good. Anyone who raised their hand, I'd think they were nuts.'"

But no matter how terrifying, no matter how dangerous their job, no matter how many buddies were lost, the Flyboys kept flying, even though if they ever said the word, they'd be relieved. Rowdy Dow, a teenager in 1945, later told me how the Flyboys flew through their fears:

Once my plane was going down and I thought this was the end. We were trained that we had eighteen seconds to put our parachutes on and get out of that turret. I grabbed my parachute but was doing this under the terrific strain of centrifugal force.

We didn't crash. We made it back to the carrier. I was trying to talk, but nothing would come out. I lost my speech because of the terror I had experienced. The intelligence officer said, "Don't worry. Go to sick bay, get a half a pint of brandy, and you'll be fine." He was right. I recovered.

Any one of us could have said "I don't want to fly" at any time. No one made us get in those planes. I'd look out the window thousands of feet up and see one of their shells come right up to the airplane, as big as a plate. That one shell could have put us up in heaven.

Everybody was afraid. We knew this was a risky business. We weren't afraid like a kid afraid of the dark. It was about going down where no one would find you, of not seeing your mom, your dad, and the girl you want to marry. That's afraid.

Your brain tells you not to get into the airplane; you'll die a nasty death. But our brain also told us that we had to do something for our country.

If we had given in to our fears, we wouldn't have won that war. There were no replacements out there. Our country was depending on us, and we were all ready to die for our country. There was a job to do. We did it.

Except for submarine duty, flying into battle off an aircraft carrier was the riskiest duty in WWII. Death was a common occupational hazard, and for the Flyboys, a lonely one. Marines fighting on land saw their buddies cut down, but for the Flyboys there was only a void — an empty chair in the ready room. "They didn't come back," said William Raker. "That was it."

And there was no time to grieve. On the carriers there was work to do and death had to be forgotten or at least shoved into the back of one's mind. "There was so much death happening around us that you just had to deal with it," said pilot Dwight Mayo. "Somebody would go down you knew like a brother," Archie Clapp said. "But you couldn't dwell on it. You'd get briefed on the next mission and you knew it could be your turn next."

"We knew they were gone," said Ken Meredith of his lost buddies. "But the next day, we were off again. Then yesterday is history. You don't deal with the day before. You just go on and hope you'll make it through another day."

"After the first or second mission," said Vince Carnazza, "you feel like you're going to get killed, but you don't know when. It ceases to be a big deal or something to worry about." Marine pilot John Leboeuf shared a piece of ready-room gallows humor with me about airmen's life insurance. "This one sounds kind of cold," Leboeuf said, "but this is how we lived."

> *Ten thousand dollars*
> *Going home to the folks.*
> *Won't they be excited?*
> *And won't they be delighted?*
> *Ten thousand dollars going home to the folks.*

The Flyboys jokingly accepted death but were deadly serious about dealing it out to the enemy. "We hated them for what they did at Pearl Harbor," said pilot Jack Cohen. "We wanted to get back at them any way we could." "We thought the Japanese were horrible," George Bush said. "We all knew the tales of torture from Bataan. We thought they did something terrible to the United States and we were going to teach them a lesson. There was no question of who was right."

These feelings of intense hatred often led some airmen to cross the line in combat. "We'd strafe them floating in the water," recalled gunner Joe Bonn. "They were the enemy. I had no compassion for them. That's the way it was."

"Japanese pilots would bail out and our pilots would take great delight at shooting them in their parachutes," Leland Holdren said. "There was nostalgia for WWI, the Red Baron thing, but we shot them." Walter Stonebraker added, "We had no mercy. If we saw a

Japanese plane go down, we'd shoot him in his chute. If we didn't, he'd survive to fight another day. It was war."

And yet there was also a distance. Chester Bennett, a navy psychologist who evaluated hundreds of Flyboys in the Pacific, wrote to a friend, "You seldom find them expressing vindictive personal hatred for the enemy. It's a contest of mechanical skill and grand strategy. And if anyone can jump the net and shake hands with the opponent after it's all over, I think it may well be some of the fliers." David Andre told me, "The air war out there was totally impersonal. We didn't see the enemy, didn't know what he looked like. You didn't think of whether he was young, did he have a family, human characteristics — these things didn't go through your mind."

It was a distance with a difference, the quality that made WWII modern and has characterized military conflict ever since. "One of the nice things about aerial combat is that it is impersonal," explained Stonebraker. "It's machine against machine. You see plants, ships, and you know people are going to be killed, but it's impersonal. You are just doing your job." Al Lindstrom explained, "I never saw the enemy. You don't from the airplane."

"The enemy was whatever the target they sent me on," added George Heilsberg. "It could have been German or Japanese. I had no hatred of the Japanese." But there was no sympathy either. "You never see if they're dead," said Bonn. "You're going a hundred and thirty miles an hour; you just spray. It's just a revenge reaction. You can't tell if you did anything."

For many Flyboys, it was a technician's job — taking off, navigating, dropping ordnance as planned, landing back on the carrier. Like clockwork, they breezed through their routine, knowing that a friendly poker game was waiting for them back in the ready room. Even though they didn't talk about it, as the list of buddies who didn't come back lengthened, they had to wonder and worry about their own chances. John Leboeuf told me, "We tried to be strong and not show anything except complete bravery in front of our fellow airmen." But there was plenty of cruel truth in a ditty that made it around the carrier ready rooms out in the Pacific:

> *He loved his plane*
> *And he loved to fly.*

He never thought
He was going to die.

Now don't feel bad
And don't feel blue.
Who knows tomorrow
It may be you.

CHAPTER THIRTEEN

No Mans Land

This is my duty and I have got to do it.

— *George Bush*

AMERICAN Flyboys recovered from the war's early setbacks and eventually knocked Japan out of the sky. In 1941, the Mitsubishi Zero was a terror, but soon Japanese pilots were the ones trembling when a Flyboy zoomed into view. American airmen had learned from their mistakes and trained themselves to peak performance. And their machines had improved along with them. Now Hellcats, P-38 Lightnings, and Corsairs had Japanese airpower reeling. By 1944, the emperor's air forces were in tatters. Too many Japanese planes had become just another notch in a Flyboy's belt.

As American airpower gained control of the Third Dimension in the Pacific, the battlefield was transformed. Now a prediction by Billy Mitchell was becoming self-evident: He who controlled the air controlled the outcome of the war.

Admiral Chester Nimitz's strategy had called for making a beeline for Japan, as directly as possible. The Mariana Trench snakes its way from Guam, Tinian, and Saipan north to Tokyo Bay. The islands along this trench — the highest peaks of this submerged mountain range — would be the American military's road to Tokyo.

And as that road neared Japan, both sides knew that hostilities in No Mans Land would be different. Unlike Guadalcanal or Tarawa or Saipan, the islands of No Mans Land were Japanese native soil, part of the undefiled realm. No barbarian had ever set his victorious foot on Japan's sacred soil. An American invasion here would constitute the invasion of Japan. The fighting would be ferocious.

But before American rifles and Japanese swords would cross in conflict there, the Flyboys brought the war to No Mans Land.

A Japanese soldier's life on Iwo Jima and in No Mans Land in 1944 and early 1945 was tedious, dull, depressing, and dangerous. On Iwo Jima, Japanese boys dug caves and tunnels into the stinking sulfurous rock. Sweat poured off their bodies as they worked far below the surface in stifling hot, clammy caverns. Carrier planes and B-24s from Saipan would suddenly appear to make their lives even more miserable. There was no spring water on barren, sulfurous-smelling Iwo Jima, and their commander set the example for his 22,000 troops by using only one cup of water a day to bathe himself and brush his teeth.

In comparison, Chichi Jima had plenty of water and was tropical-paradise lush. But the 25,000 troops there had denuded the hills long ago by cutting down trees to build shelters and foraging for anything edible.

Besides being a communications hub, Chichi Jima was the staging area for supplies intended for Iwo Jima. Freighters and transport ships would sail the six hundred miles from Japan to Chichi Jima, where they would unload in the fine natural harbor. Then the supplies were transferred to smaller boats, which ferried them the final one hundred fifty miles to Iwo Jima. Iwo had no harbor, and the small boats would have to ride the waves onto the black sand shore or wait offshore while boats from Iwo would come out to unload at sea.

As time wore on, however, American planes and submarines made the transport of supplies from Japan to Chichi Jima and onward to Iwo Jima impossible. Only the occasional Japanese submarine could get through, and they couldn't carry much cargo.

Soon a dark, forlorn feeling of abandonment overtook the soldiers in No Mans Land. Even though the *issen gorin* knew their mission was to die for the emperor, they were human beings. It was natural for them to hope that they might survive the war and feel the embrace of their mothers, girlfriends, and wives again. But these boys could see the *gaizin* planes swarming overhead, the dwindling number of Japanese ships making it through. They understood that their Spirit Warrior masters back in Tokyo had sentenced them to *gyokusai* deaths. They knew the caves they were digging would be their tombs.

In America on July 4, 1944, Dick Woellhof's mother, Laura, was celebrating the nation's 169th birthday. She was taking charge of the Independence Day picnic at her sister Ruah's farm in Idana, Kansas.

The farm kitchen was crowded with family members working, talking, and laughing. "Laura was the oldest in the family," Ruah Sterrett told me, "so she would cook and tell everyone what to do to get things ready."

The potatoes that needed peeling were grown on the farm, as were the beans that had to be trimmed. The chicken frying in oil came from the farm also. "I laid their heads on a block," Ruah said, "and would cut them off with a hatchet. You had to be brave in those days. I don't think I could do that today."

For drinks, lemons had to be squeezed and precious rationed sugar was added to make lemonade. "We didn't serve beer at our house," Ruah remembered. "We got along fine without it."

The scent of fried chicken must have reminded Laura of her son. Dick had come back to Clay Center on leave a few times over the past two years. In one of his first letters home to his mother ("Dear Sweetheart"), he asked her to "quit talking about fried chicken in those letters as I haven't had a real good meal for three weeks and it makes me hungry. We have plenty of beans. The way we can tell it is Saturday up here is every Saturday morning we have beans as our main dish." So when he was home, Laura had fried him all the chicken he wanted and gone easy on the beans.

Dick craved another simple pleasure. "When I come home," he wrote, "I'm going to lay down on a soft bed and sleep as long as I can. A person doesn't get any too much rest sleeping in a hammock and a lot of the boys have some sore spots from falling out of the hammocks. It is about a four foot drop and the floor is plenty hard."

This July Fourth must have held special meaning for Laura. She was a single mother with both her sons off fighting for their country. She could brag about Dick in the Pacific and her older boy, Lawrence, who was a GI in Africa. Laura worried about her sons, but she hoped for the best and kept herself occupied. She still worked six days a week in her beauty salon, which had supported the family since the death of her husband. And a big family gathering like this one certainly kept her distracted. Laura had to corral someone to turn the crank on the wooden freezer to convert the sweet cream and sugar into homemade ice cream. The ice had been purchased from a neighbor who had cut it from the river in the winter and stored it packed in straw in a nearby cave. Turning the crank was hard work on a hot July day, too arduous for the kids, so Laura had to assign an available adult to do the work.

During the afternoon, the relatives visited around the backyard picnic table and on the shady porch. When the sun went down, out came the fireworks. First, sparklers for the little kids and firecrackers for the teenagers. Then the climax of any American family's Independence Day — the big rockets that only the uncles could handle.

"Everybody loved those fireworks," Aunt Ruah said. "They'd burst and go into a million pieces."

That same day, Dick was aboard the USS *Yorktown,* which had sailed north from Eniwetok on June 30, 1944. On July 3, a fighter sweep had been launched against Iwo Jima, but Japanese planes rose to intercept them. In the resulting melee, twelve Japanese planes were downed, as was pilot Arthur Ward, who "failed to return," as the ship's action report put it.

Operations began bright and early the next day, July 4. There were scattered showers as the USS *Yorktown,* just sixty-six miles from Chichi Jima, readied for launch by turning into the wind. Dick's Helldiver, piloted by Owen Hintz, with Dick behind him in the gunner's seat, took off in the predawn darkness at 5:00 A.M. On the way to the strike, Dick saw the sunrise at 5:54 A.M.

Dick and his strike force circled Chichi Jima's harbor at 11,000 feet, searching for ships and docks to bomb. At 6:40 A.M., they began their dives. The plan was to dart down from 11,000 feet, release the bombs at 2,000 feet, and pull out at 1,000 feet — a classic dive-bombing operation. Unfortunately, this plan was also perfect for the island's defenders. The harbor was a "punch bowl" surrounded by rugged hills with only a small opening in the west for escape. It was a uniquely dangerous place to dive. The antiaircraft fire came not only from below but also from all sides as the planes dove below the level of the hilltops. As the planes pulled out and escaped to the west, Japanese fire would actually come down at them from caves above.

One by one, the bombers dove and the Japanese gunners reaped their bloody harvest. Warren Wright's plane was hit and burst into flame. Witnesses saw a parachute blossom forth — it was Warren or his gunner, Fred Pryor; no one knew for sure. The jumper landed in the harbor and sank beneath the water. Just then, another plane was a burning mass. Like that, pilot Jack Drysdale and gunner Bruce Dalton were gone.

Then it was Dick's turn.

As Laura Woellhof gazed into the Kansas night sky, her face illuminated by the red, white, and blue explosions, she had no idea that on that same Fourth of July her son was observing fireworks from the opposite angle. The colored missiles he saw were tracers fired at him from the antiaircraft guns below. One of those shells found its mark and tore into Dick's plane. His pilot, Owen Hintz, was killed instantly.

Then the plane burst into a million pieces.

Now Dick found himself falling free of the destroyed Helldiver and he yanked his chute open. The shell that ripped into Dick's dive-bomber had cut into his right leg. Bleeding, in great pain, Dick floated down into No Mans Land.

He landed in the harbor with no chance of escape. As he swam ashore, three soldiers pointed their bayonets. It was a hopeless mismatch, but this former letterman for the Clay Center Tigers drew his survival knife and lunged. A bayonet thrust into Dick's shoulder ended the face-off as the Japanese bagged their first Flyboy of the day.

Dick's flying career was over. Exactly two years earlier — to the day — his mother's signature on his enlistment papers had made that July Fourth "the happiest day" of his life.

As Dick was hustled off, additional waves of planes suddenly appeared. Pilot Bill Connell from Seattle had enlisted because he thought flying would be "neat." Now he was at the controls of a two-seated dive-bomber with gunner Ben Wolf in the back. Bill and Ben had lifted off from the USS *Hornet* in the dark and now, just after 7:00 A.M., they were over Chichi Jima's harbor. "We could see two freighters entering the harbor," Bill recalled. "Those were our targets."

Just as he began his dive, a shell exploded near his plane and Bill was knocked out cold. "When I came to," he said, "I tried to regain control of the plane. I pulled the stick, but there was no response. The tail was gone and the right wing was missing. I was falling down through the air like a leaf. Going flip, flop, just swaying back and forth like a falling leaf."

Bill jettisoned his bombs and yelled, "Get out! Get out!" to Ben Wolf in the backseat. Bill could not turn to see if his gunner was alive or dead or if he was even still in the plane. To this day, Bill has no idea what happened to Ben.

"I waited a few minutes to give him a chance to get out," Bill recalled. "And then I undid my straps and jumped."

As Bill floated down from eight thousand feet, the gunners below took potshots at him. "I saw the tracers coming at me," he said, "and I had a brief thought: 'Gee, today is the Fourth of July.'"

Bill landed in the harbor, stripped off his parachute harness, and inflated his Mae West. One of the ships he had been attempting to destroy sailed by him. "They aimed their machine guns at me," he recalled, "but they didn't shoot."

Bill remained floating in the harbor for about forty-five minutes. No one wanted to come out and get him until they were satisfied the bombing runs were finished. Finally, a small vessel with ten crewmen fished Bill out.

"They dragged me aboard," he said, "and started screaming and yelling and hitting me about my head. The Japanese don't use their fists; they were striking me with their open hands on the side of my head."

Then they threw Bill down on the deck and started kicking him. Their slaps and kicks were only meant to terrorize him; they could have broken bones if they wanted to. "I was scared to death," Bill said. "I thought I was going to die."

After ten minutes of this treatment, the crew took a one-inch-thick rope and bound Bill from his knees to his shoulders "like a mummy," he said. "Then they threw this mummy onto the bow of the ship and sailed toward shore."

On shore, Bill was blindfolded and his hands were handcuffed behind his back. Just then an air-raid siren wailed as another strike force appeared overhead. Bill was tossed into the sidecar of a motorcycle and rushed into an air-raid shelter.

After the raid, Bill was driven about half a mile and lashed to a tree in a manner guaranteed to cause excruciating pain. "They blindfolded me," he said, "and tied my hands to a tree behind my back. Then they kicked my legs out from under me so my legs were stretched out in front and my butt was a few inches off the ground. The pain was terrific, I was crying, tears were coming down. It felt like my shoulders were being ripped off. I tried to dig my heels in the ground to inch my way back up the tree, but I couldn't. The guards were laughing, knowing I would fail. The pain was unbearable."

After six hours, Bill had no feeling in the upper half of his body. Another wave of air strikes hit the island, with bombs landing near Bill, now left alone by the guards.

"A big chunk of dirt landed in my lap," he said. "I didn't know what had happened; I had a wild thought that my legs were gone. I was able to peek out from under the blindfold and see that I still had legs!"

Bill was lucky that he wasn't pulverized. Planes from the USS *Yorktown* alone dropped over 110 tons of bombs on Chichi Jima that day.

After almost twelve hours, the guards finally cut Bill down. "When they untied my hands," Bill recalled, "I couldn't see between my fingers because they were swollen together. My hands looked like two big balls on the end of my arms. They were blue, and I wondered if I'd ever be able to use them again. I couldn't raise my arms for two days."

Bill spent the night lashed to a second tree, with his hands tied behind him more loosely, and this time he could sit down. While he was bound there, a Japanese civilian walked up to him and put a rifle right between his eyes.

"He made it clear," Bill recalled, "that an American bomb had killed his son and he was going to kill me. I thought, 'This is it,' but the guards shooed him away."

Finally, Bill was moved to army headquarters, where he would spend the next six days. He was tied to a tree outside the headquarters building and taken inside every day to be interrogated. "They questioned me as if I had the knowledge of an admiral," Bill said, "asking me, 'How many planes does this carrier have?' and, 'What is the mission of this other carrier?'" When Bill gave an answer the interrogator didn't like, the guards boxed the side of his head so hard that he and the chair he was bound to would topple over onto the floor. "They weren't trying to kill me," Bill said, "but it sure was uncomfortable."

Bill was fed a rice ball once a day and could have all the water or tea he wanted. When tied to the tree, he was always blindfolded. "I was very frightened," he admitted. "I was sure I was going to be executed. I thought of my folks, my sister, my aunts and uncles, my grandparents. But my life was out of my control and I was living day to day, just hoping for the best.

"One day I heard voices," Bill told me, "and I angled my head so I could peek under the blindfold. I saw an American enlisted man in blue dungarees, blindfolded and handcuffed, being led across the courtyard to a building. He was limping."

It was Dick Woellhof.

Bill and Dick shared a similar existence during those harrowing days, but there was a big difference between the two in the minds of their Japanese captors. Bill was an officer and Dick was an enlisted man. "Being enlisted people, we were told we'd be shot right away because we didn't know enough," said gunner William Hale, recalling an intelligence briefing he received aboard his carrier. "The Japanese judged us according to their enlisted men."

Bill Connell spent seven days tied to the tree outside headquarters. Then he was bundled aboard an old seaplane and flown to Iwo Jima. He sat on the tarmac under the shade of the aircraft for five hours. Then he was tied again, blindfolded, and placed in the backseat of a two-engined bomber. Bill was headed for further questioning at the Ofuna POW camp, just outside of Tokyo.

On the flight to Japan, Bill peeked out from under his blindfold. "I saw I was sitting next to a canvas bag," he told me. "The bag was full of baseball bats! There was a leather baseball glove looped over one of the bats. Here we were fighting a war and they're flying baseball equipment back and forth."

After the war, Bill submitted an affidavit to the relevant war crimes trial about his treatment on Chichi Jima. In one of the letters from the American prosecutor, Bill learned that he had earned a unique distinction. "They said I was the last American off the island alive."

*   *   *

Iwo Jima's defenders knew they would die there, but at least they had the small comfort that they admired the man leading them to their deaths. General Tadamichi Kuribayashi was a sixth-generation samurai whose family had long served the emperor. Kuribayashi knew this would be his final battle. He wrote his wife, "Do not expect my return." To his son, he wrote, "Your father's life is like a candle in the wind."

But he did not despair, and in true samurai fashion his behavior enhanced the family name. The general shared his soldiers' privations, labored as hard as he asked his men to, and devised a brilliant defensive strategy for the island.

The soldiers on Chichi Jima were much less fortunate with the abusive General Yoshio Tachibana. "He was a hard drinker," recalled Matsuo Kagiwada, who served under Tachibana for six months. "I often had to get sake for him. He always drank himself to sleep." Tachibana was feared for his short temper and for personally beating soldiers when perturbed. He was a true product of the Spirit Warriors' upside-down system of morality. In an army that valued animal-like responses, this bully had risen to the top. Kagiwada concluded that he "always thought of General Tachibana as one who came up from the gutter."

On August 5, 1944, Chichi Jima was hit with another fierce bombing raid during which a B-24 was downed. All aboard were killed in the fiery crash except for one army crewman who crawled out alive. The raid had caused other casualties: Members of General Tachibana's 307th Battalion had been killed. With that, Tachibana had had enough. It was time for revenge.

The general had Dick Woellhof and the unidentified B-24 crewman tied to trees in front of his headquarters.

"These *kichiku* killed our fellow soldiers," Tachibana shouted to his assembled men. "Hit them as a warning to others. Kick them hard and hate them." Then the general smacked the two helpless boys, took a swig from a nearby sake bottle, and exclaimed, "I feel great. I am revenging the enemy!"

Tachibana issued a daily order later that August 5 calling for the execution of the two prisoners the next day. That evening he stood and addressed his men in the headquarters mess hall: "Tomorrow, prisoners will be disposed of. All orderlies and clerks who are not required to perform other duties will attend."

"The general," said Captain Seiji Higashigi, "mentioned that while he was a battalion commander in Manchuria, the execution of prisoners of war helped to build the fighting spirit of the troops."

On August 6, Dick and the B-24 crewman were loaded onto the rear of a truck and taken to the 307th Battalion's rifle range. Captain Higashigi, a senior adjutant to Tachibana, had ordered Lieutenant Colonel Kikuji Ito to oversee the execution as follows: "It has been decided upon that the prisoners should be executed by bayoneting. Lieutenant Colonel Ito, you supervise the execution."

Later, Ito would speculate that General Tachibana had intentionally singled him out for this unpleasant task. "It is true that I had a quarrel with the general," said Ito, "and it is a fact that the general hardly spoke to me." But all officers' orders were to be considered as commands from the emperor, and Colonel Ito thought only how to obey.

At the rifle range, Dick and the crewman, their hands tied behind their backs, were made to walk up a small hill. It was around 8 A.M.; the sun was up, with the temperature beginning its predictable rise. The two boys were not told they were about to be executed, but they must have assumed so. They watched as stakes were pounded into the ground. Then they were lashed to the stakes and blindfolded.

"After the prisoners were tied," recalled Moriko Okamoto, "Colonel Ito gave the order to worship the emperor with a deep bow."

"I gave the following speech," Colonel Ito later related. " 'Acting on orders, we are now going to execute these two prisoners.' I then walked over to the prisoners and felt their chests and with my fountain pen, I put a circle over their hearts." The instructions were the same as they had been in training: Executioners were not to pierce hearts or else the victims would die too soon. It was important that as many as possible got their chance to strengthen their *Yamato damashii.*

Colonel Ito then gave the order to begin the bayoneting. "I will make a coward stab a prisoner," he said, and selected Private Matsutano Kido. When Kido wasn't enthusiastic enough, Colonel Ito shouted at him, "Why are you hesitating to stab?"

There was no further hesitation. After the first round of stabbings by four privates, the lungs and stomachs of the two Flyboys were punctured, and aerated blood bubbled forth from their noses and mouths.

Their heads sagged to their chests. More men came forward two by two to thrust their sharp blades into the Americans' bodies.

"The flyers were groaning," recalled a soldier named Shimura. "They did not cry out or yell; they only groaned."

"After the prisoners were bayoneted," said Okamoto, "Colonel Ito beheaded them. They were still alive when he did this."

Ito later claimed he beheaded Dick and the crewman out of respect. "In Japanese bushido," Ito said, "when a man is executed, it is a sign of honoring him that he be beheaded. Although I was stepping beyond my actual orders, I honored the two prisoners by beheading them." Ito was referring to *kaishaku,* the ritual beheading administered after someone commits seppuku, or hara-kiri. A samurai would disembowel himself over a matter of honor and an assistant would then behead the suffering man to end his agony. This beheading was prearranged and agreed to by all parties. But the American boys with blood running out of their mouths were accorded no honor that day. In contorting the true essence of bushido, Colonel Ito was typical of his fellow Spirit Warriors, who bastardized Japanese history as they led their nation to ruin.

Dick's and the B-24 crewman's bodies and severed heads were placed in a previously dug hole. Dick had turned twenty years old eight days before.

On August 16, Laura Woellhof received a telegram from the navy notifying her that Dick had been shot down on July 4. The navy wrote that Dick was "missing in action" and that Laura was to wait for further word before jumping to conclusions.

It would be a year and a half before the navy would learn that Dick was dead. But Laura told her niece Laura Massaro that by then she already knew that her son's spirit had left the earth.

"Dick flew over the house," his mother told Massaro. "It was like a dream, but not a dream. I was awake. I saw him. Dick waved the American flag and said, 'Good-bye, Mom.'"

General Tachibana's temper grew hotter as the simmering summer of 1944 dragged on. Japanese military doctrine focused on taking the offensive, but on Chichi Jima there were no glorious battles to fight and no sex slaves to rape. As he awaited his own *gyokusai* death, all the general could do was order the digging of more caves.

Nobuaki Iwatake, the Hawaiian Nisei dragooned into the Japanese army, was one of the soldiers ordered to dig in the hard rock day after day. Iwatake-san later told me of his labors:

> Usually the engineers would use dynamite to open a hole at the entrance. After that we used the crude hammer-and-chisel method to dig caves. It was difficult to dig those caves due to the rocky nature of the landscape. Because of the hard labor and scarce food rations, many of us got sick.
>
> Actually, there was a large stockpile of rice, dried vegetables, dried tofu, and canned goods on the island. But the Chichi commanders cut rations because they expected a long war and the island was completely isolated.
>
> While digging caves, our food ration consisted of a small portion of rice gruel. We all talked about the delicious food we used to eat before life on Chichi. I even dreamed about the good food I used to eat in Hawaii, especially the whole barbecued pig we'd eat at picnics.
>
> While we were digging caves, we were constantly under attack from carrier planes and B-24 Liberators from Saipan. Once while we were taking a rest outside our cave, we heard the sound of planes approaching the island. Everyone ran for cover into the cave. I was the last one to take cover, and just as I entered the cave, there was a terrific explosion. When we went out to see what happened, there was a large crater only twenty feet from where I was standing. A B-24 had dropped a five-hundred-pound bomb. The others said to me, "You were a lucky guy."
>
> I noticed that during bombing and strafing attacks, the first ones to take cover were married men. I realized later that they had their wives and children waiting for them at home.

Iwatake and his fellow soldiers labored in the caves seven days a week. There were no weekend breaks. So on Saturday, September 2, 1944, as the dawn once again anointed No Mans Land the spot where Japan's sun is first seen, Iwatake arose to another day of drudgery.

That same dawn shone on the USS *San Jacinto,* an American aircraft carrier steaming only fifty miles west of Iwatake's cave. Flyboy George Bush was just leaving the ready-room briefing on the day's strike. His buddy Ted White saw him and asked, "What are you hitting today, George?"

"The radio station on Chichi Jima," Bush answered.

George, who had celebrated his twentieth birthday just two months earlier, had bombed Chichi the day before, but the damage had been slight. His instructions this day had been brief: "The radio station is your primary target."

Ted and George had first met on board the *San Jacinto,* but they had a special connection through their fathers. Ted's father had been a Yale classmate of George's father, Prescott, and twenty-six-year-old Ted was himself a graduate of Yale, the university George planned to attend. Family ties sure to strengthen after they both returned home to civilian life bound their friendship.

George had planned to fly that day with his regular crew, gunner Leo Nadeau and radioman John Delaney, but Ted asked if he could replace Leo. Ted was the ordnance officer for the squadron and he wanted to go on a strike as a turret gunner.

"We're moving out later today, and this may be the last time I can go with you," Ted said. "How about it?"

"It could be a rough trip," George warned.

By now, George knew all about rough trips. He had been flying in the Pacific for almost five months. He had flown into antiaircraft fire over Guam, Saipan, Wake Island, and Marcus Island. George had sunk ships and had a few close calls, including a harrowing sea ditching. Eventually, he would fly 58 strikes, make 126 carrier landings, and log 1,228 hours. At twenty years of age, George was the youngest pilot in the squadron. Like so many Flyboys, he was a kid doing a man's job.

And a dangerous job too. After George's very first combat run, a strike over Wake Island on May 23, he had experienced the spooky, empty pang of loss unique to the Flyboys' existence. George had flown off that day to bomb Wake while his roommate, pilot Jim Wykes, flew antisubmarine patrol. Jim and his crewmen, Bob Whalen and Chuck Haggard, never returned. There was no distress signal, no debris found in the water, just a heartsick void when, after waiting and hoping, the Flyboys aboard the *San Jacinto* realized their buddies were gone for good. Young George had displayed a stiff upper lip to his comrades, but when he returned to the room he and Jim had shared the night before, he boosted himself into his top bunk, curled up, and cried.

George knew that Chichi Jima presented a dangerous challenge — he had seen the flak coming at him the day before — but Ted White persisted. George said it was OK with him if the flight leader approved, which he did. Ted would fly in the turret that day in place of Leo Nadeau.

At 7:15 A.M., after a breakfast of powdered eggs, bacon, sausage, dehydrated fried potatoes, and toast, George lifted his torpedo plane off the carrier with Ted White and John Delaney in back. Each boy wore a Mae West over his flight suit. George's plane carried four 500-pound bombs.

As the Flyboys winged toward Chichi Jima, the enemy was monitoring their progress, Emperor Hirohito's antiaircraft gunners scanning the telltale pips on their radar screens.

At 8:15 A.M., George and his squadron initiated their glide-bombing run. Mount Yoake and Mount Asahi and their radio stations were easy targets to spot. The twin peaks rose abruptly from the Pacific to a height of about one thousand feet and were distinguished by their forests of antenna towers, which served as the Japanese military's radio transmitters and receivers. Surrounding these radio towers were nests of antiaircraft guns and radar facilities, now homed in on George and his group.

The lead plane went down through black clouds of antiaircraft fire, followed by the second. The two dropped eight bombs — two tons of explosives — on the radio complex. Now, however, the Japanese gunners had the Flyboys' range in their sights. George was the next to dive. He could see that he had to fly into the middle of intense antiaircraft fire.

Fifty-seven years later, I asked George Bush what it was like to dive straight toward antiaircraft gunners trying to blow him out of the sky.

"You see the explosions all around you," he said, "these dark, threatening puffs of black smoke. You're tense in your body, but you can't do anything about it. You cannot take evasive action, so you get used to it. You just think to yourself, 'This is my duty and I have got to do it.'"

Bush paused for a moment and then added, "And of course, you always thought someone else was going to get hit."

But on September 2, that "someone else" was George Bush. At release altitude, a Japanese shell tore into his plane.

"There was a fierce jolt and it lifted the plane forward," he recalled. "We were probably falling at a speed of a hundred and ninety miles per hour. Smoke was coming up from the engine; I couldn't see the controls. I saw flames running along the wings to the fuel tanks. I thought, 'This is really bad.' But I was thinking of what I was supposed to do. And what I was supposed to do was drop those bombs and haul ass out of there."

The twenty-year-old, not yet old enough to vote or drink in a bar, was now at the controls of a burning, falling plane with two buddies in the back. A potential explosion loomed. Flight leader Don Melvin, hovering nearby in a torpedo plane, later said, "You could have seen that smoke for a hundred miles."

Amazingly, George stayed on course long enough to drop his bombs on target, as instructed. Later he would be awarded the Distinguished Flying Cross for his bravery. His flight leader wrote, "Bush continued his dive, releasing his bombs on the radio station to score damaging hits. He then turned sharply to the east to clear the island of Chichi Jima, smoke and flames enveloping his engine and spreading aft as he did so, and his plane losing altitude."

Once the bombs were away, it was time to escape. "Hit the silk! Hit the silk!" George shouted into the intercom, telling Ted White and John Delaney to bail out. "Then," he told me, "I turned the plane starboard to take the slipstream pressure off the door near Delaney's station." Bush was riding a volatile fireball, but he still thought to maneuver the plane in such a way to give his crewmen a better chance of survival, though it would hinder his own ability to get out. By dipping the right wing slightly and turning the tail rudder to the left, George caused the plane to "skid" sideways through the air, thus relieving air pressure on the crew door and providing them a better opportunity to escape. It was a maneuver that used up precious time and delayed his own exit.

Finally, it was time for George to save himself. "I unfastened my seat belt and dove out and down to avoid the tail," he told me. "But I pulled the cord too quickly, and the tail came up and hit me in the head."

Now George had a big bleeding gash above one eye, and there was more. "Then the parachute hooked on the tail and tore a few panels out," he said. "As a result, I was falling faster than normal."

"Bush's plane was smoking like a two-alarm fire," said radioman

Richard Gorman, "then I saw a chute blossom out." Gorman saw Bush "hit the drink" and at the same instant, he saw a "a huge ball of fire." Bush's bomber had exploded.

George had the presence of mind to unsnap his parachute chest strap just as he slammed into the water. He put his hands up, and the parachute blew away from him toward Chichi Jima. He splashed down about four miles northeast of the island and swam to a collapsible yellow one-man life raft dropped from another plane. He inflated it and climbed in. He had no paddles, and the wind was blowing him toward Chichi Jima.

"I could see the island," Bush told me. "I started paddling with my hands, leaning over the front of the raft, paddling as hard as I could. A Portuguese man-of-war had stung my arm and it hurt. I had swallowed a few pints of water and I was vomiting. My head was bleeding. I was wondering about my crewmen. I was crying. I was twenty years old and I was traumatized. I had just survived a burning plane crash. I was all alone and I was wondering if I'd make it."

George scanned the horizon looking for his crewmen. He saw nothing. Witnesses later said that only two chutes came out of the plane. One was George's, but it was unclear who was in the other. Neither Ted White nor John Delaney survived.

George was in even more trouble than he could imagine. Not only was the current pushing him toward Chichi Jima, but some small boats had been launched from the island to capture him.

"I saw those small boats heading his way and thought, 'Oh, he's a goner,'" said gunner Charles Bynum. Two American planes dove and strafed the boats. Battle reports later noted that "*San Jacinto* ordnance records indicate 1,460 rounds of machine gun bullets were fired at the would-be Bush captors."

For the moment, the boats retreated, but Bush's fellow pilots could only help for so long. They were running low on fuel and had to return to their carriers. The flight leader radioed George's location to the rescue submarine USS *Finback,* which was standing by for just such an emergency.

For what seemed like an eternity, George paddled and hoped and paddled some more. "I had seen the famous photo of the Australian pilot being beheaded," Bush told me, "and I knew how Americans were treated at Bataan. Yes, I had a few things on my mind."

Nobuaki Iwatake had been digging in a nearby cave when the strike force appeared overhead. "Someone yelled, 'Plane down!'" Iwatake-san recalled. Along with the others, he ran to follow the action. From the vantage point of a high cliff, the soldiers saw the submarine long before Bush did.

After paddling his raft and praying for three hours and thirteen minutes, George saw a black dot emerge from the water about a hundred yards away. "The dot grew larger," he recalled. "First a periscope, then the conning tower, then the hull of a submarine emerged from the depths." Bush had no idea that anyone had radioed his position. "At first I thought maybe I was delirious," he said, "and when I concluded it was a submarine all right, I feared that it might be Japanese. It just seemed too lucky and too far-fetched that it would be an American submarine."

Five submariners threw Bush a line, pulled him alongside the sub, and helped the soaking-wet and exhausted Flyboy aboard. George managed just four words to his saviors: "Happy to be aboard."

George spent a month on the *Finback,* which gave him plenty of time to reflect on his brush with death. He would often stand the midnight–4 A.M. watch while the sub was surfaced. Later, he recalled those reflective moments:

I'll never forget the beauty of the Pacific — the flying fish, the stark wonder of the sea, the waves breaking across the bow. It was absolutely dark in the middle of the Pacific; the nights were so clear and the stars so brilliant. It was wonderful and energizing, a time to talk to God.

I had time to reflect, to go deep inside myself and search for answers. People talk about a kind of foxhole Christianity, where you're in trouble and think you're going to die, and so you want to make everything right with God and everybody else right there in the last minute.

But this was just the opposite of that. I had already faced death, and God had spared me. I had this very deep and profound gratitude and a sense of wonder. Sometimes when there is a disaster, people will pray, "Why me?" In an opposite way I had the same question: why had I been spared, and what did God have in store for me?

One of the things I realized out there all alone was how much family meant to me. Having faced death and been given another chance to live, I could see just how important those values and principles were that my parents had instilled in me, and of course how much I loved Barbara, the girl I knew I would marry.

As you grow older and try to retrace the steps that made you the person that you are, the signposts to look for are those special times of insight. I remember my days and nights aboard the Finback as one of those times — maybe the most important of them all.

In my own view there's got to be some kind of destiny and I was being spared for something on earth.

Many years after those Pacific nights, I interviewed former President Bush about the events of that tragic September day in 1944. When we finished, I was shutting my computer down and we were making idle conversation. Out of the blue, he asked me if I had any additional information about the fates of his crewmen, Ted White and John Delaney.

I was surprised by the question because I assumed it had been answered long before. If there was anything new to learn, surely the press would have dug it up during his four campaigns for vice president and president. But no one knew exactly what happened to Ted and John that day, only that they both died.

I told the president I had no additional information.

"It still plagues me if I gave those guys enough time to get out," he said with a pained grimace.

At that moment, I was looking into the eyes of arguably the most accomplished and successful man alive. George Herbert Walker Bush had led a storied life as an athlete, war hero, businessman, congressman, ambassador to the United Nations, ambassador to China, head of the CIA, vice president, president, and father of the current president. He had been in love with one woman since he was seventeen and they were approaching sixty years of marriage.

But in George Bush's eyes, I could see the same survivor's guilt — however illogical and unfounded — I had observed in other war veterans. I thought of my father, how he never got over the torture death of his buddy Ralph on Iwo Jima.

"I and everyone else thinks you did all you could, Mr. President," I said. "And I am sorry you had to be put into the position where you have these feelings still today."

For a few heartbeats we were both still. Then, as if to break the emotion of the moment, he uncrossed his legs, stood, and pushed his chair against the wall as I went back to putting my computer away.

I glanced up when he didn't walk back to his desk. He was standing at his large office window. His hands were in his pockets, causing his sport jacket to rumple a bit. The Texas sunlight illuminated President Bush's face.

Staring at the sky, the former Flyboy said, "I think about those guys all the time."

By February of 1945, the awesome might of the American military machine began the endgame of grinding Japan down to defeat. More than eight hundred American ships rendezvoused in Saipan to prepare for the invasion of Japan. Soon eighty thousand marines, my corpsman father, John Bradley, among them, would sail to invade Iwo Jima, the first Japanese soil upon which the barbarians' boots would tread.

As the Americans moved into the North Pacific in force, soldiers on Chichi Jima found themselves scurrying into their caves day and night for protection from marauding American planes. Lieutenant Mitsuyoshi Sasaki, who was a surgeon based on Chichi, later recalled the extreme conditions on that isolated island in February of 1945:

There were four to five raids during the day and two to three at night. There was no end to the number of casualties resulting from these raids. During the day there may be twenty or thirty people killed by bombings and also many people may be trapped in caves. The amount of sleep the soldiers could get at night was negligible.

The amount of ammunition was for just one battle in repelling the invasion forces. The amount of provisions was for several months. The amount of medical supplies was almost nothing.

In the sick bay there were many cases in which maggots came out of the wounds. Surgery was done in caves where there was a lot of dust.

Our supply route was cut. We would have to wait several months for supplies. The [daily] food ration was fifteen hundred calories, and every laborer was forced to work on this.

Together this physical and spiritual fatigue caused our power to dissolve and the work did not go ahead. The ability to work was getting lower. Everybody did not volunteer for work and they showed tendencies to try to keep from doing anything. The number of people arriving at the hospital showed many signs of strain. I had four or five people actually go mad; because of these the psychological aspects of the men on Chichi Jima were not normal.

One of those "not normal" men serving on Chichi Jima was a Major Sueo Matoba, commander of the 308th Battalion. Hard-drinking Major Matoba had been stationed in Singapore when the Japanese army mounted thousands of heads on roadside poles as a reminder of the fate awaiting any resisters. "The rumor was that he played a part in the capture of Singapore," said Captain Noboru Nakajima. "He often sang a song about the triumphal entry into Singapore. He spoke admiringly of the 3,000 Chinese heads put on display there." Later, he had participated in the Rape of China, during which he raped and killed women and beheaded prisoners.

One of the mythic heroes for Japanese officers like Matoba was Colonel Masanobu Tsuji. Tsuji had planned the blindingly successful invasion of Malaya and quickly become known as the "God of Strategy." It was Tsuji who had ordered the massacre of the Chinese in Singapore and that their heads be displayed on pikes. Tsuji was also known to boast that one of the secrets to his success was the "special medicine" he imbibed. This medicine was brewed from the livers of prisoners.

When I visited Chichi Jima years later, I sat crouched in Major Matoba's cave. About twenty yards deep and six feet high, chiseled out of hard volcanic rock, it looks out onto a beautiful beach. The contrast is dramatic. It is dank and dark in the cave, but you gaze out upon a postcard-worthy scene of brilliant sunlight, white sand, and gorgeous blue ocean. How many times Major Matoba must have sat in that darkness with his sake bottle, angry that he was unable to step out on that beach because of bombs falling from the Flyboys' planes. How often in his drunken stupor he must have dreamed of venting his impotent rage.

As the American juggernaut approached in February of 1945, General Kuribayashi told his men on Iwo Jima to "pray for a heroic fight."

But "praying" and "heroism" weren't macho enough sentiments for hard-drinking Spirit Warrior Tachibana on Chichi Jima. That month, he called his commanders together to deliver his version of a motivating *Yamato damashii* speech in preparation for the mass *gyokusai* death he expected of them.

"General Tachibana said that supplies would diminish and ammunition would run short," recalled Matoba, "and in the end men would have to fight even with rocks. He also said we would be forced even to eat our own comrades killed in combat, and the flesh of the enemy *kichiku* should be eaten."

Lieutenant Jitsuro Suyeyoshi also heard General Tachibana's speech and the specific reference as to how all captured Americans would be treated: "General Tachibana said that all POWs would be executed and their flesh would be eaten."

Some of the assembled officers thought this was just the general employing motivational hyperbole. But Major Matoba had experience in such matters and took him literally. As Matoba later admitted, eating the flesh of prisoners "was a practice I had grown fond of in China."

CHAPTER FOURTEEN

No Surrender

Meet the expectations of your family and home community by making effort upon effort, always mindful of the honor of your name. If alive, do not suffer the disgrace of becoming a prisoner; in death, do not leave behind a name soiled by misdeeds.

— *"Imperial Japanese Army Field Service Code"*

In the European war, Germany did not surrender until Allied troops invaded its heart. But Japan would be defeated by Flyboys. The beginning of the end for Japan came on February 16, 1945.

On that Friday morning, the largest and most powerful naval attack force ever assembled, with more than twelve hundred planes, launched the first carrier raid on Tokyo since Jimmy Doolittle's almost three years before.

It was a dangerous mission. Three days earlier, the air group commander on the USS *Randolph* had assembled all his Flyboys and announced, "Fellows, we're on our way to Tokyo." There was a moment of silence as the thought sunk in. Then the Flyboys broke out in loud cheers and applause. A moment later, a pilot turned to Bill Bruce and said, "My God, why am I clapping?"

That wintery day's weather was murky, cloudy, windy, rough, cold, and wet. Flyboys like Bill Hazlehurst and Floyd Hall now appreciated all the damp flying they had done in Oregon.

The strike force lifted off early, plane after plane aloft with clockwork precision. Gunner Robert Akerblom did not fly that day, but he listened for news of his buddies' progress. "Our ship piped a Japanese radio station through the loudspeakers," Robert said. "Our first wave was supposed to hit Tokyo at six A.M. At exactly six A.M. they went off the air. We cheered."

The Flyboys came in low, within antiaircraft range, and they took a beating. "Charlie Crommelin had over two hundred holes in his plane when he returned," remembered fighter pilot Alfred Bolduc. "He had fifty-four holes in one gas tank."

With so many planes over Tokyo that day, there were close calls. Fighter pilot M.W. Smith was strafing a train at an altitude of one hundred feet. "The fellow behind me shot his rocket right as I was going over that train," Smith recalled. "He shot three holes as big as fists in both of my wings."

The Japanese were surprised and unprepared. As a result, the carrier planes wreaked havoc on factories, shipyards, supply depots, and railroad yards. But bombing the Japanese mainland still brought a special terror. "We were scared," said Hazlehurst. "It was disconcerting bombing Japan in part because there wasn't open water to ditch in. You had to crash over land, and that meant you'd probably be captured."

Charlie Brown was caught when his two-seater SB2C Helldiver was shot down near Tokyo. "We were bombing a factory," he told me later. "We got hit; the engine was on fire. I saw a lake and made a water landing. As the plane was sinking, my crewman, J. D. Richards, was already in the life raft." A farmer in a rowboat came out. Charlie and J. D. got into his boat. When they reached shore, another farmer swung a club at Charlie's head. "If he had hit me," Charlie said, "he would have killed me." Some Japanese soldiers appeared with a thick rope. "Oh, my God!" thought J. D. "It's a lynching!" But the soldiers merely tied their prisoners together and marched them along a road. The procession would stop from time to time to allow women to beat the flyers with their *geta* — wooden shoes.

"Americans would be hitting just as hard if the situation was reversed," Charlie said with a chuckle years later. "Emotions run high in the immediate area; people get upset when they're bombed."

Eventually, the party made its way to a railroad station. His captors took Charlie outside and made him kneel in the dirt and lean forward. "I had seen the photo of the Australian pilot about to be beheaded," Charlie said. "Someone shoved me so my head was parallel with the ground. Then I heard sharp orders. I thought I was about to have my head cut off."

But Charlie Brown would live to see another day.

Because the weather worsened around Tokyo on February 17, the carrier force headed south to pound Iwo Jima. Then they sailed to bomb Chichi Jima the next day.

On a cold Sunday morning, February 18, five Flyboys awoke ready to tackle their first combat missions. This was the day they had prepared for. In the month they had been at sea, they had had plenty of time to think about what that first taste of combat would be like. Now they were about to learn.

On the USS *Randolph,* pilot Floyd Hall would wing into action with his gunner, Glenn Frazier, and his radioman, Marve Mershon. On the nearby USS *Bennington,* radioman Jimmy Dye and gunner Grady York readied for their flight. Jimmy, Glenn, Marve, and Grady were all just nineteen years old. Floyd must have been one of the "old men" to them, because he was already twenty-four.

The boys were briefed on the day's target, the airfields and radio stations on Chichi Jima. "Chichi Jima was a *mean* place," said pilot Phil Perabo. "They had very good gunners there. When you hit Chichi, you were hitting a valley between two mountains."

Fellow pilots Leland Holdren and Fred Rohlfing would fly into battle with Floyd that day. "Floyd, Fred, and I were a division of three," Leland told me decades later. "This strike on Chichi was our first time in battle. We were greenhorns. You can imagine our anxiety."

The winter sun did not rise until 7:12 A.M. on the morning of February 18, 1945. The USS *Randolph* began launching her planes at 10:54 A.M. The plane carrying Floyd, Glenn, and Marve was in the last group and launched after noon. They flew off into rainy, overcast skies.

Over on the USS *Bennington,* Jimmy Dye and Grady York were in their ready room being briefed on the same target. They would fly that day with pilot Bob King. "Our mission that day," remembered Ralph Sengewalt, "was to bomb Chichi Jima's small airstrip. They said we'd have limited opposition."

February 18 in the Pacific was February 17 back home, and it marked two years to the day since Jimmy had enlisted. "We hadn't been in cold climates until then," Vince Carnazza remembered. "I had a black navy-issue sweater and Jimmy asked if he could borrow it. I gave it to him and said, 'If I don't get that sweater back, it's your ass.'"

As they were headed out the door, Jimmy did something that Ralph Sengewalt will never forget. "Jimmy stopped at the door," Ralph told me, "turned around, and with a smile, tossed his wallet to someone who was remaining behind. As he did it he called out, 'Just in case I don't come back, see to it that my mom and dad get this.'"

Kidding was one thing, but Flyboys almost never spoke so directly about death.

"When Jimmy said that," Ralph recalled, "I had a strange feeling then and there. We never talked about not coming back."

The assault two days earlier on Tokyo had been considered dangerous, but that day's strike against Chichi Jima was anticipated to be relatively easy, a "milk run." That's why so many of the inexperienced airmen, like Bob King, Jimmy, and Grady, were heading out. But Jimmy must have had a sixth sense about the danger that awaited him. And radioman Ken Meredith learned that Grady had had his qualms too.

"When Grady and I shook hands on the flight deck," Ken recalled, "he said, 'I'm really scared.' Grady always smiled when he talked. But at that moment he wasn't smiling. Just then I felt Grady had a premonition. Even at that young age, I could feel it."

Jimmy had tossed his wallet, but he did keep something for good luck that day. His girlfriend, Gloria Nields, later told me: "In the last letter I got from Jimmy he wrote, 'I am flying off now with your white scarf on.'"

With that, the three American boys took off in their Avenger, pilot King, radioman Jimmy, and gunner Grady. Two of the three had signaled that this flight held special danger for them. King, also on his first combat flight, had not expressed any qualms. Only one of them would return.

The briefers had been wrong. The antiaircraft opposition was fierce that day.

"The antiaircraft fire was very heavy and very accurate," said gunner William Hale. "There was black smoke everywhere, and we were getting bounced around with the concussion of the shells. I was facing aft with a pair of machine guns in my hands, looking for something to shoot at and wishing we could get the hell out of there."

"It was overcast over the island," remembered pilot Dan Samuelson. "There was a hole in the clouds. A lot of the planes were going through that hole, and the Japanese gunners just plugged that hole with antiaircraft fire."

One after another, the carrier pilots made their glide-bombing runs over Chichi Jima. Pilots Leland Holdren, Fred Rohlfing, and Floyd Hall — the "division of three" — circled above, waiting their turn.

"The most dangerous time is when you're just hanging out, going slow," said Robert Akerblom. "Once you're in the dive, you feel the speed and it relieves the tension."

"We had to keep circling until the others made their dives," Leland Holdren said. "As you circle, you fly away from the optimum point from which to make your dive. If you dive relatively straight down over the target, you go in fast. But we were circling wide, and when it came time to make our dives, we dove in a less severe angle and didn't generate as much speed as the guys before us."

Leland began his dive into the flak with Fred Rohlfing and Floyd following behind. "When the antiaircraft fire comes up," said fighter pilot Alfred Bolduc, "you see little red dots. When they get closer, they're about the size of a baseball bat diameter. They're coming at you by the hundreds."

Two of those hundreds of red dots found their mark: Both Fred's and Floyd's planes were hit. Rohlfing's Avenger burst into flame and he, radioman Carrol Hall, and gunner Joe Notary never made it out.

Floyd's plane did not catch fire, but it was fatally damaged and it was all he could do to make a safe water landing. Leland had flown off at the completion of his run, and since Floyd's was the last plane, no one saw him or his crew land in the water. Letters from the navy to the parents of the three downed boys would later say that the probability of their having survived the landing "was extremely low."

But Floyd, Marve, and Glenn made it out of the plane safely and inflated their Mae Wests. They were wet, cold, and scared, but they were alive. They had landed between Chichi Jima and Ani Jima, a small uninhabited spit of land hardly big enough to have its own name. For some reason, Glenn split off from the other two and made his way to Ani Jima, while Floyd and Marve swam to Chichi Jima.

Floyd and Marve were now in the same general area that George Bush had found himself in six months earlier, though George had landed a bit farther out. Soldiers standing on the same cliffs where Nobuaki Iwatake had observed George's rescue now saw Floyd and Marve in the water. Fisherman Maikawa Fukuichiro and Warrant Officer Saburo Soya were told to bring the Americans in. They paddled out about a hundred yards and found Floyd and Marve in the frigid water, "almost half paralyzed and . . . on the point of sinking," as Fukuichiro later recalled. "Their lips were blue and they looked cold."

On the beach, the boys were allowed to warm themselves by a fire. Floyd was dressed in his one-piece flight suit and Marve was down to his white woolen long johns. Warrant Officer Soya told Fukuichiro to phone the headquarters of the 308th Battalion. The officer on the other end of the line ordered the flyers brought to the 308th, which would get credit for their capture.

At the 308th Battalion headquarters, the soldiers searched the prisoners and relieved Floyd of his pistol and Marve of his survival knife. These trophies were dispatched to Major Matoba.

But soon everyone on the island had to take cover once again. More waves of Flyboys were approaching. Floyd and Marve were bundled into an air-raid shelter.

Major Matoba retreated to his cave. As the falling bombs exploded in the sunshine outside, Matoba examined Floyd's pistol and Marve's knife. In the blackness, the major ran his hands over the Flyboys' possessions as he drank and thought.

The swarms of carrier planes kept the island hopping that day.

"The February eighteenth raids were the fiercest air raids we experienced," said antiaircraft gunner Usaki. "During the day about a thousand planes raided the island. As antiaircraft personnel, we were almost always at our battle stations and at night we also had to go to battle stations. We were very tired and every chance we got we slept in the quarters but stayed on the alert."

The gunners were tired but dedicated. "We often had to eat our meals at our positions," said Lieutenant Jitsuro Suyeyoshi. To the Flyboys, it seemed the emperor's gunners didn't pause for a bite. "There was so much flak, you could walk on it," said Robert Akerblom. Ralph Senge-walt added, "It looked like every tree on the island was firing at us."

And still the Flyboys came. Pilot Jesse Naul was flying behind Bob Cosbie's plane, which in turn was to the right of Bob King's Avenger, with Jimmy Dye and Grady York aboard. Jesse later told me what happened:

We came in at about nine thousand feet and we were getting ready to go into our dive. I was behind Cosbie's plane. Suddenly, antiaircraft fire shot Cosbie's right wing off. His plane went into a clockwise spin, spinning clockwise down toward the right, where his wing had been.

Cosbie's plane flipped upside down and went sideways. It slammed into King's plane. Cosbie's left wing hit King's plane between the turret and the vertical stabilizer. At the same time, Cosbie's propeller hit King's left wing and chewed off four feet of it.

King's plane then went into a spin. King thought they would crash, so he told his crew to bail out. Jimmy and Grady bailed out. My crew yelled, "We see two chutes."

King had his seat belt off, fixing to bail out, and to his surprise, he got the plane straight. He "caught it," meaning he caught the spin and righted the plane. He kept flying.

As Grady and Jimmy bailed out, Cosbie's Avenger went into a fatal spin. Cosbie, gunner Lou Gerig, and radioman Gil Reynolds never made it out. Jesse Naul speculated on what their last minutes might have been like:

Cosbie went into his spin at nine to ten thousand. His plane just spun and spun. Let's say they were all alive when the plane went into that spin. Even though they were healthy American males, the centrifugal force would have pinned them to the walls and they wouldn't have been able to get out.

If they were conscious, they knew what was happening and were fighting to get out. They'd be trying to unhook their seat belts and pop the doors off, but they wouldn't have been able to get out of their seats.

When a loaded seventeen-thousand-pound plane is spinning, it creates a lot of force. It's like a saucer at an amusement park that is spinning and pinning you back. It's the same thing. The force of the spin would force them to remain in the position they were in when they started going down. Finally, they smacked into the water and that was it.

Jimmy and Grady floated down in the midst of exploding shells. "Their chutes were surrounded by antiaircraft bursts," recalled Joe Bonn. "I dismissed them as shot up, dead." But amazingly, the two crewmen landed safely just off shore.

"We flew down to drop them a life raft," Ralph Sengewalt said, "but we didn't drop it because we could see Jimmy and Grady in knee-deep water, walking toward the shore. We thought they'd be prisoners and they'd be safe — at least that was our hope."

Now there were four Flyboys in Japanese hands on Chichi Jima — Floyd Hall, Marve Mershon, Jimmy Dye, and Grady York. Glenn Frazier was huddled in the bushes across the channel on uninhabited Ani Jima.

Floyd and Marve were held at the 308th Battalion headquarters for the rest of the day and overnight. Jimmy and Grady were captured by the 275th Battalion and taken to General Tachibana's headquarters.

Captain Kimitomi Nishiyotsutsuji remembered that General Tachibana encouraged anyone who wanted to beat the two bound nineteen-year-olds to do so. The general further warned that anyone who protected the boys by putting them in an air-raid shelter, or was lenient with them in any way, would face his wrath.

The next day, Monday, February 19, Jimmy and Grady were taken to Major Yoshitaka Horie's headquarters. Major Horie could speak some English and he interrogated them. Glenn remained hidden in the bushes on Ani Jima. At night he must have shivered in the winter cold. He had a canteen full of water, no food, and only a little hope.

Early in the morning of the nineteenth, Floyd and Marve were taken from the 308th Battalion to General Tachibana's headquarters, with a stop to visit Lieutenant Jitsuro Suyeyoshi's regiment. Suyeyoshi and the 308th both had a claim on the prisoners and they would later discuss who got to kill which one.

Floyd and Marve were tied up outside a guardhouse for three and one half hours, from 6:30 A.M. to 10:00 A.M. There, anyone who wanted to absorb some *Yamato damashii* kicked and slapped the two defenseless boys.

Lieutenant Suyeyoshi admired the way the two Flyboys stoically endured their punishment. He ordered his men to assemble in front of the prisoners. "I offered them a drink of whiskey from my hip flask and a cigarette," Suyeyoshi said, "and then I turned around to the enlisted men in the crowd and told them, 'These two flyers were working for their country and they are brave men, and I expect all of you to take an example from them.'"

But respect did not mean mercy. American bombs had killed some of Suyeyoshi's men the day before and he wanted revenge. Later that afternoon, Suyeyoshi spoke to Matoba about the casualties and the major promised retribution. "Lieutenant Suyeyoshi wanted a flyer to execute in order to show his men that they were personally responsible for shooting down a plane or a flyer, and to give them more fighting spirit and to build morale," Matoba said.

Floyd and Marve were loaded back into a truck and taken to Tachibana's headquarters so the general could get a few licks in. But before he had a chance, an air-raid siren sounded and Tachibana turned to scurry to his protective cave. One soldier moved toward Floyd and Marve to untie them and bring them into a shelter. General Tachibana noticed and barked, "Why are you fooling around there? We do not care if they die or not."

Later that day, Floyd and Marve were moved to Major Horie's headquarters for interrogation, where they joined Jimmy and Grady. Floyd and Marve had flown off the USS *Randolph,* Jimmy and Grady belonged to the USS *Bennington.* Here they would meet for the first time, tied up and watched by guards. They were four *kichiku* in Japanese hands — four Flyboys in big trouble.

After Jimmy and Grady had bailed out of their plane, pilot Bob King had flown back to the carrier at an altitude of one thousand feet accompanied by other squadron planes. All who saw the plane airborne with most of its left wing missing were amazed. And there was more. The back of the plane was bent where Cosbie's nose had struck. "Like a playing card bent in half," Jesse Naul said later. "It was bent in the middle and drooped."

"We told him his landing gear wouldn't work, that he shouldn't even try," Jesse said. "We told him he'd have to make a water landing." King smacked his plane down on the ocean, bending it with the impact.

"I tossed King a life raft," said Robert Akerblom. "I opened the door, holding it. 'Now,' my pilot yelled."

King had taken a bad jolt when he hit the water and spent the night in sick bay, but he was alive — more than alive: He returned to flying the next day. But the young pilot was a changed man.

"King was the most heartbroken man I ever saw in my life," Ralph Sengewalt told me. "He lost two men and lived. He didn't say much. I think he never really recovered from that flight, he was so moved. We knew what he went through; no one blamed him. What he did was almost miraculous."

"All he'd say was, 'I had my seat belt off,'" Jesse Naul remembered. "Everybody would have done the same thing. King gave Jimmy and Grady an opportunity to get out. He was looking out for his guys like he was supposed to. He was ready to bail when the plane righted. He was surprised when it did. He had his seat belt off, ready to jump."

Back on the USS *Randolph,* the surviving Flyboys mourned the loss of their three buddies.

"When someone was gone," said Bill Hazlehurst, "they were just gone. There were no questions, no discussion, and no speculation. It was really bad for me when Floyd didn't return. Really bad."

"The planes and the people just disappeared," flight commander Tex Ellison told me years later. "There was no ceremony; there isn't much you can do. When there are no remains, all you can do is bundle up their personal effects and send them on."

Enlisted friends of Glenn and Marve boxed and labeled their belongings. Bill Hazlehurst and Joe White, who had spent so many "hellacious weekends" with Floyd, were assigned to pack his things.

"We spent a morning going through Floyd's stuff in a meticulous fashion," Bill told me. "We folded everything neatly. We tossed some pictures of him in nightclubs with girls that we didn't think appropriate to send on."

Floyd's parents would later receive his belongings in the mail with a memo dated March 7, 1945, that inventoried their son's last possessions. They were "cuff links, Kodak camera, eversharp pencil, Naval Aviator certificate, Kodak pictures, sewing kit, fishing gear, leather wallet, shoe shine kit, razor, shaving brush, and leather slippers."

I asked Bill Hazlehurst if he and Joe White commented on Floyd's premonition that he would not come back from battle in the Pacific.

Floyd had told them of his belief back in California, when he stopped going out with his buddies and decided to live with one woman.

"Later we talked about it a lot," Bill said, "but not that day. That day we just consoled each other over our lost buddy and said, 'What a goddamn shame that a nice guy like Floyd had to bite the dust.'"

Flyboys also felt loss over on the USS *Bennington.*

"It was at the debriefing that it all came together," said Ken Meredith. "We went back to the ready room. The guys who aren't there, the empty chairs — those are the guys who didn't come back. I made a statement about what I saw to the air combat intelligence officer. As the debriefing went on, a total picture was developed. Then we realized Grady and Jimmy were gone."

"The planes didn't come back," said radioman Bob Martin. "There was nothing you could do. That's the way it was; it could happen to anyone. We just all figured our time would come."

Ken Meredith was chosen to sort Grady York's things. "I didn't have to throw anything of Grady's away," said his buddy. The boy whose worst epithet was "skillyboo" had nothing that his mother couldn't see.

The entire island of Iwo Jima is only five miles long. At its southern tip is Mount Suribachi, a dormant volcano approximately 555 feet high — almost exactly as tall as the Washington Monument. It is a "mount" rather than a mountain.

Standing atop Mount Suribachi, gazing at the invasion beach below, one is struck by how intimate the killing here was back in 1945. When American boys landed on that beach, the Japanese holed up in Mount Suribachi could not only see them, but were close enough to make out the insignia patches on their arms. The Marines were ducks in a shooting gallery, walking into preregistered firing patterns that had been rehearsed for months.

Easy Company, my father's unit, landed on the sands of Iwo Jima just five to six hundred yards from Mount Suribachi. My navy corpsman dad was teamed with the finest amphibious assault warriors of WWII. Yet it took four days of hellish fighting for these tough and motivated Marines to crawl just a few hundred yards. The rocky terrain from the beach to the mountain was slathered with American blood.

The reason Iwo Jima was worth such horrific sacrifice involved the Flyboys.

The Pacific war was fought over the largest theater in the history of warfare. Islands — sometimes spits of sand or hard, unforgiving rocks like Iwo Jima — determined America's strategy. The Marianas — Guam, Tinian, and Saipan — provided the long airfields needed for the B-29s to bring the war to the island of Japan.

The B-29s were the long-haul truckers of America's air fleet. They were ninety-nine feet long and fit ten men comfortably. The biggest obstacle a B-29 pilot faced on his bombing run from the Marianas to Japan was presented by Iwo Jima. Lying in the direct path to Japan, the island was almost exactly halfway between the Marianas and Japan and boasted two airstrips and a radar station. As the B-29 Superfortresses approached Iwo, that radar station gave mainland defenders a two-hour early warning. There were additional risks. Although American pilots had established overall superiority in the Pacific, the gigantic B-29s lumbering north to attack the empire made easy targets for Japan's remaining small, quick Iwo-based fighter planes. Then, after enduring antiaircraft fire and dogfights over Japan, the B-29s, often damaged, would again be forced to face the Iwo-based fighters on their return trip. Too many pilots and crew were being lost to watery graves. General Curtis LeMay, commander of the Twentieth Air Force, warned that his pilots could not sustain these losses much longer. Iwo Jima would have to be eliminated as a threat for the Flyboys to effect the downfall of Japan.

The Joint Chiefs gave the job of conquering the island to America's oldest fighting force, the United States Marines. There were plenty of army soldiers in the theater, but only Marines could take a citadel like Iwo. As noted historian Stephen Ambrose wrote, "The Marines were the best fighting men of World War II." Approximately 70,000 leathernecks trained for the invasion of Iwo Jima for almost a year. (My dad's company practiced the invasion on Iwo-like volcanic terrain on the "Big Island" of Hawaii. They even found a Mount Suribachi "look-alike" there and scaled its rocky sides.)

Flyboys bombed Iwo Jima for seventy-two straight days before the February 19 invasion. After the war, navy analysts declared the tiny island the single most intensely bombed spot of the Pacific war. Two thousand seven hundred sorties dropped 5,800 *tons* (11,400,000 pounds) of bombs. In one square mile of Iwo Jima, U.S. aerial photographs revealed 5,000 bomb craters. Admiral Nimitz thought American forces were dropping bombs "sufficient to pulverize everything on the island." Meanwhile, a vast American armada of 880 ships forming a line seventy miles long sailed in. Those ships, carrying a total of 110,000 men, eventually surrounded Iwo Jima.

The vast wealth and power of the United States were obvious from the fact that 1,322 pounds of supplies backed up each of the 70,000 assault troop Marines at Iwo. The armada hauled enough food to keep the city of Atlanta going for a month. They were Marines, so they packed a hundred million cigarettes.

All this for a tiny speck of cooled lava in the middle of the vast Pacific. Driving your car on the highway, it takes just five minutes to go five miles. It took the slogging, dying Marines thirty-six days to conquer the same distance. The beaches of Normandy were safe enough to have a tea party there less than twenty-four hours into the battle. Yet on Iwo Jima, with a landing beach only two miles long, an area of battle much more compact than that of Normandy, American boys died on the beach for weeks.

The terror of Iwo Jima was that one side was not fighting for victory. The Japanese knew in advance that they were going to lose. They were not even fighting for survival. General Kuribayashi composed orders he called "Sacred Battle Vows" and ordered them posted in every blockhouse, cavern, and cave. He didn't write, "Kill ten Americans for victory," or "Kill ten Americans and we have a chance." He wrote, "Kill ten Americans *before you die.*"

Fighting on Iwo Jima was like being confronted in your garage at night by an attacker who will not stop if you stab him, who will keep on coming if you shoot him, who will grab you by the throat with his left hand if you cut his right hand off, an attacker you can mangle but who will still crawl malevolently toward you with his last ounce of life. Kei Kanai, a POW captured unconscious on Iwo Jima, told me of the advice his schoolteacher had given him about going into battle: "My teacher told me that even if I had no arms or legs on my body and had only my mouth left, I was to spit at the enemy."

Knowing they would die, the Japanese went underground and became "cave kamikaze" to cause maximum casualties. They dug sixteen miles of tunnels on a five-mile-long island. These tunnels with their shellacked walls were large enough for troops to run through standing up and they boasted electric lights to illuminate the way. Japanese engineers had constructed a multilayered military city far below the island's surface. General Kuribayashi's command post was seventy-five feet under ground. The island's hospital was forty-six feet under ground, its beds carved into the walls. The whole of Mount Suribachi had been hollowed out into a fantastical seven-story subterranean world, fortified with concrete revetments and finished off with plastered walls, a sewer system, and conduits for fresh air, electricity, water, and steam. Japanese soldiers armed with guns of every conceivable size and design filled the rooms and tunnels.

Before the Marines ascended Mount Suribachi on February 23, navy and Marine carrier planes zoomed in to soften it up. "They dropped napalm for an hour and a half," Marine Don Howell told me years later. "Suribachi was a wall of flame from top to bottom."

Napalm was invented by Harvard president James Conant, and scientists at MIT, DuPont, and Standard Oil. They found that mixing naphthenic and palmitic acids (hence na-palm) with gasoline produced a sticky Vaseline-like yellow paste that stuck to materials and burned slowly. It was a perfect incendiary. This jellied gasoline would stick to anything — roofs, walls, humans — and it could not be put out. Water only splattered it. If a glob landed on the back of your hand, it would burn until it consumed itself. If you patted the burning napalm in an attempt to extinguish it, the result would be scorched fingers and a burned hand.

"The pilots were dropping napalm jelly around the side of the top cone of the mountain," said Howell. "That napalm would run down the side of the mountain. The whole thing was aflame. The planes toasted Suribachi before we walked up. We wondered how anyone could live through that."

Don Howell, climbing just ahead of my dad, peered into some of the caves. He saw Japanese soldiers who were alive but hardly moving. "They sat there looking stunned, dazed, like they were all drunked up," he said. "Their eyes were open, but they were lethargic, not even reaching for their rifles. They were dressed well in uniforms, but they were laid back, like they were in a stupor."

Contrary to later garbled press reports and John Wayne's celluloid heroism in *Sands of Iwo Jima,* not one Japanese bullet was fired at the forty boys who first ascended Mount Suribachi. Not one Japanese leaped out with a sword to attack the Marines. No Japanese grenades were tossed.

"We were tense," said Robert Leader, "thinking the enemy would suddenly jump out, or one of us would step on a mine. But it was completely quiet. Not a shot was fired. It took us about forty minutes to get to the top."

No one knows exactly why the tenacious Suribachi defenders did not lash out one last time. None of the stunned Japanese soldiers in the caves lived to later tell their tale. ("You didn't give them a chance," Howell told me. "You just shot them or threw in a hand grenade.") But the most probable reason is that the Flyboy rain of napalm fire had sucked the oxygen out of the mountain, suffocating the Japanese inside to death, or at least into the stuporous state Don Howell described.

The photo of the flag raising on Iwo Jima would win a permanent place in the world's heart and go on to become the single most reproduced image in the history of photography. But until now, almost no one knew that at about the same time Indian Ira Hayes was helping to raise that flag on Iwo Jima, another Indian Marine was in trouble 150 miles away.

Earlier in the week, Marine Lieutenant Warren Earl Vaughn had been waiting on a destroyer as part of a replacement pool of pilots. When the USS *Bennington* — Jimmy Dye's and Grady York's carrier — asked for pilots to replace their losses, Warren Earl was sent over. He flew air patrols over the carriers on February 20, 21, and 22. The February 23 strike against Chichi Jima was his first combat flight.

Archie Clapp flew behind Warren Earl that day. "It was a terrible target for us," Archie told me. "Because of the intense antiaircraft fire, it was like coming down the rails at a carnival with you as the sitting duck. Vaughn's plane got hit. His wing was clipped off. When I flew over the target, I could see him going down in a chute. When he hit the water, he swam toward shore."

Warren Earl's actions after being hit were normal for a *gaizin.* He bailed out of his Corsair, opened his parachute, and then swam ashore to avoid dying quickly of hypothermia in the chilly North Pacific waters. But to his soon-to-be captors watching him swim into their grasp, Warren Earl had disgraced himself by saving his own life.

And Warren Earl's captors were not hypocrites. They didn't think he should die only because he was an American. They weren't the type to kill a POW and then beg for their own lives. Honorable warriors should never become prisoners, they believed.

Back on Iwo Jima, friends of the men who captured Warren Earl were demonstrating this code of honor with their lives.

After the first flag was raised on Iwo Jima, Don Howell, who would later be awarded a Navy Cross for heroism, went inside Mount Suribachi's rim to check for Japanese caves:

We were scouting quietly with our rifles ready. Suddenly, a Japanese emerged from a cave. He had a rifle in his hands, but it wasn't pointed at us. He was just carrying it by his side with no intention of shooting us. He came out screaming like a wild man, squawking. He must have known we'd shoot if he screamed like that. If he had come out quietly without a weapon, with his hands up, we would have taken him prisoner. We dropped him.

Others came out. They came out one at a time, disorganized. We did not encounter any organized resistance. They were like wild men running around with rifles or swords. They were announcing their presence. They knew it was the end, their suicide. They wanted to go to their happy hunting grounds by dying for their country.

That's the way they were. Nobody could understand them.

Just as back on Chichi Jima, nobody could understand Warren Earl's desire to live. A soldier's duty was to die and never surrender. War, the Japanese knew, was about victory or death.

It was a lesson the Cherokee in No Mans Land would soon be taught.

CHAPTER FIFTEEN

Kichiku

It is better not to have persons on Chichi Jima, even if they do good, if they disobey orders. My policy is to execute all persons who do not obey orders.

— *Captain Shizuo Yoshii, Guam War Crimes Trial, 1946*

As Associated Press photographer Joe Rosenthal's camera shutter immortalized six boys raising Old Glory on February 23, 1945, Warren Earl Vaughn parachuted into the water 150 miles north of Mount Suribachi. He landed near a cliff, where Private Yukutaro Ishiwata of the 307th Battalion tossed him a rope and pulled him out of the water. The soldiers gave him a cigarette and allowed him to warm up by their fire.

Now there were two pilots — Warren Earl Vaughn and Floyd Hall — and three enlisted men — Jimmy Dye, Marve Mershon, and Grady York — in custody on Chichi Jima. Glenn Frazier remained hidden on Ani Jima.

The soldier who escorted Warren Earl to General Tachibana's headquarters described his prisoner as "an officer, over six feet tall, very handsome, medium dark complexion with long brown hair." Another soldier also described the prisoner: "His skin, as an American, was very dark, and he had a very furious look on his face. He was tall and his body was strongly built."

When Warren Earl arrived at Tachibana's headquarters, the general had already decided some fates. Floyd Hall, Jimmy Dye, Marve Mershon, and Grady York had spent the last five days at Major Horie's headquarters being interrogated. Now things were about to change.

"General Tachibana said that all flyers would be executed as soon as Major Horie was through with them," Major Matoba recalled. The enlisted men — Jimmy, Grady, and Marve — would go first.

Jimmy and Grady were sent to Tachibana's headquarters, where they would spend three days tied to trees with Warren Earl. Marve was dispatched to Major Matoba's 308th Battalion headquarters. "The feeling of hatred was running very high in the 308th Battalion and at General Tachibana's headquarters," admitted Major Horie.

After the fierce bombing raids of February 18, Major Matoba had promised Lieutenant Suyeyoshi that he could execute a prisoner. Now the major kept his word. Marve, clad only in his white long johns, was moved from Matoba's headquarters to Lieutenant Suyeyoshi's. There he awaited his fate tied to a tree.

February 23 was the fifth day of the battle for Iwo Jima. The United States had no intention of invading Chichi Jima — taking out the radio station and interrupting the shipping lines was all the U.S. planned to do. But the Japanese didn't know that. Given Chichi Jima's location as the next island on the way to the mainland, it was natural to assume the Americans would arrive there any moment now. "We thought we were the next to die," said Lieutenant Minoru Hayashi. Thus, the Japanese soldiers on Chichi were like prisoners in a holding cell, hearing friends being tortured in the next room, awaiting their own turn. A Lieutenant Wantanabe later recalled the mood of the men:

> The despair of the soldiers was very great. Most of the personnel thought that after the fall of Iwo Jima, the enemy would come to Chichi Jima.
>
> The air raids were very frequent and especially during February it was most fierce. During the day we were attacked by rockets and strafing, and they did a very thorough job. At night they dropped time bombs, and during the daytime as the planes came strafing, we could not be too careful. At night when an air raid sounded, we had to take shelter in the air raid shelter so we could only sleep about two hours.
>
> Concerning provisions, the supply route to Japan was cut. All the units

were cut down on their rations and because of this they were using all sorts of edible grass, snails, et cetera, to supplement their diet.

Because of these reasons the troops were suffering from something like a nervous breakdown.

At one point, Lieutenant Suyeyoshi gathered his soldiers around the prisoner. He gave Marve a swig of whiskey and a cigarette. Then he turned to the assembled soldiers and said, "We are very tired from fighting air raids every day, building positions and working hard. The prisoner is also tired and war is hard on both sides. We have fought very courageously up to now on Chichi Jima. This prisoner has come through a sheet of bullets. Even as an enemy he is courageous. He has shed no tears."

Even though he had requested a prisoner to execute, for some reason Lieutenant Suyeyoshi did not take this opportunity to make Marve's beheading a public spectacle. The lieutenant simply ordered Lieutenant Hironobu Morishita to "dispose" of the prisoner. Morishita decided that the island's cemetery was the best place to do the deed and late in the afternoon he assembled a crew.

"There was an order for a working party to fall out," a soldier named Iwakawa later testified. "So I took a shovel and went to the cemetery. I was told to dig a hole."

There is no record of what Marve was told about his forthcoming fate, but he must have assumed he was about to die. He walked along the road with his hands tied, accompanied by a party of soldiers carrying shovels. A samurai sword dangled from Lieutenant Morishita's side.

As Marve was walking to the cemetery, his gunner, Glenn Frazier, arrived at Major Matoba's 308th Battalion headquarters with a bag of biscuits.

Earlier that day, Glenn had awoken on Ani Jima, his fifth morning on the tiny uninhabited island. He had his canteen with him and still had a little water left, but he had had no food since the February 18 breakfast aboard the USS *Bennington*. He decided he couldn't go on.

Glenn normally weighed 110 pounds, but by now the nineteen-year-old boy must have been well under 100 as a result of the lack of food and dehydration. He saw two fishermen, Maikawa Fukuichiro and Tsutomu Yamada, out in the strait between Chichi Jima and Ani Jima. Fukuichiro was one of the men who had pulled Glenn's buddies

Floyd Hall and Marve Mershon out of the water when Glenn swam the other way.

When American planes had appeared overhead that morning, the two fishermen paddled to nearby Ani Jima, beached their craft, and hid behind some rocks. When the air raid was finished, they shoved off again. Then they heard someone calling from the beach.

The two men turned and saw Glenn walk out from behind some bushes with his hands up. He pointed to his mouth in a gesture the fishermen understood meant he was hungry.

"I yelled, 'Come here,'" recalled Fukuichiro. "The flyer walked out on the pier. We thought that the flyer wouldn't shoot us, so we paddled back and Yamada put the flyer in the canoe." Fukuichiro was "amazed at how small he was. The flyer was a very small man, so that Yamada did not have much trouble with him."

Glenn was wearing a reddish-brown leather jacket with a fur collar, blue dungarees, brown boots, and a blue shirt. He wore a silver ring and had his survival knife on his belt and carried his canteen. Fukuichiro described Glenn as having "fiery red" hair.

In the boat, Glenn, using hand signals, asked for food. The fishermen had none but offered him some raw squid, which Glenn refused. When they beached on Chichi, the fishermen took Glenn to their nearby fishing shack, where they gave him some biscuits and water. Glenn slipped off his ring and gave it to Fukuichiro-san in gratitude for the biscuits he was hungrily devouring. Fukuichiro remembered, "The flyer was crying, he was so thankful.

"As soon as I gave the flyer biscuits," Fukuichiro said, "he was eating them so fast that I could not find out anything. His mouth was full all the time."

Orders soon arrived to deliver Glenn to the 308th Battalion headquarters. A truck came to get him.

At the 308th headquarters, Captain Yoshikaru Kanmuri took charge. Glenn was in such an obviously weakened state that his captors didn't even bother to tie him up. Instead, they just left him on a mat in front of the guardhouse.

Major Matoba was hosting a conference of his commanders in the headquarters building that day. The "conference" consisted of Spirit Warrior officers feasting and drinking themselves silly while the enlisted men hacked out caves on meager rations.

Matoba and his fellow revelers had already been imbibing for three hours when, at 4 P.M., they were told that an American prisoner was outside. Prisoners were supposed to proceed to General Tachibana's headquarters, but this would have interrupted the party, so Matoba ordered Glenn held until the next morning.

One of the officers swigging sake with Major Matoba was Captain Noboru Nakajima, a notoriously violent drunk. Nakajima was well-known for always carrying a club to beat his soldiers. The weapon was about three feet long and one inch thick, made from the core of a tree, so it was dense and heavy, like a billy club. Many Japanese soldiers had felt its crunching impact.

As the afternoon wore on and the sake flowed, Captain Nakajima became so obviously inebriated that even Major Matoba scolded him for overdrinking. Nakajima got up from his table in a huff, grabbed his club, and stormed out of the party around 6 P.M.

Captain Kesakichi Sato was interrogating Glenn in a nearby building. Captain Nakajima approached.

"He was very drunk," recalled Corpsman Kanemori, who was one of approximately ten soldiers on the scene. "When Nakajima gets drunk he is like a madman. It is impossible to stop him. Therefore, when he approached us, we drew back."

Captain Nakajima barked questions at Glenn. The boy not only didn't understand a word of Japanese, he must have been terrified and probably confused. His withered body was just now digesting its first food in days and he had been knocked to the ground by Captain Sato's blows several times.

"I stuck out my arms," Nakajima later testified, "and tried to ask how many big and small airplanes were around Iwo Jima, and how many planes crashed and were shot down." The drunken captain, who wasn't using an interpreter, said he expected Glenn to answer his questions "by signs."

When the disoriented nineteen-year-old Kansan wasn't quick enough with answers for his growling, inebriated interrogator, Nakajima lashed out. "Captain Nakajima started to beat the prisoner with his club," Kanemori remembered. Glenn was seated in a chair when Nakajima first struck him. The heavy blows drew blood. Glenn absorbed three whacks and then fell backward onto the floor. He groaned as the thick club cracked his skull. Ten blows left Glenn's face and head a bloody pulp and Nakajima panting.

Later, the captain informed Major Matoba that he had beaten the prisoner to death. "Major Matoba told me that by rights he should kill me for killing the flyer," Nakajima said. But it wasn't the loss of a life that concerned the major. "Major Matoba said he should kill me because I killed the flyer before they could extract any information from him, and not just because I killed the flyer."

Soldiers dug a hole nearby and placed Glenn's blood-soaked, emaciated body in it. They buried him with his canteen. There was no marker, and no one even bothered to record his name in a report. Glenn was always referred to as just "the prisoner" or "the flyer."

"I did not know the name of the prisoner," Captain Nakajima later admitted. "I didn't take the trouble to find out. I did not even ask the name of the flyer that I beat to death."

At dusk, just after Glenn was killed, his radioman, Marve Mershon, reached his final resting place. The cemetery was up a small rise from the main road. Lieutenant Morishita paused at the side of the road with his prisoner. The men with shovels proceeded up to the cemetery. After a few minutes, Morishita then led Marve up the small hill.

Years later, I trod that same path. One can sense the unmistakable stillness of a cemetery. The canopy of overhanging trees must have darkened the dusk. In just a few steps up the hill, grave markers become visible. The stone sentries are tall and narrow, different than squat American tombstones, but Marve would have recognized it as a cemetery. And there was a freshly dug grave.

Lieutenant Morishita gave Marve a cigarette as they stood beside the new hole. Marve remained calm and smoked quietly.

Radioman Mershon was blindfolded and instructed to kneel beside the hole.

What did it feel like at that moment? Pilot Charlie Brown had thought he was about to have his head chopped off after he was shot down over Tokyo on February 16. He was blindfolded and made to kneel and extend his neck. "I thought, Here it comes," Charlie said. "But there was no fear or panic when I thought my head was going to be chopped off. Actually, it was the reverse: A calm went through me.

Maybe it was blood rushing out of my head like I was about to faint. My life didn't flash in front of me; there was just calmness. All I remember thinking was, I hope my parents don't find out how I died."

Dr. Sherwin Nuland, in his book *How We Die,* suggests that Charlie's feeling of calm had a medical basis. Nuland writes that the body releases self-generated opiates called endorphins when confronted with terror. "Endorphin elevation appears to be an innate physiological mechanism to protect mammals and perhaps other animals against the emotional and physical danger of terror and it probably appeared during the savage period of our prehistory when sudden life-threatening events occurred with frequency." Commenting on the case study of one murdered young girl, Dr. Nuland writes, "I am convinced that nature stepped in, as it so often does, and provided exactly the right spoonful of medicine to give a measure of tranquillity to a dying child."

Marve, clad in his long underwear, knelt in the freshly dug earth.

"Lieutenant Morishita aimed his sword and raised it up," said a soldier named Yoshia. "Then he told us to move back because the blood might splatter us."

"Lieutenant Morishita aimed his sword two or three times at his neck," recalled Iwakawa. "We in the working party didn't want to look, so we retired several meters to the rear."

The sword came down and sliced through Marve's neck. "When the flyer was struck," Iwakawa said, "he did not cry out but made a slight groan."

As Morishita withdrew his weapon, Marve tumbled forward into his grave. Lieutenant Morishita ordered the soldiers to cover Marve with dirt. When Iwakawa looked at Marve's body lying there, he saw that the lieutenant had done an incomplete job.

"The head was not completely severed from the body," Iwakawa said. "It was almost severed off, but it was held on by the skin of his throat." If Marve's inert corpse were held upright at that moment, his head would have hung upside down against his chest dangling by the skin of his neck.

As the sun dipped below the horizon, Los Angeleno Marve Mershon was buried in his long johns. Marve had lived exactly nineteen years, six months, and two days. It had been almost twenty months since he had enlisted, at his brother Hoyt's suggestion, to get his life together.

*   *   *

The day after Marve died, Saturday, February 24, Major Matoba met with General Tachibana at the general's headquarters. They were both aware of the ferocity of the fighting on nearby Iwo Jima, where their comrades were being mown down. On Chichi, their soldiers were suffering from overwork, limited rations, and the anxiety of expecting imminent attack. Even though it was just after noon, the major and the general were engaged in their favorite pastime — drinking sake. Whether they were getting drunk or getting drunker is the only question. "Major Matoba told me that he had been drinking for three days," Captain Shigeo Ikawa later testified.

"At the general's headquarters," Matoba recalled, "sake was served and the conversation turned to the Japanese forces that had been stationed in New Guinea. General Tachibana and I talked about how the troops there had lacked provisions and eventually had to eat human flesh to survive."

The two Spirit Warriors were discussing a topic that must have held a morbid fascination for their alcohol-soaked minds. The Spirit boys in Tokyo had dispatched more than 150,000 Japanese troops to New Guinea. They planned the invasion "off the map," with little knowledge of the horrible tropical conditions there. Instead of responsibly backing the troops up with sufficient supplies, they blithely gave instructions for the Japanese boys to survive by "local provisioning." But New Guinea could barely support its few tribal inhabitants; the land was not rich like that of China. And when shipping lines were cut by American naval might, the Tokyo armchair generals simply wrote their stranded troops off.

This was a death sentence for almost all the Japanese soldiers in New Guinea. With no food, they began to eat their dead. Sipping their sake, General Tachibana and Major Matoba spoke of the situation with a perverse admiration.

In the middle of the afternoon, Colonel Takamune Kato, who was in charge of the 307th Battalion, phoned General Tachibana's headquarters to invite the general and Major Matoba over to his headquarters for a drinking party.

"We walked to Colonel Kato's quarters," Matoba said, "and when we arrived, we found that Colonel Kato did not have enough drinks and things to go with the drinks." Ikawa recalled, "We only had two bottles of sake. Major Matoba began to shout for drinks."

Everybody knew where plenty of sake was stashed — back at Tachibana's headquarters. Ikawa phoned there and ordered some bottles brought over.

A sukiyaki-style meal of meat and vegetables had been set out on a table. To make sukiyaki, a heavy pan full of liquid is heated and then fish, meat, vegetables, noodles, and other ingredients are cooked by dipping them.

General Tachibana took one look at the spread of meat and vegetables and murmured that there wasn't enough meat to go around.

"Major Matoba was very angry," said Ikawa, "because the 307th Battalion did not have enough meat on the table to go with the vegetables."

As the terrified hosts tried to figure out how to secure more meat and avoid a beating, General Tachibana, who had been knocking back drinks for hours by now, had a creative idea. "The general asked me about the execution and about getting some meat," Matoba said. Tachibana told his hosts, "One had to have enough fighting spirit to eat human flesh." When he spoke of eating human flesh, the general used the word *kimo*. *Kimo* refers specifically to the liver and more generally to the internal organs. The word can also refer to spiritual or mental strength. In Japanese, one can say *"kimo ga ookii,"* literally, "he has big *kimo,"* meaning "he is bold and daring," or "he has a lot of guts." So when Tachibana spoke of eating Marve's *kimo,* he was using a term that referred to an organ but had much more meaning.

At about 4:30 P.M., Major Matoba called his headquarters, the 308th Battalion. "Matoba sounded drunk on the phone," said Captain Kanmuri, who took the call. Matoba ordered the captain to cut *kimo* from Marve's body.

"I told the major that the body had already been buried and so please give up the idea of getting any flesh from it," said Kanmuri. "Although I tried to advise the major by telling him not to take any flesh from the body, he ordered me to order the medical officer to have the body exhumed and to have flesh cut away from it and delivered to him."

Orders are orders. Captain Kanmuri told the battalion surgeon, Dr. Teraki, to do the dirty work. Corpsman Kanemori was working that afternoon and later recalled events:

Doctor Teraki came into the sick bay accompanied by two soldiers and told me to get some surgical instruments ready. He did not tell me what for. I thought this was an emergency call, so I prepared a kit with emergency gear. The doctor said, "Follow me."

It was dusk when we reached the cemetery. Someone pointed out the location of the grave and the doctor ordered the two soldiers to dig.

The doctor told me that he had received orders from Major Matoba and that we were to dissect the body and take out the liver. Whereupon I objected, as I knew the flyer was executed the previous day and the body would be decomposed. However, the doctor said it was an order.

The enlisted men dug up the body, which had on long underwear. The body was decapitated, although the head was hanging by a little skin. The neck was about seven tenths severed.

After the body was exhumed, Doctor Teraki took a scalpel from my hands and informed me that he was going to dissect the body.

Doctor Teraki ordered me to cut the leg. I asked him, "Why?" He answered, "It is Major Matoba's order." It was a custom in the Japanese army that when the whole body could not be given a proper burial, we would sometimes just cut off a hand or a foot and give this portion a proper burial. Therefore, I thought the same thing was desired of this body, and I started to cut off one of the feet.

Then Doctor Teraki said, "You should not cut there at the foot. You must cut the thigh." I asked him, "Why should I cut the thigh?" Then he told me, "You should not ask questions. It was an order."

Then I asked him, "Must I cut the whole thigh off, right into the bone?" Doctor Teraki replied, "No, just remove the flesh."

Doctor Teraki cut open the chest and took out the liver. I removed a piece of flesh from the flyer's thigh, a piece weighing about six pounds and measuring four inches wide, about a foot long.

The doctor wrapped up the liver and flesh in white cellophane paper.

I had brought gauze bandages and cotton from the sick bay. I placed the gauze over the leg wound and then started to bandage it. I brought out a needle and thread and asked the doctor if he was going to sew up the body and he told me that as it was too late, he was not going to sew it up. Then the doctor turned to the men and told them to bury the body.

About twenty minutes after we had removed the liver and flesh, Sergeant Sugiyama came and the package was turned over to him by Doctor Teraki.

Sergeant Sugiyama delivered the package of flesh to the 307th Battalion headquarters. Marve's liver and thigh were cut up and put on the table next to the sukiyaki pan for cooking.

"Major Matoba and General Tachibana asked for the meat and I served them," said Ikawa. "Major Matoba said, 'You have to eat this kind of meat to become a strong fighter.'"

The general ordered others to eat, saying they had to demonstrate the "necessary courage." Matoba commented, "Human liver is a good medicine." But the broader feast was not to be. "Major Matoba and General Tachibana had eaten most of their portions," Kanmuri later recalled. "Then the air-raid siren went off."

Kanmuri spirited the wobbly general out to a nearby air-raid shelter. "Matoba did not come, as he said bullets and bombs would not hurt him," said Kanmuri.

"After the air raid, Tachibana was so drunk that he couldn't move," Kanmuri remembered. Finally, the snoring Spirit cannibal was bundled into a car and driven to his headquarters to sleep off the day's drinking. Major Matoba had passed out on the floor of the headquarters building, where he lay until the next day. Captain Ikawa said the men "did not even cover him up with a blanket."

The next morning, Major Matoba ordered the remaining hunk of Marve's flesh sent to General Tachibana's headquarters. Later, he couldn't recall giving that specific order, but the major did admit there was a good chance that since he had started drinking early again that day, he probably was just too drunk to remember.

No crime was committed by eating Marve Mershon. It was legal for Spirit Warriors to eat *kichiku*. The Australian National Archives preserved the original of a secret order found by Australian forces in New Guinea that addressed the subject. The Australian archivists titled it "Captured Document number 80.107," an order written by Major General Kikutaro Aotsu, commanding general of the Forty-first Infantry Group. He had the order stamped "Most Secret," and it is dated November 18, 1944. Addressing "all Force Commanders," Aotsu explains that he is writing because "Recently, offences, especially murder, robbery and the acquisition of human flesh have been frequent within the detachments' jurisdiction and this has had a great influence on the army's morale." He goes on to address the problems of — and punishments for — murder and robbery. Then he moves on to the "frequent" problem of "acquisition of human flesh" and writes: "Those who have consumed human flesh (excluding enemy) knowing that it is human flesh, will be sentenced to death as for the worst human crime."

Excluding enemy.

This document is curious, not just because it approved cannibalism of *gaizin*, but because it had to be written at all. As far as I can determine, the British, French, German, and American armies did not have to address the problem of cannibalism in their ranks. Only the Spirit Warriors' army.

In August of 2002, I interviewed a soft-spoken eighty-year-old Australian man by the name of Bill Hedges. Bill served as a corporal in the Australian army in New Guinea. During training, he struck up a friendship with Private George Bliss. Bill told me that George "was a happy country boy" and that the two were "good mates." They slept in the same tent and were typical twenty-year-old buddies who shared stories of home.

In early 1943, Bill and George were fighting on the Kokoda Trail in New Guinea, one of the most godforsaken places in the world. Bill led a forty-man patrol into battle and was ambushed by the Japanese, who were well hidden by the concealing jungle. Six of his men were killed, including George Bliss, who was felled "right alongside" Bill. Bill was not hit because a tree shielded him, but he had to retreat and leave George's body where it lay.

The next day, replacements arrived, and one day later the Australians counterattacked. The denseness of the jungle now worked to the Australians' advantage as they caught the Japanese soldiers by surprise. The Japanese fled for their lives, leaving their equipment and supplies strewn about.

Bill stepped warily over the ground where his buddies had been downed only forty-eight hours earlier. He came to the spot where Private Bliss had fallen and found George's body still there — what was left of it.

"His uniform had been torn off and the flesh stripped all off his arms and his legs," Bill told me. "They butchered him."

Farther on, Bill found suspicious-looking meat in Japanese eating tins. An Australian doctor confirmed that it was human flesh.

At the time, Bill was shocked but preoccupied with survival. "We had trouble coping with it," he said, "but we were getting shot at and had to look after ourselves." Later, Bill was debriefed by Australian Army Intelligence and was ordered to sign a pledge that he would not speak of this incident for twenty-five years.

Bill told me that after he left New Guinea, the memory dogged him. Some of his friends never recovered. He said they were "brain damaged" after seeing Private Bliss's hacked skeleton. When I asked Bill why his opponents were eating humans, he said he really didn't know, but that "some said it gave them more fighting spirit, the feeling of being superior to their enemy."

Eighty-year-old Bill Hedges still has "bad dreams now and again." The image of George Bliss's stripped body comes up all the time. Said Bill, "Sixty years after the fact, I can see it now as if I was there."

U.S and Australian WWII archives hold many files detailing numerous acts of Japanese army cannibalism. For example, of those 157,646 sons of Japan sent to New Guinea, only 10,072 survived. Allied bullets killed relatively few. The vast majority were felled by disease and starvation. General Aotsu was aware of the plight of his men. He wrote that incidents of cannibalism in New Guinea were "frequent." Japanese boys were starving and had to eat whatever they could find. Often, all they could find was one another.

Harumichi Nogi, the chief of a Japanese naval police force stationed in the South Pacific, later recorded in his memoirs a story told to him by an army lieutenant:

> There was absolutely nothing to eat, and so we decided to draw lots. The one who lost would be killed and eaten. But the one who lost started to run away so we shot him. He was eaten. You probably think that many of us raped the local women. But women were not regarded as objects of sexual desire. They were regarded as the object of our hunger. We had no sexual appetite. To commit rape would have cost us too much energy, and we never wanted to. All we dreamt about was food. I met some soldiers in the mountains who were carrying baked human arms and legs. It was not guerrillas but our own soldiers who we were frightened of. It was such a terrible condition.

Of course the emperor's soldiers preferred to eat non-Japanese when the opportunity presented itself. In New Guinea, Japanese soldiers referred to the Allies as "white pigs" and the local population as "black pigs." Australian and American archives cite many examples of Japanese troops harvesting Allied dead killed in battle. As historian Yuki Tanaka has written, "It seems clear that Japanese soldiers removed the bodies of Allied soldiers from the area in which fierce combat was occurring and carried them to a staging area to be cooked and consumed, while others held back the Allied forces in order to prevent them from recovering the bodies. This indicates that these incidents were not isolated or sporadic acts but part of an organized process."

On January 23, 1943, U.S. Army private E. Dickson and Corporal Clinne Lamb of Company F, 163rd Regiment, serving in New Guinea, found the remains of their sergeant, who had been missing for four days. The two American boys swore to the following: "The flesh part of the thigh and each leg had been cut away. The abdominal cavity had been opened by cutting away the skin and flesh under each lower rib. The face had not been mutilated, thus making identification possible. A stew pot in a nearby Japanese bunker contained the heart and liver of approximate size of that [of a] human."

On May 20, 1945, Australian army warrant officer C. Hugo swore an affidavit that he had found the body of a buddy in New Guinea in this condition:

(a) All clothing had been removed.

(b) Both arms had been cut off at the shoulder.

(c) The stomach had been cut out, and the heart, liver and other entrails had been removed.

(d) All fleshy parts of the body had been cut away, leaving the bones bare.

(e) The arms, heart, liver and entrails could not be found.

(f) The only parts of the body not touched were the head and feet.

(g) A Japanese mess tin in which appeared to contain human flesh was lying four to five yards from [his] body.

Starving Japanese combat troops used battles as a hunt for food, but noncombat units had to devise other means. Japanese officials dispatched an engineering battalion deep into the interior of what is now Indonesia. The engineering battalion used Indo-Pakistani POWs, former Commonwealth soldiers captured in the fall of Singapore, as slave laborers. One of those soldiers was Pakistani Hatam Ali. Ali had been aware that sick prisoners unable to work were immediately shot or given lethal injections and then eaten by the Japanese. But by 1944, the Allies were closing in, supply lines had been cut, and the Japanese had started to eat live, healthy prisoners. Ali told his harrowing story to Australian investigators: "Those selected were taken to a hut where flesh was cut from their bodies while they were alive and they were then thrown into a ditch alive where they later died. When flesh was being cut from those selected terrible cries and shrieks came from them and also from the ditch where they were later thrown. These cries used to gradually dim down when the unfortunate individuals were dying. We were not allowed to go near this ditch, no earth was thrown on the bodies and the smell was terrible."

The reason the Japanese butchers didn't kill the prisoners outright was that in the tropics, with no refrigeration, the meat quickly rotted. So they would just hack off parts of the body to provide a meal without killing the prisoner, then toss him into a ditch, where he would survive another day or two, thereby ensuring that his internal organs remained fresh for later consumption. Ears, noses, lips, cheeks, toes, palms, buttocks, shoulders, and thighs were cut and eaten while the main course remained preserved.

The abandonment of troops with no concern for their welfare was a monstrous crime committed by the Spirit Warriors. The starving Japanese boys were brutalized too. But debased officers like General Tachibana and Major Matoba, rather than seeing the horror in their comrades' predicament, reveled in the morbid stories as they drank themselves into their nightly stupors.

Radioman Jimmy Dye, gunner Grady York, and pilot Warren Earl Vaughn sat tied to trees outside General Tachibana's headquarters from the afternoon of Friday, February 23, to Monday, February 26.

For all his bravado, there is no record of Major Matoba's ever laying a hand on any of the prisoners. Glenn and Marve had been outside his headquarters on February 23, but Matoba never interrupted his partying long enough to even view them. On February 24, the major was drinking at General Tachibana's headquarters and once again, there is no record that he made an effort to get even one *Yamato damashii* kick in against Jimmy, Grady, or Warren Earl.

Indeed, except for Captain Nakajima's drunken beating death of Glenn Frazier, there never was any frenzy of hatred toward the prisoners. There were many thousands of Japanese soldiers on the island armed with rifles and knives. Any one of them could have wounded or killed an American. But the Flyboys were not shot or cut, just socked and kicked — de rigueur for members of the emperor's army.

It seems that the Japanese soldiers, tired from overwork, undernourished, depressed by their prospects, and perhaps only narrowly following orders, mostly ignored the prisoners. Jimmy, Grady, and Warren Earl were certainly roughed up as they sat tied to trees those three days. But presumably this was mostly because soldiers coming and going from the general's headquarters had to demonstrate their toughness to their commander. The boys were tied there as trophies of General Tachibana, who demanded that his men show proper Japanese spirit.

Under the cover of darkness, however, one soldier showed mercy. Captain Tadaaki Kosuga wanted to help the bound Americans but dared not disobey General Tachibana's prohibition against feeding them. But he found a way to give the boys something to eat while remaining true to the letter of his commander's order. "The cakes that I gave to the prisoners were not military-supplied food," said Kosuga, "but cake which I bought with my own money. Therefore, I thought it would be all right."

By Monday, February 26, General Tachibana apparently tired of the three dirty and bruised flyers. He decided to send Warren Earl Vaughn to Major Horie (who still had Floyd Hall) for questioning. The 275th and the 307th Battalions would execute Jimmy Dye and Grady York. Colonel Kato's 307th Battalion would get first choice. "I heard the general say that he was sending a flyer to Colonel Kato because of the number of casualties in his battalion," said Captain Ikawa.

"We took back the smallest of the three prisoners," said Sergeant Masao Kishimoto of the 307th. They had chosen five-foot-four-inch Grady York, who probably weighed less than 100 pounds by then, considering his fighting weight was only 106.

"We took one prisoner and brought him back to the 307th Battalion headquarters," recalled Corporal Shinosuke Taniyama, who never learned Grady's name. "This flyer had black hair, was about 1.7 meters tall, and was wearing a leather fur-lined jacket. We tied this prisoner to a telephone pole in front of our headquarters. We took turns guarding him until after noon."

Inside the headquarters, Colonel Kato was deciding who would execute Grady. He had a clerk find out what companies within the battalion had men killed by American bombs. He then selected five men from those companies, to be led by Captain Masao Yamashita. Yamashita was told they should kill Grady with sharpened bamboo spears and bayonets.

After Grady was taken away and Warren Earl was dispatched for interrogation, Jimmy was left alone outside Tachibana's building. The general then gave the order for the 275th Battalion, the group that had captured Jimmy and Grady on the beach, to execute Jimmy.

"Have that flyer executed with bamboo spears," Captain Kosuga remembered General Tachibana ordering him. Kosuga phoned the 275th Battalion to express the general's wishes. Soldiers from the 275th headquarters drove to Tachibana's headquarters to pick up Jimmy while other soldiers dug his grave and nailed a wooden crossbar to a nearby tree. Jimmy would be tied to the cross and pierced with bamboo spears.

But before the soldiers from the 275th Battalion arrived, someone else came to claim Jimmy.

"A car from the wireless station came," Kosuga recalled, "and a sailor got out and said he came to get a flyer. He said there was an arrangement between Captain Yoshii, the commander of the radio station, and General Tachibana. I went to the general's room and told him that the car had come to take a flyer to the Yoake wireless station. The general said, 'All right,' and the flyer was sent." Days earlier, navy captain Yoshii had asked General Tachibana for a prisoner to assist with the radio station's monitoring of U.S. military messages. The general fulfilled his promise to the navy by handing over Jimmy. Radioman Dye had — for the moment — been spared.

Back at the 307th battalion headquarters, Captain Yamashita moved to carry out the order to kill Grady York. "Around two o'clock in the afternoon, Yamashita came and ordered us to accompany him, as the prisoner was going to be executed," Taniyama said.

Earlier that day, Grady had been separated from Jimmy for the first time since they were shot down. He had been moved to another headquarters and must have observed soldiers conferring about him. Now, when Captain Yamashita showed up, he heard barked orders and was surrounded by about ten soldiers with sharp bamboo spears and shiny bayonets.

Grady and the soldiers walked in a procession toward the execution ground. It was the same area where Dick Woellhof and the B-24 crewman had been bayoneted and beheaded. Sergeant Kishimoto was one of the soldiers in the procession. Earlier, he had picked Grady up at Tachibana's headquarters and by now had been at Grady's side for over four hours. Grady was small for an American but average size for a Japanese. Also, Grady had a swarthy complexion and black hair similar to those of a Japanese. He was not as "white" as the white devils Kishimoto had imagined Americans to be.

"The prisoner was rather small and the color of his hair did not differ from ours," Kishimoto later said, "and his face resembled the smaller brother of a friend of mine. I pitied him and tried to think of some way to escape this place, while following some distance behind the prisoner."

But orders were orders. Maybe some of the Japanese boys assigned to execute Grady detested the duty, maybe some relished it. Their feelings didn't matter.

The group soon reached the killing ground. It was about 3:30 P.M. on Monday, February 26, 1945.

"We thereupon immediately prepared for execution," Taniyama said. "We tore off the coat and shirt of the prisoner, tied him to a telephone post, and shoveled out a hole in the ground in front of him."

Grady York, the sensitive artist, the boy who never cursed and thought rough behavior was drinking on Christmas Eve, now watched soldiers dig his grave. He saw the bayonets and the sharpened bamboo spears. He stood nude above the waist, his bare back against the rough wooden pole. He must have looked smaller and younger than his nineteen years and six months. Even though his heart was probably beating wildly in that tiny frame, Grady did not squirm or struggle. Finally, Yamashita wrapped a blindfold over his eyes.

Two bamboo spears and three bayonets were thrust into Grady's body. Private Takekazu Oshida and Corporal Shoichi Morito speared Grady with the sharpened bamboo first.

"Captain Yamashita said hurry up and spear him," Oshida said. "He said it over and over. He said it to Corporal Morito and Morito pierced the flyer. Then he turned and said the same to me."

"Corporal Morito was very willing to help, very gung-ho," Kishimoto said later. "I saw Morito spear the flyer. I remember Captain Yamashita standing beside him saying, 'Spear his heart.'"

After the young soldiers had demonstrated sufficient *Yamato damashii* with their spears, the older soldiers moved in for the kill with bayonets. "At the command of Captain Yamashita," said Taniyama, "we soldiers together with Yamashita took turns in bayoneting the prisoner in the chest."

General Tachibana and Major Matoba, who assumed these executions would build fighting spirit, probably would have been disappointed by the human feelings in the breasts of some of the participants that day.

"As this was the first time I saw a man getting killed, I felt fearful," Kishimoto admitted. Private Oshida had been ordered to spear Grady, but he hurried from the scene as soon as he had done so. "After using the spear, I stepped down the hill and stood on the path about eight yards away," Oshida said. And when Captain Yamashita later informed Colonel Kato that the execution had been carried out, he added, "I hate to receive orders of that nature."

"We completed the execution in two or three minutes," Taniyama said. Added Kishimoto, "The prisoner died and was in a half fallen position with his face looking upward."

"This prisoner did not cry out, not even a groan from start to finish," Yamashita recalled. "He also did not show any tears from start to finish. He struck me as being a very brave man."

"The bayoneted prisoner was buried in the hole we had dug for him," concluded Taniyama. "His body was amply covered with earth and, our duties completed, we were ordered to return."

The United States Navy telegram informing Grady's parents that Grady had been shot down and was missing reached their Jacksonville home after Grady was already dead. Betty Huckleberry, Grady's cousin, was there. "Mr. York got the telegram at home," she said. "Mrs. York wasn't there; she was in church. Mr. York telephoned the pastor, DeWitt Mallory. The pastor told Mrs. York at the altar."

Grady's mama was where he would have wanted her.

She was in church. Praying for him.

*   *   *

Now there were three Flyboys alive on Chichi Jima that Monday, February 26, 1945. Pilots Floyd Hall and Warren Earl Vaughn were at Major Horie's headquarters. Radioman Jimmy Dye was in a car winding his way up to Mount Yoake.

The imperial navy's Mount Yoake radio station had two missions: to relay Japanese military information between the troops out in the Pacific and Tokyo and to eavesdrop on U.S. military radio communications. Because of the inferior state of Japanese radio receivers at that time, these jobs could not be done in Tokyo — a presence in No Mans Land was necessary. Captain Yoshii hoped that Jimmy could help his team understand the American codes they intercepted.

Or maybe Captain Yoshii had another motive. The navy and the army had separate operations on Chichi Jima and the two services seldom fraternized. But the captain was one navy man who did cross that line. And he had an unsavory army acquaintance.

"Major Matoba was quite a good friend of Captain Yoshii's," said a navy petty officer who served at Mount Yoake. The relationship between the army major and the navy captain was based on more than an interest in interservice cooperation: They both loved the bottle and partied together at army headquarters and on Mount Yoake. Indeed, Matoba and Yoshii had a lot in common. "Captain Yoshii did not recognize ordinary men as human beings," one who served under him later testified. "He would do things without thinking of anything or anyone. He was sort of a bully and a despot."

As they drank together, Captain Yoshii absorbed some of Major Matoba's ideas about killing POWs and about eating *kimo.* "I heard Yoshii talking with some officers in the mess hall about eating a portion of the human body as medicine," his orderly Suzuki later testified.

Jimmy was brought to Captain Yoshii's office near the radio station atop Mount Yoake. Yoshii only spoke Japanese, so he had one of the radio station's English speakers, Petty Officer Fumio Tamamura, there to translate.

Fumio Tamamura was born twenty years before in San Francisco. His father left Japan in 1906; he ran a small shop on Grand Avenue and had been chairman of a local merchants' association. Young Fumio had walked across the new $35 million Golden Gate Bridge the day it opened in May of 1937. But he was not long for his native land.

"Fumio, if you finish college in America, you'll become too Americanized," he remembered his dad telling him. His mother took him back to their hometown of Kyoto, where he studied until it was time to make a decision. "The navy seemed a safer place than the army," Tamamura-san told me.

He served in the navy's communications school as a civilian employee. When he was about to be shipped overseas, he said he'd like to continue his status as a civilian employee. "Tamamura, you don't know the score, do you?" he remembered a superior telling him. "'You're not going to come back alive. You should become a petty officer for your mother's pension.' So I became a petty officer."

Tamamura arrived on Chichi Jima in March of 1944. He had been serving under Captain Yoshii at the Mount Yoake radio station for eleven months. "Yoshii was a career navy man," Tamamura-san said. "I had a formal reporting relationship with him. I was young enough to be Yoshii's son and he looked at me that way. I saw him as a father figure."

With Petty Officer Tamamura interpreting, Captain Yoshii questioned Jimmy. "We learned that he came from an American task force in the vicinity," Tamamura-san said. "He said his home carrier was the USS *Bennington*. He told us the dates the carrier left Pearl Harbor and later Ulithi. He gave his name and rank as James Dye, Aviation Radioman third class."

Tamamura-san remembered Jimmy as "tall, with a light complexion, light-colored hair, wearing a leather jacket, dark green trousers, and field shoes. Also, he was wearing a white silk scarf."

Yoshii told Tamamura to take the prisoner to the radio station and put him to work listening to American messages. "Report on your progress," the captain ordered.

But Jimmy was in no condition to make any progress. His characteristic cheerfulness had long since abandoned him. Jimmy was nineteen years old, far from home, and very scared.

"He was in a nervous state of mind," Tamamura-san said. "I knew he could not do any work, so I let him sit in front of a receiving set and we talked a lot."

Jimmy spoke of New Jersey and life in the navy. He showed Tamamura his hands and explained that they hurt from being tied up at

Tachibana's headquarters. He said he was worried about Grady, his tail gunner. And, after the relationship between them warmed, Jimmy fingered his scarf and told Tamamura that it held special meaning for him. "He said he got it from his sweetheart," Tamamura-san remembered.

"Dye and I discussed mostly other things than our business," Tamamura-san said. "As he was a little tired out, I thought it would be unreasonable to start work from the beginning. So we never did get started on our work."

Others noticed.

Jimmy, in his agitated state, couldn't have impressed Captain Yoshii much at their interview. And it was easy to see that Jimmy wasn't going to pull himself together enough to be of assistance.

Lieutenant Minoru Hayashi observed the prisoner sitting with Petty Officer Tamamura in the radio station. It was only the second time he had seen a foreigner. "He was young and skinny," Hayashi-san remembered. "He was slumped over somewhat. He looked like he had lost his personal power. He looked unhappy, limp — like he gave up. I felt sorry for the prisoner. He wasn't some big guy to hate."

Tamamura did not tell Captain Yoshii the prisoner never buckled down to work in the two days he was there. But there were about twenty others working in the radio station, and word got around. "I heard that he was not very good in intercepting and translating messages," Petty Officer Shohei Shiina said.

As word spread, Yoshii's first impression was reinforced, and he made a decision. "Yoshii called me to his office," Tamamura-san said, "and told me, 'The Americans may land tomorrow or in a few days. You, all of us, should be prepared to die. And today at four P.M., we are going to execute the prisoner.'"

"Why did Captain Yoshii order Jimmy's death?" I asked Tamamura-san years later. He explained:

For Yoshii it was an effort to raise morale. He had to prepare everyone for dying. We were all going to die, we thought. We knew the American instruments of death were going to come at us and that we had no hope. We were all going to die together; the prisoner would go first. "It can't be helped," everyone thought. It's a mass hysteria, wartime hysteria. It's impossible to analyze it unless you were in that bizarre situation. The reactions of a cornered rat are not normal. And besides, when the Americans came and we were all going to die, how could we hold on to a prisoner?

Tamamura tried to cover for Jimmy, promising Yoshii that the prisoner would be a big help in the future. "I told the captain that Dye was working and to have his life saved, but it was impossible," Tamamura-san later testified. "The captain told me in front of some officers, 'You tried to save his life, didn't you? That is not good.' Later I heard that a number of times."

As young Tamamura made his way back to Jimmy in the radio station, he wondered, "Should I tell him he is going to die this afternoon? Or should I not? If I was in his shoes, which would I prefer? I could not tell him. I thought that in his nervous mental state, it would have been too much for him.

"We sat and talked all morning," Tamamura said. "He talked a lot about the gunner on his plane. Dye was always worried about him."

As Jimmy and Fumio chatted in the radio station, Captain Yoshii announced plans to the others in the mess hall. Lieutenant Shinichi Matsutani later recalled, "After the morning meal, the captain said, 'Today at four o'clock we shall execute the prisoner. I shall have the young officers execute him to build up their nerve. Hayashi and Matsutani, both of you will cut.'" Then Yoshii turned to the unit's doctor, Mitsuyoshi Sasaki, and ordered, "You will remove the liver."

Lieutenants Matsutani and Hayashi and Dr. Sasaki were dumbstruck.

"I was very troubled because it was so sudden," said Matsutani. "I asked the captain, 'If the army is supposed to handle the prisoners, is it all right for the navy to do such a thing?' In answer to this, Captain Yoshii did not say anything but just glared at me."

"When I received this order, I thought a terrible thing had happened," Lieutenant Hayashi-san, who was just twenty-two years old at the time, later told me. "I protested that this embarrasses me, but the captain just said, 'This is an order; you must do it.' As I was before many officers, I could protest no further because I was afraid I may be shamed." Dr. Sasaki was so shocked all he could do was mumble a yes and then leave the room.

After breakfast, the three who had been ordered to take part in

Jimmy's execution went individually to Captain Yoshii to protest. Yoshii had said he was going to have the "young officers" behead Jimmy, but he could have said "young and unruly." Both Lieutenants Matsutani and Hayashi had had their run-ins with the captain in the past. Yoshii was a career military man, but Matsutani and Hayashi had been students and, of course, Dr. Sasaki was an educated man. All three remembered the captain's oft-repeated notion: "People who come from schools have democratic leanings; that is why I am going to hammer this out of you with strict training." He had never trusted them and was not shy about reminding them of their fates if they displeased him. Once, Lieutenant Matsutani failed to perform some coding correctly. He wasn't trained sufficiently for it, but the captain saw it strictly as a matter of discipline. "What do you think orders are?" Captain Yoshii bellowed at young Matsutani. "Up to now I have many times reminded you of your disobedience to orders, but from now on I will never forgive you. In case of disobedience, I will punish you and have this spread throughout the whole navy."

"Punishment would have meant being reported in the navy bulletin, published throughout the navy," Matsutani recalled. "Punishment is the most disgraceful thing in the military service. As a result of such punishment, when the time for promotion comes, I would not be promoted."

But even with this history, Lieutenant Matsutani went to Captain Yoshii's office to argue his case. "The prisoner was borrowed from the army for monitoring purposes, and what is the reason for his execution?" Lieutenant Matsutani asked. "In answer to this question, the captain said, 'You do not have to ask questions; rely on me.'"

"I said, 'I cannot possibly cut a human being,'" Matsutani recalled. 'If you are going to execute him, choose someone else.' In answer to this, the captain said, 'You will have to do this nevertheless. I have spoken many times about what would happen if you disobey orders; you should know this.'"

Like Matsutani, Lieutenant Minoru Hayashi was no blood-and-guts fighter, but that was the point: Captain Yoshii was picking on him because he was the runt of the litter. Hayashi was small and mild-mannered, the least likely person to slice off someone's head. He came from the country town of Kofu, where, as a high school student, he had observed the workings of an army base there. "I found the soldiers were badly treated," Hayashi-san told me years later. "I came to hate the army. They were serving as worse than servants to their superiors. They competed with each other to loosen their superiors' foot bindings. Superiors hit their subordinates. The army was brutal." So when he was forced to quit college after two and a half years and enlist in a service, Hayashi chose the navy, where he became a technical officer. On Chichi Jima, it was his job to keep the radar equipment working. Yoshii had singled out a meek, quiet technician to perform a grisly deed.

"When you got an order from an officer, you were to treat it as if it came from the emperor," Hayashi-san told me. "Ever since I entered the navy, we had been taught that a subordinate is not to inquire about the orders from the superior officer."

But Lieutenant Hayashi was troubled.

"I was an officer, so I had a sword," Hayashi-san told me, "but I had never used one. I had no such experience and I desperately wanted to escape. But we were on an island. There was no escape.

"I was young," he added, "and Captain Yoshii was an older military person. His eyes were sharp and scary. He had a threatening atmosphere about him. I was scared of him."

In spite of "emperor's orders," a lifetime of having been trained not to question authority, and Yoshii's well-known threat — *My policy is to execute all persons who do not obey orders* — Lieutenant Hayashi mustered his courage and entered the captain's office.

"I told Yoshii I didn't want to behead the prisoner," Hayashi-san recalled. "Captain Yoshii said, 'You know what happens to an officer who refuses an order.'

"At that point," Hayashi-san said, "I expected to be executed if I did not obey, or at least receive life imprisonment. I did not like it, but I accepted the order."

"Today at four o'clock, the execution shall be held in front of the fuel storage house," Captain Yoshii sternly instructed his young charge. "And you will be there."

When Dr. Sasaki, who had been ordered to cut out Jimmy's liver, told the captain, "I cannot possibly do such a thing," Yoshii's face turned red and he shouted, "What are you saying? Are you going to disobey my order? The young people now do not have any nerve."

Dr. Sasaki realized he had no choice and he quietly left.

"There was no other way than to obey," Tamamura-san later told me. "There just wasn't any disobedience at that time in Japan. We were all covered by society's huge blanket and it was impossible to go against the tide. Disobedience was not something that was recognized within the framework of the military or society. Disobeying would be a strictly personal action and he'd have to pay for it. With his life."

Jimmy and Tamamura chatted at the radio station all morning and through lunch. At 2 P.M., Captain Yoshii's orderly came by and told Tamamura that the captain wanted Jimmy's leather jacket and white scarf. Tamamura told Jimmy to hand them over. He did so, but this must have alarmed him. It was February, the nights were chilly, and everyone else had a jacket; now Jimmy didn't. And his last connection with home — Gloria's white silk scarf — was now gone.

The two boys continued their chat. Then, about 4 P.M., the orderly returned. It was time to go.

Fumio Tamamura looked into Jimmy Dye's blue eyes. They had been born just a few months apart on opposite coasts as Americans. Tamamura thought of what to say. "I told him that Captain Yoshii is going to parade you in front of the men and then you'll come back," Tamamura-san recalled years later. "I just said you are going to be exhibited to the men on the hill. To this day I still think it was better not to tell him."

Jimmy and Tamamura walked about fifty yards from the radio station toward a crowd gathered near a freshly dug hole. Conspicuous were Captain Yoshii and two lieutenants in dress uniform with sheathed swords. Tamamura told Jimmy to sit at the edge of the hole with his feet dangling. Then he was blindfolded. He must have sensed what was next.

"I told him to sit still and that the commander was going to question him," Tamamura-san said. "He didn't say anything. But he was pretty nervous."

In Jimmy's last letter to his father, he had written, "I'm still just a boy." That boy was terrified.

Captain Yoshii now addressed the assembly: "Watch closely. What today is another's fate may be your fate tomorrow."

"It was a rephrasing of an old Japanese saying," Tamamura-san said. "It's used when someone has an unfortunate accident. Something to the effect that what happens to someone else may happen to me tomorrow."

Tamamura-san told me, "When Captain Yoshii said, 'Watch closely,' the atmosphere was very somber. We felt these were not light words. We felt it was the truth. The American navy surrounded the island. We really did think we would die the next day."

"Kire!" Captain Yoshii barked. "Cut!"

Lieutenant Hayashi obediently came forward. He described what happened next: "'I will start,' I said to the captain, saluting. I stepped to the rear of the prisoner. I saluted the prisoner and cut."

"Lieutenant Hayashi was trembling when he executed the American," added Petty Officer Kaoru Sakamoto. "Everyone knew that Lieutenant Hayashi was not the man to do the job."

"The first blow cut into the flyer's neck about one inch," Petty Officer Rokuro Kuriki later testified. "The flyer's head fell forward a little, but the body did not fall over."

Jimmy had probably lost consciousness. An inch-deep cut would have severed his spinal cord. Witnesses testified that they saw blood coming from a wound on the back of his neck. "Hayashi cut just a little," Tamamura-san said, "but that was enough to break Dye's backbone."

The grisly scene engendered little of the *Yamato damashii* fervor Captain Yoshii had hoped for. Hayashi later said, "After I struck the blow, I dived among the crowd." Petty Officer Sakamoto testified, "When the first blow struck, most of the men turned their backs. The flyer was groaning." Petty Officer Shohei Shiina said, "I ran away after the first blow."

"Lieutenant Matsutani was supposed to be the second executioner," Tamamura-san said, "but he faltered and was standing there frozen."

"I trembled when I saw Lieutenant Hayashi cut," Matsutani testified. "I thought that the prisoner had already died. But the captain said, 'Next, Lieutenant Matsutani cut.' I saluted the captain and stepped two or three steps toward the prisoner. Then the captain came up to me and advised, 'A person who is going to cut for the first time, if he puts too much strength in it, he will cut himself, so do not put too much strength in.'"

"The second blow cut at least half of the neck, because his head fell forward," said Kuriki.

"After the second blow, Dye's body fell forward into the hole," Tamamura-san said. "As he was sitting, he just toppled over."

"After the second stroke," Petty Officer Teresada Aruga recalled, "I and other men broke ranks and ran away."

A Flyboy had been killed, but there was no cheering. "There was just silence," Tamamura-san said.

Captain Yoshii motioned to Dr. Sasaki, who came forward.

"The doctor cut open the abdomen," said Kuriki. "He took out the liver. This was put in a box and taken to the galley."

"Six or seven people — including Yoshii — surrounded the body as the liver was being taken out," Tamamura-san said. "I was there, but I did not care to see the body. I saw the liver being carried away toward the HQ building of the radio station."

"After the liver had been removed," Tamamura-san added, "the doctor looked up — I think it was to the officer of the day, standing quite a distance away from the spot, and asked him, 'I think that is enough. I don't want to cut any more. Don't you think that is enough?' The officer replied, 'Yes, don't cut any more.'"

"After I removed the liver," Dr. Sasaki testified, "I sewed up the incision and with the remaining thread sewed the neck. I cleaned off the blood. After I finished this, I placed his hands together and I saluted the body. When I did this, there were some people who laughed, but as for myself, I felt that I should give the body every respect possible."

Jimmy was buried in the hole where he lay.

"I don't think there was any formal dismissal," Tamamura-san told me. "They just dissolved, went their own way. It was a clear, sunny day."

Twenty-year-old Petty Officer Tamamura walked from the scene back to his post at the radio station.

"I felt confusion, sadness, horror," he remembered. "I had never seen anyone killed before. Taking someone's life is not something to be taken lightly. When something like that occurs and everybody has shared the knowledge, you don't talk about it."

And the executioners hardly reveled in the memory.

"I hate to remember it," Hayashi-san told me. "I never discussed it with Matsutani. We didn't do it willingly. Matsutani was not the type of person to do it either. He was a sensitive person, a Tokyo University graduate."

*   *   *

By ordering the beheading, navy captain Yoshii had proven he was a big brave Spirit Warrior like army major Matoba. Now he would prove he was Matoba's equal as a Spirit cannibal.

"I believe it was dark when a sailor brought in a package of something wrapped up in a newspaper," Yoshii's orderly, Suzuki, later testified. "The sailor told me it was sent by the captain and that I should keep custody of it. Therefore, I left it in the galley. Later on in the evening, the captain requested me to bring this package to him. Yoshii said, 'Bring me the flesh which is in your keeping.'"

Suzuki unwrapped the package for Yoshii. "It was a very dark-colored piece of flesh," Suzuki said. "I did not know whether liver looks like this, and I cannot say that it was liver."

Yoshii was alone in his quarters with the package when Suzuki left him. But there was a sake-drinking party going on in the nearby officers' mess.

"I understood the officers had a party," Tamamura-san said. "I wasn't there, but I understand that part of the liver was served to all of the officers at the party that night, and they were forced to eat it by Captain Yoshii. They could not refuse."

"I heard that Yoshii had liver cooked and put it on the table and told everyone to eat it," said Hayashi.

"I heard that Yoshii brought the liver personally to the officers' mess," said Petty Officer Sakamoto, "and that most of the officers deserted the captain's table when he brought liver and ordered them to eat it."

(Rumors swirled around Mount Yoake the next day, and still exist today on the island, that Jimmy Dye's body was hacked up and served in the enlisted men's soup. Other than the persistent rumor, I can find nothing to substantiate this. Apparently, the extraction of his liver led to exaggerated stories among the enlisted men of his entire body being cut up.)

Spirit cannibal Yoshii kept the remainder of Jimmy's liver in his room. "Every time an officer went into Captain Yoshii's room," Tamamura-san said, "he would offer them a part of the liver, and they were afraid to eat it and afraid to refuse to eat it."

Later in life, Tamamura read about the practice of combatants eating the livers of their enemy. "This is not a Japanese tradition," he explained. "Chinese warriors would eat enemies' livers with the idea that it would transfer power. Captain Yoshii, being of the old school, probably felt it would. Eating the liver is supposed to arouse hatred or animosity, I guess. Devouring the liver is one way to overcome the enemy.

"Captain Yoshii gave me a little piece of Jimmy Dye's liver," Tamamura-san told me. "I didn't know what to do with it. I felt it was part of a body and I shouldn't just chuck it away. So I passed a needle through it and strung it up and left it hanging. Eventually, it got moldy and I had to throw it away."

Jimmy had been dead for a week when his parents received the March 7, 1945, telegram that began with the dreaded words, "The Navy Department deeply regrets to inform you . . ."

But the telegram said only that their son was "missing in action." And a letter from Jimmy's commander assured Mr. and Mrs. Dye that he had "landed safely with his parachute on."

The Dyes had hope. Even after the war, they expected Jimmy to emerge from a prisoner-of-war camp any day. Jimmy's friends and family hoped and prayed for a year that he was alive. They just didn't know.

But Gloria Nields did.

"I had a big eight-by-ten framed picture of Jimmy," she told me decades later. "It was the shot of him in his sailor uniform with a big smile. Every night I would kiss his picture and sleep with it. One night it fell on the floor and broke. I woke up and it scared me. I knew something had happened. Later I learned that was when Jimmy died."

CHAPTER SIXTEEN

Fire War

Please try to understand this. It's not an easy thing to hear, but please listen. There is no morality in warfare. You kill children. You kill women. You kill old men. You don't seek them out, but they die. That's what happens in war.

— *Paul Tibbets, quoted in* Duty: A Father, His Son, and the Man Who Won the War

AFTER Marve Mershon, Grady York, and Jimmy Dye were taken away on Friday, February 23, Floyd Hall was alone at Major Horie's headquarters. His solitude lasted until Monday, February 26th — the day Jimmy and Grady were taken to their deaths — when Warren Earl was transferred from General Tachibana's to Major Horie's headquarters. There, the two pilots met for the first time.

Major Horie was a small bookish man who limped because of a leg injury suffered while serving in China. An intelligence officer with a clerk's demeanor, he had a low opinion of Tachibana and Matoba and shared none of their hatred of POWs. Friends at navy headquarters in Tokyo had informed him that Japan's fleet was gone, and Horie realized Japan's defeat was only a matter of time. As a result, he thought that abusing POWs was senseless and even dangerous if America won the war. When he told Tachibana and Matoba of his opposition to killing flyers, they scoffed. Major Horie's intelligence operation was a sideshow, without operational authority. He could not determine policy, but Floyd and Warren Earl were safe as long as they were in his custody.

In Major Horie's care, there was little discipline. Floyd and Warren Earl walked about freely, were fed well, and were not beaten. If either had been violent or run away, there would have been consequences, but they behaved themselves. They knew they were trapped on an island with no hope of escape.

After a few interrogation sessions, there wasn't much else to be gleaned from the two pilots. Warren Earl told Major Horie that he had come from Ulithi, that he had "transferred to a destroyer about a hundred miles south of Iwo," and that he had been on his "first real flight," but nothing of value. Floyd and Warren Earl had been briefed on their missions just hours before flight time. They had no knowledge of long-range strategy.

Major Horie spoke rudimentary English and wanted to improve. He asked Floyd and Warren Earl to give him English lessons.

"The war will be over soon," the boys told the major. Horie would need some practical survival skills. It was time to learn how to go out at night in America.

"They taught me how to enter a nightclub, to order drinks, to do checks and other such things," Horie later wrote. In one lesson, Warren Earl even took the major's hand to teach him how to snuggle a honey on the dance floor.

Two peaceful days passed. Floyd and Warren Earl enjoyed the security of being in each other's company. Perhaps they would make it out alive.

Then Captain Yoshii appeared.

On February 28, 1945, the day after he had Jimmy Dye beheaded, Yoshii informed General Tachibana that he needed another prisoner. Captain Tadaaki Kosuga remembered Yoshii telling Tachibana, "The prisoner did not help in the interception of broadcasts. Therefore, I had two of my youngest officers kill him."

"Is that so?" the general replied. "It was just an ordinary conversation between the two," Kosuga recalled.

Yoshii learned that Major Horie had two Americans in his care and he asked the general if he could have one to replace Jimmy Dye. Tachibana assented, and Yoshii brought Warren Earl up to the Mount Yoake radio station.

Captain Yoshii put Petty Officer Tamamura in charge of the new prisoner. "I did not like the idea," Tamamura-san recalled, "because I knew what he had done with Jimmy Dye." Tamamura was protective of his new charge. Warren Earl lived in Tamamura's own room in the radio station, shielded by a cloth curtain. "I did not like anyone to come to the room with him, except the men in my group, and we had a fine time," Tamamura-san said.

Vaughn worked with Tamamura in the receiving room. "I was not very busy at that time," Tamamura-san recalled, "and we talked about a lot of things, and we listened to the shortwave radio. Captain Yoshii told me to get all the information possible out of him."

Yoshii came by the radio station every day, badgering Tamamura for information from the prisoner. Warren Earl told Tamamura that "he was off the *Bennington,*" he flew "a single-cockpit fighter plane," he was from Texas, and he was "part Cherokee Indian." Together they listened to intercepts from nearby carriers and Warren Earl gave Tamamura routine information.

Yoshii read Tamamura's reports but wasn't satisfied.

"Yoshii said, 'I know that Vaughn knows more than what you are telling me,'" Tamamura-san remembered. "He said it was funny that the lieutenant did not know more."

Tamamura told his prisoner that Captain Yoshii wanted more in-depth information. Tamamura-san remembered the moment: "Vaughn told me that he knew more information than what I got out of him, and I could kill him, but I would not get the information from him."

It was clear that Tamamura was running out of ammunition in his battle to protect the American. Some Japanese sailors were not even willing to wait for Yoshii to step in. "A group of navy officers got drunk," Tamamura-san said. "They came and wanted to beat the flyer. They were outside demanding I turn him over. I said, 'No, sir.' They said, 'We are officers and we are giving you an order.' One said, 'Tamamura, I am going to chop your head off for this disobedience.' He pulled out a sword. Petty Officer Kagaya got up and said, 'God damn you, stay out of here and leave the prisoner alone.'"

The drunken officers later complained to Yoshii about Tamamura's obstinacy. "I was called to the captain's room," Tamamura said. "He said the prisoner was in my care and I did the right thing."

As Warren Earl spent his days in front of the radio monitor, he often found himself seated next to a shy young man who, like himself, was new to the radio station. The man was born in Hawaii and spoke English. He wanted to be on Chichi Jima about as much as Warren Earl did. His name was Private Nobuaki Iwatake.

Iwatake had been in the hospital suffering from diarrhea when, on February 19, there was an announcement: "U.S. TROOPS HAVE LANDED ON IWO JIMA. THIS IS AN EMERGENCY. ALL TROOPS WHO CAN WALK MUST RETURN TO YOUR UNITS." He returned to "pounding on rocks, hammering away with steel bars every day." Then one morning, his commander took him to battalion headquarters. "Here's a guy who speaks English," the commander told a colonel. "I order you to the naval communications unit on Mount Yoake," the colonel said. "Your work there is valuable; you must proceed immediately."

Iwatake arrived at the radio station just after Jimmy Dye was killed. He was introduced to Warren Earl but was wary.

"At first I didn't say much to him," Iwatake-san said. "We were told to be careful." But soon the two American-born boys, both in their early twenties, struck up a friendship. "I told him I was from Hawaii," Iwatake-san said. "He said he was from Texas. He was a very friendly guy, and we started talking a lot. Even though he was a prisoner, he used to tell us jokes." Decades later, Iwatake-san could still recall Warren Earl's humor:

A rough-hewn country boy was invited by a sophisticated girl to her home. She sat him on the couch. She started to play the piano. Her dog Fido was under the couch.

The boy had some gas. He thought no one would hear if he tooted quietly into the couch. He farted.

The girl stopped playing the piano and said to the dog, "Fido!"

Then the smile returned to her face as she resumed her playing.

The boy thought he got away with it so he let out another quiet toot.

"Fido!" she said, then again resumed playing.

One more fart and he'd be done with it. He tooted.

The girl said, "Fido! Get away from him before he shits on you!"

Untied and unshackled, Warren Earl mingled with everyone at the radio station. Against one wall was a row of wireless radio sets where Warren Earl sat next to Iwatake as they listened to messages. Against the opposite wall were navy bunk beds. Outside was a shack that served as a kitchen, a bathhouse, and a slit trench for a toilet. Nearby was a huge cave drilled into the side of a hill used as a shelter when American planes appeared overhead. Everyone there — Warren Earl included — worked, ate, and slept in the large radio room.

"While we were monitoring, there was a can of hard biscuits," Iwatake-san said. "We'd pass it around when we were hungry. Because of the bombing, we couldn't grow anything, so our meals were mostly canned goods — fish, beef, beans — and rice. We also had dried stuff to cook — dried vegetables, dry beans, dried tofu."

It must have been surreal to Warren Earl. Atop Mount Yoake, on an island six hundred miles from Tokyo, surrounded by the enemy, he must have felt as far away from Texas as possible. But with his headset on, he was more tuned in to the American homeland than he had been for months. He tapped his toes to the Andrews Sisters' hit song "Don't Fence Me In," chuckled at Bob Hope's jokes, and was kept abreast of the European conflict by Walter Cronkite's London broadcasts.

"We listened to radio contact between ships," Iwatake-san remembered. "I heard Admiral Halsey talk about his shelling of Japan. We listened to Tokyo Rose for the good music and the Voice of America for news." Once Captain Yoshii caught Petty Officer Tamamura laughing while listening to a comedy. "He asked for a translation," Tamamura-san said. "But comedy doesn't translate so well."

"I remember listening to the Bing Crosby show once," Iwatake-san told me. "Frank Sinatra was on the program with Bing's two kids. They told Sinatra they didn't like him because 'Daddy says you are taking our bread and butter away.'"

Warren Earl listened a lot, but he didn't volunteer any inside information. Iwatake and Tamamura covered for him. "I always told Yoshii that Vaughn was working out fine," Tamamura-san said, "because I did not want him to get killed."

But everyone on the headsets could hear reports of the slaughter on nearby Iwo Jima. Japanese messages made it clear they were being obliterated; American messages spoke of territory gained and Japanese dead. American progress on Iwo Jima meant death was nearing for both Warren Earl and his captors.

"We heard many frantic messages from Iwo Jima," Iwatake-san said. "Once, I heard cries from a ship, 'This is an emergency. We've been hit by a kamikaze! Emergency!' We often heard strange voices. It sounded like code but wasn't in English. It wasn't until long after the war that I learned that it was the Navajo code talkers."

And the boys endured the daily raids against the Mount Yoake radio station. "There were craters everywhere," Iwatake-san told me. "It was a hopeless feeling with all the bombing — we always had to be ready to run for shelter."

Once, a bomb exploded just outside the radio station's window. "We were almost goners," Iwatake-san said. "Warren ran out shaking his fists and shouted at the American plane, 'You son-of-a-bitch!'"

Warren Earl also impressed his captors with his brave face.

"I didn't hear him having any concern for himself, only for his buddy [Floyd Hall]," Iwatake-san said. "He would ask, 'I wonder what happened to him?'

"The only pain I sensed from him," Iwatake-san added, "was when he talked about his girlfriend. He'd say, 'After I finish this tour of duty, I'm going to marry my girlfriend.' Only then could I see anxiety on his face."

"He was a real friend to me," Iwatake-san told me. "One night we were walking in the dark to the bathhouse. I was nearsighted and fell into a bomb hole about six feet deep. Warren pulled me out. He kept asking, 'Are you OK? Are you hurt?' He expressed real concern like someone trying to rescue his buddy. Later we were soaking up to our necks in hot water. 'This is great,' Warren said."

One night, three *kamikaze* pilots trekked up Mount Yoake just to meet the Marine Flyboy. They had heard Warren Earl had piloted a Corsair.

"I acted as an interpreter," Iwatake-san recalled. "The *kamikaze* asked, 'If I got on your tail, what would you do?' Warren stood up and towered over everyone. He motioned with his hands to demonstrate how he would roll away from them. He was eager to explain his tactics. They spoke together as pilots, not as enemies. You could see they respected Warren."

Warren Earl Vaughn and Floyd Hall were receiving perhaps the most kindly and benign treatment experienced by any captive American pilots in the Pacific war. Things were certainly different for their Flyboy brethren held in Japan.

Bill Connell, the "last man off Chichi Jima alive," and Charlie Brown, shot down over Tokyo during the February 16 strike, were held at the Ofuna prisoner-of-war camp outside Yokohama. Ofuna held about eighty prisoners in the individual six-by-eight-foot cells of three flimsy wooden buildings.

"When we were in our cells, all you could do was sit on the floor," said Bill. "There were a couple of cotton blankets we made into our bedrolls, but they were worn out and gave no warmth. In the winter, we were freezing all the time."

Every morning all prisoners had to fall into formation for calisthenics. The guards would lead the exercises. They began by facing in the direction of the imperial palace and bowing to the emperor.

"The first time, I didn't bow with the rest," Charlie remembered, "until the man behind me said, 'Dammit, bow and spit.' I bowed and observed each prisoner bow and spit. The guards didn't see it because they were bowing."

The Japanese held all prisoners in low regard, but Flyboys were the lowest of the low. At Ofuna, the war criminal Flyboys were given only two thirds of the rations served to the regular POWs. "The Japanese were hard up for food at that point anyway," said Charlie, "so the POWs didn't get much, and we got less." On one of Charlie's first days at Ofuna, he was served soup with a big fat green worm in it. He tossed it out into the corridor. "Two Americans had a head-on collision as they each grabbed for that worm," Charlie told me. "They had been there longer than me. That was the last worm I discarded."

"All we talked about was food," Connell recalled. "That's the way it is when you're hungry all the time."

Bill and Charlie described their meals in Ofuna as "mostly hot water," with various other ingredients according to availability — cucumbers, potatoes, fish eyeballs, and barley. "Once I got a chicken wing," Charlie remembered, "and I slowly chewed it over days. It was something to chew on, and I was hoping for some sustenance. I lost forty-three pounds — I came out weighing ninety-seven."

The Flyboys never once had a chance to wash their clothes in the six months they were there. A bath was a once-a-month occurrence consisting of a small bowl of water and a sliver of soap. And Flyboys were regularly beat up during their interrogation sessions.

"They set up a good cop / bad cop dynamic," Bill told me. "The guards were the bad guys, the questioners were the good guys. The questioners would give us a cigarette. If we didn't give them an answer, the guard would work us over." Charlie recalled, "The interrogation was intense, but I heard it had been worse earlier in the war. They knew dang well they were losing. Maybe that's why they weren't as ruthless as they had been. But it was rough enough."

The interrogators spoke excellent English and some had worked and studied in the United States. Flyboy Oscar Long, who went from one hundred sixty pounds to one hundred eighteen while at Ofuna, was asked if he could name a U.S. Navy carrier christened for a famous university. Long was stumped. His interrogator prompted him: The college was located in New Jersey. "I still couldn't recall the name," Long said, "so the interrogator became exasperated and asked if I didn't know the U.S. had a college named Princeton. And then he boasted that he graduated from there."

"Not all the guards were awful," Bill Connell told me. "I would say about sixty percent of the guards did what they had to do but didn't take pleasure in it. The remaining forty percent took great pleasure in making us as uncomfortable as they possibly could. They were young kids — sixteen, seventeen, eighteen years old — with a lot of energy. Even though they were young, they were vicious; they did everything they could to antagonize us, instill as much fear in us as they could. They could do anything they wanted to us, stick us with a bayonet, enough to be uncomfortable, not to fatally wound us."

Once, a guard found Bill's name, serial number, and date of entry into Ofuna scratched in the corner of his cell. Bill later recalled the punishment: "The guard made me assume the position — standing with legs spread apart — and hit me five times, knocking me down each time. Then he said, 'Sorry for that,' and gave me a cigarette."

Prisoners' "violations" were recorded, and special punishment was administered once a week. "They'd take us out one at a time and have us put our hands up against a fence," Charlie told me. "They'd take a club that was a little longer than a baseball bat. They would hit us as hard as they could against our buttocks and hamstrings. After the third swing, your muscles would tie up in a knot — muscle spasms — and you'd have to crawl back to your cell. It took hours for that to go away."

As carrier planes bombed so near to Ofuna that Charlie "could smell the burnt powder," the prisoners and guards knew the American military was drawing near. But that only made the Flyboys' status more precarious.

"The Japanese constantly told us that if Japan lost the war, we as war criminals were going to be executed," Bill recalled. "And we believed them, no doubt about it!" "I thought I wouldn't survive," Charlie told me. "I thought they'd execute me with the invasion."

The Ofuna guards who harassed Bill and Charlie probably viewed themselves as relatively benign. If the tables had been turned, the guards certainly would not have expected any better from the Americans. "I was shocked by the U.S. treatment," Yoshio Nakajima, one of the very few Iwo Jima POWs, told me. "The U.S. treated me fairly as a human. There was a huge gap between the Japanese and American forces." Another Iwo Jima POW, Masaji Ozawa, told me he believed he would have his head chopped off if he surrendered to U.S. forces. Instead, he found himself receiving medical treatment for his wounds and drinking Coca-Cola. "Our education was a military one," Ozawa-san said. "We were supposed to die for the emperor. We were small things, like bugs to be squashed. We thought the Americans would treat us as bugs, just like our army did. But instead America saved my life."

As Warren Earl passed his days in No Mans Land listening to broadcasts, Floyd Hall remained at Major Horie's headquarters, giving English lessons. Soon the soldiers began referring to Floyd as "Horie's pet." Major Horie asked Captain Yoshii when Warren Earl would be returned to him, as Yoshii had promised. "Just a few more days," the captain would always answer.

American carrier planes continued to harass the troops on Chichi Jima. And other, larger Marianas-based airplanes made their appearance also. "The B-29s would swoosh over us and drop what we thought were bombs," said Iwatake-san. "But they were just dropping empty fuel tanks on us to say hello. Those B-29s you can never forget; they were huge."

On the evening of March 9, Flyboys Floyd Hall and Warren Earl Vaughn heard something unusual overhead in the darkness. For hours, a long stream of more than 330 B-29s flew north at low altitudes over

Chichi Jima. Usually the planes flew in smaller numbers, but their concentrated roar punctuated the night.

"As the bombers were going overhead to bomb Japan," said Dr. Mitsuyoshi Sasaki, "the men on Chichi Jima would think of our brothers, sisters, and mothers and feel as if we were seeing them off to their deaths." Tamamura-san told me, "We'd wire back to Tokyo about the B-29s that were on their way. We knew what they were going to do."

But actually no one knew. No one could imagine what was about to happen during the evening hours of March 9 and the early morning of March 10. The largest slaughter of humans in world history was about to take place. The airplane, which just a few decades earlier was a frail bundle of wood most military experts judged would never be a major factor in war, would now prove itself as history's most effective killing machine.

In 1937, when Japan bombed "defenseless men, women and children" in Chinese cities, Franklin Roosevelt had called the action "ruthless" and said it "sickened the hearts of every civilized man and woman." In 1939, Germany had shocked the world by bombing Warsaw. Then, in 1940, the Luftwaffe had bombed Rotterdam, London, and Coventry. Roosevelt "again pleaded that all parties refrain from bombing civilians, and went on to 'recall with pride that the United States consistently has taken the lead in urging that this inhuman practice be prohibited.'" The British foreign office condemned the "inhuman methods used by the Germans in other countries" and declared that "His Majesty's Government have made it clear that it is no part of their policy to bomb nonmilitary objectives, no matter what the policy of the German Government may be."

Yet when the English and Americans entered the air war in force, they proved to have few qualms about slaughtering German and Japanese civilians.

On July 8, 1940, Prime Minister Churchill wrote, "When I look around to see how we can win the war I see that there is only one sure path, and this is an absolutely devastating, exterminating attack by very heavy bombers from this country upon the Nazi homeland." Yet the ability of an airplane traveling hundreds of miles an hour to pinpoint something as small as a factory or munitions dump proved to be impossible. "A chilling report in August 1941 documented that only about one bomb in five landed within even a five-mile radius of the designated target." So if the Royal Air Force could not bomb the targets they wanted to, they would bomb what they could.

The civilized English slaughter from the air was distinguished from the barbaric German and Japanese campaigns by an obfuscating cloud of euphemisms. The public was told British planes sought out strictly "military targets" and civilians were only killed by "mistake." Churchill spoke of "dehousing." Indiscriminate bombing of civilian areas was called "area bombing." One U.S. Army Air Force instructor noted, "Most of the European nations are definitely contemplating [area bombing, but it is] repugnant to our humanitarian principles." Instead, U.S. Army Air Force doctrine called for "high-altitude precision bombing." The Norden bombsight, a new high-tech aiming device, was capable of "pinpoint accuracy," the Americans claimed, able to place a bomb down a smokestack from five miles up in the sky. This technological marvel would, it was argued, make high-altitude bombing more effective and more humane. Cities could be bombed with surgical precision, targeting only key economic sites like airplane factories and oil refineries. But the tests on the Norden bombsight had been conducted in the dry, sunny American Southwest where there was maximum visibility. Bombing conditions in foggy, rainy Germany were very different.

Even though the bombs were not hitting their marks, the U.S. military kept up the fiction of high-altitude strategic bombing for stateside Americans. As British historian John Keegan writes, "[It] combined moral scruple, historical optimism, and technological pioneering, all three distinctly American characteristics."

But on the front lines, American Flyboys knew what was happening. "Don't get the notion that your job is going to be glorious or glamorous," said an American officer briefing a bomber crew. "You've got dirty work to do and might as well face the facts: You're going to be baby killers."

Bombardier Frank Clark was the son of a Wisconsin factory worker and his mission bothered him. "What I don't like, and didn't talk about to anyone," he admitted after the war, "was the fact that we were bombing industrial towns that were largely populated with working people — much like the towns a lot of us came from. . . . To me the war had a human face."

American and British bombs eventually killed more than 650,000 German civilians. (Total U.S. combat deaths in WWII were about 400,000.) Twenty percent of these — 130,000 — were German children. An additional 800,000 German civilians were maimed. With their homes burned to the ground, millions fled for their lives. In accomplishing these staggering statistics, many Flyboys perished. The Americans lost 18,369 planes and suffered 79,265 casualties in the European theater alone. Britain had about 80,000 Flyboy casualties. In comparison, the entire United States Marine Corps had 75,000 casualties in all of World War II.

And the earlier German air attacks that had been "odious" to Winston Churchill were tame in comparison to the monstrous raids he authorized. In firestorms like that at Hamburg in late July of 1943, the RAF killed more people in one stroke than would die in Britain during the entire war. At least 45,000 old men (the young men were in the service), women, and children were killed in the conflagration. Half of Hamburg was destroyed and 400,000 people were "dehoused." In Hamburg, 731 RAF bombers dropped four-pound incendiaries to start fires on roofs and thirty-pound high explosives to penetrate deeper into houses and disrupt roads to hamper fire crews. The rapidly expanding fireball created a meteorological phenomenon — a firestorm that sucked oxygen into its center with "a bellows-like draft creating terrific winds that sent bodies, trees, and parts of buildings flying through air heated to 800° centigrade." "One survivor said the sound of the wind was 'like the Devil laughing.'"

Screaming human torches ran down streets while "tiny children lay like fried eels on the pavement." Some ran to their basements or air-raid shelters. But "the fire drained these quarters of oxygen, asphyxiating inhabitants, then baking the bodies through radiant heat or, if the fire burst through collapsing walls, melting them into 'a thick, greasy black mass' or leaving behind what the Germans called Bombenbrandschrumpfleichen (incendiary-bomb-shrunken bodies)."

Sir Arthur Harris, who directed Churchill's bombing campaign, later wrote:

> Tell me one operation of war which is moral . . . Sticking a bayonet into a man's belly, is that moral? Then they say, well, of course strategic bombing involved civilians. Civilians are always involved in major war.

After all, previous wars ended up in the besieging of major cities, and in besieging a city what was the idea? To cut off all supplies, and the city held out if it could until they'd eaten the last dog, cat, and sewer rat and were all starving, and meanwhile the besieging forces lobbed every missile they could lay their hands on into the city, more or less regardless of where those missiles landed, as an added incentive to surrender.

Some, including Jimmy Doolittle, opposed the indiscriminate bombing by Americans of German civilians. One air corps general wrote, "We should never allow the history of this war to convict us of throwing the strategic bomber at the man in the street. [Such activity would] absolutely convince the Germans that we are the barbarians they say we are, for it would be perfectly obvious to them that this is primarily a large-scale attack on civilians, as, in fact, it of course will be." Another air force general protested this "baby killing plan."

But Roosevelt told Secretary of War Stimson that the enemy had to be taught a lesson. FDR wrote that it was "of the utmost importance that every person in Germany should realize that this time Germany is a defeated nation. . . . The fact that they are a defeated nation, collectively and individually, must be so impressed upon them that they will hesitate to start any new war."

Army air corps leaders had been dismayed when an Associated Press article somehow got by censors and informed the home front that "the Allied air commanders have made the long-awaited decision to adopt deliberate terror bombing of the great German population centers as a ruthless expedient to hasten Hitler's doom." One air force man warned of the "nationwide serious effect on the Air Forces as we have steadily preached the gospel of precision bombing against military and industrial targets." But FDR, now comfortable with "barbarous" methods of air war, saw something different in these holocausts: "an impressive demonstration of what America might be able to achieve in its war against Japan." As award-winning historian Richard Frank has written, "The most fundamental point about the history of bombing in Europe is that it had trampled down every moral barrier to the use of massive aerial firepower . . . even when it was clear that the destruction of the target would entail death for large numbers of noncombatants."

On February 3, 1945, American bombers killed at least 35,000 civilians in Berlin. Then, on February 14, the Anglo-Americans scorched another 40,000 to death in Dresden. Kurt Vonnegut memorialized the moment in his novel *Slaughterhouse-Five:* "Dresden was like the moon now, nothing but minerals. The stones were hot. Everybody else in the neighborhood was dead." Vonnegut described "little logs" lying on the pavement. "These were people who had been caught in the firestorm."

Today, with twenty-twenty hindsight, people speak of March 1945 as "near the end of the war." True, Germany was close to defeat. But it was a different story in the Pacific. Casualties were increasing and the fighting becoming more intense. Observed Ernie Pyle, "The Pacific war is gradually getting condensed, and consequently tougher and tougher. The closer we go to Japan itself, the harder it will be. . . . To me it looks like trying days for us in the years ahead." Ernie didn't say months — he said years.

Billy Mitchell had told America how to deal with Japan twenty years earlier: "Japan's teeming cities erected of 'paper and wood and other inflammable structures' comprised 'the greatest aerial targets the world has ever seen. . . . Incendiary projectiles would burn the cities to the ground in short order.'" Back in early 1940, AAF general Claire Chennault had written General Hap Arnold that five hundred American aircraft could "burn out the industrial heart of the Empire with fire-bomb attacks on the teeming bamboo ant heaps of Honshu and Kyushu." Hap had responded that the U.S. "was only interested in the precision bombing of military targets, and the 'use of incendiaries against cities was contrary to our national policy of attacking military objectives.'"

But the commander in chief felt differently. "Whereas Arnold and the airmen rejected the idea, Roosevelt was delighted by the proposal and ordered his top cabinet officials to work on the project." The plan soon died as Secretary of War Stimson "had moral objections to attacks on cities and civilians," and General George Marshall was focused more on the threat Hitler posed to his GIs. But as war with Japan loomed closer, Marshall had invited seven Washington journalists to a secret briefing on November 15, 1941. Off the record, Marshall told the opinion-makers that if war came with Japan, the United States would fight without mercy. American planes would be "dispatched immediately to set the paper cities of Japan on fire. There won't be any hesitation about bombing civilians — it will be all out."

In the aftermath of Pearl Harbor, the U.S. had been unable to secure landing fields close enough to bomb the island nation. As a result, it wasn't until early 1943 that the first detailed study of urban attack against Japan had been produced. It had noted that "even as small amounts as 10 tons of M-69's [small napalm-filled pipe bombs] would have the possibility of wiping out major portions of any of the large Japanese cities." By now, the Japanese had been so demonized that few Americans had a problem with what they had recently considered barbarous bombing. But the AAF was still concerned about appearances. A May 1943 memo about firebombing Japanese cities had included this telling sentence: "It is desired that the areas selected include, or be in the immediate vicinity of, legitimate military targets."

Japan is a small country, about the size of California, and most of Japan is mountainous, so there is no "interior." The largest cities hug the coastline. Manufacturing was incredibly concentrated with "about 75 percent in the half-dozen largest cities." "A line connecting the industrialized centers of Japan . . . would inscribe an elongated S, with the upper tip at Niigata, the sinuous bends encircling the great centers of Tokyo, Yokohama, Nagoya, and Kobe, and the lower tip running through Hiroshima-Kure and Yawata." These cities are all within 150 miles of one another. Whereas only 12 percent of Germany's industrial workforce lived in its fifteen largest cities, 34 percent of Japan's factory workers were crammed into its six largest cities. Berlin had 6 percent of Germany's industrial workers; Tokyo had 14 percent of Japan's. Hamburg had 6,000 inhabitants to the square mile, while Osaka had 45,000 and Tokyo's Asakusa workers' ward had more than 130,000 to the square mile.

In February 1944, Roosevelt received a plan for strategic air assault on Japan. By January of 1945, bombing studies that spoke of the "vulnerability of Japanese cities to fire" now began to consistently include the argument that cities were "a valid and eventually important military objective . . . because of the heavy dispersal of industry within the cities and within the most congested parts of them." Many family homes were also workshops where parts were fabricated for assembly in nearby factories. "Each factory was like a tree radiating a web of roots throughout the surrounding living areas from which it drew both workers and parts."

Elmer Davis, head of the Office of War Information, told the Joint Chiefs of Staff in February of 1945 how the American public felt: "There did not appear to be a great deal of opposition from the humanitarian point of view to the bombing of Japan but some opposition is being expressed to the continual bombing of Berlin." Syndicated military analyst Major George Fielding Eliot called for "the complete and ruthless destruction of Japanese industry, so that not one brick of any Japanese factory shall be left upon another, so that there shall not be in Japan one electric motor or one steam or gasoline engine, not a chemical laboratory, not so much as a book which tells how these things are made." In 1945, FDR's son and adviser Elliot Roosevelt called for bombing Japan "until we have destroyed about half the Japanese civilian population." And the B-29 made it possible.

FDR had made America's biggest WWII investments in airplanes. The most expensive — the costliest weapon of history's largest war — was the B-29. The atom bomb would cost $2 billion, but many in Washington referred to the B-29 as America's "$3 billion gamble."

The B-29 Superfortress was far from an overnight technical success. Long before Pearl Harbor, Hap Arnold had perceived the need for a large bomber able to fly long distances to defend America against the Nazi threat. After Pearl Harbor, Hap had rushed development of the B-29. He demanded that improvements that normally would take years be completed in months. The resulting plane was plagued by mechanical problems. The engines overheated and caught fire, and famous test pilots died in fiery crashes.

Not surprisingly, nobody wanted to fly the B-29, so Hap asked Jimmy Doolittle to send him his best pilot. That man was Paul Tibbets. Tibbets had flown the U.S.'s first strategic bombing sortie against the Germans. He was just twenty-nine years old, but he was a skilled pilot and a quiet yet firm leader who inspired confidence. Tibbets soon whipped the program into such snappy shape that he became known as "Mr. B-29."

The B-29 was to airplanes what rifles were to slingshots. It was the biggest, longest, widest, heaviest, fastest, and longest-flying airplane in history. Its four propellers were each sixteen feet long. It could carry ten tons of bombs and still fly 357 miles per hour. It could remain airborne more than sixteen hours while providing living room–like comfort to its eleven-man crew. Other planes required bulky clothes and cumbersome oxygen masks in the minus-50-degree cold at thirty thousand feet. But this "Cadillac of the skies" had pressurized crew quarters, so airmen could lounge comfortably in their regular clothes. And once the kinks had (mostly) been worked out, it became the most devastating weapon of WWII. Recalled pilot Harry George: "Shirtsleeve atmosphere. Flush rivets. Powerful engines. Big new type of bombsight. Altitude pressurized. We loved it. It was just a beautiful, beautiful plane."

On June 15, 1944, China-based B-29s made their first attack on Japan, against a steel mill in Kyushu. Sixty planes flying at thirty thousand feet reached the target, but only one bomb hit the plant, and seven bombers didn't return. These high-altitude daylight missions were abysmally ineffective. More bombs landed on rice paddies than on steel furnaces, and too many planes were lost.

To solve the problem and prove the B-29's ability to win the war, Hap Arnold dispatched his Top Gun out of Europe, General Curtis LeMay. Curtis was just thirty-eight years old, the youngest general in the army air force. He was personally brave and had led a number of dangerous bombing missions in Europe. He was big and beefy, but he spoke so softly it was hard to hear him from a few yards away. His round face was frozen in a perpetual scowl, the result of a mild form of Bell's palsy. Curtis was known for his immobile, unflappable style. A subordinate said he "doesn't appear to work much, but he thinks more than any man I have ever known." Said another:

> Until he made up his mind about something, he was inclined to listen and say nothing. After he had made up his mind, he remained silent long enough to figure out how he could announce it in the fewest possible words. One or two sentences was his idea of a speech. Perhaps this paucity of words was by itself a factor in riveting the men around him. He had a way of sounding as if he had considered all the options, then chosen the only possible one. And by saying so in so few words, he seemed to con-

vince everyone that, however surprising his decision might be, it was probably the right one.

A combination of General George Patton and Vince Lombardi, Curtis was totally focused on the goal; winning was the only thing. He instructed his men "that if a crew was able to get to a target, the inability to return was no reason to abort." As one Flyboy said about him, "Our job was to hit the target — planes and crews, it seemed, were expendable." Curtis had a reputation as a tough taskmaster ready to accept casualties to achieve results. One airman said, "General LeMay has taken over [and] he is going to get us all killed."

Curtis later remembered his orders as: "You go ahead and get results with the B-29. If you don't get results, you'll be fired." He wrote that he knew he was under pressure because "our entire Nation howled like a pack of wolves for an attack on the Japanese homeland."

With the capture of Saipan, Curtis moved the B-29 operation to the Mariana Islands. Now Flyboys were within reach of the Japanese empire.

Curtis initially stuck to air force dogma — high-altitude precision bombing. But at thirty thousand feet over Japan, his crews were buffeted by a series of mysterious winds no one had encountered before, as if the gods were again whipping up the *kaze* to protect the Land of the Rising Sun. This unknown witch's brew of winds would later be named the jet stream. Jet stream stratospheric blasts came howling out of Siberia across the Sea of Japan at 250 miles an hour. If a B-29 flew perpendicular to the wind, the plane "skidded" sideways. If the plane flew into the wind, it became a stationary target, a sitting duck for anti-aircraft fire. If a pilot flew with the wind, his Surperfortress would travel at a ground speed of 450 miles an hour — much too fast to aim with Norden bombsights. The divine winds also created layers of bad weather between the planes and the targets six miles below. On one run, just 24 planes out of 111 were able to sight their targets and drop their payloads anywhere near them.

Hap Arnold viewed the expensive B-29s — they cost $600,000 each — as magic silver bullets that could end the war. If Curtis didn't get results from the country's huge investment, the idea of strategic bombing would be tossed, the navy would probably commandeer the B29s, and Billy Mitchell's dream of an independent air force would be out the window. "I had to do something," Curtis said. "And I had to do something fast."

Curtis examined past AAF doctrine — daytime high-altitude precision bombing — and decided to turn it on its head. He would go in at night. He would swoop in low, below the *kaze.* In the darkness, there would be no precision and he would bomb indiscriminately.

"Going in low" might sound sensible to the reader, but to the B-29 Flyboys, it sounded like suicide. The whole point of flying high was to avoid being shot. Flyboys at thirty thousand feet could look down and see fields of flak coming up at them. Now they had to conceive of flying directly into those black puffs. This was like asking a foxhole soldier to suddenly abandon his protective cover and charge toward the incoming bullets.

But Curtis thought he had found a hole in the Japanese defenses. To some it was a wild guess, but he figured the Japanese didn't have sufficient antiaircraft coverage between three and ten thousand feet. He would thread his planes through that seam. His flak experts told him he'd lose 70 percent of his B-29s. But his gut told him otherwise. He hoped to achieve surprise and confuse Japanese antiaircraft gunners, who would be forced to attempt adjustments in the dark. He also reasoned that Japanese fighter planes would not rise to confront his planes in the dark. So, in another daring move, he decided to take the guns, ammunition, and gunners off the B-29s, enabling each plane to carry 2,700 extra pounds of napalm.

To test his theory, Curtis chose the biggest target — Tokyo — and decided not to tell his boss. As he wrote:

If I do it I won't say a thing to General Arnold in advance. Why should I? He's on the hook in order to get some results out of the B-29's. But if I set up this deal, and Arnold O.K.'s it beforehand, then he would have to assume some of the responsibility. And if I don't tell him, and it's all a failure, and I don't produce any results, then he can fire me. And he can put another commander in here, and still have a chance to make something out of the 29's. This is sound, this is practical, this is the way I'll do it: not one word to General Arnold.

On March 9, 1945, Curtis briefed his Flyboys on the mission. He spoke first of the target, the route and land-sea rescue arrangements. Then, cigar in hand, feet firmly planted, he faced the crews and announced, "I'm going to send you in at five thousand feet. And without any guns, gunners, or ammunition."

The boys were shocked. This was a death sentence issued by a maniac. "A sort of cold fear gripped the crews. Many frankly did not expect to return from a raid over that city, at an altitude of less than 10,000 feet."

"We thought LeMay was out of his mind to order anything like this," said pilot Fiske Hanley. "At these low altitudes, four thousand to six thousand feet, the Japanese could hit us with almost any kind of flak that they had."

"We thought he was crazy," echoed Newell Fears. "We just couldn't comprehend the man. We had to strip all of our ammunition. . . . It just was unthinkable." Bob Rodenhaus thought Curtis had lost his marbles: "It's putting a plane in a confrontation that it was not designed for, and we couldn't conceive of what the purpose was." "I thought it was next to suicide," said Loy Collingwood. "We were scared." Joe Tucker believed he had just heard his death sentence: "We thought, 'Oh, boy, Old Blood-and-Guts — his guts and our blood.'"

But Curtis was focused on the awful step necessary to win this war: "No matter how you slice it, you're going to kill an awful lot of civilians," he told his crews. "Thousands and thousands. But, if you don't destroy Japanese industry, we're going to have to invade Japan. And how many Americans will be killed in an invasion of Japan? Some say a million. We're at war with Japan. We were attacked by Japan. Do you want to kill Japanese, or would you rather have Americans killed?" Regarding the morality of an operation that would kill civilians, Curtis simply said, "Every soldier thinks something of the moral aspects of what he is doing. But all war is immoral and if you let that bother you, you're not a good soldier."

The B-29s began lumbering down Guam airstrips at 5:35 P.M. on Friday, March 9, 1945. On Saipan and Tinian, which were nearer to Tokyo, they began forty minutes later. The Flyboys ascended with heavy hearts. Many believed they were winging to their deaths. John Jennings, who remained behind on Guam, thought he would never see his buddies again. "We all went down to the flight line to say good-bye to our friends," he recalled. "Nobody's going in at those altitudes and coming back."

By 8:15 P.M., 334 B-29s were in the air. They formed three 400-mile-long parallel streams that roared above Iwo Jima and Chichi Jima. Two hundred million dollars' worth of hardware was in the air. This was at a time when $1,700 was a sufficient yearly salary to support a family of four, a Harvard education cost $1,000, and a good hotel room in New York cost three dollars a night.

To test napalm's potential on "industrial" Japan, the army had built a "Little Tokyo" at Dugway Proving Ground, eighty-seven miles southwest of Salt Lake City, Utah. Carpenters and designers who had worked in Japan had constructed two dozen Japanese-style homes, using authentic Japanese wood. Japanese floors — tatami mats — were hard to come by, but some were found in Hawaii and shipped in. Authentic furniture was placed in the rooms. To simulate real living conditions, clothes were hung in closets.

Throughout the summer of 1943, the army air force had dropped different mixtures of napalm on Utah's Little Tokyo. The winner was a new bomb called the M69. The M69 didn't look like a bomb; it looked like a section of pipe twenty inches long and three inches in diameter, and was not round but hexagonal with blunt ends. Inside the pipe was napalm packed in cheesecloth bags. The entire assembly weighed just six and a half pounds. This pipe bomb was dropped from a plane and floated to earth attached to a three-foot-long streamer that slowed its descent, preventing it from falling so fast that it would go right through a building and into the basement.

When the M69 hit the ground, it lay still for about five seconds — just an inert pipe. Then, with a bang, it shot out the cheesecloth bags. If there were no obstructions, the bags traveled a distance of a hundred yards. If the cheesecloth bag struck an object, its projectile force burst the bag and the flaming goo broke into hundreds of small chunks and splattered up to fifty feet in all directions.

Other incendiaries burned intensely, but they burned in one place. An old-fashioned incendiary might crash through your roof and start your floor afire, but the fire was localized and you might be able to put it out. The M69 didn't start one fire, it started hundreds. And they kept burning.

The popular *Collier's* magazine highlighted the perfection of the M69 napalm bomb in a breezy article entitled "Tokyo Calling Cards." Accompanying the article was a colorful illustration of Little Tokyo on the barren Utah salt flats. The article said the M69 was first tested against civilian homes. "Having proved itself in the comparatively simple job of demolishing houses, the bomb had to be capable of doing an equal job on industrial buildings, too, or the Army didn't want it. During an incendiary bomb attack some houses do get burned — by accident — but the prime target is the enemy's industrial plant." The article did not question why, if industrial targets were the priority for destruction, meticulously constructed homes were the first targets of the tests.

For decades the Japanese government had known its cities were uniquely vulnerable to firebombing. But if the Spirit Warriors admitted this vulnerability to the populace, their prestige might be questioned. So even after the fall of Saipan, the Spirit Warriors elected "to give priority to production over civilian protection."

As a result, the entire city of Tokyo had only eighteen concrete air-raid shelters. These had room for five thousand of the city's six million inhabitants. Only eight thousand firemen were available. The standard method of protection for the people of Tokyo was little dugouts beside their houses. Yoshiko Hashimoto, a twenty-four-year-old mother living with her parents and sisters, remembered that her family's dugout was built up above ground because of the high water table around their home. "I wondered if it would protect us," she told me decades later.

Neighborhood associations of ten to twenty families each were organized into an air-raid defense network. "The military instructed us civilians," Yoshiko Hashimoto said. "They would toss a mock bomb that generated smoke. We threw water on it. We had bucket brigade practice. We learned how to care for the wounded, how to put them on stretchers."

Against 334 $600,000 bombers winging to Japan with 3,334,000 pounds of deadly napalm, Tokyoites were armed with wet mops, sandbags, and buckets of water.

March 9, Hashimoto-san remembered, was "very windy and cold." A north wind was blowing over fifty miles an hour, "violent as a spring typhoon." As the leading B-29 "pathfinder" planes winged toward the empire, radiomen tuned in to Tokyo Rose. Crewmen glanced at one another as they heard the song "Smoke Gets in Your Eyes." Just before midnight, a spokesman for Imperial General Headquarters went on the radio to remind Tokyo residents that Army Day would be celebrated the next day, March 10. There would be a big parade in the center of Tokyo. As he signed off, he encouraged his listeners to keep their chins up. His last words were "The darkest hour is just before dawn."

Minutes later, the pathfinder planes came whooshing over Tokyo at a height of only five hundred feet. Releasing their jellied gasoline, they seared a flaming X across the city.

"They took the most experienced crews and put them up about forty-five minutes before the bulk of the bomber stream arrived," pilot Charlie Phillips said about the pathfinders. "They drew a fiery X on the ground. That formed four quadrants. We would have a designated quadrant to put our bombs into as we arrived."

Then the bombers arrived in groups of three, homing in on the flaming X. The B-29s had timing devices called intervalometers that planted the five-hundred-pound clusters of incendiaries every fifty feet. "In this way, the bomb load of each bomber covered a strip 350 feet by 2,000 feet."

The 334 B-29s dropped 8,519 bombs weighing 500 pounds each. These bombs burst open 2,000 feet above Tokyo and released a total of 496,000 individual 6.2-pound cylinders containing jellied gasoline. The cylinders floated down slowly with their little parachutes.

Back on Guam, General Curtis LeMay sat in the control room smoking a cigar.

"I'm sweating this one out myself," he told an aide. "A lot could go wrong. I can't sleep. I usually can, but not tonight."

Finally, the first bombs-away message arrived: "Bombing the primary target visually. Large fires observed. Flak moderate. Fighter opposition nil." Curtis wouldn't know much detail until reconnaissance planes returned with photos the next evening, but out of a corner of his mouth, he mumbled, "It looks pretty good." Then "he shifted his cigar and for the first time he smiled."

Seventeen-year-old Miyoko Takeuchi had jumped into the family dugout when the alert sounded. "I saw American planes dropping incendiaries like a shower, like a Niagara Falls of fireworks," she said. "Everyone there in the dugout said 'How beautiful!'" From the distant hills of the Jesuit Sophia University, Father Gustav Bitter thought the scene of falling cylinders with their parachutes resembled "a silver curtain falling like . . . the silver tinsel that we hung from Christmas trees in Germany . . . and where these silver streamers would touch the earth, red fires would spring up." Danish diplomat Lars Tillitse later said the incendiaries "did not fall, they descended rather slowly, like a cascade of silvery water. One single bomb covered quite a big area, and what they covered they devoured."

Thousand of fires sprang to life. "The wind acted like a lid on the fire, keeping the heat low and forcing the flames to spread out instead of up. Smoke and sparks were everywhere, and white-hot gusts came roaring down narrow streets." Individual fires merged into whirlwinds of flame that lashed out like dragons' tongues. Within thirty minutes, the fire department was completely defeated. "At one station, the fire left only a tangle of corpses around a melted fire engine." Recalled one pilot, "The whole area was lighted as if it were broad daylight when we entered the drop zone."

Curtis's hunch had been correct.

"It turned out that the Japanese had built a great deal of antiaircraft fire that went up to about 5,500 feet," said Flyboy John Jennings. "They had quite a bit of medium that went from around 10,000 up to 20,000 and then from 20,000 to 30,000, but they had built nothing between 5,500 and 10,000. Who would be crazy enough to come in at those altitudes?"

Yoshiko Hashimoto was asleep with her one-year-old son and three sisters, mother, and father when the attack began. Her husband was away on duty. She heard the air-raid siren. She ran with her baby to the family's dugout for protection. Her mother and father and sisters — Chieko, nineteen; Etsuko, seventeen; and Hisae, fourteen — came next.

Her father immediately sensed that this raid was different from the smaller ones Tokyo had already endured. "It's dangerous to stay in the dugout, let's run away!" he shouted to his wife and daughters.

"I tied my baby on my back and covered him with a big maternity cover," Hashimoto-san told me. "I carried diapers, milk, and important family documents." She didn't yet grasp that this night would be a flight for survival.

The family took shelter underneath an elevated railway. But in just seconds, her father yelled again, "Let's go!"

"I looked to the west — it was red like the sun setting," Hashimoto-san said. "I saw many pillars of fire sprouting from the ground. Many B-29s were dropping bombs. They were flying so low I wondered if they'd hit the utility poles. They were so large and their bellies were red from the reflected fire.

"Days earlier, the B-29s were small dots in the sky with a tail," she told me. "But that night they were so big. And the sound of so many incendiaries going off was like listening to a train rushing by. The town was like day even though it was night.

"The fire was moving fast, driven by the wind," she said. "It was a storm rushing at us with sparkles of fire inside."

Nineteen-year-old sister Chieko decided to remain under the train tracks to guard the family possessions.

Now six family members ran from the galloping flames. Yoshiko carried her baby boy on her back as her family "took flight before the flames, through smoke that hung so thickly in places that they could not see more than ten feet, all panting 'huh, huh, huh' as they ran." She tried to hold her younger sister Etsuko's hand, but seventeen-year-old Etsuko felt it was her responsibility to clutch a big pot of rice with both hands in case the family needed it. Etsuko fell behind and in the push and shove of the crowd, Yoshiko shouted back to her, "Little Etsuko, are you OK?"

"Big sister, please wait for me!" Etsuko screamed.

"The distance between us widened," Hashimoto-san told me through tears. "I lost her in the crowd of people. I am eighty-one years old now. But I still hear her voice, 'Big sister, please wait for me!'"

The seven members of the Hashimoto family now numbered five. The baby boy on Yoshiko's back was screaming nonstop. The wind and the heat levitated whole portions of sheet-metal roofs that sliced through the air like Frisbees. Sparks, bedding, and burned clothes whizzed past them.

Gunner David Farquar, high above the flames, remembered, "The missions were so low, the fires were so intense, that oftentimes scraps and bits of burning material would end up in our bomb bays — little pieces of shingle or little pieces of scraps and bits of things that had been burned." The tremendous heat tossed planes five thousand feet above the flames. "The turbulence was so bad that some aircraft were flipped over on their back, the whole crews," remembered pilot Harry

George. "Imagine a piece of paper in a leaf pile," gunner Ed Ricketson said. "Now imagine an entire city." "My chair was bolted to the floor and tied to me with the seat belt," radio operator George Gladden said. "When the wave hit, it jerked the bolts out, and I was stuck against the ceiling with a chair tied to me."

The fire was so hot that "superheated vapors rushing ahead of the wall of flames killed or knocked unconscious its victims even before the flames reached them." The temperature reached 1,800 degrees Fahrenheit. Babies exploded on mothers' backs, and cars on streets were "consumed like crumpled paper."

Iwao Ishikawa remembered being trapped by the fire in a group of about forty people. "Because of this inferno, this burning hell, a young father right next to me didn't seem to know that the child on his back was on fire," Ishikawa said. "People on the outer edge of the group fell one by one, dead from inhalation."

Rivers of fire flowed down the streets. Canals boiled and humans burst spontaneously into flames, blazing like matchsticks. People's heads exploded in the heat, the liquid brains in their burst skulls bubbling an eerie fluorescence. The feet of the fleeing masses scrunched eyeballs that had popped from sockets under pressure.

Miho Yoshioka ran into a temple for safety. She remembered thinking that she saw "a lot of statues of guardian deities inside, just like the ones outside. I suddenly realized they were really burned bodies, still standing upright."

Nineteen-year-old Kimie Ono saw a mother and child running. "Suddenly the firestorm swept out a finger to lick them, and in a second the mother and child burst into flames. . . . Their clothes afire, they staggered and fell to the ground. No one stopped to help them."

Hidezo Tsuchikua rushed with his two children to the Futaba School, famous for its large swimming pool. He went to the roof, where flames lapped at them. Inside the school building, thousands were baked to death and "looked like mannequins, some of them with a pinkish complexion." Tsuchikua will always remember the sight of the pool: "It was hideous. More than a thousand people, we estimated, had jammed into the pool. The pool had been filled to its brim when we first arrived. Now there wasn't a drop of water, only the bodies of the adults and children who had died."

Yoshiko Hashimoto, with her baby boy on her back, continued to run with her parents and youngest sister toward the river. They dodged billboards and debris whirling through the heated air. Finally, they reached the bridge.

"People were burning to death on the bridge," Hashimoto-san said. "Clothes would burst into flames. Everybody was stamping out fires. My hair caught on fire. Everyone was screaming." And the little boy on her back had been yelping as loudly as anyone.

"Suddenly, I heard a *big* scream from him," she told me. "I turned to see he had sparkles of fire in his mouth. His mouth was red inside. I scraped the burning sparkles out with my hand."

The baby boy was the pride of the all-female family. Hashimoto-san placed him on the ground and wrapped her body around him for protection. Her mother and father did the same for her. They covered themselves with the maternity coat, but it caught fire.

"We'll all die here!" Hashimoto-san remembered her father crying.

"At that moment I did think I was going to die," she told me. "It's so hard to realize you're going to die."

"Yoshiko! Jump in the river!" her mother screamed. "Jump! Jump!"

"It was March; the river was cold," she remembered. "I had a baby in my arms. I didn't have the courage to jump. But I had to."

The metal bridge railings had been ripped out earlier to be melted down for weapons. Now the railings were logs, which were ablaze. To jump in, Hashimoto-san had to place her feet in the fire. She hesitated.

"My mother took her fire hood off and put it on my head," she told me. "We were four girls in the family and I had the first son. Everybody loved the boy. We didn't have many things. Our general mood was dark. For my mother, watching the baby boy grow was her only joy. I still remember her face. Her hair was standing on end, blown by the hot wind. The red of the nearby flames reflected in her face. I cannot forget her face. It was the last time I saw her."

Yoshiko stepped onto the burning rails and leaped with her baby in her arms.

"I went from the heat to the piercing cold of the water," she said. "The baby's eyes opened wide. The water was cold and right above it was hot like a furnace. You know when you put something in a furnace and it immediately catches fire? That's what it was like.

"I was swimming with one arm, holding the baby with the other arm. A raft of logs came along. I put my baby on a corner of the raft. I hung on. I repeatedly put water over his head. I sunk my head in the water and kept putting water on my baby.

"Right next to the raft was a small boat with two men on it. I screamed to those men — 'Please, save my baby. Only my baby is fine, you don't have to take me.' They came close to the raft. They took my baby and let me on the boat. We floated downstream."

The two men saved Yoshiko and her little boy. She spent the night in and out of consciousness as the boat inched along with the roasted corpses.

"I heard moans all night," she told me. "I still hear them moaning. Groaning and moaning like hungry big toads. All the rest of my life I hated hearing toads making that noise."

Kosuke Shindo was a twenty-two-year-old student. His dad was a local air-raid warden who stood his ground and died. Kosuke ran. "I looked up and saw B-29s circling," he remembered. "Their planes were red with the reflected fire. Those pilots must have thought it was fun to see us ant-sized people fleeing in the flames. I could almost see the smiles of the laughing faces of the American soldiers. Devils. Sons-of-bitches. I almost boiled with bitterness. Since that moment I started to hate America from the bottom of my heart."

But the American devils in their $600,000 planes weren't smiling or laughing. In fact, they weren't thinking much about the human toll at all.

"We weren't worried about the civilians," Loy Collingwood later told me. "We were worried about thirty-six hundred miles with a B-29 that wasn't as reliable as some thought and the Japanese hitting us."

"We didn't think of what we were doing," added Ed Ricketson. "We were surviving. We were trying to do our job and go home. We did what our commander told us to do. We didn't question it."

"We weren't gung ho for dropping bombs on people," Collingwood explained. "But when you put the twenty-one military targets in a three-square-mile area, you can't hit those targets without killing people."

"At five thousand feet, you could smell the flesh burning," remembered Chester Marshall. "It's kind of a sweet smell. We said, 'What is that I smell?' Somebody said, 'That's flesh burning.'" Pilot Harry George disagreed: "The smell of burning flesh was putrid. It wasn't nice at all."

"It was what I would think looking into hell would look like," Fiske Hanley recalled. "We felt bad, but that's the way you win war. Total war."

The all-clear signal sounded at 2:37 A.M., March 10. The Flyboys had dropped gasoline on Tokyo for about two hours and forty minutes. The conflagration continued through much of the night as the Flyboys headed home. "We could see the fires for a hundred miles or more still burning," said Newell Fears.

At dawn, Yoshiko Hashimoto forced her soot-caked eyes open.

"I looked above and wondered if it was the moon, but it was the sun," she said. "It looked like a turbid moon, the end of the world. The sun that had lost its light."

The men who had rescued them took Yoshiko and her baby to a medical facility, one of the few still standing. She remembered seeing "bodies like dead trees, faces swollen to double, triple the size" and smelling a "stinky burnt-flesh smell."

She and two of her sisters survived. Her mother, father, and one sister perished. Her baby recovered.

Yoshiko was lucky. Almost 100,000 others were not.

The largest single-day killing in world history had just taken place. The dead would surpass the later atomic toll at Nagasaki. Only Hiroshima would see more — slightly more — dead.

The survivors trudged through the moonscape like silent ghosts. Many had been literally toasted, their skin darkened for the rest of their lives. A low roof of smoke hovered over the still-smoldering landscape. Masuko Harino remembered gazing at "swollen, contorted, blackened bodies that resembled 'enormous ginseng roots.'" Nobody could tell if they had once been men or women.

Iwao Ishikawa searched for his wife. "Because of the oily smoke, it was difficult to open my eyes," he said. "I forced them open with my thumb and index finger." He eventually found what he believed were the charred corpses of his wife and two daughters. Their clothes were burned off, but he guessed it was they because of the tiny charred body he found under his wife. "My wife was pregnant and was overdue by three or four days," Ishikawa said. "Probably she gave birth just before she was burnt to death."

Yoshie Kogure was fourteen years old as she staggered through the

Bill Doran and Stripe, the "best hunting dog in the world." It was a conversation with Bill in his Iowa home that started my quest for the stories of the Chichi Jima Flyboys. As Bill told me, "All these years I had this nagging feeling these guys wanted their story told."
(James Bradley)

Warren Earl Vaughn flying his Corsair in a photo he sent home to his mother, 1944.
(Courtesy of Billye Winder and Ann Crockett)

Warren Earl Vaughn in 1944. A relative said, "I can tell you one thing for
certain: Warren Earl Vaughn was as good-looking a man as I've ever seen."
(Courtesy of Billye Winder and Ann Crockett)

TELEGRAM
(M I A)

IDENTIFICATION
NUMBER **029620-1**

DGU -296 - **hms**

FROM: COMMANDANT OF THE MARINE CORPS

TO: **MRS EVIA MCDONALD (MOTHER)**

400 AVENUE F SOUTHEAST

CHILDRESS TEXAS

DEEPLY REGRET TO INFORM YOU THAT YOUR
RELATIONSHIP
RANK-NAME } **SON SECOND LIEUTENANT WARREN E VAUGHN USMCR**
CLASSIFICATION

IS MISSING IN ACTION IN THE PERFORMANCE OF HIS DUTY AND SERVICE OF

HIS COUNTRY. I REALIZE YOUR GREAT ANXIETY BUT DETAILS NOT AVAILABLE

AND DELAY IN RECEIPT THEREOF MUST BE EXPECTED. TO PREVENT POSSIBLE

AID TO OUR ENEMIES DO NOT DIVULGE THE NAME OF HIS SHIP OR STATION.

LETTER FOLLOWS.

RELEASED BY **M G CRAIG**

DATE **7 MARCH 1945**

A A VANDEGRIFT
LIEUT GENERAL USMC
COMMANDANT OF THE MARINE CORPS

016232

The telegram to Evi McDonald saying her son, Warren Earl Vaughn, was
missing.
(Courtesy of Billye Winder and Ann Crockett)

Warren Earl Vaughn's mother, Evi, waiting for her son to return. A relative said, "When Warren Earl was declared missing, it threw Evi into a nervous breakdown." (Courtesy of Billye Winder and Ann Crockett)

Lieutenant (j.g.) George Bush in the cockpit, wearing his parachute harness over the Mae West life jacket, 1944. His radio headset allowed him to communicate with his aircraft carrier and his crewmen.
(George Bush Presidential Library)

George Bush being rescued by five members of the *Finback*'s crew on September 2, 1944. From 16mm film shot by Ensign Bill Edwards.
(George Bush Presidential Library)

A U.S. Navy SB2C Helldiver over Chichi Jima. Futami Bay Harbor, into which Dick Woellhof and Bill Connell parachuted, is clearly visible. At far right is the strait between Chichi Jima and Ani Jima, where Floyd Hall, Marve Mershon, and Glenn Frazier crash-landed.
(Robert Stinnett)

Smoke rises from the radio stations on Chichi Jima's Mounts Yoake and Asahi after a U.S. bombing run.
(Robert Stinnett)

A 25mm dual-purpose Japanese antiaircraft gun like the ones the Flyboys faced bombing Chichi Jima.
(Robert Stinnett)

Radio worker on Chichi Jima. Flyboy Warren Earl Vaughn sat at similar controls.
(Robert Stinnett)

Pilot Bob King flying his damaged TBM Avenger after Jimmy Dye and Grady York parachuted over Chichi Jima, February 18, 1945.
("Press Association, Inc.," courtesy of Vincent C. Carnazza)

General Curtis LeMay said, "We scorched and boiled and baked to death more people in Tokyo on that night of March 9 to 10 than went up in vapor at Hiroshima and Nagasaki combined."
(National Archives)

Flyboys in a carrier ready room, February 1945
(National Archives)

B-29s flying unchallenged near Mount Fuji symbolized that the war was lost, but Japan would not surrender.
(National Archives)

Incendiary bombs hang in the bomb bay of a B-29. On the evening of March 9, 1945, 334 B-29s dropped 496,000 individual 6.2-pound cylinders of napalm on the city of Tokyo.
(U.S. Air Force)

B-29s dropping incendiaries on Yokohama on May 29, 1945.
(National Archives)

A B-29 Superfortress firebombing
Osaka in June 1945.
(National Archives)

Yokohama burning, May 29,
1945.
(National Archives)

The city of Toyama was 99.5 percent destroyed the night of August 1, 1945. (National Archives)

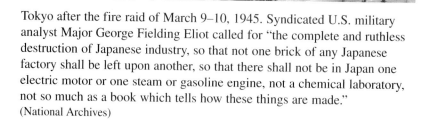

Tokyo after the fire raid of March 9–10, 1945. Syndicated U.S. military analyst Major George Fielding Eliot called for "the complete and ruthless destruction of Japanese industry, so that not one brick of any Japanese factory shall be left upon another, so that there shall not be in Japan one electric motor or one steam or gasoline engine, not a chemical laboratory, not so much as a book which tells how these things are made." (National Archives)

Tokyo after the fire raid of March 9–10, 1945. The head of the Tokyo fire department informed the emperor that "the United States had the capability to burn down all Japan's cities and that he and his men could do little to stop the fires."
(National Archives)

"SOME NEW JAPANESE PRINTS."

This caricatured, subhuman Japanese views the results of the fire war as published in the *New York Times*'s Sunday edition, May 20, 1945.
(© New York Public Library, Art Resource, NY)

A Japanese mother and baby burned by American napalm. FDR's son and adviser Elliot Roosevelt called for bombing Japan "until we have destroyed about half the Japanese civilian population,"
(National Archives)

Napalm—jellied gasoline—killed more Japanese than the atomic bombs did. Radio Tokyo referred to the U.S. fire war as "slaughter bombing."
(National Archives)

Commodore Perry's thirty-one-star flag, which flew in Tokyo Bay in 1853, on display on the USS *Missouri* for the surrender ceremony on September 2, 1945. (For some reason the flag was hung backward.)
(National Archives)

A show of force by fifteen hundred navy carrier aircraft and five hundred B-29s over the USS *Missouri* on September 2, 1945.
(National Archives)

Surrender on Chichi Jima. Left to right: unknown, General Tachibana, Major Horie, unknown, Admiral Abe, unknown, Major Matoba
(Everett Harvey)

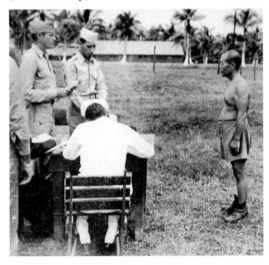

In an apparent effort to humiliate him, General Tachibana is read his death sentence stripped to his shorts.
(Robert Stinnett)

Major Sueo Matoba going to the gallows on September 24, 1947.
(Robert Stinnett)

Captain Shizuo Yoshii as he goes to the gallows on September 24, 1947.
(Robert Stinnett)

President Bush and author James Bradley atop Mount Suribachi, Iwo Jima, Japan, on June 17, 2002. Bradley's foot is on the exact spot where his father and his friends raised the American flag on Iwo Jima. The famous "Sands of Iwo Jima" can be seen in the background. President Bush was the second U.S. president to stand atop Mount Suribachi. President Eisenhower was the first.
(James Bradley)

Former American devil Bush and former Japanese devil Iwatake on Chichi Jima, June 18, 2002, at the spot where Warren Earl Vaughn was killed.
(James Bradley)

Yoshiko Hashimoto. When she was twenty-one years old, Hashimoto-san jumped from a Tokyo bridge during the March 9, 1945, U.S. fire raid to save her baby son. This statue in front of the Tokyo Daikusyu / Sensai Shiryo Center (Center of the Tokyo Air Raid and War Damages) memorializes the moment.
(James Bradley)

Minoru Hayashi and James Bradley. Hayashi-san told Bradley how Captain Yoshii ordered him to behead Jimmy Dye. He spent seven years in prison for the deed.
(James Bradley)

Masayo Enomoto and James Bradley. Young Enomoto-san helped wreak havoc in China as a soldier in the Japanese army but is now welcomed there for his truth telling. He says, "It was the emperor system that allowed such atrocities to take place. We have to eradicate militaristic thinking from this earth."
(James Bradley)

Fumio Tamamura in Yokohama. Born in San Francisco, Tamamura-san later walked Jimmy Dye to his death on Chichi Jima. Now a Rotary International pin sparkles from his lapel.
(James Bradley)

smoky ruins. "I saw so many dead bodies," she said. "I had to push them with my feet to walk. We went to the subway station. There were people with all their clothes burnt off. There was a man standing and I wanted to ask him directions. I touched his body and he fell. He was dead and I screamed."

It took twenty-five days for Japanese officials to count the dead. It was an inexact science. Almost two million people had evacuated Tokyo before the raid, so the officials did not have an accurate base to work from. Also, the raid disrupted the bureaucracy. Dead people without homes could not report to dead officials with no offices. One method of tallying was to add up one fire helmet, five buttons, and the metal frame of a wallet to equal "one person."

Eventually, the authorities came up with totals of 83,793 killed and 40,918 injured. But this tallied only the identified and counted bodies. The authoritative U.S. Strategic Bombing Survey report acknowledged that many dead were never found and never counted. "Later a figure of 90,000 to 100,000 came to be accepted, but even these immense totals are sometimes challenged as too low." Curtis would write, "We scorched and boiled and baked to death more people in Tokyo on that night of March 9–10 than went up in vapor at Hiroshima and Nagasaki combined." Not quite, but he came close.

In one night, at a cost of only fourteen planes lost, General LeMay's gamble burned out sixteen square miles of Tokyo. Sixty-three percent of the commercial district was ash, 18 percent of Tokyo's industrial capacity was gone, and a quarter of all its buildings had vanished. And there were a million traumatized homeless *shinmin* scavenging for their next meal.

Curtis had outsmarted the *kaze* and brought hell to the Land of the Rising Sun. And the fire war was just beginning.

CHAPTER SEVENTEEN

Enduring the Unendurable

If we are prepared to sacrifice 20 million Japanese lives in
kamikaze *effort, victory will be ours.*

— *Admiral Takijiro Onishi, quoted in* Hell in the Pacific

THE experts who had warned against General Curtis LeMay's
hunch had been wrong about American losses over Tokyo. Instead of
70 percent casualties, he had suffered less than 5 percent. Further-
more, flying at low altitudes had proved much less demanding on the
B-29 engines and consumed less fuel. Curtis had hit the jackpot and
immediately ordered more fire war. "It would be possible, I thought, to
knock out all of Japan's major industrial cities during the next ten
days."

Back in the U.S., General Hap Arnold was in an air force hospital.
He had just suffered his fourth major heart attack, which many attrib-
uted to anxiety over his "$3 billion gamble." Finally, with this napalm
attack on Tokyo, Hap could see the beginning of the end. In a "My
dear Curt" letter, he wrote: "I want to commend you and your Command on the superb operations you have conducted. A study of the
Tokyo attack of March 10 and knowledge of the fact that by July 1 you
will have nearly a thousand B-29s under your control, leads one to
conclusions which are impressive even to old hands at bombardment

operations. Under reasonably favorable conditions you should then have the ability to destroy whole industrial cities should that be required."

Curtis had burned out the heart of one of the world's great cities with 334 B-29s on his first try. Hap was now promising him three times that number to torch Japan.

Back home, *New York Times* headlines proclaimed, "B-29s FIRE 15 SQUARE MILES OF TOKYO," hitting "Thickly Populated Center of Big City." A day later, the paper's headline drove home the same message: "CENTER OF TOKYO DEVASTATED BY FIRE BOMBS," with "City's Heart Gone." The *Times* measured the destruction using a comparable area of Manhattan. The article referred to "jellied gasoline," and a correspondent who accompanied the mission reported, "I not only saw Tokyo burning furiously in many sections, but I smelled it."

Airmen in Washington were worried that if the public understood that Americans were pouring gasoline indiscriminately on civilians, there would be complaints — and with reason. One of General MacArthur's aides, Brigadier General Bonner Fellers, described the Tokyo raid in a confidential memo as "one of the most ruthless and barbaric killings of non-combatants in all history." But instead of halting such raids, Washington sent a message to Curtis stating that U.S. "editorial comment [is] beginning to wonder about blanket incendiary attacks upon cities therefore [we] urge you [to] continue hitting hard your present line that this destruction is necessary to eliminate home industries and that it is strategic bombing." Just to make sure he got the point, the message ended, "Guard against anyone stating this is area bombing."

At a March 23 Washington press conference, army air force spokesmen didn't speak of human carnage. Instead, everything was reduced to dry cost-benefit statistics: "1,200,000 factory workers . . . made homeless," and "at least 100,000 man-months" of labor lost to Japan, and "360,000,000 sq. ft. of highly industrialized land . . . leveled to ashes." As to the use of napalm, it was just "the economical method of destroying the small industries in these areas . . . of bringing about their liquidation." When asked about "the reasoning behind this switch from explosives to incendiaries," the spokesman dodged the question, claiming that the mission was still "the reduction of Japanese ability to produce war goods."

In 1937, when Japan first bombed Chinese cities, the *New York Times* headlined two hundred deaths as a "Slaughter of Noncombatants." The very idea of airplanes killing "civilian victims" was shocking front-page news. Now the press followed the American government line. Newspapers noted, "Tokyo is a prime military target, so recognized under the rules of war and . . . civilians remain there to man Japan's armament industries at their own peril." And in case anyone was feeling bad about napalming women and children, the *New York Herald Tribune* assured its readers that "the incendiary raids cause little loss of life but drive inhabitants into the country and destroy their industrial utility."

But Radio Tokyo referred to the new U.S. policy as "slaughter bombing." The Tokyo fire chief informed the emperor that "the United States had the capability to burn down all Japan's cities and that he and his men could do little to stop the fires."

Of course, if the Spirit boys had been rational, there never would have been a Tokyo fire raid. Saipan's fall in the summer of 1944, combined with knowledge of how the U.S. had bombed Germany, made it obvious that the Americans could obliterate Japan's cities. But even now that the worst had happened, the military retained a stiff upper lip. A foreign diplomat serving in Tokyo later wrote, "No Japanese would yet let himself say the forbidden words 'Nippon maketa'— Japan is beaten — but one could see the thought lurking behind the wooden faces." That included the emperor, who finally — eight days after the raid — "set forth in a general's uniform and riding boots" to survey the damage. Hirohito silently observed his huddled *shinmin* atop the scorched earth. Then the Boy Soldier returned to his palace in his sparkling limousine with its imperial flag snapping in the wind. And the holy war continued.

Six hundred miles south of the imperial palace, the boys monitoring the radios on Chichi Jima were perhaps better informed than Hirohito about Japan's ultimate fate. "Members of my army unit would ask me how the war was going," Nobuake Iwatake recalled. "When I told them Japan was losing, they called me a traitor. They had no idea."

The Tokyo raid did not immediately change Warren Earl Vaughn's surreal life. He remained a captive of the Japanese, yet he soaked in tubs with them and listened to Bing Crosby. Warren Earl and Iwatake were both on night duty on March 14, 1945. "All of a sudden Warren stood up, took his headphones off, and told us that the Americans had just announced, "All organized resistance on Iwo Jima has ended," Iwatake-san remembered. "Warren told us the news calmly, but inside he must have felt differently. Tamamura-san was with us, so he gave the message to Captain Yoshii." Yoshii immediately passed the message up the chain to imperial headquarters in Tokyo. So in all probability, the emperor learned that Iwo Jima was lost as a result of a message intercepted by a Flyboy on Chichi Jima.

Disorganized resistance continued in spurts. Two days later, on March 16, a besieged General Kuribayashi radioed from Iwo Jima: "The battle is approaching its end. Since the enemy's landing, even the gods would weep at the bravery of the officers and men under my command."

The next day, March 17, Prime Minister Kuniaki Koiso, Tojo's replacement, went on the radio and called the fall of Iwo Jima "the most unfortunate thing in the whole war situation." He was quick to add, however, that the nation would fight to the last man "to shatter the enemy's ambitions."

Captain Yoshii had had enough. He spoke to his friend Lieutenant Yasua Kurasaki, who was in charge of the torpedo boat squadron down on the shore of Futami Bay.

Late that morning of March 17, Warren Earl and Iwatake took a break from their duties. They lounged in the sun outside the radio station, leaning against the concrete wall. A truck with five navy men came over the hill. Iwatake had never seen them before. They were from the torpedo boat squadron.

"Warren sensed they came for him," Iwatake-san told me. "He stood up, turned to me, and shook my hand. 'They came to get me,' he said. He had a sad look in his eyes. I felt it was the final good-bye, the way he said it and the way he looked at me."

Twenty-two-year-old Iwatake watched his twenty-four-year-old buddy walk away with the navy men. They got in the truck and drove down the hill.

Warren Earl was taken to the torpedo boat squadron headquarters on the edge of Futami Bay. At about 3 P.M., a crowd of 150 gathered near a bomb crater there. Lieutenant Yasuo Kurasaki was in charge.

Captain Yoshii watched. They were good Spirit Warriors. They were drunk.

Kurasaki spoke to Warren Earl in halting English. He told the Cherokee he was about to have his head chopped off. Kurasaki asked him if he was ready to meet death. "Yes," Warren Earl replied. Is there anything you would like to say? "No," Lieutenant Vaughn answered.

Kurasaki gave a speech similar to the one his friend Yoshii had made prior to Jimmy Dye's execution, something to the effect that "we are now going to execute an American flyer, and maybe one day you all will be in the same situation, so have a good look and remember all of the details."

Kurasaki called for a volunteer to kill Warren Earl.

Nobody came forward.

He called upon Ensign Takao Koyama.

"When Lieutenant Kurasaki told Koyama to perform the execution, Koyama refused," a witness later testified. In front of everyone, the lieutenant reminded the ensign he had been given an order. Koyama had no choice. "Lieutenant Kurasaki was drunk and said he himself would perform the execution. But he did not do it. He picked out Koyama because he was an expert in kendo."

Warren Earl knelt on a mat at the rim of the bomb crater. A later report noted, "In a gesture of defiance he insisted on rolling down his own collar for the execution." He was then blindfolded.

With one stroke, Ensign Koyama decapitated Warren Earl, who fell forward into the crater.

Lieutenant Kurasaki shouted for Dr. Kanehisa Matsushita to come forward. A witness said, "Captain Yoshii ordered Dr. Matsushita to dissect the flyer and remove his liver."

Back atop Mount Yoake, Iwatake wondered what had happened to his friend. Some navy guys walked by the radio station and casually remarked, "The prisoner who was with us was executed."

"I thought, how cruel," Iwatake-san told me. "How could they do such a cruel thing? I was so sad. I hated Captain Yoshii because I heard he was the leader of the group who killed Warren."

In his shock and grief, Iwatake felt he had to do something. But what?

"I kept wondering what I could do to carry on Warren's memory,"

Iwatake-san said. Then Iwatake had an idea. He would have to keep it secret on Chichi Jima, but he would not forget.

After Warren Earl's execution on March 17, pilot Floyd Hall was the last Flyboy left on Chichi Jima. Floyd had told his buddies Bill Hazlehurst and Joe White that he wouldn't return alive, but he hoped he might make it off Chichi Jima in one piece.

By now, Floyd had spent a month at Major Horie's headquarters, where he had continued the English lessons Warren Earl and he had begun. As Floyd taught the major English, he also picked up some Japanese. The meek intelligence officer and the buoyant Flyboy seemed to be opposites, but as they taught each other, the differences melted away. Horie later wrote about Floyd, "I talked with Hall frequently. I ate with him often. He was lively and intelligent, and gave me great pleasure."

"He was born in Missouri," Horie elaborated.

He was still single because he had postponed his marriage on account of the war. He said that he intended to return home and marry his sweetheart as soon as peace was declared. He said if I ever came to the United States in the future he would guide me everywhere. I also told him that if I lived and if he ever came to Japan I would have him sleep at my home and would guide him. At that time there were many air raids, and we did not know when the American forces might land on Chichi Jima. Under such conditions he consoled my heart and gave me comfort more than anything else could do.

One soldier remembered that Floyd was "on good terms with Major Horie and very friendly with everyone. He was always joking he was going to give Major Horie a good time in the States, and that he wanted to visit Japan. Everybody was friendly with Hall. Hall learned quite a number of words in Japanese."

Every day, Floyd must have grown more confident of his chances for survival. He was in the care of a relatively high-ranking man — a major — was never tied up, and enjoyed complete freedom. Floyd attended parties and drank sake with his captors. When American bombers appeared overhead, Floyd ran into caves along with the Japanese. Floyd had always been clever — this was a guy who had worked his way up from enlisted man to officer, from cook to Flyboy. Now he was teaching himself the Japanese language and customs well enough to use chopsticks and joke with his captors. Maybe he would be lucky.

But Major Horie had no operational power. He was an intelligence man, subservient to the warriors. And Floyd's death sentence had already been issued, although Horie and Floyd didn't know it. On March 9, almost three weeks after Floyd was shot down, Major Matoba issued his order:

I. The battalion wants to eat flesh of the American aviator, Lieutenant (Junior Grade) Hall.

II. First Lieutenant Kanmuri will see to the rationing of this flesh.

III. Cadet Sakabe (Medical Corps) will attend the execution and have the liver and gall bladder removed.

Date: 9th March 1945

Time: 9 A.M.

Place: Mikazuki Hill Headquarters

Battalion Commander: Major Matoba

Two weeks went by. Then, on March 23, a surprise message from Iwo Jima was received at the Mount Yoake radio station. General Kuribayashi's March 16 message from Iwo Jima was assumed to be the last one that would come from the American-conquered island.

"The Japanese government had announced the fall of Iwo Jima," Tamamura-san recalled. "We thought everyone was dead on Iwo Jima. But later we received a signal. They had portable radio transmitters. We got a message that there were thirty survivors on the northern cliffs. That night they were going to make a banzai charge." Horie remembered the message as, "Good-bye to our friends on Chichi Jima."

This message apparently shook up the command on Chichi Jima. Various headquarters were consolidated to prepare for imminent American attack. Major Horie was ordered to General Tachibana's headquarters as the general's new chief of staff. Now the major could no longer protect his American friend. Major Matoba's order would be carried out.

On the evening of Friday, March 23, Major Horie and Floyd Hall had a last supper together in the major's quarters. Horie told Floyd he would be "moved" but did not tell him he was to be executed. Floyd and the major spoke hopefully of a postwar world in which they would visit each other's countries as friends.

The next day, Major Horie telephoned Captain Kanmuri of the 308th Battalion, who had received the order to kill Floyd from Major Matoba. Major Horie told him to come get the prisoner.

"Major Horie told me not to kill Hall in any inhuman way because Hall was very much in his favor," Kanmuri said. "I understood that Hall was to die but to do the job as humanely as possible."

Floyd stayed in a guardhouse at Major Matoba's 308th Battalion headquarters overnight. His hands were tied in front of him, but he was not tethered to anything. He could walk around. He was fed well and given cigarettes.

Floyd must have sensed he was in trouble. He wasn't being abused, but he felt the rough rope against his wrists. Yet Floyd wasn't giving up hope. "The flyer was talking to the people around him in broken Japanese," one witness said. A Korean laborer later testified, "I saw the flyer joking with a navy man. The man had a beard the previous day and during the night he shaved it off. They were joking about it." Floyd, hands tied, held in a guardhouse, was trying to make human connections with anyone. Maybe . . .

Major Matoba ordered Dr. Teraki, who had dissected Marve Mershon, that he was to do the same with Floyd. Teraki told the corpsmen there would be a demonstration the next day. One corpsman recalled, "It was just an order that the prisoner was to be executed, and after the execution the body would be dissected; and all of the corpsmen should be present at the dissection in order to study the human body."

On Sunday, March 25, Major Matoba bestirred himself and gave the order for Floyd to be executed. It was a routine matter.

"All the Japanese on Iwo Jima were lost," Matoba said. "No one on this island had the least idea of returning to Japan alive. Therefore it was just an understanding that all captured flyers were to be executed."

But the brave major wouldn't do the dirty work himself. He barked to Captain Kesakichi Sato, "Behead the flyer today."

"I cannot do so," Captain Sato replied. Major Matoba eyed his subordinate coldly. He reminded him that it was "an order." As Matoba departed, Sato commanded that Floyd be taken from the guardhouse to a nearby crater for execution.

Sato realized he had to carry out the order, but Matoba had not told him to kill Floyd personally. Captain Sato had been born into a Buddhist home and taught never to kill anything that was living. "To kill persons who are defenseless was against bushido," he said. So, in the tradition of other Chichi Jima Spirit Warriors, Captain Sato passed the buck. He eyed Sergeant Furushika nearby and said, "I have been ordered to execute the prisoner by Major Matoba. You do it."

Sergeant Furushika refused. Captain Sato told him it was "an order." The sergeant said yes.

A crowd milled around Floyd at the guardhouse. "All of the men were talking about the coming execution," said Corpsman Kanemori, who had assisted Dr. Teraki with the dissection of Marve.

But Floyd couldn't understand enough to know the men were speaking of his execution. He kept his cool and continued joking.

"The prisoner knew many words in Japanese," Kanemori said. "We were all fooling around with him and just talking. We gave him cigarettes and so forth."

After about ten minutes, a guard came and took Floyd to the bomb crater. The crowd followed.

Captain Sato walked out of the headquarters building and was about to follow the crowd to the execution site when he realized the assigned head-chopper, Sergeant Furushika, had disappeared.

"I went to Sergeant Furushika's quarters, but I could not find him," Sato said. "I told an orderly to find him and bring him to the scene."

Floyd stood with about fifty Japanese soldiers at the edge of a bomb crater on Mikasuki hill, about three hundred yards from 308th Battalion headquarters.

Captain Sato approached. He told Floyd he was going to be executed. He gave Floyd a final cigarette. Floyd smoked it slowly, not speaking. He was offered a glass of whiskey, which he drank.

Floyd was blindfolded. He was made to sit on the edge of the crater, facing west, away from the imperial palace.

Twenty minutes had elapsed since the group had arrived at the crater, but the assigned executioner, Sergeant Furushika, still hadn't appeared. Now Sato was in a bind. He had to get the show on the road.

"I looked around and saw Corporal Nakamura with a sword," Sato said. "I went over to Nakamura and ordered him: 'Execute the prisoner.'"

Now Corporal Nakamura would be the third to refuse an order to execute the American devil.

"When Captain Sato said that I should do it," Nakamura said, "I didn't want to. I said, 'You have a man scheduled to do it.' "

Captain Sato walked across the road to consult with Dr. Teraki. The captain and the doctor came back to Corporal Nakamura.

"Dr. Teraki walked up and said that he was going to be late for the dissection," Nakamura said. Then Captain Sato grunted, "Behead the flyer." It was "an order." Nakamura said yes.

All this time, Floyd was sitting blindfolded and silent on the edge of the crater. Now Nakamura reluctantly pulled out his sword. He wiped it with a handkerchief. He approached Floyd from the rear. He aimed twice, slowly swinging the blade up and down. He struck. He stepped away.

"Corporal Nakamura did not entirely decapitate the flyer," a corpsman said. "His sword entered about two thirds of the flyer's neck."

Private Iso remembered, "Immediately after the blow was struck, blood gushed out of the wound. It made me feel sick and so I left."

"After Corporal Nakamura beheaded the flyer," Sergeant Mori said, "the body rolled over. I was just there as a witness, but before the beheading, Captain Sato told me to borrow a rifle and bayonet and stand by. Now Captain Sato told me to bayonet him. I didn't refuse the order because it was public and in front of the enlisted men. Although I did not like to do it, I did it anyway. I still do not know why I was made to bayonet a dead body."

It was about 11 A.M. on Sunday, March 25, 1945. The boy from Sedalia, Missouri, who had enlisted the day after Pearl Harbor, had lived twenty-four years and eight months.

Dr. Teraki came forward and said to the assembled corpsmen, "The body will be dissected and all corpsmen are to study the anatomy of the human body." A guard stood at the perimeter of the dissection area and prevented additional onlookers from coming close.

Later, one corpsman gave this account:

I saw the bloody body was placed on its back. I heard Doctor Teraki order all corpsmen present to come near the body, as he was going to dissect the flyer. There were five of us corpsmen. Corpsman Kanemori took off the clothing of the flyer. He stripped his chest and abdomen bare. Doctor Teraki instructed corpsmen while he dissected the body.

Doctor Teraki made an incision from the flyer's chest to the abdomen and laid open his chest. We examined all of the intestines, and the doctor cut right down to the insides. The doctor lifted up the lungs and heart and let all of the corpsmen examine them. He lifted out the stomach and had it examined. He later cut out the liver and wrapped it in cellophane paper.

"I knelt at the doctor's left side," Kanemori said. "He cut into the left thigh. Every time he came upon a sinew, he took the scissors out of my hand to cut it. While he was cutting around the thigh, he told me to hold on to the flesh because he did not want to get any dirt on it. I complied with this request."

Kanemori wrapped Floyd's liver and thigh meat ("about eight pounds") in cellophane. A soldier took it from him and brought it to Major Matoba's headquarters. One of the corpsmen found two photos in Floyd's pocket, which he replaced. Soldiers shoveled dirt onto Floyd, lying at the bottom of the bomb crater.

That night, Major Matoba and a number of other army officers brought a delicacy to Admiral Kinizo Mori's headquarters. Matoba had had Floyd's liver prepared specially for the party. "I had it pierced with bamboo sticks and cooked with soy sauce and vegetables," Matoba said.

"Major Matoba came to my headquarters and was very drunk," Mori recalled. "The meat was cut in very small pieces and pierced together by bamboo spits."

The officers remarked how liver was good for the stomach. The drunken major repeated this several times. Matoba remembered: "Admiral Mori mentioned that during the Chinese-Japanese war human liver was eaten as a medicine by the Japanese troops. All the other officers agreed that liver was good medicine for the stomach."

All the soldiers on Chichi Jima believed that, like the executed Flyboys, they would soon be in their graves. They were wrong. Chichi Jima was not invaded. The focus was now on burning down mainland Japan.

In the summer of 1945, the army air force issued an astonishing document. It was a map of Japan with the cities listed that General

LeMay had scorched. It detailed the percentage of each city burned and compared each city in size to an American city.

Here's a sampling:

Kawasaki	35%	Portland
Shimizu	42%	San Jose
Hiratsuka	46%	Battle Creek
Toyohashi	67%	Tulsa
Hammatsu	60%	Hartford
Kofu	78%	South Bend
Hitachi	72%	Little Rock
Tokyo	40%	New York
Yokohama	57%	Cleveland
Chiba	41%	Savannah
Nagoya	40%	Los Angeles
Gifu	69%	Des Moines
Takahatsu	67%	Knoxville
Himeji	49%	Peoria
Kobe	55%	Baltimore
Osaka	35%	Chicago
Shimonoseki	37%	San Diego
Moji	24%	Spokane
Nagaoka	55%	Madison

These percentages refer not to area bombed or area damaged but to area obliterated, gone, burned, turned to ash. This wasn't artillery damage in which one wall crumbled and the family huddled in another room. These percentages referred to wastelands — flat, desolate ash deserts.

This was unprecedented urban damage. The 1871 Chicago fire destroyed three square miles and the 1906 San Francisco earthquake destroyed four square miles. Chicago's mate city on the air force map, Osaka, lost more than twice as much area as those two disasters combined: 16.4 square miles.

Japan was being burned into the Stone Age. Millions took to the hills, roaming the countryside. One Japanese author wrote: "It was possible to look across acres and acres of desert-like space where once

had stood a bustling community of workers' homes and small factories. Now there was nothing but heaps of ashes, bits of corrugated iron,
bricks, concrete blocks, a few twisted girders, and here and there the
shell of a burned-out concrete building. Skeletons of motor vehicles,
including fire engines, dotted the landscape."

Curtis was clearly much more effective than the American bombers
had been in Europe. Bombing destroyed seventy-nine square miles of
Germany's urban area. Curtis destroyed more than twice as much urban area in Japan: 178 square miles. Germany's capital, Berlin, lost 10
square miles. Tokyo lost 56.3 square miles. In fact, the damage in just
two Japanese cities, Tokyo (56.3 square miles) and Osaka (16.4 square
miles), nearly equaled all the damage done to all German cities put
together.

Hap Arnold now told President Harry Truman that "conventional
bombing could easily end the war." And Curtis told the Joint Chiefs
in Washington, "We could bomb and burn them until they quit." His
only problem was that "by October he would run out of cities to
burn." Already American napalm had killed more than 400,000
Japanese and injured nearly 500,000. It had destroyed 2.5 million
homes. Thirty percent of the urban population — 9 million people —
was homeless, trudging through the land with vacant stares and empty
bellies.

Flyboys completely dominated Japan's skies. Curtis later wrote that
by this time, "it was actually safer to fly a combat mission over Japan
in a B-29 than it was to fly a B-29 training mission back in the United
States. Truth. The fatality rate in the training program was higher than
the rate in combat." And after the B-29s burned out all of Japan's
cities, there were other aggressive plans if Japan did not surrender.
"The rice paddies might be sprayed with oil, defoliants, or biological
agents, and the production of fertilizer further attacked."

Total war indeed. Even before Pearl Harbor there had been food
shortages in Japan. Now "theft of produce still in the fields led police
to speak of a new class of 'vegetable thieves' and the new crime of
'field vandalizing.'" A majority of the population was malnourished.
"Workers had to barter for food in the countryside and absenteeism
rose to 40% in the major cities." "Food rationing was so strict then
that we had no salt or soy sauce, and only about a thumbnail-size dol-
lop of miso paste per person per day," Motokazu Kumagaya remem-

bered. "For vegetables we were lucky to be able to eat the leaves grown in a vacant lot. I was so hungry that it was a chore to climb the stairs. One day when we returned home, we found that even though we had locked the house tightly, a thief had entered. Nothing was missing except our small amount of rice and miso soup. We looked dumbfounded at each other, amazed that someone was worse off than we."

The Spirit Warriors, who continued to enjoy fine meals in Tokyo, showed their concern by promulgating a document entitled "Eat This Way — Endless Supplies of Materials by Ingenuity." Pulitzer Prize–winning historian John Dower described it:

> The emperor's loyal subjects were encouraged to supplement their starch intake by introducing such items as acorns, grain husks, peanut shells, and sawdust to their household larder. (Sawdust, it was explained, could be broken down with a fermenting agent, transformed into a powder, and mixed in a ratio of one to four with flour to make dumplings, pancakes, or bread.) For minerals, people were encouraged to introduce used tea leaves and the seeds, blossoms, and leaves of roses to their diet. Protein deficiencies could be remedied by eating silkworm's cocoons, worms, grasshoppers, mice, rats, moles, snails, snakes, or a powder made by drying the blood of cows, horses, and pigs. Well sterilized, the researchers reported, mice and rats tasted like small birds, but it was important to avoid eating their bones since it had been demonstrated that this caused people to lose weight.

There were similar articles, such as "How to Eat Acorns" and "Let's Catch Grasshoppers." People spoke of an "onion existence, with the clear implication of weeping as one peeled off layer upon layer of precious belongings" to trade for some barley or potatoes. Sumo wrestlers were not fat anymore. The zoos were empty; the animals had been eaten.

With the labor force enfeebled and raw materials scarce, industrial production shrank to 50 percent of what it had been before Pearl Harbor. These material statistics demonstrated that Japan had lost the war. "But in Japanese military doctrine, material things did not signify. Spirit was crucial. A white soldier might be twice as big as a Japanese soldier, but that meant nothing, because the white man's heart was small." The Spirit boys made this point by exhibiting a crashed B-29 in a Tokyo park. Next to the enormous American airplane was a replica of the tiny pursuit plane that had rammed the B-29 to bring it down. It was proof that small could conquer big.

As a further example, after sixty-seven days of being tortured by the Kempetei, Flyboy Hap Halloran was tossed in the back of a truck and taken to the Tokyo zoo. He was stripped naked and tied to the bars of a monkey cage to show the malnourished and burned *shinmin* that they could still win.

"The purpose was to let civilians come by," Hap recalled. "Do not fear these B-29 people. Look at this one. My body was covered with running sores from the bedbugs, lice, and fleas, and I had lost ninety pounds by then. You're standing there just kind of holding on trying to act like an air corps guy, you know, with dignity. Maintain your dignity the best you can."

The French ambassador to Japan wrote to Paris about the Spirit Warriors' mind-set: "Are they sincere or are they intoxicated? The only thing certain is that they refuse to see the possibility of defeat. As for the people, they have no definite attitude; they are resigned to all physical suffering and . . . [are] confident in their leaders."

When their Nazi allies surrendered in May, Tokyo residents heaped ridicule on Germans in the streets. A diplomat commented, "The Tokyo papers blamed Germany's defeat on its lack of bushido. With bushido . . . one never dies, never surrenders unconditionally."

The Spirit boys prepared for the "final decisive battle."

The battle plan was called *Ketsu-Go* or "Decisive Operation." The entire civilian populace — armed with bamboo spears and plenty of *Yamato damashii* — would shatter-jewel the hell out of the *gaizin.*

On June 8, the emperor sanctioned *Ketsu-Go* as "The Fundamental Policy to Be Followed Henceforth in the Conduct of the War," which "proclaimed that Japan must fight to the finish and choose extinction before surrender." The Spirit Warriors were ready and eager to sacrifice any and all Japanese to their impossible dream. The Americans would be fought "in the interior" rather than "at the water's edge." Japan would use "sure victory weapons," "body-smashing" or "special attack" weapons. These kamikaze tactics would "exchange" the life of a pilot for a military gain. Japan would become one big Iwo Jima. The army and the emperor were going to manage the war from vast underground caves in the Matsuhiro Mountains northwest of Tokyo. Every citizen was mobilized for the glorious effort. All men ages fifteen to sixty and all women ages seventeen to forty were organized in the "Patriotic Citizens Fighting Corps." All school classes were suspended under the "Decisive Battle Educational Measures Guidelines." Students would fight, and their schools would become military bases.

"Special attack" or suicide tactics, it was announced, would save the realm. The "Divine Wind Special Attack Corps" would *kamikaze* American ships. Powerful motorboats —"Ocean Shakers"— with large dynamite charges in their bows would ram ships that approached Japan's shores. "Turning of the Heavens" was the name for a human-guided torpedo shot from a submarine that left no chance for the human's survival. "Crouching Dragon" men wore underwater breathing suits and huddled on the ocean floor waiting to poke surface-landing craft with explosive-tipped poles. Tiny biplanes would ram B-29s. Children trained to carry backpacks of explosives and to throw themselves under the treads of tanks were called "Sherman carpets." Meanwhile, the biological-warfare Unit 731 developed "Cherry Blossoms at Night," a plan to have *kamikaze* pilots infest California with disease. Planes loaded with plague-infected fleas would take off from a submarine and contaminate San Diego.

It was madness, but the Japanese leadership saw only wisdom in this leap into the pit. Foreign Minister Shidehara wrote a close friend, "If we continue to fight back bravely, even if hundreds of thousands of noncombatants are killed, injured, or starved, even if millions of buildings are destroyed or burned there would be room to produce a more advantageous international situation for Japan." And it wasn't only high officials who were ready to toss the *shinmin* into the cauldron. One army officer in Osaka wrote, "Due to the nationwide food shortage and the imminent invasion of the home islands, it will be necessary to kill all the infirm old people, the very young and the sick. We cannot allow Japan to perish because of them."

It was all so simple. As Admiral Takijiro Onishi, the father of the "special attack" idea, declared, "If we are prepared to sacrifice 20 million Japanese lives in *kamikaze* effort, victory will be ours!" But 20 million was an understatement. "Behind the suicide craft were nearly three million well-rested troops and 32 million civilians who were being trained in the use of primitive weapons in order to make a heroic last stand." This was "more than the combined armies of the United States,

Great Britain and Nazi Germany." But Japan lacked cloth for uniforms. So henceforth, the combatants would all be in civilian dress. "By deliberately eliminating any distinction between combatants and noncombatants, they would compel Americans to treat all Japanese as combatants or fail to do so at their peril. It was a recipe for extinction."

Years later, I asked Fumio Tamamura about Japan's final plans. "The military encouraged a strong belief in *kamikaze*," Tamamura-san said. "Some divine providence would do away with the invaders. There was no counter to the military. There was no resistance movement in Japan. If the Americans had invaded, the Japanese would have fought to the last man."

The overall American invasion plan was called "Downfall." The first phase was "Operation Olympic," a frontline assault on the southern island of Kyushu by 767,000 troops planned for November 1, 1945. Kyushu would then be the staging area for "Operation Coronet," the March 1, 1946, invasion of the main island of Honshu.

General MacArthur told Secretary of War Stimson that the invasion would "cost over a million casualties to American forces alone." A War Department report concluded that "defeating Japan would cost the Japanese five to ten million deaths and the United States between 1.7 and 4 million casualties, including 400,000 to 800,000 fatalities." President Truman later said, "If we had had to invade Japan, a million soldiers on both sides would have been killed and a million more would have been maimed for life." But secret intercepts indicated that Japanese defenses were far in excess of original estimates, meaning casualties would be much worse.

History's biggest bloodbath was in the making. U.S. Navy losses in just the battle of Okinawa — which followed the battle of Iwo Jima — had "exceeded the Navy's total losses from *all previous wars combined.*" D-Day at Normandy was accomplished with 175,000 invading troops. Seven *million* American troops were in the Pacific now. Normandy's casualties would be easily surpassed in the sideshow invasion of the Malay Archipelago, where 200,000 British troops were scheduled to fight for *seven months* to retake Singapore. The U.S. Office of War Information recommended efforts to gird the nation "for the heavy losses which undoubtedly would occur."

At the time, Japan held 350,000 Allied prisoners of war. Vice Minister of War Shitayama issued an order to POW camp commandants instructing them what to do in the event of an invasion:

> When the battle situation becomes urgent the POWs will be concentrated and confined in their location and kept under heavy guard until preparations for the final disposition will be made. Although the basic aim is to act under superior orders, individual disposition may be made in certain circumstances. Whether they are destroyed individually or in groups, and whether it is accomplished by means of mass bombing, poisonous smoke, poisons, drowning, or decapitation, dispose of them as the situation dictates. It is the aim not to allow the escape of a single one, to annihilate them all, and not to leave any traces.

Flyboy Charlie Brown, shot down on February 16, was wasting away in the Ofuna POW camp when he got the word. "It was a casual comment as one of the guards was tapping me on the head with a bamboo stick," Charlie told me. "The guard said, 'If there is an invasion you will all die.'"

Flyboys were already dying. As revenge for B-29 attacks in May and June, Professor Fukujiro Ishiyama, director of external medicine at Kyushu Imperial University, had strapped eight captured American crewmen to operating tables. The professor didn't administer an anesthetic. He began to cut.

He sliced out one Flyboy's lung and placed it in a surgical pan. The patient was alive. Then he slit his lung artery and watched the boy gurgle to death in his own blood. Another boy had his stomach cut out — while conscious. Professor Ishiyama then cut five of the boy's ribs, slit an artery, and watched to see how long his heart would pump before he died. Professor Ishiyama bored a hole in one Flyboy's skull. Then he inserted a knife and twisted it around in his brain. The professor wanted to see what parts of the boy's body jumped and jerked with each turn of the knife.

On July 26, 1945, President Truman issued the Potsdam Declaration. "Japan shall be given an opportunity to end the war," it stated. Japan could surrender or face "utter and complete destruction."

On August 1, American napalm burned out 80 percent of Hachioji, a major rail terminus near Tokyo. On the same day, Nagaoka, about the size of Madison, Wisconsin, was 65 percent destroyed. B-29s dropped 1,466 tons of napalm on Toyama on the west coast of Honshu and burned out a remarkable 99.5 percent of that city.

On August 2, "Mr. B-29," Paul Tibbets, along with his bombardier, Tom Ferebee, walked into Curtis LeMay's office on Guam. "The cigar-chomping LeMay was almost casual as he led his visitors to a map table and uncovered the charts and reconnaissance photos that were taped to its surface. 'Paul,' he announced through a cloud of cigar smoke, 'the primary's Hiroshima.'"

Hiroshima housed the headquarters of the army that would defend Kyushu from American landings. Forty-three thousand soldiers crowded among Hiroshima's 280,000 civilians, and there were a number of military installations and factories manufacturing military supplies.

On August 4, "720,000 leaflets were dropped on [Hiroshima] urging everyone to get out and indicating that the place was going to be (as the Potsdam Declaration had promised) obliterated." The leaflets warned, "Evacuate now!" A day later, the cities of Nishinomiya-Mikage, Saga, Maebashi, and Imabari (which had also been warned by leaflets) were aflame.

At 2:45 A.M. on August 6, Paul Tibbets took off from Tinian in a B-29. He had named the plane after his mother, *Enola Gay.* At 5:55 A.M., he looped around Iwo Jima's Mount Suribachi as he waited for two other B-29s to catch up with him. Looking down from the cockpit, he ruminated that the horrendous battle for Iwo Jima had been worth its cost: "The island, which had become Japan's prime defensive outpost, lay directly on the route our bombers flew on their mission from the Marianas to Tokyo. Without it, our mission would have been more difficult." At 6:07 A.M., the three planes rendezvoused over Mount Suribachi and headed for Japan.

At 08:15:17, Tom Ferebee sighted Hiroshima's Aioi Bridge in his Norden bombsight and yelled, "Bomb away!"

Just over one pound of uranium —.85 kilograms — fell through the air. It traveled nearly six miles in forty-three seconds. At 8:16 A.M., the uranium detonated 1,900 feet above the Shima Hospital, 550 feet from the Aioi Bridge aiming point. The explosion created "a blinding pulse of light for perhaps only a tenth of a second."

"Pika-don," the survivors called it. *Pika* (flash) *don* (boom). Flash-boom. *Pika-don*. Thirty seconds after the *pika,* explosive wind blew out windows 6.6 miles away. Within eight minutes, a mountain of smoke and debris arose as tall and massive as Mount Everest. An estimated 140,000 people would die.

To Curtis and many Flyboys, the atomic bomb was not the destructive quantum leap many have since claimed. Plain old fire killed most of the Hiroshima victims, and Curtis had killed almost as many in Tokyo with napalm. The U.S. Strategic Bombing Survey stated that the atomic bomb at Hiroshima was the equivalent of 220 fully loaded B-29s. "Accordingly, a single atomic explosion represented no order-of-magnitude increase in destructiveness over a conventional air raid."

Likewise, Curtis did not think a moral boundary was crossed. Later, he wondered if people thought it "much more wicked to kill people with a nuclear bomb, than to kill people by busting their heads with rocks. I suppose they believe also that a machine gun is a hundred times wickeder than a bow and arrow."

"Having found the bomb," President Truman said, "we have used it. We have used it to shorten the agony of young Americans." A few days later, he explained his motives in a letter to the U.S. Federal Council of Churches of Christ. He told the Christian leaders, "When you have to deal with a beast you have to treat him as a beast."

Few people now reflect that samurai swords killed more people in WWII than atomic bombs. WWII veteran Paul Fussell wrote, "The degree to which Americans register shock and extraordinary shame about the Hiroshima bomb correlates closely with lack of information about the Pacific war."

Marine veteran and historian William Manchester wrote, "You think of the lives which would have been lost in an invasion of Japan's home islands — a staggering number of Americans but millions more of Japanese — and you thank God for the atomic bomb." Winston Churchill told Parliament that the people who preferred invasion to dropping the atomic bomb seemed to have "no intention of proceeding to the Japanese front themselves."

Japanese pilot Mitsuo Fuchida led Japan's attack on Pearl Harbor. In 1959, Fuchida told Paul Tibbets: "You did the right thing. You know the Japanese attitude at that time, how fanatic they were, they'd die for the Emperor. . . . Every man, woman, and child would have resisted that invasion with sticks and stones if necessary. . . . Can you imagine what a slaughter it would be to invade Japan? It would have been terrible. The Japanese people know more about that than the American public will ever know."

But perhaps the greatest lifesaving function served by the atom bombs was that they shortened LeMay's firebombing of Japan. Secretary of State James Byrnes said the atom bombs did not cause "nearly so many deaths as there would have been had our air force continued to drop incendiary bombs on Japan's cities." In March, Curtis had dropped 13,800 tons of liquid fire on Japan. Beginning in September, he was prepared to drop 115,000 tons a month.

Perhaps the most shocking aspect of the atomic bombing at Hiroshima was that it didn't motivate the Spirit Warriors to save the lives of their countrymen. But then again, what did 100,000 deaths matter to them? These were the guys who wrote off 150,000 Japanese boys in New Guinea. They still controlled coastal China and Manchuria. Singapore was secure. There was a little trouble in the Philippines, but the Japanese hadn't surrendered to MacArthur yet. The samurai-imposters still held thousands of teenage sex slaves who were being raped forty to seventy times a day. The Spirit boys were ready to sacrifice 20 *million* civilians. So what if atom bombs were killing civilians? What was the big deal? Let them eat acorns.

The military sent a delegation of seven to survey the damage at Hiroshima. As they landed in the atomic wasteland, an officer ran up to their plane. He had a harlequin face — one half was scorched, oozing red pus. The other half, unexposed to the bomb's rays, was normal. He proved himself to be a true-blue Spirit guy when he pointed to his face and exclaimed, "Everything which is exposed gets burned, but anything which is covered even only slightly can escape burns. Therefore it cannot be said that there are no countermeasures."

"Hiroshima brought no instantaneous prostration of the Japanese military," Curtis recalled. "We were still piling on the incendiaries. Our B-29s went to Yawata on August 8th, and burned up 21 per cent of the town, and on the same day some other 29s went to Fukuyama and burned up 73.3 per cent. Still there wasn't any gasp and collapse when the second nuclear bomb went down above Nagasaki on August 9th. We kept on flying."

On August 9, a *pika-don* over Nagasaki killed 70,000. Japan had some other bad news that day. At 1 A.M. that morning, over one million Soviet troops had invaded Manchuria. Three months earlier, Joseph Stalin had signaled his intention to fight when he allowed the USSR-Japan Nonaggression Act to lapse. In response, the Spirit Warriors withdrew many of their troops to the Korean border. Millions of Japanese civilians living in Manchuria — the emperor's "pioneers" — were not told they had been abandoned by their military. At least 180,000 Japanese civilians died when the Soviets raped and tortured them, and the Manchurian natives rose up with pitchforks against their recent Japanese masters. Fleeing Japanese mothers were forced to abandon thousands of children to the care of the locals. The Soviets dragged 700,000 Japanese prisoners back to the gulag, many never to return.

That same day, the six-man Supreme Council for the Direction of the War met in Tokyo. Any rational military person might have admitted to having a bad day. The Japanese people were starving. Curtis was toasting their ancient cities off the map. *Pika-dons* were vaporizing neighborhoods. Hundreds of thousands of Japanese civilians were scrambling for their lives in the Manchurian wilderness.

But the war minister urged his colleagues to look at the bright side. No sense in being gloomy. General Korechika Anami ticked off Japan's remaining strengths. He reminded the cabinet that all Japanese men from fifteen to sixty and all women from seventeen to forty were now in the fight. Japan had 32 million warriors out there practicing with *really sharp* bamboo spears. Why give up before the real fight began?

"With luck, we will repulse the invaders before they land," added General Yoshijiro Umezu.

Luck? The Americans had a $3 billion airplane dropping $2 billion bombs. Luck.

Elderly prime minister Kantaro Suzuki tried to state the obvious to the War Cabinet. "We cannot carry on this war indefinitely," he said. "There is no way left for us but to accept the Potsdam Proclamation."

War Minister Anami's face flushed. Where was the prime minister's *Yamato damashii?*

"Who can be one hundred per cent sure of defeat?" General Anami thundered. "We certainly can't swallow this proclamation."

"We fought," soldier Koshu Itabashi later observed, "until the very end. No one considered the possibility that Japan could lose. We were like Sergeant Yoko and Lieutenant Onoda — the men who emerged from the jungles, one in Guam, the other in the Philippines, in the 1970s — who couldn't imagine that Japan had been defeated. That's the way the whole country felt."

But Suzuki was right. The end had come and even the emperor realized it.

"Went to Kumagaya on August 14th," Curtis wrote. "[Forty-five] per cent of that town. Flew our final mission the same day against Isezki, where we burned up 17 per cent of that target. Then the crews came home to the Marianas and were told that Japan had capitu lated."

Later that day, in an amazing display of Orwellian doublespeak, Emperor Hirohito portrayed himself in his surrender speech as a peace-loving guy who had suffered some setbacks in his efforts to help Asia. He said it was "far from Our thought either to infringe upon the sovereignty of other nations or to embark upon territorial aggrandizement," and that "We declared war on America and Britain out of Our sincere desire to assure Japan's self-preservation and the stabilization of East Asia." Hirohito's "stabilization" had brought final "peace" to almost 30 million Chinese, 4 million Indonesians, 1.8 million Indians, 1 million Vietnamese, 2.5 million of his own people, and hundreds of thousands of American, Korean, Australian, New Zealand, British, Dutch, Filipino, and Malaysian dead. The emperor never said the words "surrender," "defeat," "apologize," or "sorry." He just told his *shinmin* they had to "endure the unendurable and bear the unbearable."

Flyboy Charlie Brown remembered the last day of the war at the Ofuna POW camp:

We had heard from an American prisoner shot down on August seventh that the Americans had dropped a bomb on a city and wiped it out. We thought he was mentally off.

On August fourteenth, the guards lined up in front of the office. We could tell from their demeanor the war was over.

First they started drinking. One drunken guard tried to kill himself. He sat down on a step and stuck a knife in his stomach. They took him off to the hospital in an ambulance.

And that was all Charlie Brown remembered. The doctors later told him he had no memory of the next two weeks because of a vitamin A deficiency. Like injured Flyboy Phil Vonville, who lost consciousness only after he had eased his plane onto the carrier deck, Charlie's spirit had kept his weak body alive. Then, after he realized his side had won, his system shut down to rest.

Flyboy Bill Connell, the last man off Chichi Jima alive, was digging caves on a work detail the day of the surrender. Now only one hundred pounds hung on his six-foot frame. Two weeks later, he sent a message home. "The telegram said, 'I'm well, happy, flying home.' That's the first time my mom and dad even knew I was alive."

Flyboy Robert Goldsworthy recalled his first moments of freedom aboard a U.S. hospital ship: "We lived like pigs for so long. All of a sudden there were nurses with starched uniforms, clean, smelling good. But my greatest thrill took place a few hours earlier, when I first boarded the ship. I had beriberi, my ankles were swollen. I had amoebic dysentery and I had yellow jaundice, and I weighed about eighty-five pounds. I was lifted onto the deck by two sailors and I stumbled over to the railing and looked at Omori prison camp and shook my fist and yelled, 'You bastards, I beat you.'"

Now the 31,617 American POWs were free. And after fourteen years of war, Japan also released all its Chinese POWs. There were 56.

George Bush was training with a new squadron in Virginia Beach when he heard the news:

It was unbelievable joy, rejoicing with our fellow pilots down the street, with this tremendous outpouring of emotion. We were free to live normal lives. The killing would be stopped — nine of the fourteen original pilots of our squadron had been lost.

I remember laughing, yelling — crying, too. The impact of the announcement was unbelievable. We jumped and yelled and cried like kids. We were kids — seasoned by war, but kids.

301

*   *   *

Billy Mitchell begat Hap Arnold who begat Curtis LeMay. They were right. Flyboys could win a war. Japan was defeated without an invasion. For the first time, a nation was defeated by air power. The navy Flyboys had cleared the air of opposition and then the army air force Flyboys had burned down Japan.

Dutch Van Kirk, the navigator on the *Enola Gay*'s Hiroshima mission, told me, "The atom bomb didn't end the war. It helped the emperor make a decision." Prime Minister Kantaro Suzuki said, "It seemed to me unavoidable that in the long run Japan would be almost destroyed by air attack so that merely on the basis of the B-29's alone I was convinced that Japan should sue for peace. . . . I myself, on the basis of the B-29 raids, felt that the cause was hopeless." Emperor Hirohito wrote, "Thinking of the people dying endlessly in the air raids I ended the war." Prince Fumimaro Konoe said, "Fundamentally the thing that brought about the determination to make peace was the prolonged bombing by the B-29s." "After the war, pollsters asked civilians why they came to doubt that Japan would win the war. The largest response for one category (over one-third) was 'air attack.'"

The U.S. Strategic Bombing Survey concluded:

> It seems clear that, even without the atomic bombing attacks, air supremacy over Japan could have exerted sufficient pressure to bring about unconditional surrender and obviate the need for invasion.
>
> Based on a detailed investigation of all the facts, and supported by the testimony of the surviving Japanese leaders involved, it is the Survey's opinion that certainly prior to 31 December 1945, and in all probability prior to 1 November 1945, Japan would have surrendered even if the atomic bombs had not been dropped, even if Russia had not entered the war, and even if no invasion had been planned or contemplated.

Many more Japanese civilians died from gasoline in the fire war than were killed by atomic energy. Japan was in ruins. Five months of napalm rain had burned out an incredible 20 percent of Japan's housing. An astonishing 15 million people were homeless.

America paid a price for operations over Japan. In all, 544 navy aircraft were lost during operations against the home islands, or about 19 percent of total losses during the Pacific war. B-29 losses for all operations totaled 414. B-29 aircrew casualties numbered 2,897, of which 2,148 were deaths. Another 334 Superfortress crew members were listed as captured or interned, of whom 262 survived.

On Wednesday, August 29, 1945, navy lieutenant John Bremyer took off in an airplane from Iwo Jima bound for Tokyo Bay. John was exhausted. He was on the last leg of a record-breaking 120-hour, 9,500-mile-long trip that had taken him through twelve time zones. His journey began at Annapolis the Thursday before, on August 23. His mission was to deliver a wooden box to Admiral Bull Halsey on the USS *Missouri.* Lieutenant Bremyer had been ordered never to allow the box out of his sight. He slept with the box, it was at his side when he ate, he even took it to the bathroom.

On that Wednesday, Lieutenant Bremyer completed his mission when he handed the box to Admiral Halsey on the *Missouri.* Then the weary lieutenant slept for two days.

Inside the box was a linen bag. Wrapped carefully in the bag was a ninety-two-year-old American flag that had been displayed at the Naval Academy's museum. It had thirty-one stars. It was the flag Commodore Perry had brought ashore to Japan in 1853. Perry's visit had "propelled Japan onto its ultimately disastrous course of global competition with the Western powers." Now the Americans would return to the same spot, once again supremely powerful.

On September 2, 1945, the USS *Missouri* lay just four and one half miles northeast of the spot where Commodore Perry had anchored his ship. No one remarked on it at the time, but General MacArthur and Admiral Chester Nimitz were ferried out to the *Missouri* in the destroyer *Buchanan,* named for the first U.S. military man to set foot on Japanese soil.

Two hundred and sixty "Allied ships ringed the *Missouri* in concentric circles of power." A nine-member Japanese delegation traveled from Tokyo to Yokohama for the surrender ceremony. They traveled the same route that emissaries had trod to shuttle messages between Commodore Perry and the last shogun. Now they passed through burned-out cities.

The Japanese signed the surrender document at 9:04 A.M. The war had lasted 1,364 days, 5 hours, and 44 minutes. General MacArthur signed for the United Nations. Admiral Nimitz signed for the United States.

At the end of the ceremony, MacArthur walked over to Admiral Halsey and asked, "Bill, where the hell are those airplanes?" Halsey gave the signal, and soon Flyboys provided the thunderous exclamation mark to the proceedings. Fifteen hundred navy carrier aircraft and five hundred B-29s darkened the sky over Tokyo Bay.

Both President Truman and General MacArthur addressed the U.S. in a live radio hookup. Like their counterparts in the nineteenth century, they couched their remarks with repeated references to "civilization" and their Christian god. Truman's speech was almost religious in tone. The Japanese were "forces of evil" who had posed a "mighty threat to civilization." It was "God's help" that "brought us to this day of victory" over those who were out to "destroy His civilization." Truman used the words "God" and "civilized" five times each — as often as he said the word "America."

MacArthur called the war a "holy mission" in which a "merciful God" had ensured "the survival of civilization." He seemed to be offering Japan one last chance at civilization when he intoned: "We stand in Tokyo today reminiscent of our countryman, Commodore Perry, 92 years ago. His purpose was to bring to Japan an era of enlightenment and progress by lifting the veil of isolation to the friendship, trade and commerce of the world. But alas the knowledge thereby gained of western science was forged into an instrument of oppression and human enslavement."

The rhetoric was high blown, but most on the *Missouri* had more mundane feelings of relief. "Well, it was over and done," Curtis LeMay later wrote. "And whoever was down was down, and whoever was living was living. Like many other folks, probably, I stood there and felt pretty tired."

On October 4, 1945, just one month after the surrender ceremony, a storm began to form in the Pacific. The winds started slowly in the Marianas, where Curtis's B-29s had once taken off to strike Japan. As if in a revengeful fury, the storm gathered mass and strength as it blew northward. Navy weathermen tracked the storm for days and predicted it would sputter into China. But on October 9, the *kaze* seemed to change its mind and headed straight for where the Americans were massed on Okinawa.

By 2 P.M., the *kaze* was blowing ninety-five miles an hour. The rain blew "horizontal, more salt than fresh." Huge U.S. Navy ships anchored off Okinawa were blown sideways, their heavy anchors dragging the bottom. Forty-foot walls of water came roaring through like locomotives. A midday darkness fell on "a scene of indescribable confusion as dragging ships collided or . . . disappeared into the murk."

By 4 P.M., the *kaze* was blowing 115 miles an hour with gusts up to 140 miles an hour. As if to intentionally inflict maximum damage, the wind then shifted and tore grounded boats off reefs and blew them back across the bay, "dragging their anchors the entire way." Ashore there was only misery. "Twenty hours of torrential rain soaked everything, made quagmires of roads and drowned virtually all stores, destroying most of the tents and flooding the rest." Some Quonset huts were lifted whole and moved hundreds of feet, others were torn to bits, the galvanized iron sheets ripped off, the wallboards shredded and the curved supports torn apart. The *kaze* destroyed 80 percent of Okinawa's houses.

When it was over, 12 ships lay on the bottom of the ocean and 222 were grounded. One hundred thirty-three of these were damaged beyond repair. Famed U.S. Navy historian Samuel Morison later concluded: "This was the most furious and lethal storm ever encountered by the United States Navy."

In 1281, the *kamikaze* killed 150,000 Mongols who dared to attempt to invade the land of the gods. That typhoon left the Japanese mainland unscathed. It seemed to target the seaborne invaders.

The October 1945 typhoon also skipped the main islands of Japan. If the Flyboys had not brought Japan to its knees and it had continued with the war as the Spirit Warriors had insisted, the typhoon off Okinawa that day would have torn through a U.S. invasion fleet of thousands of ships and millions of American boys.

CHAPTER EIGHTEEN

Casualties of War

If I had lost the war, I would have been tried as a war criminal.

— *General Curtis LeMay, quoted in* Dark Sun:
The Making of the Hydrogen Bomb

WHEN Warren Earl was declared missing, it threw Evi into a nervous breakdown," Evi's niece Billye Winder told me. "Warren Earl was her only son and she worshiped him." Warren Earl's cousin Ethelyn Goodner said, "His mother lost her mind about him being a POW. She just lost it. It took the wind out of her life. She was never the same."

Floyd Hall's sister, Margie, remembered, "When we got the report he was missing, my mother went wild. She really fell apart. She was crying constantly. It was hard. When she was alone, she'd think about it and the tears would come."

Kathryn Dye had her husband write a series of letters to the navy seeking more information on Jimmy. Mr. Dye even wrote to their congressman, Charles Wolverton. The navy responded politely to each inquiry, but the answer was always "No further information is available."

Mr. Hall wrote the Navy about Floyd: "Since March 7 we've heard nothing further concerning our son's welfare, and we are anxious to know if further info is not available at this time." The response: "No further information is available."

Evi wrote many letters to the Marine Corps, hoping her persistence would turn up information on Warren Earl. Each response noted, "I regret to advise you we have no additional information."

Evi grasped at straws. In November of 1945, she bypassed the Marines and sent a picture of released American POWs from her hometown newspaper to the Treasury Department. She wrote, "The one with the circle drawn around it resembles my son. I am asking you to let me know if you have the names of those in the picture as I haven't heard anything and it would help some." She ended the letter, "I'm enclosing a self addressed envelope."

The Treasury Department forwarded her letter to the Marines, who answered, "It is with regret that I must inform you that no additional report has yet been received regarding him. He will be continued on the records as 'missing in action.'"

MIA. For over a year, each mother awoke to gray days of not knowing. Her boy was "missing." When Laura Woellhof received Dick's MIA telegram, she said defiantly, "That don't mean dead."

But if he wasn't dead, where was he? On a life raft being roasted by the sun, slowly starving to death? Injured and in pain, crying for his mama? The mothers' minds were stretched like rubber bands by the not knowing.

Two months into her nightmare, Evi wrote in a letter to one of Warren Earl's buddies, "I still cling to the faint hope that Warren is alive, yet I do have my low moods in regards to him."

"It was terrible because she didn't know if he was dead or missing," said Warren Earl's cousin Madeline Riley about Evi. "She would cry a lot. The fact there was no further information about Warren Earl's status had a profound, debilitating effect on Evi. She was never again the same person, living her life without joy or peace."

Kathryn Dye literally could not sit still thinking about Jimmy. She contacted everyone who knew him and asked them to come visit her. If they couldn't come, she hit the road to see them. She stayed a week with Grady York's family in Jacksonville. She and Marie York shed tears together but had no new information to share.

Kathryn Dye and her husband drove to Wheeling, West Virginia, to see Jimmy's buddy Ralph Sengewalt. They stayed for four days at Ralph's parents' home.

"Mrs. Dye was a distraught mother anxious for her son," Ralph told me. "She said, 'If he was killed and there was a body, I could accept it. But there was no body, so I can't accept it.' I couldn't help much. All I could tell them was we saw Jimmy and Grady walking up on shore. I saw her cry many quiet tears."

Glenn Frazier's buddy Lyle Comstock visited Glenn's mother in Kansas City after the war. They sat in the living room for a while and visited. Lyle showed Mrs. Frazier a knife Glenn had given him. "If something happens to me, you can have this," Glenn had told Lyle. Lyle offered Glenn's knife to Mrs. Frazier, but she told him to keep it. "I still have it," Lyle told me.

Mrs. Frazier asked Lyle to come upstairs with her. On the wall of one room was a large map of the Pacific. "I can't find Chichi Jima," she told him. Lyle pointed to the tiny island on the map. Mrs. Frazier looked for a second and gushed, "Oh! It's so far away." Then she broke down and sobbed in Lyle's arms.

On Saturday, October 6, 1945, the U.S. Navy destroyer USS *Trippe* sailed into the harbor at Chichi Jima. It was commanded by Marine colonel Presley M. Rixey. His mission was to disarm the soldiers on Chichi Jima and repatriate them to the Japanese mainland.

Major Horie and an interpreter came aboard. After settling details, Colonel Rixey asked Major Horie, "And what became of the American flyers you captured on these islands?"

The Americans had no firm information that any flyers had been captured at Chichi Jima. As Rixey later wrote, "The American Navy probably thought that those lost in combat flights had gone down at sea." The colonel was merely baiting Major Horie to see if he could get some information.

To Colonel Rixey's "utter surprise," Major Horie responded immediately.

"Yes," Major Horie said. "We captured six. All Navy, I think. They received very kind treatment. Two were sent to Japan by submarine. The last four unfortunately were killed by your own bombs in an air raid against these islands during the capture of Iwo Jima. They were blown up by a direct hit. Nothing remains. I am so sorry this happened. I was very beloved of them and wished them no harm. We buried what remained of the bodies after cremation. This is Japanese custom."

Rixey later wondered to himself, "Why did Horie admit that aviators had been shot down and captured? He must have suspected that we knew more than we did! Somehow his story did not ring true, yet we nodded our heads in belief."

Rixey ordered that the Japanese officer who had been responsible for the prisoners appear on the destroyer the next day. Rixey was told the officer was Major Sueo Matoba.

When Major Horie and his party returned to Chichi Jima, the translator of the meeting on the *Trippe,* Cadet Oyama, warned him: "Do not be too sure. Maybe you have not fooled the Americans. They are thorough and you will hear more of this from them."

"It is done," Major Horie said. "We must stick to our words. I believe our prepared story will deceive them. They will find no evidence. Bones and belongings have been thrown into the sea by orders of General Tachibana."

The next day, Major Matoba and Major Horie reported to Colonel Rixey on the *Trippe.* Rixey recalled Matoba as a large "cruel"-looking man with a "bull throat" and "very short cropped hair" who held himself "very erect," bowed "only half as low as the others," and "folded his hands on the table in an arrogant manner." Rixey observed that Matoba had "the most cold-blooded eyes I had ever looked into."

"Major," Colonel Rixey began, "why did you not protect these flyers like you protected yourself and your men in air-raid shelters?"

"Sir, I regret the neglect of my troops," Major Matoba answered stiffly. "My adjutant was given strict instructions to properly care for the Americans. I believe your raid came upon us so quickly that my men had little time to act."

"You were responsible as Commanding Officer for their safe-keeping," Colonel Rixey told him. "You should have quartered them in a well-protected shelter. Your neglect has violated the rules of International Law. I shall hold you personally responsible. There will be further investigations. Tomorrow, you will produce the enlisted men who were actually on watch over the prisoners."

As his words were being translated, Colonel Rixey watched Matoba closely. "Sparks seemed to jump from his eyes and he rubbed his neck vigorously."

"Were the ashes of these Americans buried as prescribed by the rules of war?" operations officer Captain Kusiak asked Major Horie. "And did you or Major Matoba erect a cross over the site of the graves as is usually done in the Christian religion?"

"Yes, sir," Horie answered. "A large cross was placed over the American grave. We rendered military honors."

Colonel Rixey informed the two Japanese majors that he would come ashore the next day to view and photograph the grave. As they were being rowed ashore after the interrogation, Major Matoba asked Major Horie how to construct a Christian cross.

The next day, Colonel Rixey was escorted to the cemetery where Marve Mershon had been bayoneted. Rixey recalled, "Everything was in order as had been said. But the cross itself was of new wood. It bore no sign of having been exposed to the elements longer than the day before."

Suspicious, Colonel Rixey had Matoba's four enlisted men interrogated separately. "Each man questioned told exactly the same story of the unfortunate deaths of the flyers," Rixey wrote. "Mind you, this had happened eight months previously yet each machine gunner recalled the exact spot, the exact time of day *to the minute,* the direction of flight of the American plane and the number of bombs dropped. Yet when questioned as to what the flyers were wearing, all remained mute and shook their heads. Their Major Matoba had forgotten to tell them what to say about this important point! They looked worried when they reboarded their wooden landing craft."

The repatriation of Japanese from Chichi Jima was a low priority for the American military. Most navy ships were being used to return U.S. servicemen to the United States. Colonel Rixey's men had destroyed some Japanese armaments on the island, collected others, and repatriated just 3,000 (out of 25,000) Japanese soldiers by the end of 1945. Rixey was suspicious about the fate of the Flyboys, but he had no leads.

Then, in December of 1945, a Japanese coast guard cutter arrived at Chichi Jima with civilians who had been evacuated from the island two years earlier. Among them was Fred Savory, great-grandson of the island's founder, Nathaniel Savory. Fred approached Colonel Rixey with a startling story.

"Sir," Fred Savory began, "in Japan I heard rumors spoken by the soldiers you shipped from Chichi Jima. They are saying that their officers executed American flyers. And there is a rumor that Major Matoba ordered his medical officer to remove an aviator's liver after execution and to deliver it to his orderly. A member of this battalion believes that Matoba and a few of his officers ate this liver at a sake party the next day."

"We were flabbergasted," Rixey recalled. "We had suspected beheadings, of course, but never cannibalism!"

Rixey decided on a course of action. He singled out Major Horie for special attention, inviting him as the only Japanese to attend parties with American officers. Then, on New Year's Day 1946, after a few bourbons, Colonel Rixey made his pitch.

"Major Horie," the colonel began, "as a military man, I appreciate what you did for your Emperor and your country. I consider you my friend and I need your aid. You may not know it, but I have much information about what went on in these islands. I know of executions and other facts that followed. I also know that you are not involved. Those guilty must be punished. I will protect you because I know you are innocent of any wrongdoing. You lied to me on the *Trippe* but I forgive that. You were acting under orders of your senior officers and it is understandable. But now I appeal to your friendship and your honor as a true and brave solider." Major Horie complied.

When the armed Marines dispatched to arrest him surprised Major Matoba in his hut, he was sitting in a chair, listening to a record on his phonograph. He was dressed in his favorite pink bathrobe.

Emperor Hirohito was a war criminal if there ever was one. Under the Meiji Constitution he had the "right of supreme command." He was responsible for sanctioning military initiatives, promoting officers, and approving budgets. "Much of Japan's aggression was formulated outside the cabinet in conferences involving only the military and its commander in chief." Soldiers like Masayo Enomoto who garroted Chinese farmers were raised to believe they were performing these deeds in the emperor's name and with his approval. No general could be promoted, no ship launched, without Hirohito's knowledge and assent.

Many agreed with Prince Konoe, a former prime minister, when he proclaimed that Hirohito was "the major war criminal." Some of the emperor's staunchest western allies, like former ambassador to Japan

Joseph Grew, concluded, "Hirohito will have to go." The president of prestigious Tokyo Imperial University "argued that Hirohito should abdicate on moral grounds." Even those in court circles accepted "the notion that he should somehow assume responsibility for the war." On August 29, two days before the conquering *gaizin* arrived in Japan, Hirohito spoke to an adviser "about abdication as a way of possibly absolving his faithful ministers, generals, and admirals of responsibility for the war." The emperor "had his officials brief him on the practice of abdication in the British monarchy." Hirohito's uncle Prince Higashikuni — serving as prime minister — "met privately with his nephew and recommended that he step down," and Prince Mikasa, the emperor's younger brother, "urged the emperor to take responsibility for defeat."

The Japanese public would have accepted Hirohito's abdication. They had assented to his decision to surrender and would have obeyed his wishes regarding his own future. An American intelligence unit monitoring Japanese opinion reported, "Informed sources claim that many people have reached a state where it is almost immaterial to them whether the Emperor is retained or not. People are more concerned with food and housing problems than with the fate of the Emperor." The U.S. Strategic Bombing Survey found only 4 percent checked off "worry about Emperor, shame for Emperor, sorrow for him" when asked their feelings about Japan's surrender. "A poll conducted in Osaka found over a quarter of respondents in favor of Hirohito abdicating right away or at an opportune moment." Millions were dead as a result of the emperor's "holy war." Abdication would have enhanced the moral integrity of the imperial institution.

On the other side of the Pacific, a Gallup poll conducted just before the war's end "indicated that 70 percent of Americans favored executing or harshly punishing the emperor." Washington ordered General MacArthur to investigate the emperor's culpability in the war, especially his approval of the attack against Pearl Harbor. If the emperor had the power to stop a war with one speech, wasn't he also responsible for its beginning and continuation?

With the slightest effort, American authorities could have mustered voluminous evidence that "at the end of the war, at its beginning, and through every stage of its unfolding, Emperor Hirohito played a highly active role in supporting the actions carried out in his name." Just a trip to a Tokyo corner newspaper stand would have done the trick. On October 9 and 27, the *Asahi Shimbun* published stories confirming that Hirohito had approved the decision to go to war and known of the plan to attack Pearl Harbor.

But when American war crimes prosecutors arrived in Tokyo, they "found the war leaders all saying virtually the same thing." The line was the same whether spoken by a Japanese politician or an American general. Hirohito was innocent. He had opposed the war. He was a hero for single-handedly ending the conflict.

The fix was in. General MacArthur laid out the logic in a report to Washington:

> His indictment will unquestionably cause a tremendous convulsion among the Japanese people, the repercussions of which cannot be overestimated. He is a symbol which unites all Japanese. Destroy him and the nation will disintegrate. . . . It is quite possible that a million troops would be required which would have to be maintained for an indefinite number of years.

Tremendous convulsion? Japan disintegrate? Most Japanese had only been aware of their emperor for a small fraction of their 2,600-year history. When Perry's Black Ships revealed the impotence of the Tokugawa regime, "the Japanese had discarded their feudal Shogunate . . . cast them off like worn-out garments after almost eight centuries of exalted existence." Hirohito had proven himself more than impotent. He had been defeated by *gaizin* and allowed a foreign army into the land of the gods. Why would Japan disintegrate if a loser was replaced? Japan had lost a war and disarmed peacefully. There were no outbreaks of violence, no terrorist attacks on the American occupiers. But MacArthur, well in advance of the surrender, had apparently succumbed to the Spirit Warriors' Oz-like hype about the emperor's being eternal. Months before the war ended, General MacArthur approved the plan to save the emperor, reasoning that "unlike Christians, the Japanese have no God with whom to commune," that the Japanese needed Hirohito as a Christ-figure, and that "it would be a sacrilege to entertain the idea that the Emperor is on a level with the people or any governmental official. To try him as a war criminal would not only be blasphemous but a denial of spiritual freedom." American officials wrote, "Hanging of the Emperor to them would be comparable to the crucifixion of Christ to us." MacArthur agreed: "You cannot remove their Emperor worship from these people by killing the Emperor . . . any more than you remove the godhead of Jesus and have any Christianity left."

General Bonner Fellers had been one of the very first Americans in Japan after the surrender, a passenger on the plane that first brought MacArthur. General Fellers immediately "went to work to protect Hirohito from the role he had played during and at the end of the war." He spent five months coaching war crimes suspects on how they should testify. In one conversation with a high-ranking Japanese official, Fellers pointed out that the Russians wanted to try Hirohito as a war criminal. Fellers said, "To counter this situation, it would be more convenient if the Japanese side could prove to us that the emperor is completely blameless. I think the forthcoming trials offer the best opportunity to do that. Tojo, in particular, should be made to bear all responsibility at his trial. In other words, I want you to have Tojo say as follows: 'At the imperial conference prior to the start of the war, I had already decided to push for war even if his majesty the emperor was against going to war with the United States.'"

Instead of investigating the emperor as he was ordered, General MacArthur forbade it. In a secret cable he assured Washington: "Investigation has been conducted. . . . and no evidence has been found that connected Hirohito to political decisions during the past decade." And chief prosecutor Joseph Keenan informed his prosecutors that they were not to go after the emperor. Any evidence that led to the top would be suppressed, and if they would not assist in the cover-up, they should "by all means go home immediately." Rather than serve to prosecute justice, "the prosecution functioned, in effect, as a defense team for the emperor."

Former Prime Minister Tojo and twenty-seven other military and government officers were charged as Class A war criminals. The main charge was that they were part of a "conspiracy" to "wage wars of aggression, and wars in violation of international law."

A law passed after the occurrence of an event that retrospectively changes the legal consequences of the event is called an ex post facto law. The United States Constitution has two clauses prohibiting ex post facto laws. But the charge of "waging aggressive war" was a charge invented by the victors after World War II. U.S. Brigadier General Elliott Thorpe was one who shared the job of choosing which war criminals would be tried. "I still don't believe that was the right thing to do," Thorpe later said. "I still believe that it was an ex post facto law. They made up the rules after the game was over." Thorpe thought the trials were not about justice but revenge. "We wanted blood and, by God, we had blood," Thorpe said. And General William Chase wrote, "We used to say in Tokyo that the U.S. had better not lose the next war, or our generals and admirals would all be shot at sunrise without a hearing of any sort."

Prosecutor Keenan tried to make the case that the inept Spirit Warriors, the guys who in reality had stumbled from event to event, were actually master conspirators who worked their evil over a fourteen-year period, from 1928 to 1945, hiding it from their boss. But the name of the only official who held power throughout those fourteen years was never mentioned. It was like making the case that the Model T automobile sprang from workers' coffee breaks and Mr. Ford just happened to have a big office.

Chief Judge William Webb of Australia later criticized the fact that the "leader of the crime, though available for trial, had been granted immunity." Judge Henri Bernard of France wrote that Japan's crimes "had a principal author who escaped all prosecution and of whom in any case the present Defendants could only be considered as accomplices." Former Prime Minister Tojo was happy that "nothing was carried up to the emperor and on that point I am being comforted." On the day the Class A conspirators were sentenced, prosecutor Keenan enjoyed a three-hour lunch with Emperor Hirohito at the palace.

Seven Class A prisoners were hanged, including Tojo. Six others died in prison and two were released insane. Thirteen were later paroled, serving at the most eight years for crimes against millions of people.

But in many cases, it seemed the bigger the crime, the more likely the criminal was to get off scot-free. Colonel Masanobu Tsuji, the "God of Strategy" who planned the southern advance, had Chinese heads displayed in Singapore, and inspired Major Matoba with his habit of eating enemy livers, was one who escaped prosecution. Douglas MacArthur's intelligence chief, General Charles Willoughby, had damning evidence that Colonel Tsuji had beheaded Flyboy Lieutenant Benjamin Parker and eaten his liver. But Willoughby was concerned about the spread of Communism in postwar Japan and "Tsuji's anti-communist bona fides, together with his renowned planning skills, made him a valuable property for postwar Japan; and one thus worth protecting." Tsuji not only avoided prosecution but was later elected to the lower house of the Japanese Diet.

Perhaps Japan's most egregious war crime was the biological and chemical warfare waged in China by Unit 731. General MacArthur and a number of other American officers knew that Unit 731 had experimented upon and killed captured American POWs. But when the diabolical doctors offered the U.S. valuable information based on their gruesome experiments in exchange for immunity, MacArthur immediately approved this devil's deal.

In 1979, fourteen Class A criminals were secretly enshrined as patriotic "martyrs" in Tokyo's Yasukuni Shrine, which honors Japan's war dead. Among those enshrined were Tojo and General Iwane Matsui, whose troops were responsible for the Rape of Nanking.

Today many complain that Japan has not taken full responsibility for its involvement in World War II. But by letting the chief culprit off, by contorting justice with ex post facto laws, and by hiding some of Japan's most horrific crimes, the Allies rendered justice arbitrary and made a mockery of any attempt to fix historical blame. If Hitler had been coddled and defended by the American conquerors, would the average German be expected to reflect upon his guilt?

Lieutenant Bill Doran had just graduated from the U.S. Naval Academy in 1946 when he was ordered to observe the Guam War Crimes trials of the Chichi Jima accused. This trial was one of hundreds that took place throughout the Pacific. It was conducted under conditions of extreme secrecy in a "humungous" metal Quonset building.

"The Japanese prisoners sat at a long table," Bill recalled. "There was a huge Marine standing behind each prisoner. Each Marine carried the weapon of his choice, magnums, semi-automatics, shoulder holsters, pearl-handled thirty-eight specials. Plus, all the Marines carried big ebony clubs, three times the size of regular policemen's billy clubs. Each Marine was at 'parade rest,' with his back to crowd, legs apart. They had their left hand on the chair of each prisoner, and the club in their right hand behind their back. Once in a while the portable electrical generator would cut out. When it did, the interior of the hut went completely pitch-dark. When this happened, the Marines would instantly move their left hand from the back of the prisoner's chair to the back of his neck. And they would bend over the prisoner and put the club just over the prisoner's head. We would see this scene briefly when the lights went back on."

Fourteen Japanese officers, soldiers, and doctors were tried as Class B criminals by a military commission on Guam. Eight American military officers from various services sat as judges. American and Japanese civilian lawyers served as defense counsel. Class B crimes included murder, ill treatment of prisoners, failure to give an honorable burial, and failure to control the unlawful behavior of subordinates. The navy searched for past instances of war criminals being charged with cannibalism, but no one at The Hague or Geneva had ever anticipated the need to criminalize the eating of the enemy. The charge of "failure to give an honorable burial" was substituted.

Bill Doran, who spent his life as a lawyer, told me many years later: "I've read thousands of trial transcripts. All war crimes trials have people accusing one side of doing something, the other side denying it, and then courts make a decision. Here, you have all the testimony coming from one side, all the witnesses are Japanese themselves. The Japanese are admitting that they were cannibals, in their own words."

In his opening statement, prosecutor Daniel Flynn warned that some of the alleged "acts are so revolting to the human mind that man long ago decided it unnecessary to legislate directly against their commission. [The charges] rank with the most startling ever to be heard in the criminal court. It is our hope that never again will the like of these cases have to be presented." Prosecutor Fredric Suss called the accused "inhuman savages . . . who have torn and mutilated the bodies of our defenseless brothers in the most primitive and barbaric fashion." He suggested that the Chichi Jima soldiers were "typical representatives of this diabolical evil force . . . the ambitious Japanese military that infected their country like a dangerous disease and spread with cruelty as the deadly plague over Asia and the Pacific."

"But the information about the Americans having their heads chopped off and livers taken out wasn't supposed to get back to the United States," Bill said. "The Marine guards told me the navy didn't want people back home to know that their sons were eaten."

The prosecution called forty-three witnesses. Major Horie, in khaki shorts, was the star witness. Behind the scenes, General Tachibana called Horie "an American dog." "You are not Japanese," the general told him.

"The navy kept the Japanese prisoners all together in a big penned area," Bill said. "Inside were barracks. The pen was made of heavy wire mesh. One night, Matoba tore a hole in that fence, big enough to get his head through. The guards caught him the next morning. None of the Marine guards could rip the material the slightest bit."

General Tachibana denied everything. He said he didn't know about the killing of any flyers and that he never ate human flesh. And at first, Major Matoba tried to pass blame off on underlings, though he finally came clean. He dispelled the idea that the cannibalism occurred because of hunger. "My battalion still had sufficient food," he said.

"Yes [I am a cannibal]," Major Matoba testified. "I was a madman due to the war and that is the only reason I can give for being a cannibal."

Captain Yoshii, who ordered the deaths of Jimmy Dye and Warren Earl Vaughn, refused to answer questions. Instead, he submitted a statement noting, "Not one war criminal has been found among the victorious nations." He wrote that the "War Crimes Trials are [an] emotional act of revenge against the defeated nations." Yoshii instructed his interrogators: "Do not judge the guilty, before you have judged yourself. Therefore, before you charge anybody, charge yourself first." He quoted the Book of Saint Matthew: "Judge not, that ye be not judged. For that judgment ye judge, ye shall be judged; and with what measure ye mete, it shall be measured to you again. And why beholdest thou the mote that is in thy brother's eye, but considerest not the beam that is in thine own eye?"

Yoshii refused to testify until the commission answered how they, as Christians, could answer why he was being judged and no Allied war criminals were. The mistreatment of POWs was a perfect example. There was no doubt that Japan had perpetrated an enormous crime. Japan had held 132,134 western POWs and 35,756 of them died in detention, a death rate of 27 percent. In contrast, only 4 percent of the POWs held by the Germans and Italians died. "Moreover, the postwar death rate among surviving POWs of the Japanese was also higher."

But one of the judges at the Tokyo war crimes trial was from the Soviet Union. America's ally still held up to 700,000 Japanese prisoners captured in Manchuria. As the Tokyo trial wore on and a Soviet sat in judgment over Japanese, their countrymen were being worked to death in Soviet prison camps. More than 62,000 Japanese POWs — almost twice as many as Allied POW deaths — would die in the gulag.

Captain Yoshii never addressed the commission.

General Tachibana, Major Matoba, and Captain Yoshii were high-ranking officers who ordered Flyboys' deaths. It was easy to assign them guilt. The lower-ranking Japanese soldiers who had been ordered to serve as executioners assumed that the blame would stop at the officer level and not reach them. After all, Japanese soldiers *had* to follow orders. But they were shocked to learn that for the purposes of the trial, they would be retroactively transferred to an ethical sphere they never could have imagined. These soldiers were informed that they had been individuals on Chichi Jima who had exercised free will. And to their astonishment, the soldiers learned that they had been responsible for their actions and superior orders were no excuse.

The interpreters must have had a difficult time conveying these foreign concepts to the *shinmin* — "people who obediently comply with their orders." Rights? Free will? The responsibility to disobey? And what exactly was an illegal order? These soldiers had operated in a moral universe where it was illegal to disobey a superior's order. The backbone of the Japanese military was obedience. These soldiers were not citizens; they had no rights. They were Hirohito's *issen gorin.*

Private Matsutano Kido was one of four soldiers ordered to stab Dick Woellhof. His defense counsel noted, "Private Kido was an uneducated man who received an order. He obeys that order and a year later finds himself charged with violation of the laws and customs of war. . . . What does Kido know about the laws and customs of war? Kido can barely read and write — yet now he is supposed to know all about International Law and proper treatment of prisoners and the Geneva and Hague conventions."

But despite such pleadings, the prosecution maintained that the Geneva convention held sway on Chichi Jima. Hirohito might be protected, but not these men.

The Japanese defendants were thus held to a different standard than U.S. troops would have been in the same situation. Army chief of staff George Marshall had decreed that when an accused American's acts "were done pursuant to order of a superior or government sanction [such a superior order] may be taken into consideration in determining culpability." So an American serviceman could use superior orders as a defense. But at the Guam trials, the prosecution decreed that Japanese soldiers could not: "Superior orders . . . are no defense to the commission of crime, for a man is not obliged to obey an unlawful order."

Sergeant Takano was another who had bayoneted Dick Woellhof. He was shocked to learn that he bore responsibility for carrying out an order. "I cannot understand how my superior officers on Chichi Jima could make it possible for me to be accused of murder because they ordered me to carry out their orders," Takano testified. "I had no will to kill any prisoner. . . . I blindly carried out an order with only the idea that to do so is the right thing. I trust implicitly my superior officers and never for one moment doubted but that their orders were to be carried out."

Arguing that the Japanese soldiers' lot was "little better than [that of] slaves," defense counsel said, "It is a crime against humanity to lay responsibility upon those whose acts are limited by their superiors. It is cruel to condemn those to heavy punishment who do not know the law." Major Horie testified, "The fundamental basis for the Army is absolute obedience to any order — unquestioning obedience." And Captain Masao Yamashita, who carried out the order to kill Grady York, told the commission: "I was educated since I was young to give absolute obedience to orders. I carried it out much against my will as I did not have any other alternative." Private Taniyama, another who had speared Dick Woellhof, said, "We did not have any freedom at all to judge the right or wrong of given orders. We were all puppets who have been deprived of our own will and freedom." Corporal Nakamura, who had reluctantly chopped Floyd Hall's head off, said, "The order was given on the front line of battle. I knew that to refuse such an order meant sure death." Lieutenant Hayashi, who sliced Jimmy Dye, reminded the commission of the "seriousness of the crime of disobedience" in the Japanese military. And Colonel Kato, who had ordered Grady York's death and accepted full responsibility, urged the commission to "understand the position of absolute obedience" in which the executioners had found themselves: "I plead that you fully understand that their actions were not committed by them of their own free will."

A voice from the grave supported this claim. Ensign Takao Koyama, who had chopped off Warren Earl Vaughn's head, had committed suicide over his guilt. He left a note. In it he wrote, "I now say my actions were wrong [but] I believe I have done right as a military man [because] the carrying out of orders from superior officers was more important than death."

The defense recalled the extraordinary time in which the executions occurred, with daily air raids and the fear of an American invasion, when "obedience to orders was most rigidly required." One defendant said, "During a period of war an order is something more absolute than any moral obligation." A defense lawyer pointed out that "orders under the grueling, pounding stress of battle assume a far different aspect than they do in peaceful surroundings on a quiet military installation." He said that to expect a Japanese soldier "to refuse to obey such an order is to be entirely ignorant of the Japanese mind and temperament." Another defense lawyer put it in terms the American commission members could understand. He maintained that "if a comparable order had been given by a Marine Corps major to a Marine Corps first lieutenant to take a firing squad and shoot a Jap prisoner on Iwo Jima at the same time that these events took place on Chichi Jima — the first lieutenant would not have hesitated any longer nor protested any more than [the Japanese] did."

In September of 1947, five Spirit Warriors — General Tachibana, Major Matoba, Colonel Ito, Captain Yoshii, and Captain Nakajima — were hanged and buried in unmarked graves on Guam. Most of the other accused were sentenced to prison terms and served their time in Tokyo's Sugamo prison.

Newspapers in Japan and America reported snippets of the trial and the hangings. The news accounts were sensational but short on detail.

Time magazine's headline was "Unthinkable Crime." The *New York Times* referred to the proceedings as the "CANNIBALISM TRIAL." The trial of former Prime Minister Tojo and the other Class A criminals dominated the news, and the Guam trials were relegated to the inside pages. The names of the Chichi Jima Flyboys were never mentioned.

Almost two hundred war crimes trials took place throughout Asia after World War II. The trials were held in many countries and jurisdictions, and there is no accurate tabulation of the final results. But as far as can be determined, approximately 5,700 Japanese were indicted for war crimes. About 920 were executed, 525 received life sentences, 2,944 were sentenced to more limited prison terms, 1,018 were acquitted, and 279 were never brought to trial. No Americans were tried.

After the emperor surrendered, General Tachibana had ordered the Flyboys' bodies uncovered, cremated, and their ashes thrown into the sea. Soldiers opened the graves and poured oil on the bodies to burn them. Marine lieutenant Robert Frazer later testified that American investigators found very little. In one grave they discovered a mechanical pencil with the words "Glenn J. Frazier" on it, a piece of rope, and three bones. In a nearby grave they found a jumble of burned bones. At Omura Cemetery the U.S. team found a box of ashes and a few charred bones. These combined remains were assumed to be those of Glenn Frazier, Marve Mershon, and Floyd Hall, who had flown together.

In Jimmy Dye's grave near the Mount Yoake radio station, the investigators found a few bones and "considerable amounts" of brown hair.

In the area where Dick Woellhof and the B-24 pilot were killed, one grave yielded a single vertebra. Pieces of rope and segments of wooden stakes were found in the other. In 1946, each of the families was told that "remains" of their boys had been reinterred at the American cemetery on Iwo Jima. Pilot Floyd Hall, radioman Marve Mershon, and gunner Glenn Frazier flew together, crashed together, and were buried together. The families were told that "individual identification [was] impossible."

In 1947, the U.S. government removed the remains of all Americans from Iwo Jima. Floyd, Marve, and Glenn were formally buried in the Santa Fe National Cemetery in Santa Fe, New Mexico, on Friday, July 2, 1948. The headstone of their common grave reads:

> Floyd Ewing Hall
> Ensign
>
> Glenn Frazier Jr
> AOM2C
>
> Marve William Mershon
> ACM3C
>
> US Naval Reserve
>
> February 19 1946

The most popular tourist attraction in Hawaii is not the USS *Arizona* memorial or a volcano, but "Punchbowl" cemetery. Its official name is the National Memorial Cemetery of the Pacific. One glance at the graceful sloping crater in which the cemetery lies and one understands its nickname.

More than thirty-five thousand veterans of America's wars are buried there. The centerpiece of the beautiful cemetery is a striking "Court of Honor" dominated by a thirty-foot statue of Columbia, in whose name American pioneers first moved west. (Columbia was featured in the opening montage of the TV program *Hawaii Five-0.*)

The families of Dick Woellhof and Warren Earl Vaughn were told that when the graves of their boys were opened on Iwo Jima, there were no "remains" to be found. The Punchbowl's "Courts of the Missing" — ten granite monuments on either side of the ascending stairway leading up to Columbia — honor the vanished. An inscription reads:

> In These Gardens Are Recorded
> The Names of Americans
> Who Gave Their Lives
> In the Service of Their Country

And Whose Earthly Resting Place
Is Known Only to God

Among the 28,788 names chiseled into the Courts of the Missing are these two:

Vaughn Warren Earl
Second Lieutenant USMC Texas

Woellhof Lloyd R
AVN Radioman 2C USNR Kansas

Jimmy Dye always wanted to stand out from the crowd, so perhaps it is fitting that he is the only Chichi Jima Flyboy with a grave all his own. Jimmy's "remains" are buried at Punchbowl cemetery, his tombstone at "Plot N 1291," flush with the grass, reading:

James Wesley Dye Jr.
New Jersey
ARM3 US Navy
World War II
Nov 27 1925 Feb 25 1945

Two of the Flyboys are also memorialized elsewhere. Dick Woellhof's name is chiseled on a stone at Greenwood Cemetery in his hometown of Clay Center, Kansas. And today when students enter the lobby of Smith-Cotton High School in Sedalia, Missouri, they see a photo collage of the sixty students from that little school who died in World War II. One of the photos is of handsome Floyd Hall, the Flyboy who liked blondes and knew he would never come back.

Two Flyboys have no memorial. No one knows the identity of the B-24 airman killed with Dick Woellhof. And when Grady York's grave was opened on Iwo Jima there was nothing there. In an oversight, Grady's name never made it to the Courts of the Missing. The religious skillyboo boy who hoped someone would "Pray for me" has nowhere for anyone to pray for him.

*   *   *

For one year after the initial MIA telegrams the postman brought reminders of the Flyboys back home but no new information. Letters from Flyboy buddies, chaplains, and commanding officers recounted fond memories of brave boys but offered no real hope to anxious families. The mothers' hearts must have beat faster whenever official letters arrived from the navy, but the envelopes only contained routine paperwork. Each mother had to sign for a box containing the possessions her boy had left behind in his ship's locker before his last flight. Marve Mershon's earthly possessions were listed as "bible, log book, key ring, penknife, address book, bedroom slippers, sheath knife, gym pants, billfold containing ID, photos and $55.28." When Dick Woellhof's belongings arrived, his mother didn't open them right away. "I want to do that when I'm alone," Laura Woellhof told her sister.

Then, in February of 1946 — one year after the boys' deaths — the families received telegrams and letters that repeated Major Horie's big lie. Evi's telegram told her that Warren Earl had been:

KILLED ON 15 MARCH 1945 IN AN AERIAL BOMBARDMENT
AT OMURA CHICHI JIMA. HE IS CARRIED ON THE RECORDS
OF THE MARINE CORPS AS KILLED IN ACTION. NO
INFORMATION AVAILABLE REGARDING DISPOSITION OF
HIS REMAINS. PLEASE ACCEPT MY HEARTFELT SYMPATHY.

Some accepted this news, others were in denial. Warren Earl's high school buddy Harold Waters visited Evi soon after she learned of her only child's death. "She had his room exactly like he left it," Waters told me. "She didn't touch a thing. Evi wasn't accepting his death. She said she knew he was going to come back."

Floyd Hall's memorial service was at the Broadway Presbyterian Church in Sedalia, Missouri. "We had Floyd's photo on the altar with a few flowers," his sister, Margie, told me. "It was hard to just look at a picture." Dick Woellhof's aunt Ruah Sterrett said, "We had a memorial service for Dick at the church. It was hard with no body."

"In June of 1946, we read an article in *Life* magazine about Chichi Jima and the torture and things done there," Jimmy's brother Ronnie Dye told me. The *Life* article mentioned that General Tachibana and Major Matoba were accused of executing "American fliers shot down

325

in the Bonins and, even more revolting, of practicing cannibalism on them." There was "evidence of American fliers being clubbed, bayoneted and beheaded, of their bodies being mutilated, of their livers being served in sukiyaki, and strips of their flesh used to flavor soup."

"My mom read that *Life* article and got hysterical," Ronnie Dye said. "She cried for years and years. It was never out of her mind. My mother never recovered. She was in a doctor's care for the rest of her life." Because the articles offered no American names and only sketchy rumored details, relatives were left in an anguished limbo. Mr. Dye wrote the navy requesting they stop sending letters to the house because "my wife suffers a nervous condition." Subsequently, Jimmy's navy record states that letters should be "addressed to the local Veterans Assistance Office which will in turn contact Mr. Dye personally so that the mother of James will not have to suffer the pains she has already suffered in connection with her son's death."

Finally, one and a half years after their deaths, their families recieved letters in the fall of 1946 with the navy's final censored version of the boys' demises. The letters recounted the boys' shoot-downs and gave bare details, like Jimmy Dye was "sent on to Yoake wireless station for the purpose of helping decode messages," Dick Woellhof "remained about a month" on Chichi Jima, and Marve Mershon was "cremated and buried in Omura Cemetery; 20 Jan 46, remains exhumed and delivered to Iwo where reburied 14 Nov 46." No mention was made of beheading or the desecration of their corpses.

Many years later, I obtained the Chichi Jima Flyboys' military service records. These records are still withheld today from the families. I obtained them through sources I choose not to reveal. Their service records show clearly that the navy knew who was bayoneted, beheaded, and/or cannibalized. But these details were never passed on, despite desperate pleas from mothers wishing to know what happened to their babies.

Some families imploded, the grief too overwhelming to address. "Floyd's memory was about silence," his brother James later told me. "There was no counseling then, and we all dealt with it internally, by ourselves. In 1955, my parents went to see his grave. They didn't say much about it."

Other families exploded. Marve's death blew the Mershon family apart. With no body, little information, and no counseling, there was no outlet for their grief. Already hard drinkers, Marve's parents —

Hoyt Sr. and Clarinda — and his brother, Hoyt Jr., upped their intake to drown their sorrow. Hoyt Jr. suffered a special survivor's guilt. He was the one who had talked Marve into enlisting. And after a few drinks one night, Clarinda compounded her son's suffering when she told Hoyt Jr., "I wish it had been you that died."

Clarinda and Hoyt Sr. abandoned their city life and moved to Cathedral Canyon, California, where they lived in a garage on the edge of the desert. They cooked on a hot coil, slept on army cots, and poured alcohol over their grief. A relative told me, "Clarinda would wander in the desert for weeks at a time and no one knew where she was."

Like many fathers, Hoyt Sr. ("a big jolly man") kept his grief inside, unexpressed. He died in 1951, at the age of fifty-nine, of a heart attack. Clarinda passed away in 1955, also at the age of fifty-nine. On her death certificate, the "Reason for death" is listed as "Cirrhosis of liver." On the line that requests "How long condition?" there is one word: "Years."

Hoyt Mershon Jr. never shook his guilt over persuading Marve to enlist in the navy. He died in 1958 at the age of thirty-eight. His death certificate says he had "Cirrhosis of the liver for three years plus" and "chronic alcoholism for ten years plus."

Hoyt Jr. had buried his mom and dad in the Santa Fe National Cemetery near Marve. Expressing his guilt to the end, Hoyt Jr. had himself buried apart from the rest of the family, in Inglewood Memorial Park in Inglewood, California.

Many years later, I spoke with Hoyt Jr.'s three daughters, Susan, Linda, and Carol. They are now in their fifties and though they were vaguely aware of their father's feelings regarding his brother's fate, they knew nothing about how Marve perished. They always thought he had "died when his plane crashed."

After I told Susan Mershon that Hoyt Jr. knew that his brother had not died in a crash and that Marve had made it onto Chichi Jima alive, she was quiet for a while. Then Susan said, "So that's why when I was a little girl my father was always alone in that room at night. He would sit there in the dark just smoking, drinking, and crying."

Unlike some other families, who were silent about their loss, the Yorks often discussed Grady. "My mom would cry and talk about what a good boy he was," Grady's sister Pearl Diffenderfer told me. "I remember her saying many times that he was so different. He was a good Christian boy. He didn't go out drinking; he believed in God and doing something for his country."

Grady's mother devoted a small shrine to her lost son. As Pearl later told me, "Mother kept Grady's things in a cedar chest. She placed the chest in the foyer close to her bedroom. She had a scarf over it and put Bibles on top. She would get on her knees and go through his things silently. Reading the letters and looking at the pictures. I must have seen her kneeling there a hundred times or more."

And Laura Woellhof kept Dick's memory alive. "Till her dying day, she had his navy picture displayed," Ruah Sterrett told me. "It was on a table in the living room, a big picture of Dick in his navy uniform."

Warren Earl's mother, Evi, struggled for the rest of her life. In a letter to one of Warren Earl's Flyboy buddies, she wrote, "I will never get over losing my son." She tried to console herself with religious thoughts: "I will live a clean Christian life, and when my work in this wicked world is finished, I know I will meet my darling son, for I have the assurance that he was a Christian. He has gone to his permanent home, and I must try to think, it will just be a short separation, and then I will see him again."

But, as her nephew Ralph Sides told me, "After Warren Earl was killed, Evi wasn't right anymore." Ethelyn Goodner said, "Her personality changed. She was very sad and had nothing to say. She took shock treatments for a while." Billye Winder remembered, "Through the years Evi attempted suicide. Her second husband divorced her." Ralph Sides said, "She had a few nervous breakdowns. She married her third husband on a whim. She didn't even know the fellow. It only lasted a month."

Evi spent most of her life in nursing homes, dying in one at the age of eighty-seven in 1991. Columbus Lewellen was one of her pallbearers. He often visited her in her last years. "She never gave me any details about her son being killed," Columbus told me. "But she said she didn't care if she lived or died after he didn't come back. Evi had a fine mind the day she died. But she was a brokenhearted woman."

There were broken Japanese hearts also. Haro Iketani's young daughter was strafed and killed by an American Flyboy as she ran across a field. "My daughter died after living only sixteen years," Iketani said.

"A miserable ending. I loathe and hate that enemy from the bottom of my heart. I want to trace the single shot back to the pilot who shot my daughter and I want to shoot the person who killed my daughter."

Kazuyo Funato was a little girl when her family ran from the napalm flames in Tokyo on March 10. In the melee, she and her father were separated from her mother, who was carrying her baby boy on her back. In the morning, Kazuyo and her father returned to the family home, now reduced to a pile of ash. They waited for her mother to return. After a while, they realized she was already there; they just hadn't recognized her. The mother was sitting on the ground covered by an army blanket. Her clothes were charcoal, her hair burned.

Kazuyo asked about her baby brother. "What's happened to Teruko-chan?"

Kazuyo's mother was silent. Kazuyo looked closely at her mother when she didn't answer. "I could see she had been holding Teruko-chan on her back," Kazuyo said. "Where Teruko-chan's legs had touched her body there were horrible burns. Her elbows, where she was probably holding him to keep him from falling off, were burned so that you could see the raw flesh. She could barely walk."

Kazuyo's mother lost two of her children — Teruko-chan and Hiroko-chan — in the Tokyo fire raid. Flames burned Teruko-chan off her back.

"I used to take her to pray at their graves," Kazuyo said. "She'd pour water on them and say, 'Hiroko-chan, you must have been hot. Teruko-chan, you must have been hot.'"

Nations tend to see the other side's war atrocities as systemic and indicative of their culture and their own atrocities as justified or the acts of stressed combatants. In my travels, I sense a smoldering resentment toward WWII Japanese behavior among some Americans. Ironically, these feelings are strongest among the younger American generation that did not fight in WWII. In my experience, the Pacific vets on both sides have made their peace. And in terms of judgments, I will leave it to those who were there. As Ray Gallagher, who flew on both atomic missions against Hiroshima and Nagasaki, argues, "When you're not at war you're a good second guesser. You had to live those years and walk that mile."

If anyone has a right to hate, it is Glen Berry. Berry was on the

Bataan Death March ("heads chopped off, bodies all over the road"), endured two Hell Ships ("one hundred thirty degrees down in the hold, guys went crazy"), and had medical experiments performed on him at Fukuoka prison camp ("I don't remember anything for a three-month period"). He told me, "It's a matter of indoctrination. Their soldiers were taught that their emperor was a descendent of the sun goddess. They were taught not to have regard for human life, not even their own lives.

"I have forgiven the Japanese. I have Japanese friends. I make it clear that I have respect for the Japanese now because they have changed their attitude. I believe any culture can be indoctrinated into any attitude that the leaders want to teach them."

Masayo Enomoto, who as a young soldier helped bring terror to China, agrees. Now the Chinese welcome him to their country because he tells the truth about Japan's past. As I sat in his suburban living room sipping tea, Enomoto-san told me:

> It was the emperor system that allowed such atrocities to take place. People thought that they could do anything for the sake of the emperor. The soldiers were prepared to die for the emperor. And they thought they could do anything in China. The militarism and imperialism was because of the emperor system. Others helped, but in the end it's the emperor who is responsible. I do have grudges against the emperor.
>
> I want to make known what we did in China. We have to eradicate militaristic thinking from this earth.

Flyboy Oscar Long almost died in Ofuna prison camp. When he returned and his sister saw his emaciated body, she cried and had a deep contempt for all Japanese. But Oscar explained to her: "The Japanese were doing what they were commanded to do. It was no different from me doing what I was commanded to do. I killed people with the bombs I dropped. It was my job to do it, and it was their job to do what they did."

Singaporean Elizabeth Choy was a victim of brutal Japanese torture. After the war, she argued that her torturers should not be executed: "It's the war that is so wicked. If it hadn't been war, if they were in their own homes, they would be just like you and me. They have got their families, they have got their father, they have got their mother and they have got their wives and they've got their children, and they've got their jobs, so they are ordinary people. Because of the war they are forced to be so cruel and brutal. So I say I forgive them."

Researching this book was often a disorienting experience. Early on, I thought I knew where justice lay. But as I listened to stories in Japan and America, I wasn't so sure.

I know former Flyboys who napalmed a horrible war to an end. And in Tokyo I spent a day with eighty-one-year-old Yoshiko Hashimoto, who jumped into the icy river to save her baby. Throughout the interview we passed a box of Kleenex back and forth. When she finished her story, I asked her how she felt about Americans.

Hashimoto-san said, "A chaplain told me that if you kill one person it's murder, but if you kill many you're a hero. Those people who killed many in Tokyo are heroes in the U.S., I guess. But our Japanese soldiers were killing in China. At that time Japan praised that killing as a great achievement. We all do the same bad things. War is like that."

On a trip to Japan in the summer of 2001, I spent a day in Yokohama with seventy-six-year-old Fumio Tamamura, the San Francisco nisei who as Petty Officer Tamamura had walked Jimmy Dye to his death. A Rotary International pin sparkled from his suit lapel. "Japan is the number two Rotarian country, you know," Tamamura-san proudly noted.

We spoke all morning and into the afternoon. Only at three P.M. did we part. I was jet-lagged and tired. At four P.M. I drew my hotel room drapes to block the sunshine. I lay down for a nap.

A ringing awakened me. The clock said I had slept just forty minutes. It was Tamamura on the phone. He asked if I would like to speak with a former Japanese Imperial Navy lieutenant. Minoru Hayashi had spent seven years in Sugamo prison for following Captain Yoshii's orders to kill Jimmy Dye.

"I phoned Hayashi just now, after I got home," Tamamura-san said. "I told him to speak with you. He was hesitant. Hayashi said, 'No, I don't speak to anyone about that time. Not even my children know.'"

Tamamura continued, "But I told him to speak with you anyway."

From my darkened hotel room, I asked Tamamura-san, "Hayashi must be near eighty, so his kids are in their forties or fifties right? Why do you think he will speak to me when he hasn't even told them?"

Tamamura-san responded, "I told him your father had served on Iwo Jima and that you are fair. I told him just now, 'Bradley will write the story with or without you. Hayashi, this is the time for you to talk.'"

So the next morning I boarded a train. As I gazed at the countryside speeding by, I wondered what it would be like to meet the man who fifty-six years earlier had sliced Jimmy Dye's neck.

Hayashi-san was mild-mannered and conservatively dressed in a blue suit, white shirt, and red tie. He reminded me of my father, in the sense that there is something torn in those who have killed unwillingly. I asked him repeatedly, "You had to obey Yoshii's order . . . don't you think seven years in prison was too much?" No, he answered. He thought his sentence was fair. Japan lost the war. He had expected to die. "America treated me well," he assured me.

At the end of our time together I said, "Hayashi-san, of course you realize I am going to write facts about you that your children still don't know."

"My plan is to tell them before I die," Hayashi-san said, his eyes moist. "Or maybe they will find out from you. Please write a good book."

When I returned home from Japan, I phoned Jimmy's Flyboy buddies to tell them more of his fate. One day I was speaking with Joe Bonn, who saw Jimmy parachute off Chichi Jima. Bonn is a straight-ahead, no-nonsense sort of guy. He had told me of the mutual hate in the Pacific and how he had strafed helpless Japanese soldiers and civilians. "That's the way it was," he had explained. I wondered how he would react to the news that I had met with a Japanese who had swung a sword at his friend.

I explained how Hayashi-san had unwillingly followed an order under the duress of strict command. Lieutenant Hayashi, the meek radar technician, had had no animosity in his heart when a drunken Spirit Warrior forced him to wield his untested sword. Hayashi had been just one of Japan's many good children scarred by the Spirit Warriors' non-Bushido mania. Drunken cannibal officers abusing their troops are not part of the samurai tradition.

After I told Bonn about Jimmy's last moments, there was a silence on the telephone line.

"That's a hell of a thing," he finally said.

After a few seconds I asked, "What's a hell of thing?"

"Well, I don't think it was right to cut Jimmy's head off," he answered.

Now it was my turn to be still. I could agree with Bonn, but just days before I had had tears in my eyes as I listened to Hayashi-san. I took a chance and said, "Yes, but maybe the civilians you strafed thought *that* was a hell of a thing."

Now there was an even longer silence.

I wasn't sure if I had gone too far.

Finally the former Flyboy sighed. "Yeah, I guess it just matters what side you're on."

George Bush made his peace with his former enemy. He had many friendly dealings with Japanese in his long career as a businessman, U.N. ambassador, and America's envoy to China. In 1989, President Bush endured political heat for attending the funeral of Emperor Hirohito. And at a Pearl Harbor remembrance ceremony in Hawaii on December 7, 1991, he stood before American and Japanese veterans and declared, "I hold no rancor in my heart for my former enemy."

By 2002, the former Flyboy was seventy-eight years old. He had been mostly silent about the flames, the explosion, the blood, the ghosts. But in his dreams, did he see a small island where, young and hopeless, he feared he would die? And what about his two lost Flyboy buddies? I had heard him say, "I think about those guys all the time." And I learned just how much when he phoned me one day and asked me to take him back — back in time to when he was just George, a twenty-year-old Flyboy in big trouble.

So on Tuesday, June 17, 2002, I stood on Iwo Jima's tarmac watching President Bush's jet arrive. I greeted him, "Welcome to Iwo Jima, Mr. President."

We walked the black sands and then ascended Mount Suribachi. "Here's where the boys raised that flag," I said. Dwight Eisenhower is the only other American president to have walked that sacred ground.

On June 18, 2002, we awakened to an Iwo Jima sunrise. It is at Iwo Jima that the goddess Amaterasu's rays first shine upon Japan. Her sunlight initially warms Iwo, then travels up the No Mans Land archipelago to mainland Japan. Only then does the Land of the Rising Sun pass light on to the rest of the world.

Later that morning, Japanese Flyboys whisked us by helicopter to Chichi Jima. When we touched down, my eyes searched the happy crowd for a friend from my previous visits. When I noticed him — handsome, suntanned, and fit — I motioned him forward to the edge of the landing pad.

He was Abel Savory. Nathaniel Savory, a founder of Chichi Jima, had greeted Commodore Perry in 1853. Now, 149 years later, Nathaniel's great-great-great-grandson would do the honors. Abel Savory beamed, "Welcome to Chichi Jima, Mr. President."

The whole island — all two thousand people — turned out to welcome President Bush. Four-foot-tall Japanese women squealed and hugged his legs as smiling men shook his hands.

Two veterans with their own Chichi Jima wartime memories accompanied us. They were former United States Navy lieutenant Bill Connell and former Imperial Japanese Army private Nobuaki Iwatake.

Bill Connell, the "last American off Chichi Jima alive," vanquished old ghosts at the tree to which he had been tied for seven days. Warren Earl Vaughn's old buddy Iwatake-san and I took President Bush to the cliff from where, on September 2, 1944, Private Iwatake had seen Flyboy Bush crash into the Pacific. As former Japanese devil Iwatake and former American devil Bush squinted out to sea, Iwatake-san told the president, "Do you know what the Japanese soldier next to me said when we saw the submarine that rescued you? He said, 'Americans sure take good care of their pilots!' Sending a sub for one pilot was something Japan would never have done."

Out in the Pacific, off the coasts of Chichi Jima and Ani Jima, I snapped a photograph of George Bush placing two wreaths on the water in memory of Gunner Ted White and radioman John Delaney. The whirr of my camera was the loudest noise.

Atop the two peaks Commodore Perry had written of, the president discovered that Flyboys had caused little actual damage to the Japanese radio stations. Their three-foot-thick concrete-and-steel-reinforced walls still stand. The ceilings are damaged only because Colonel Rixey's Marines dynamited them after the war.

Iwatake-san led President Bush to the outside wall of the Mount

Yoake radio station, where he had bid farewell to Warren Earl Vaughn. As Iwatake told the story, tears ran down our cheeks. Then it was on to the sunlit shore where the handsome twenty-four-year-old Texan had rolled down his collar. The two former foes, Bush and Iwatake, placed one flower each to mark Warren Earl's death spot. They lingered to speak privately. I knew President Bush held Iwatake-san in special esteem.

Earlier I had told the president how Iwatake-san's life story seemed to sum up all the twists, turns, and contradictions of Japanese-American relations in the twentieth century. He was born Nobuaki Iwatake, the American son of Japanese immigrants. He recited the Pledge of Allegiance in Hawaiian grade school. Later, the Japanese army drafted him from a Tokyo college and slapped *Yamato damashii* into him. Then American submarines torpedoed him and Flyboys flung bombs at his head. Awaiting slaughter by the expected soon-to-invade American devils, he assisted Japanese intelligence while seated at a radio console trading jokes with a Cherokee Marine. Having formed a close bond with this *kichiku,* he came to loathe Captain Yoshii for ordering Warren Earl's death. Months later, on August 6, 1945, Iwatake-san was still atop Mount Yoake with his headsets. He was startled to hear about an explosive device called the atomic bomb. His extended family lived in Hiroshima. He later learned that his younger brother had been vaporized near the detonation point. Bearing no grudges, he promoted friendship between America and Japan as a longtime employee in the press section of the United States embassy in Japan. Iwatake-san is retired now and lives in a comfortable section of Tokyo. He holds Japanese and American citizenship.

Standing where Warren Earl had died, I was moved by the sight of the old Flyboy and the old *issen gorin* together — once boys whose divine mission had been to kill each other, now wiser men lost in the quiet murmurs of mutual understanding.

The Flyboy who got away became president of the United States. What might have been for Warren Earl, Dick, Marve, Glenn, Floyd, Jimmy, the unidentified airman, and all the Others who had lost their lives? A Nobel prize, a wife's love, a daughter's soft memory? And what might have been for those millions of doomed Japanese boys, abused and abandoned by their leaders? War is the tragedy of what might have been.

On Chichi Jima in March of 1945, twenty-two-year-old Private

Iwatake had promised himself he would honor the memory of his friend Warren Earl Vaughn. After he returned to Japan, he followed through, taking a name that reminds him daily of what might have been.

In 2001, Iwatake-san was the first person I phoned in my search for the Chichi Jima Flyboys. Fifty-six years had passed since that final handshake, and I was curious about Iwatake's dreams. I touched his Tokyo number on my telephone keypad.

From across the Pacific — as if borne by god winds — I heard his aged voice.

"Hello," he said, "this is Warren."

Acknowledgments

War has always interested me; not war in the sense of maneuvers devised by great generals . . . but the reality of war, the actual killing. I was more interested to know in what way and under the influence of what feelings one soldier kills another than to know how the armies were arranged at Austerlitz and Borodino.

— *Leo Tolstoy, quoted in* On Killing: The Psychological Cost of Learning to Kill in War and Society

IRIS Chang and Bill Doran inspired me to search for the memories of the Chichi Jima Flyboys. I thank them and all those interviewed for the book. I also appreciate the kind help offered by Mark Bradley, Chris Cannon, Isabel DeSouza, Hill Goodspeed, Mako Hanyu, John McGuire, Liz Nagle, Mickey Russel, Barbara Russo, Abel Savory, Rocky Savory, Yoshikuni Taki, Betsy Uhrig, Richard Wheeler, and Yuko Yoshioka.

I owe special thanks to Audrey Manring, who single-handedly organized thousands of pages of trial documents from the National Archives.

I am fortunate to be represented by the world's finest literary agent, Owen Laster. And I sleep well knowing I have professionals like Max Eisikovic and Robert Rapoport advising me.

Great editors don't get enough credit. Geoff Shandler acquired this book in the idea stage and never flagged in his enthusiasm. Geoff's emotional commitment to the Flyboys was evident from the beginning. His laserlike focus on excellence helped immeasurably in creating a worthy testament. The reader cannot identify Geoff's many important contributions, but I can and I will always remember.

I have lived and worked in Japan and have warm friendships with a number of Japanese. Nothing I have written detracts from the deep respect I have for Japan and its people.

My admiration for the Flyboys is boundless. As Rowdy Dow told me, "If we had given in to our fears, we wouldn't have won that war. There were no replacements out there. Our country was depending on us and we were all ready to die for our country. There was a job to do. We did it."

Philosopher Immanuel Kant wrote, "With men the normal state of nature is not peace but war." This state of nature can change. To that end, proceeds from this book will fund scholarships for American students to attend high school and university in Japan. If you are interested in contributing to this cause, or if you know a worthy student, please visit my Web site at: http://www.JamesBradley.com/scholarships.cfm.

James Bradley
June 24, 2003
Rye, New York

Notes

Chapter 2: Civilize-ation

p. 9 ". . . with plants and animals to which they were accustomed." Richard Drinnon, *Facing West: The Metaphysics of Indian-Hating and Empire Building* (Minneapolis: University of Minnesota Press, 1980), xiii.

p. 10 ". . . made them all in the same mould, has imposed on them the duty to help one another." Alexis de Tocqueville, *Democracy in America,* vol. 2, ed. J. P. Mayer and Max Lerner, trans. George Lawrence (London: Collins/Fontana Library, 1968), 971.

p. 10 ". . . where the barbarian peoples of the world hold sway." Drinnon, *Facing West,* 232.

p. 11 ". . . as righteous and beneficial a deed as ever took place on the frontier." Thomas G. Dyer, *Theodore Roosevelt and the Idea of Race* (Baton Rouge, LA: Louisiana State University Press, 1980), 79.

p. 11 ". . . I shouldn't like to inquire too closely into the case of the tenth." Ibid., 86.

p. 11 "half-savage, half-civilized race." Sam W. Haynes, *James K. Polk and the Expansionist Impulse* (New York: Longman, 1997), 169.

p. 11 "they want nothing but tails to be more brutes than the Apes." Ibid., 101.

p. 11 "melt away as the Indians before the white man." Ibid., 169.

p. 11 "we were sent to provoke a fight." Ulysses S. Grant, *Personal Memoirs of U. S. Grant* (New York: Dover Publications, 1995), 16.

p. 11 ". . . a stronger nation against a weaker nation." Ibid., 21.

p. 12 ". . . most cordially and intensely ashamed of it." Center for Research on North America (CISAN), National Autonomous University of Mexico, *Voices of Mexico,* #41.

339

p. 12 "... a vast field of warm-blooded oil deposits known as sperm whales." Nathaniel Philbrick, *In the Heart of the Sea: The Tragedy of the Whaleship Essex* (New York: Viking, 2000), xi.

p. 12 Herman Melville estimated the American whaling industry employed 18,000 men aboard 700 ships, reaping a harvest of $7 million annually. Peter Booth Wiley, *Yankees in the Land of the Gods: Commodore Perry and the Opening of Japan* (New York: Viking, 1990), 30.

p. 12 ... scarcely charted wilderness larger than all the earth's landmasses combined. Philbrick, *In the Heart of the Sea*, xi.

p. 13 Chichi Jima: The island had many names over the years given to it by English, American, and Portuguese explorers. I use its eventual Japanese name, which translates as "Father Island."

p. 14 "... by establishing the quickest lines ... turn [these channels] through the U.S." Wiley, *Yankees in the Land of the Gods*, 92.

p. 14 It was clear to the congressmen that Maury was suggesting no less a prize than commercial domination of the Pacific. Ibid., 92.

p. 16 "One and all rushed out to see him, crowding all the roads." George Elison, *Deus Destroyed: The Image of Christianity in Early Modern Japan* (Cambridge, MA: Council of East Asian Studies, Harvard University, 1988), 321.

p. 16 "... They are truly the delight of my heart." Matthew C. Perry, comp. Francis L. Hawks, *Narrative of the Expedition of an American Squadron to the China Seas and Japan Performed in the Years 1852, 1853, and 1854, Under the Command of Commodore M. C. Perry, United States Navy, by Order of the Government of the United States* (New York: D. Appleton and Company, 1857), 30.

p. 16 "Once the people's allegiance has been shifted, they can be manipulated and nothing can be done to stop it." Wiley, *Yankees in the Land of the Gods*, 266.

p. 17 "... 'Common people who behave unbecomingly to members of the military class ... may be cut down on the spot.'" Ibid., 252.

p. 18 "... laws imposed from on high governed the tiniest details of life in Japan." Ibid.

p. 18 Japan was the most urbanized country in the world, with almost 7 percent of the population living in cities, compared with 2 percent in Europe. James L. McClain, *Japan: A Modern History* (New York: W. W. Norton and Company, 2002), 54.

p. 18 "majestic citadels ... loomed over the countryside as awesome symbols of their prodigious strength." Ibid., 5.

p. 19 "the facts of that case are of a character to excite the indignation of the people of the United States." Wiley, *Yankees in the Land of the Gods*, 40.

p. 19 "The nation stands upon strong vantage ground. We want accommodations for fuel and a depot for our steamers and we have a good cause for a quarrel." Ibid.

p. 19 "trample on [a brass crucifix] by putting the left foot on the cross and then the right foot." U.S. Senate, *Official Documents Relative to the Empire of Japan,* 32nd Congress, 1st Session, Executive Document #59, Message from the President, April 12, 1852, 12.

p. 19 . . . the *kamikaze* "would blow them away by aid of their priests." Ibid., 21.

p. 20 . . . the "real object of the expedition should be concealed from public view." Wiley, *Yankees in the Land of the Gods,* 73.

p. 20 ". . . the United States' global rivalry with England and the need to secure ports on a Pacific steamship line were its real raisons d'être." Ibid., 124.

p. 20 The big event for the islanders was the arrival of whaling ships, which called for fresh water, supplies of fresh turtle and fish, vegetables, fruits, liquor, and occasional sexual services. Mary Shepardson, *The Bonin Islands: Pawns of Power* (C. Barbara Shepardson and Beret E. Strong, Unpublished, 1998), 35.

pp. 20–21 ". . . edged with coral reefs." Perry, *Narrative of the Expedition of an American Squadron to the China Seas and Japan,* 231.

p. 21 ". . . They are clearly seen on entering the harbor." Ibid., 246.

p. 21 . . . for a price of fifty dollars, four cattle, five Shanghai sheep, and six goats. Samuel Eliot Morison, *Old Bruin: Commodore Matthew C. Perry, 1794–1858, the American Naval Officer Who Helped Found Liberia* (Boston: Little, Brown and Company, 1967), 312.

p. 21 "first piece of land bought by Americans in the Pacific." Shepardson, *The Bonin Islands,* 61.

p. 23 Thousands of armor-encased soldier-archers with eight-foot longbows and pikes stood by. Rhoda Blumberg, *Commodore Perry in the Land of the Shogun* (New York: Lothrop, Lee and Shepard Books, 1985), 30–31. (Much of the colorful information on Perry's landing in this chapter is from *Commodore Perry in the Land of the Shogun.*)

p. 23 "Your letter being received, you will now leave." Wiley, *Yankees in the Land of the Gods,* 322.

p. 24 "would produce a decided influence upon [the] government and cause a more favorable consideration of the President's letter." Ibid.

p. 24 The original is from Morison, who reported, "Buchanan replied that the United States Navy operated under American law wherever it went," which I have rendered as, "The United States Navy operates under American law wherever we go." Morison, *Old Bruin,* 326.

p. 26 *Shinmin* meant "people who obediently comply with their orders." Herbert P. Bix, *Hirohito and the Making of Modern Japan* (New York: HarperCollins, 2000), 30.

p. 26 ". . . but should treat them in the same way as do the Western nations." McClain, *Japan: A Modern History,* 293.

p. 26 ". . . The Strong Eat up the Weak." John Toland, *The Rising Sun: The Decline and Fall of the Japanese Empire, 1936–1945* (New York: Random House, 1970), 21.

p. 27 "... trying to develop civilization and a country that inhibits the progress of civilization." McClain, *Japan: A Modern History,* 300.

p. 27 "a character suitable for great achievements in the world." Ibid.

Chapter 3: Spirit War

p. 29 "I was thoroughly well pleased with the Japanese victory," Raymond A. Esthus, *Theodore Roosevelt and Japan* (Seattle: University of Washington Press, 1966), 24.

p. 31 "Neither Trafalgar nor the defeat of the Spanish Armada was as complete and overwhelming." Ibid., 71.

p. 31 "the great civilizing force of the entire East." Ibid., 41.

p. 31 "but ... I am far stronger pro-Japanese than ever." Ibid., 96.

p. 31 "... just as the United States has a paramount interest in what surrounds the Caribbean." Ibid., 41.

p. 31 "just like we have with Cuba." Ibid., 101.

p. 31 "Korea should be entirely within Japan's sphere of interest." Ibid.

p. 31 "It is like the stampede of rats from a sinking ship." Ibid., 110.

p. 34 "map exercises, military history; the principles of military leadership, tactics ... strategy and chess." Bix, *Hirohito and the Making of Modern Japan,* 44.

p. 34 "training in horsemanship and military drills by junior army officers." Ibid.

p. 34 "had a trench dug inside the crown prince's compound so that Hirohito could practice firing machine guns." Ibid., 48

p. 34 "played war-strategy games with him." Ibid.

p. 34 "... the small group of talented officials who had assisted him." Ibid., 27.

p. 34 "hand-to-hand combat rather than firepower determined victory or defeat in battle." Ibid., 47.

pp. 34–35 "... 'military spirit education' in general should be encouraged." Robert J. Butow, *Tojo and the Coming of the War* (Princeton, NJ: Princeton University Press, 1961), 23.

p. 35 "Every facet of the curriculum was permeated with emperor worship and militarism." Sabura Ienaga, *Japan's Last War: World War II and the Japanese, 1931–1945* (New York: Pantheon Books, 1978), 327.

p. 35 "... three toy soldiers with the caption 'Advance! Advance! Soldiers move forward!'" Ibid., 106.

p. 35 "... Music classes were to reverberate with war songs." Ibid., 24.

p. 35 "... I was prepared to serve the emperor in any way possible." I became aware of Masayo Enomoto's experiences in the Imperial Japanese Army through the kindness of someone at the BBC who sent me an interview with him. I later journeyed to Enomoto-san's living room, confirmed segments of his previous interviews (the BBC interview and the documentary *Japanese Devils* are just two examples of Enomoto-san's telling his tale publicly), and learned new facts from this fascinating man. At first it seems strange that Enomoto, a man who admits he ate a Chinese woman, is welcomed to and respected in China. Why? Because he is Japanese and tells the truth.

p. 36 ". . . you'll have to kill a hundred, two hundred Chinks." Ibid., 107.

p. 36 ". . . we had to stand at attention and salute." Haruko Taya Cook and Theodore F. Cook, *Japan at War: An Oral History* (New York: The New Press, 1992), 235.

p. 36 ". . . You simply bore up under it, your teeth clenched." Ibid., 235.

p. 36 ". . . and is advancing with the times to lead the entire world." Bix, *Hirohito and the Making of Modern Japan,* 200.

p. 36 ". . . she would shrivel up and die." Butow, *Tojo and the Coming of the War,* 25.

p. 37 ". . . They were non-persons." Ienaga, *Japan's Last War,* 51.

p. 37 ". . . The result was an officer corps of rigid mentality and limited experience." Ibid., 48.

p. 38 ". . . 'absolute obedience to superiors.' " Ibid.

p. 38 ". . . who concedes a strategic area to the enemy shall be punishable by death." Ibid., 49.

p. 38 "This act typifies the glorious spirit of the Imperial Army." Ibid.

p. 39 ". . . It was the last primitive infantry army of modern times." Frank Gibney, trans. Beth Cary, *Senso: The Japanese Remember the Pacific War* (Armonk, NY: M. E. Sharp, 1995), 23.

p. 39 ". . . My uniform froze." Ibid., 28.

p. 39 ". . . They thought that beatings were a form of education." Ibid., 27.

p. 39 ". . . I nearly fainted in agony." Ibid., 54.

p 39 ". . . I wonder what my parents would have felt had they seen me in this state." Ibid., 28.

p. 40 ". . . obedience to them had to be absolute and unconditional." Bix, *Hirohito and the Making of Modern Japan,* 55.

p. 40 "We learned that the senior soldiers were gods," Gibney, *Senso,* 54.

p. 40 ". . . held the soap for the NCOs and washed their backs." Ienaga, *Japan's Last War,* 53.

p. 40 ". . . men who would carry out our superiors' orders as a reflex action." Gibney, *Senso,* 54.

Chapter 4: The Third Dimension

p. 41 "You just got in and flew." Craig Nelson, *The First Heroes: The Extraordinary Story of the Doolittle Raid — America's First World War II Victory* (New York: Viking, 2002), 39.

p. 43 "... so tomorrow we shall write of battles in the skies." Isaac Don Levine, *Mitchell: Pioneer of Air Power* (New York: Duell, Sloan and Pearce, 1958), 388.

pp. 43–44 "... or disaster in war." Ibid., 317.

p. 44 "... she would still be able to get home." Ibid., 240.

p. 44 "... and half a hundred newspapermen." Ibid., 241.

p. 44 "... flyers will never sink the *Ostfriesland.*" Ibid., 239.

p. 44 "... by officers of the navy department in high authority." Ibid., 311.

p. 45 "... while others hid their faces behind handkerchiefs." Ibid., 256.

p. 45 "... It is evident to everyone who attended the demonstration that history is being made." Ibid., 260.

p. 45 "'... with sufficient airplane and submarine protection this country was perfectly safe from attack.'" Ibid., 268.

p. 45 "... and Constellation be converted into aircraft carriers." Ibid.

p. 45 "the battleship is still the backbone of the fleet and the bulwark of the nation's sea defense." Ibid., 269.

p. 46 "... I have never seen anything like it." Ibid., 295.

p. 46 "... care must be taken that it is not underestimated." Ibid., 298.

p. 46 "... may end up by developing the greatest air power in the world." Ibid., 299.

p. 46 "... take us at least two years to get on a par with ... Japan." Ibid., 304.

p. 46 "... as things stand now, would probably be with the Japanese." Ibid., 337.

p. 46 "... You have got to look ahead." Ibid., 304.

p. 46 "... to humiliation, demotion and discipline." Ibid., 307.

p. 47 "knocking a butterfly out of the air with water from a garden hose." Gen. William Mitchell, "Building a Futile Navy," *Atlantic Monthly,* September 1928.

p. 47 "... bore the mark of a single bullet hole." Levine, *Mitchell: Pioneer of Air Power,* 316–17.

p. 47 "... proved the exact opposite." Ibid.

p. 47 "... anti-aircraft devices remain the 'backbone' of coast defense." Ibid.

p. 47 "jar the bureaucrats out of their swivel chairs." Ibid., 318.

p. 48 "... openly tell falsehoods about aviation to the people and to the Congress." Ibid., 327–28.

p. 48 "... I would certainly be tried for it." Ibid., 329.

p. 48 "... exceedingly dangerous undertaking and precedent." Ibid., 342.

pp. 48–49 "... which is being ignored in the administration of national defense." Ibid., 343.

p. 49 ". . . The last war taught us that man cannot make a machine stronger than the spirit of man." Ibid., 363–64.

p. 49 ". . . with forfeiture of all pay and allowances for five years." Ibid., 368.

p. 49 "to seize Alaska, Hawaii and the Philippines." Ibid., 375.

p. 49 ". . . a surprise move while negotiations would be going on behind diplomats' doors." Ibid.

p. 49 "Japan never declares war before attacking." Ibid., 389.

p. 50 ". . . had not entirely dissuaded the Japanese from making the attempt." "United States Strategic Bombing Survey Summary Report (Pacific War)" (Washington, DC, July 1, 1946), 28.

p. 50 ". . . apparently was regarded by both as a minor auxiliary." Nelson, *The First Heroes*, 102.

p. 50 ". . . our planes should be designed to attack Japan." Levine, *Mitchell: Pioneer of Air Power*, 395.

p. 50 ". . . a little while we will be as easy to attack as a large jellyfish." Ibid., 397.

p. 51 "The American people will regret the day I was crucified by politics and bureaucracy." Ibid., 399.

Chapter 5: The Rape of China

p. 52 ". . . we will make the whole world look up to our national virtues." Butow, *Tojo and the Coming of the War*, 46.

p. 53 "Japan's holy mission beckoned: defend the imperial way and build a paradise in Asia!" Ibid.

p. 53 ". . . Where should we find an outlet for these millions?" Ienaga, *Japan's Last War*, 11.

p. 53 ". . . save its 600,000,000 from 'imperialistic oppression.'" Butow, *Tojo and the Coming of the War*, 32.

p. 53 ". . . Three or four divisions and a few river gunboats will be quite enough to handle the Chinese bandits." Ienaga, *Japan's Last War*, 85.

p. 54 ". . . Spies! This was war." All quotes from Shozo Tominaga are from Haruko Taya Cook and Theodore F. Cook, *Japan at War* (this quote from page 44).

p. 54 . . . Chinese troops were not "soldiers," but "bandits." Russell, Lord of Liverpool, *The Knights of Bushido: A Short History of Japanese War Crimes* (New York: Berkley Publishing, 1958), 34.

p. 54 "if you kill them there will be no repercussions." Katsuichi Honda, *The Nanjing Massacre: A Japanese Journalist Confronts Japan's National Shame* (Armonk, NY: M. E. Sharp, 1998), 171.

pp. 54–55 ". . . nor act in accordance with, all the concrete articles of the Treaty Concerning the Laws and Customs of Land Warfare and Other Treaties Concerning the

Laws and Regulations of Belligerency." Bix, *Hirohito and the Making of Modern Japan,* 359.

p. 55 The same directive ordered "staff officers in China to stop using the term 'prisoner of war.' " Ibid.

p. 55 ". . . decision to remove the constraints of international law on the treatment of Chinese prisoners of war." Ibid.

p. 55 ". . . massacred, tortured, or drafted into Japanese labor camps." Russell, *The Knights of Bushido,* 34.

p. 57 ". . . It was to make the prisoners last as long as possible." Gibney, *Senso,* 65.

p. 58 ". . . and here would come thousands of Japanese to take away what the natives had." Ibid., 206.

p. 58 ". . . to ensure no one could report where the invaders slept." Jonathan Lewis and Ben Steele, *Hell in the Pacific: From Pearl Harbor to Hiroshima* (London: Channel 4 Books, an imprint of Macmillan Publishers, 2001), 42.

p. 59 ". . . the soldiers had sliced off his flesh to feed to the dogs." Honda, *The Nanjing Massacre,* 98.

p. 59 ". . . only his torso remained on the ground." Gibney, *Senso,* 30.

p. 60 ". . . I'd order the one I planned to kill to dig a hole, then cut him down and cover him over." Cook and Cook, *Japan at War,* 151–57.

p. 60 Newspaper contest quotes from Honda, *The Nanjing Massacre,* 125–27.

p. 60 "'. . . It's a valuable weapon.' " Gibney, *Senso,* 96.

p. 61 ". . . spread of such a disease would weaken the strength of the Army considerably." Yuki Tanaka, *Hidden Horrors: Japanese War Crimes in World War II* (Boulder, CO: Westview Press, 1998), 96.

p. 61 ". . . 20,000 comfort women were required for every 700,000 Japanese soldiers, or 1 woman for every 35 soldiers." Ibid., 99.

p. 61 "32.1 million condoms were sent to units stationed outside Japan." Ibid., 96.

p. 62 "The caption below read simply *Totsugeki* — 'Charge!' " Honda, *The Nanjing Massacre,* xx.

Chapter 6: The ABCD Encirclement

p. 63 ". . . ATTACKS TERMED ILLEGAL." *New York Times,* September 23, 1937.

p. 63 ". . . CIVILIANS VICTIMS." *New York Times,* September 23, 1937.

p. 63 ". . . ENVOY CITES SLAUGHTER OF NONCOMBATANTS." *New York Times,* September 24, 1937.

p. 63 "campaign of death and terror." *New York Times,* September 24, 1937.

p. 64 ". . . make war indiscriminately upon noncombatants and combatants alike." *New York Times,* September 22, 1937.

p. 64 "... contrary to principles of law and of humanity." *New York Times,* September 28, 1937.

p. 64 "... developed as an essential part of modern civilization. John Dower, *War Without Mercy* (New York: Pantheon Books, 1996), 38.

p. 64 "... profoundly shocked the conscience of humanity." Robert Dallek, *Franklin D. Roosevelt and American Foreign Policy, 1932–1945* (New York: Oxford University Press, 1979), 39.

p. 64 "... inhuman bombing of civilian populations." Dower, *War Without Mercy,* 39.

p. 64 "... have aroused horror and indignation throughout the world, and solemnly condemns them." *New York Times,* September 28, 1937.

p. 65 "What the United States would do if the protest should go unheeded was not revealed." *New York Times,* September 23, 1937.

p. 65 "... neither her people nor her government wishes to become embroiled in the Far East." *New York Times,* September 25, 1937.

p. 65 "... a program to keep the United States out of war and safeguard the democracy they fought to save twenty years ago." *New York Times,* September 22, 1937.

p. 65 ... the Oxford antiwar oath: "I refuse to support the Government of the United States in any war it may conduct." *New York Times,* April 23, 1937.

p. 65 "... Ask the American Indian or the Mexican how excruciatingly trying the young United States used to be once upon a time." Butow, *Tojo and the Coming of the War,* 107.

p. 66 "... now cry, 'Thief!' if Japan even so much as looked at a neighboring territory?" Ibid., 25.

p. 66 "... the white miners who have been strongly attracted there by reports of rich deposits of the precious metal." Dee Brown, *Bury My Heart at Wounded Knee: An Indian History of the American West* (New York: Henry Holt and Company, 1970), 284.

p. 67 "... do a great many evil things. .... This war has come from robbery — from the stealing of our land." Ibid., 299.

p. 67 "... to the greatness of the race and to the well-being of civilized mankind." Dyer, *Theodore Roosevelt and the Idea of Race,* 78.

p. 67 "... wholly alien race which holds a coveted prize in its feeble grasp." Ibid.

p. 68 "would be like granting self-government to an Apache reservation under some local chief." Drinnon, *Facing West,* 298.

p. 68 ... found only three who recommended independence for the Philippines. Stuart Creighton Miller, *Benevolent Assimilation: The American Conquest of the Philippines, 1899–1903* (New Haven, CT: Yale University Press, 1982), 16.

p. 68 "Has it ever occurred to you that Jesus was the most imperial of the imperialists?" Ibid., 18.

p. 68 "... Filipinos were savages no better than our Indians." Drinnon, *Facing West,* 297.

p. 68 "no one even bothered to respond." Miller, *Benevolent Assimilation,* 250.

p. 69 . . . it was impossible to recognize "the actively bad from only the passively so." Ibid., 210.

p. 69 ". . . 'Buenos Dias, Senors' (means good morning)." Ibid., 182.

p. 69 ". . . killed every native we met, men, women and children." Ibid., 220.

p. 69 ". . . Everyone was crazy." Ibid.

p. 69 ". . . the more you kill and burn the better it will please me." Ibid.

p. 69 . . . kill all those above "ten years of age." Ibid.

p. 69 ". . . and then turned over to the men for their pleasure." Ibid., 241.

pp. 69–70 ". . . 'picking off niggers in the water' was 'more fun than a turkey shoot.'" Ibid., 67.

p. 70 ". . . I am doing everything I can for Old Glory and for America I love so well." Ibid., 88.

p. 70 "routinely firing on Filipinos carrying white flags." Ibid., 238.

p. 70 "ordered to take no prisoners and to kill the wounded." Ibid., 188.

p. 70 ". . . who had been taken before they learned how not to take them." Ibid., 188.

p. 70 "by lot select a POW — preferably one from the village in which the assassination took place — and execute him." Ibid., 209.

p. 70 ". . . he made forty-seven prisoners kneel and 'repent of their sins' before ordering them bayoneted and clubbed to death." Ibid., 238.

p. 71 ". . . His suffering must be that of a man who is drowning, but he cannot drown." Drinnon, *Facing West,* 319.

p. 71 ". . . for the triumph of civilization over the black chaos of savagery and barbarism." Miller, *Benevolent Assimilation,* 251.

p. 71 ". . . the most glorious war in the nation's history." Ibid., 250.

p. 71 "act of discrimination carrying with it a stigma and odium which it is impossible to overlook." Butow, *Tojo and the Coming of the War,* 11.

p. 71 . . . denying visas to Japanese and other Asians. Ibid., 21.

p. 72 "'. . . condemn the late-coming nations to remain forever subordinate to the advanced nations.'" McClain, *Japan: A Modern History,* 394.

p. 72 ". . . 'as much as possible to grant de jure equality' to foreign subjects living in their territory." Ibid.

p. 72 ". . . Japan had made Manchuria into an island of stability and prosperity." Ibid., 414.

p. 73 "According to an opinion poll, 75 per cent of the American public agreed." Dallek, *Franklin D. Roosevelt and American Foreign Policy,* 236.

p. 73 ". . . then the three countries will fight resolutely." *Asahi Shimbun,* October 5, 1940.

p. 74 "lecturing the Japanese about the 'principles of good behavior.'" Dallek, *Franklin D. Roosevelt and American Foreign Policy,* 76.

p. 74 ". . . no alteration to the status quo except through peaceful means." Ibid.

p. 74 ". . . staff conversations at Singapore with high-ranking British, Dutch, Australian, New Zealand, and Indian officers in April." Ibid., 272.

p. 74 . . . that threatened the Philippines, East Indies, Malaya, and Thailand, and peaceful relations with the United States. Ibid., 309.

p. 74 Roosevelt proposed that the Japanese "dispel the dark clouds." Ibid.

p. 74 ". . . the only way to break the stalemate in China was to risk a war with the whole world." Cook and Cook, *Japan at War,* 27.

p. 75 ". . . 'if the Japanese government were to fail to speak as civilized twentieth-century human beings.'" Dallek, *Franklin D. Roosevelt and American Foreign Policy,* 237.

p. 75 . . . chain them together and transported them by barges for days as they roasted under a tropical sun. Dower, *War Without Mercy,* 331.

p. 76 ". . . That had been four years ago and the fighting was still in progress." Butow, *Tojo and the Coming of the War,* 254.

p. 76 ". . . With what confidence do you say 'three months'?" Ibid.

p. 76 ". . . putting anyone on the spot was considered a rather drastic thing to do." Ibid.

p. 76 The U.S. annually produced twelve times the steel, five times the number of ships, one hundred and five times the number of automobiles, and five and a half times the amount of electricity that Japan did. Cook and Cook, *Japan at War,* 171.

p. 76 ". . . the Americans, being merchants, would not continue for long with an unprofitable war, whereas we . . . could carry on a protracted war." Lewis and Steele, *Hell in the Pacific,* 49.

p. 77 The Chichi Jima signals described a "two-prong" attack, one going east from Japan, the other south. Robert B. Stinnett, *George Bush: His World War II Years* (Washington, DC: Brassey's, 1991), 2.

p. 77 ". . . AN AGGRESSIVE MOVE BY JAPAN IS EXPECTED WITHIN THE NEXT FEW DAYS." Chief of Naval Operations message 272337, November 27, 1941, drafted by Rear Admiral R. K. Turner, Director of War Plans.

p. 77 . . . General Hirofumi Yamashita landed his 20,000 troops on the east coast of Malaya. Tanaka, *Hidden Horrors,* 81.

Chapter 7: Flyboys

p. 80 . . . "the typical American reaction that we had better do something about this." Joe Hyams, *Flight of the Avenger: George Bush at War* (New York: Berkley Publishing Group, 1992), 39.

p. 80 ". . . my thoughts immediately turned to naval aviation." George Bush with Victor Gold, *Looking Forward* (Garden City, NY: Doubleday, 1987), 30.

p. 81 ". . . Western economies were firmly in the era of the internal combustion machine." Eric M. Bergerud, *Fire in the Sky: The Air War in the South Pacific* (Boulder, CO: Westview Press, 2001), 317.

p. 81 ". . . moved over poor roads to the large naval air base at Kagamigahara prior to its initial flight." Ibid., 321.

p. 82 "future adventurous young men who sought glory in war would tend to seek it as pilots." Tom Wolfe, *The Right Stuff* (New York: Bantam Books, 1980), x.

p. 82 . . . "only in the moment in this strange, unmortal space, crowded with beauty, pierced with danger." A. Scott Berg, *Lindbergh* (New York: Berkley Publishing Group, 1999), 64.

p. 82 ". . . you didn't have to have a license to fly an airplane in 1923." Ibid., 70.

p. 82 ". . . so they felt they had received their money's worth." Ibid., 65.

p. 82 ". . . worthwhile trade for an ordinary lifetime." Ibid., 66.

p. 82 . . . "I won't need any more, and if I don't get to Paris, I won't need any more, either." Ibid., 115.

p. 82 ". . . either the happiest day in my whole life, or the saddest." Ibid., 117.

p. 83 " Not even Columbus sailed alone." Ibid., 120.

p. 86 . . . " 'I'm going in.' " Bush, *Looking Forward,* 31.

p. 86 . . . "It was the first time I had ever seen my dad cry." Hyams, *Flight of the Avenger,* 43.

p. 90 ". . . represented a step up the economic ladder." Bergerud, *Fire in the Sky,* 317.

Chapter 8: Doing the Impossible

p. 100 "won nearly every aviation trophy there was." Carroll V. Glines, *The Doolittle Raid: America's Daring First Strike Against Japan* (New York: Orion Books, 1988), 17.

p. 100 ". . . almost black out a number of times from the pain." Nelson, *The First Heroes,* 45.

p. 101 ". . . It could be done, as long as an engine didn't skip a beat." Edward Oxford, "Against All Odds" (privately published essay).

p. 101 "We're in for something really big." Duane P. Schultz, *The Doolittle Raid* (New York: St. Martin's Press, 1988), 58.

p. 101 ". . . This mission was very important if he was involved in it." Dr. James C. Hasdorff, "Interview of Brig. Gen. Richard A. Knobloch." United States Air Force Oral History Program, July 13–14, 1987 (Maxwell Air Force Base, AL: Air Force Historical Research Agency), interview with Col. James Macia.

p. 101 ". . . We were ready for anything." Nelson, *The First Heroes,* 32.

p. 102 ". . . No questions asked." Glines, *The Doolittle Raid,* 31.

p. 102 ". . . give the Japs a dose of their own medicine." Nelson, *The First Heroes,* 61.

p. 102 "The sailors I saw were jumping up and down like small children." James Merrill, *Target Tokyo: The Halsey-Doolittle Raid* (Chicago: Rand McNally and Company, 1964), 41.

p. 103 ". . . We're not supposed to do this to one another." Lewis and Steele, *Hell in the Pacific,* 106.

p. 103 "They know we're here." Gen. James H. "Jimmy" Doolittle with Carroll V. Glines, *I Could Never Be So Lucky Again: An Autobiography* (Atglen, PA: Schiffer Publishing, 1995), 4.

p. 103 ". . . who really believed he would complete the flight safely." Col. C. Ross Greening, *Not As Briefed* (St. Paul: Brown and Bigelow, 1945), 22.

p. 103 "And nobody batted an eye." Helena Pasquarella, "Moorpark Man Recalls a Fateful Flight over Japan During WWII," *Los Angeles Times,* July 22, 1993.

p. 104 ". . . thought the only thing short of being destroyed over the target area would be to end up as a prisoner of war." Hasdorff, "Interview of Brig. Gen. Richard A. Knobloch."

p. 104 ". . . a twenty-four-knot headwind all the way to Honshu." Nelson, *The First Heroes,* 123.

p. 104 "And they were tame compared to this thing." Cindy Hayostek, "Exploits of a Doolittle Raider," *Military History,* March 1996.

p. 105 ". . . I'm sure many thought they wouldn't be able to make it either." Doolittle, *I Could Never Be So Lucky Again,* 7.

p. 105 "I put down ten dollars at even money that less than half of them would get off." Alvin Kernan, *Crossing the Line: A Bluejacket's World War II Odyssey* (Annapolis, MD: Naval Institute Press, 1994), 31.

p. 105 "like circus elephants against their chains." Nelson, *The First Heroes,* 128.

p. 105 "'. . . He can't make it!'" Ibid.

p. 105 ". . . since we had the best pilot in the Air Force flying with us." Greg DeHart, *One Hour Over Tokyo.* History Channel, May 26, 2001.

p. 105 "We watched him like hawks." Ibid.

p. 105 ". . . could even hear it above the roar of their props." Nelson, *The First Heroes,* 126.

p. 105 ". . . I could not say good-bye to anyone — just a thumbs-up as each took off." *Keesler Field* (Mississippi) *News,* May 27, 1943.

p. 106 ". . . We knew when we started that it wasn't going to fit." Nelson, *The First Heroes,* 133.

pp. 106–107 ". . . each man to decide what he will do." Glines, *The Doolittle Raid,* 65.

p. 107 ". . . I guess the Imperial forces want to impress the people that they are fully prepared." Stan Cohen, *Destination: Tokyo* (Missoula, MT: Pictorial Histories Publishing Company, 1983), 48.

p. 107 "... that was no mile." Merrill, *Target Tokyo,* 79.

p. 107 "Our houses are only made of wood, while yours are of stone." Tom Bernard, "Japs Were Jumpy After Tokyo Raid," *Stars and Stripes,* April 27, 1943.

p. 108 "... move the patients out of harm's way, flabbergasted at the Americans' barbaric act." Nelson, *The First Heroes,* 148.

p. 108 "... I raked the length of the deck from stern to bow." Ibid., 152.

p. 108 "... But after they shot at us, I changed my mind." C. Hoyt Watson, *The Amazing Story of Sergeant Jacob DeShazer* (Winona Lake, IN: Life and Light Press, 1950. Reprinted as *DeShazer,* Croquitlam, British Columbia: Galaxy Communications, 1991), 21.

p. 108 "... ditching among them would be very appealing." Doolittle, *I Could Never Be So Lucky Again,* 9.

p. 109 "... a tailwind of about 25 miles per hour and eased our minds about ditching." Ibid.

p. 109 "This meant that the chance of any of us getting to the destination safely was just about nil." Ibid., 10.

p. 109 "... I bent my knees to take the shock." Ibid.

p. 110 "... six elementary or secondary schools, and innumerable nonmilitary residences." Merrill, *Target Tokyo,* 102.

p. 110 "... such a great difference between the battle front and the home front." Saburo Sakai, with Martin Caidin and Fred Saito, *Samurai* (New York: E. P. Dutton, 1958), 148–49.

p. 110 "... We then began to doubt that we were also invincible." Glines, *The Doolittle Raid,* 145.

p. 110 "... avenged the raid on Pearl Harbor." Ibid., 148.

p. 111 "'... 2,600 years of her glorious history' was going to be destroyed." Ibid., 149.

p. 111 "... the Commander-in-Chief of the China Expeditionary army will begin the operation as soon as possible." Shultz, *The Doolittle Raid,* 239, citing D. Bergamini, *Japan's Imperial Conspiracy* (New York: William Morrow, 1971).

p. 112 "... lead to the torture and death of their friends." Glines, *The Doolittle Raid,* 152.

pp. 111–112 "... and forced his wife to set her husband on fire." Nelson, *The First Heroes,* 227.

p. 112 "... you can't miss the savage nature of the Japanese army." Shultz, *The Doolittle Raid,* 239, citing Father George Yager and Bishop Charles Quinn in the *New York Times,* May 26, 1943.

p. 112 "... these Japanese troops slaughtered every man, woman and child in those areas." Glines, *The Doolittle Raid,* 151.

p. 112 "A quarter million Chinese soldiers and civilians were killed in the three-month campaign." Ibid.

p. 112 ". . . with bubonic plague, pneumonia, epidemic hemorrhagic fever, typhoid, and syphilis." Nelson, *The First Heroes,* 227.

pp. 112–113 ". . . This is what actually happened." Lewis and Steele, *Hell in the Pacific,* 213.

p. 113 ". . . death of seventeen hundred Japanese soldiers and the injury of ten thousand more." Nelson, *The First Heroes,* 228.

p. 113 ". . . I can kill you this afternoon and no one will ever know who did it." Lewis and Steele, *Hell in the Pacific,* 157.

p. 113 ". . . He and his family would be disgraced forever." Russell, *The Knights of Bushido,* 46.

p. 113 ". . . Inevitably this attitude was applied with equal vigor towards enemy POWs." Lewis and Steele, *Hell in the Pacific,* 157.

p. 114 ". . . After the war ended, all of the POWs were safely returned to Russia." Tanaka, *Hidden Horrors,* 72.

p. 114 ". . . to attain the national objectives within the bounds of international law." Ienaga, *Japan's Last War,* 136.

p. 114 ". . . so that nothing will miscarry in the attainment of our war aims." Ibid.

p. 114 ". . . Today such a need no longer applies." Lewis and Steele, *Hell in the Pacific,* 68.

p. 115 ". . . and all of the Japanese soldiers laughed merrily and walked away." Lester I. Tenney, *My Hitch in Hell: The Bataan Death March* (Washington, DC: Brassey's, 1995), 42.

p. 115 ". . . I guess I looked stunned, so he added that it was a sanitation measure." Cook and Cook, *Japan at War,* 378.

p. 116 ". . . forcing the pencils up and down causing the skin to break." Glines, *The Doolittle Raid,* 170.

p. 116 ". . . If you use this method, ninety percent of them talk." Cook and Cook, *Japan at War,* 154.

p. 116 ". . . after about five minutes of that my knees were so numb I couldn't feel anything else." Chase Nielson, Testimony Before U.S. Military Commission, Shanghai, China. February 27, 1946.

p. 116 ". . . I felt more or less like I was drowning, just gasping between life and death." Ibid.

p. 116 ". . . Rest assured, it's strictly a one-way ticket." "Threat to Fliers," *New York Times,* April 22, 1943.

Chapter 9: Airpower

p. 118 ". . . shipped six hundred thousand gas masks to the Western Defense Command." Nelson, *The First Heroes,* 218.

p. 120 "... the most impressive sight of the day." Lewis and Steele, *Hell in the Pacific*, 110.

p. 120 "... though it was still a long and harrowing distance in the future." David M. Kennedy, "Victory at Sea," *Atlantic Monthly,* March 1999.

p. 121 "... With that, they dismissed us." Hasdorff, "Interview of Brig. Gen. Richard A. Knobloch."

p. 121 "... even in the event of an exchange of war prisoners they may not be repatriated to the United States forces." Glines, *The Doolittle Raid,* 216.

p.122 "... I want you to know that I died fighting for my country like a soldier." Letters from 1946 Tokyo War Crimes Tribunal.

p. 122 "... That was all that was said." Glines, *The Doolittle Raid,* 181.

p. 122 ... "Face the target!" Ibid.

p. 122 "... were captured and court-martialed and severely punished according to military law." Nelson, *The First Heroes,* 301.

p. 124 ... "All of us who soloed thought we were ten feet tall." Hyams, *Flight of the Avenger,* 55.

p. 124 ... when he was a kid and war was something in the history books. Hyams, Ibid., 54.

p. 132 "... some of our most important victories would not have been possible." Capt. Robert Allen and Lieutenant Otis Carney, *The Story of SCAT 253* (SCAT publication, 1943), 14.

p. 132 "... SCAT moved 43,626,495 pounds of cargo plus 235,596 passengers carried in 34,834 trips." Col. W. K. Snyder, USMCR (Ret.), *The History of Marine Corps Transport Squadron VMJ 253* (SCAT publication, 1944), 13.

p. 132 "... Kimball loaded his casualties aboard and took off." Allen and Carney, *The Story of SCAT 253,* 16.

Chapter 10: Yellow Devils, White Devils

p. 133 "... who fell into Japanese hands as an incident of warfare." Glines, *The Doolittle Raid,* 208.

p. 134 "... TOKYO STANDS ALONE AS A CRUEL CAPTOR IN DEFIANCE OF GENEVA CONVENTION." *New York Times,* April 23, 1943.

p. 134 "... more determined than ever to blot out the shameless militarism of Japan." Glines, *The Doolittle Raid,* 208.

p. 134 ... they must be "utterly destroyed." Nelson, *The First Heroes,* 296.

p. 134 Chase Nielson's mother and Mrs. John Meder quotes. Ibid., 296.

p. 136 "... I wanted a mental bath after looking at them." John Dower, *Japan in War and Peace: Selected Essays* (London: HarperCollins/Hammersmith, 1995), 258.

p. 136 ". . . I feel exceedingly proud of being Japanese." Ibid., 275.

p. 136 . . . "savage . . . barbaric tribe of Americans are devils in human skin" with as much worth "as a foreign ear of corn." Dower, *War Without Mercy,* 247.

p. 136 ". . . These terms were widespread in Japan." Cook and Cook, *Japan at War,* 452.

p. 136 ". . . If you fail to destroy him utterly you can never rest in peace." Lt. Col. Dave Grossman, *On Killing: The Psychological Cost of Learning to Kill in War and Society* (New York: Little, Brown and Company, 1995), 165.

pp. 136–137 ". . . It caused them to feel that invasion of other countries and annihilation of other races was justified." Gibney, *Senso,* 9.

p. 137 ". . . depicted bombs falling on a frantic pack of yellow rats." Dower, *Japan in War and Peace,* 264.

p. 137 ". . . They were wiping out dirty animals." Quoted in Andrew A. Rooney, *The Fortunes of War: Four Great Battles of World War II* (Boston: Little, Brown, 1962), 57.

p. 137 ". . . you know: the grin, the slanty eyes, the glasses, the Jap, or the Nip." Lewis and Steele, *Hell in the Pacific,* 92.

p. 138 "A Jap's a Jap . . . we will be worried about [them] until they are wiped off the face of the map." Ibid., 94.

p. 138 ". . . When the word Japanese was inserted into the question, the percentage really wanting to kill the soldier jumped to 44 percent." Ibid., 144.

p. 138 ". . . the word was that we were to take no prisoners." Ibid., 169.

pp. 138–139 ". . . The scavenger grumbled and continued extracting his prizes undisturbed." E. B. Sledge, *With the Old Breed at Peleliu and Okinawa* (New York: Oxford University Press, 1991), 120.

p. 139 ". . . he had refused to accept a letter opener made of the bone of a Japanese." Dower, *War Without Mercy,* 330.

p. 139 "I want no prisoners. Shoot them all." Lewis and Steele, *Hell in the Pacific,* 169.

p. 139 ". . . They were pretty brutally treated." Ibid.

p. 139 ". . . when they hit the water they were nothing but a piece of meat cut to ribbons." Dower, *War Without Mercy,* 66.

p. 140 ". . . the commander's 'overwhelming biological hatred of the enemy.'" Ibid., 330.

p. 140 ". . . You can't be sporting in war." Ibid., 67.

p. 140 ". . . And more Japs meet their ancestors. The show's over, boys." Lewis and Steele, *Hell in the Pacific,* 100.

p. 141 ". . . Perhaps he is human. Nothing on Attu indicates it." Robert Sherrod, "The Nature of the Enemy," *Time,* August 7, 1944.

p. 142 ". . . One or two of you doesn't mean anything." Cook and Cook, *Japan at War,* 269.

p. 142 ". . . one of His Majesty's children." Ibid., 279.

p. 142 ". . . Hardened combat veterans used to say, 'On the battlefield ruthlessness is sometimes a virtue.' " Ienaga, *Japan's Last War,* 182.

p. 142 ". . . I know tears don't erase my sin." Cook and Cook, *Japan at War,* 279.

p. 143 . . . "And if they didn't use it, we'd cut their jugular vein." Holland M. Smith and Percy Finch, *Coral and Brass* (Nashville, TN: The Battery Press, 1989), 193.

p. 143 ". . . by practicing on the Japanese stragglers living in central and eastern parts of the island." Lewis and Steele, *Hell in the Pacific,* 183.

p. 143 ". . . and blow themselves and the other fellow to pieces with a hand grenade." Richard B. Frank, *Downfall: The End of the Imperial Japanese Empire* (New York: Penguin Books, 2001), 28.

p. 143 ". . . they were wearing gas masks as protection against their own dead." Karl Doenitz and R. H. Stevens, with David Woodward, *Memoirs: Ten Years and Twenty Days* (Cleveland: World, 1959), 341.

p. 144 ". . . the Japanese garrison lost 4,938, with only 79 taken prisoner, a fatality rate of 98.4 percent." Frank, *Downfall,* 28.

p. 144 "The real war is starting now." Cook and Cook, *Japan at War,* 263.

p. 144 ". . . no post-mortem analysis on the influence its Midway losses might have on future operations." Bix, *Hirohito and the Making of Modern Japan,* 450.

p. 144 "And when are you ever going to fight a decisive battle?" Ibid., 466.

p. 145 ". . . The only thing left is to wait for the enemy to abandon their will to fight because of the '*Gyokusai* of the One Hundred Million.' " Haruko T. Cook, "The Myth of the Saipan Suicides," *Military History Quarterly,* 7.3 (Spring 1995): 12–19.

p. 145 ". . . I strongly hope [you] will increase aircraft production." Ibid.

p. 146 ". . . It didn't make any difference if you shot one, five more would take his place." Ibid.

pp. 147–148 ". . . Do the suicides of Saipan mean that the whole Japanese race will choose death before surrender?" Sherrod, "The Nature of the Enemy." (All preceding Sherrod quotes are from this article.)

p. 149 ". . . TOGETHER WITH THE BRAVE MEN." Haruko T. Cook, "The Myth of the Saipan Suicides." (Preceding Japanese newspaper quotes and headlines are also from this article.)

p. 149 ". . . in the time of the airplane, a great admiration for hara-kiri!" Ibid.

p. 149 ". . . it will be necessary to invade the industrial heart of Japan." Ibid.

p. 150 ". . . achieve a splendid victory like at the time of the Japan Sea Naval battle [in the Russo-Japanese War]." Bix, *Hirohito and the Making of Modern Japan,* 476.

p. 150 ". . . make it terrible, and the war will stop." Justice M. Chambers, Oral History Collection, Marine Corps Historical Center.

Chapter 11: To the Pacific

p. 153 ". . . holding my sword, I made them kneel down." Cook and Cook, *Japan at War,* 111.

p. 153 In 1944, Japan evacuated about seven thousand. Paul Sampson, "An Era Ends for the 'Yankee' Isles: The Bonins and Iwo Jima Go Back to Japan, Civilians," *National Geographic,* vol. 123, no. 1, July 1968, 127.

p. 153 "Japanese anti-aircraft gunners were transferred from the Akasaka Palace of Emperor Hirohito." Stinnett, *George Bush,* 104.

p. 154 ". . . It wasn't long before we became very good instrument flyers." Lewis and Steele, *Hell in the Pacific,* 139.

p. 164 . . . their ability to dig in and their ability to endure the most god-awful shelling from the sea and bombing from the air. Joseph H. Alexander, *Storm Landings: Epic Amphibious Battles in the Central Pacific* (Annapolis, MD: Naval Institute Press, 1997), 110.

p. 167 "a suitable place to slaughter the American devils." Dower, *Japan in War and Peace,* 276.

p. 167 "are sent to hell, the cleaner the world will be." Ibid., 277.

Chapter 12: Carrier War

p. 169 "the equivalent of sending an Anzio beachhead fighter all the way back to Kansas City for his two weeks." James Tobin, *Ernie Pyle's War: America's Eyewitness to World War II* (New York: The Free Press, 1998), 228.

p. 170 ". . . The walls were covered with bulletin boards, charts, maps, posters, and briefing guides." Hyams, *Flight of the Avenger,* 126.

p. 172 . . . "If he hadn't been there, I wouldn't be telling this." Lt. Cdr. Roy W. Bruce, USNR (Ret.), and Lt. Cdr. Charles R. Leonard, USN (Ret.), *Crommelin's Thunderbirds: Air Group 12 Strikes the Heart of Japan* (Annapolis, MD: Naval Institute Press, 1994), 56.

p. 172 ". . . The machine gun sprayed the flight deck and ship's superstructure with .50-caliber bullets." Ibid., 78.

p. 173 ". . . and everybody snapped back." Hyams, *Flight of the Avenger,* 121.

p. 174 ". . . It was the way I went out." Bruce and Leonard, *Crommelin's Thunderbirds,* 62.

p. 174 ". . . Sure, why not?" Ibid., 110.

p. 179 ". . . I think it may well be some of the fliers." John C., McManus, *Deadly Sky: The American Combat Airman in World War II* (Novato, CA: Presidio Press, 2000), 243–44.

Chapter 13: No Mans Land

p. 189 "always thought of General Tachibana as one who came up from the gutter." Maj. Yoshitaka Horie, *Ogasawara Sendan No Saigo (The Tragic End of the Soldiers Sent to Ogasawara)* (Ogasawara Sen you kai, 1969), 222.

p. 189 ". . . I am revenging the enemy!" Ibid., 221.

p. 190 ". . . All orderlies and clerks who are not required to perform other duties will attend." All quotes from members of the Japanese military on Chichi Jima are from the Guam War Crimes trial transcripts, located in the National Archives, unless otherwise noted.

p. 192 . . . "The radio station on Chichi Jima." Hyams, *Flight of the Avenger,* 142.

p. 193 "The radio station is your primary target." Ibid., 7.

p. 193 . . . "It could be a rough trip." Ibid., 142.

p. 194 . . . a breakfast of powdered eggs, bacon, sausage, dehydrated fried potatoes, and toast. Ibid., 8.

p. 195 "You could have seen that smoke for a hundred miles." Ibid., 144.

p. 195 ". . . smoke and flames enveloping his engine and spreading aft as he did so, and his plane losing altitude." Stinnett, *George Bush,* 147.

p. 196 . . . "a huge ball of fire." Ibid., 160.

p. 196 ". . . 1,460 rounds of machine gun bullets were fired at the would-be Bush captors." Ibid., 147.

p. 197 ". . . then the hull of a submarine emerged from the depths." Ibid., 156.

p. 197 ". . . It just seemed too lucky and too farfetched that it would be an American submarine." Hyams, *Flight of the Avenger,* 160.

p. 198 ". . . there's got to be some kind of destiny and I was being spared for something on earth." Ibid., 178–79.

p. 200 ". . . He spoke admiringly of the 3,000 Chinese heads put on display there." Horie, *Ogasawara Sendan No Saigo,* 224.

p. 201 "was a practice I had grown fond of in China." Hyams, *Flight of the Avenger,* 217.

Chapter 14: No Surrender

p. 202 "My God, why am I clapping?" Bruce and Leonard, *Crommelin's Thunderbirds,* 30.

p. 203 "Oh my God!" thought J. D. "It's a lynching!" Ibid., 41.

p. 213 "The Marines were the best fighting men of World War II." Stephen Ambrose, *To America: Personal Reflections of an Historian* (New York: Simon and Schuster, 2002), 107.

p. 214 "sufficient to pulverize everything on the island." Smith and Finch, *Coral and Brass,* 243.

Chapter 15: Kichiku

p. 224 ". . . it probably appeared during the savage period of our prehistory when sudden life-threatening events occurred with frequency." Sherwin B. Nuland, *How We Die: Reflections on Life's Final Chapter* (New York: Vintage Books, 1995), 133.

p. 224 ". . . exactly the right spoonful of medicine to give a measure of tranquillity to a dying child." Ibid., 132.

p. 230 ". . . It was not guerrillas but our own soldiers who we were frightened of. It was such a terrible condition." Tanaka, *Hidden Horrors,* 114.

pp. 230–31 . . . Japanese soldiers referred to the Allies as "white pigs" and the local population as "black pigs." Ibid.

p. 231 ". . . This indicates that these incidents were not isolated or sporadic acts but part of an organized process." Ibid., 119.

p. 231 ". . . A stew pot in a nearby Japanese bunker contained the heart and liver of approximate size of that [of a] human." Ibid., 118.

p. 231 ". . . A Japanese mess tin in which appeared to contain human flesh was lying four to five yards from [his] body." Ibid., 115.

p. 232 ". . . We were not allowed to go near this ditch, no earth was thrown on the bodies and the smell was terrible." Ibid., 121.

Chapter 16: Fire War

p. 257 ". . . it is no part of their policy to bomb nonmilitary objectives, no matter what the policy of the German Government may be." Dower, *War Without Mercy,* 39–40.

p. 257 ". . . absolutely devastating, exterminating attack by very heavy bombers from this country upon the Nazi homeland." Frank, *Downfall,* 41.

pp. 257–58 ". . . only about one bomb in five landed within even a five-mile radius of the designated target." Ibid., 41.

p. 258 ". . . repugnant to our humanitarian principles." Kenneth P. Werrell, *Blankets of Fire: U.S. Bombers Over Japan During World War II* (Washington, DC: Smithsonian Institution Press, 1996), 16.

p. 258 "[It] combined moral scruple, historical optimism, and technological pioneering, all three distinctly American characteristics." John Keegan, "We Wanted Beady-Eyed Guys Just Absolutely Holding the Course," *Smithsonian* 14, no. 5 (1995): 34–55.

p. 258 ". . . You're going to be baby killers." Frank Clark, "The 36th Mission," *American Heritage* (May–June 1995): 46, 48.

p. 258 ". . . to me the war had a human face." Ibid.

p. 259 Half of Hamburg was destroyed and 400,000 people were "de-housed." Donald L. Miller, *The Story of World War II* (New York: Simon and Schuster, 2001), 253.

p. 259 ". . . bodies, trees, and parts of buildings flying through air heated to 800° centigrade." Michael S. Sherry, *The Rise of American Air Power: The Creation of Armageddon* (New Haven, CT: Yale University Press, 1987), 153.

p. 259 ". . . the sound of the wind was 'like the Devil laughing.'" Grossman, *On Killing,* 100.

p. 259 "tiny children lay like fried eels on the pavement." Quoted in Martin Middlebrook, *The Battle of Hamburg: Allied Bomber Forces Against a German City in 1943* (London: Allen Lane, 1980), 276.

p. 259 ". . . Bombenbrandschrumpfleichen (incendiary-bomb-shrunken bodies)." Sherry, *The Rise of American Air Power,* 153.

p. 260 ". . . as an added incentive to surrender." Gwynne Dyer, *War* (New York: Crown Publishers, 1995), 18.

p. 260 "baby killing plan." Ronald Schaffer, *Wings of Judgement: American Bombing in World War II* (New York: Oxford University Press, 1985), 92.

p. 260 ". . . must be so impressed upon them that they will hesitate to start any new war." Ibid., 88.

p. 260 ". . . to hasten Hitler's doom." Sherry, *The Rise of American Air Power,* 261.

p. 260 ". . . preached the gospel of precision bombing against military and industrial targets." Ibid.

p. 260 "an impressive demonstration of what America might be able to achieve in its war against Japan." Ibid., 156.

p. 260 ". . . the destruction of the target would entail death for large numbers of noncombatants." Frank, *Downfall,* 48.

p. 261 . . . "These were people who had been caught in the firestorm." Kurt Vonnegut, Jr., *Slaughterhouse-Five or the Children's Crusade* (New York: Dell, 1969), 128–31.

p. 261 ". . . To me it looks like trying days for us in the years ahead." Ernie Pyle, *Ernie's War: The Best of Ernie Pyle's World War II Dispatches,* ed. David Nichols (New York: Simon & Schuster, 1987), 567.

p. 261 "'. . . Incendiary projectiles would burn the cities to the ground in short order.'" Frank, *Downfall,* 51.

p. 261 ". . . fire-bomb attacks on the teeming bamboo ant heaps of Honshu and Kyushu." Werrell, *Blankets of Fire,* 41.

p. 261 ". . . 'use of incendiaries against cities was contrary to our national policy of attacking military objectives.'" Ibid.

p. 261 ". . . ordered his top cabinet officials to work on the project." Ibid.

p. 261 "had moral objections to attacks on cities and civilians" Ibid.

p. 262 ". . . There won't be any hesitation about bombing civilians — it will be all out." Ibid., 46.

p. 262 ". . . the possibility of wiping out major portions of any of the large Japanese cities." Ibid., 51.

p. 262 "It is desired that the areas selected include, or be in the immediate vicinity of, legitimate military targets." Ibid.

p. 262 "about 75 percent in the half-dozen largest cities." Frank, *Downfall,* 452.

p. 262 ". . . and the lower tip running through Hiroshima-Kure and Yawata." Ibid.

p. 262 "vulnerability of Japanese cities to fire." Werrell, *Blankets of Fire,* 151.

p. 262 ". . . heavy dispersal of industry within the cities and within the most congested parts of them." Ibid.

p. 263 ". . . from which it drew both workers and parts." Frank, *Downfall,* 7.

p. 263 ". . . but some opposition is being expressed to the continual bombing of Berlin." Sherry, *The Rise of American Air Power,* 264.

p. 263 ". . . not so much as a book which tells how these things are made." Dower, *War Without Mercy,* 54.

p. 263 "until we have destroyed about half the Japanese civilian population." Ibid., 55.

p. 264 ". . . It was just a beautiful, beautiful plane." Quotes from interviews with the following B-29 airmen appear courtesy of Mark Natola: Loy Collingwood, David Farquar, Newell Fears, Harry George, George Gladden, Hap Halloran, Fiske Hanley, John Jennings, Chester Marshall, Charlie Phillips, Ed Ricketson, Bob Rodenhaus, and Joe Tucker.

p. 264 ". . . he thinks more than any man I have ever known." Keith Wheeler and the Editors of Time-Life Books, *Bombers Over Japan* (Alexandria, VA: Time-Life Books, 1982), 166.

p. 265 ". . . however surprising his decision might be, it was probably the right one." Thomas M. Coffey, *Iron Eagle: The Turbulent Life of General Curtis LeMay* (New York: Crown Publishers, 1986), 160.

p. 265 ". . . planes and crews, it seemed, were expendable." Werrell, *Blankets of Fire,* 117.

p. 265 "General LeMay has taken over [and] he is going to get us all killed." Ibid., 139.

p. 265 ". . . If you don't get results, you'll be fired." Gen. Curtis E. LeMay, USAF (Ret.), with MacKinlay Kantor, *Mission with LeMay: My Story* (Garden City, NY: Doubleday and Company, 1965), 347.

p. 265 "our entire Nation howled like a pack of wolves for an attack on the Japanese homeland." LeMay, *Mission with LeMay,* 322.

p. 265 . . . just 24 planes out of 111 were able to sight their targets and drop their payloads anywhere near them. Wheeler, *Bombers Over Japan,* 102.

p. 266 ". . . And I had to do something fast." Werrell, *Blankets of Fire,* 156.

p. 266 ". . . This is sound, this is practical, this is the way I'll do it: not one word to General Arnold." LeMay, *Mission with LeMay,* 348.

p. 267 ". . . And without any guns, gunners, or ammunition." Coffey, *Iron Eagle,* 157.

p. 267 ". . . Many frankly did not expect to return from a raid over that city, at an altitude of less than 10,000 feet." Ibid.

p. 267 ". . . Do you want to kill Japanese, or would you rather have Americans killed?" Coffey, *Iron Eagle,* 161.

p. 267 ". . . But all war is immoral and if you let that bother you, you're not a good soldier." Quoted in Richard Rhodes, *Dark Sun: The Making of the Hydrogen Bomb* (New York: Simon and Schuster, 1995), 21–22.

p. 269 ". . . but the prime target is the enemy's industrial plant." David O. Woodbury, "Tokyo Calling Cards," *Collier's,* April 14, 1945, 43.

p. 269 "to give priority to production over civilian protection." Frank, *Downfall,* 5.

p. 269 . . . 3,334,000 pounds. "United States Strategic Bombing Survey Summary Report: Pacific War."

p. 269 "violent as a spring typhoon." Frank, *Downfall,* 3.

p. 270 they heard the song "Smoke Gets in Your Eyes." Col. Robert Morgan, USAFR, Ret., with Ron Powers, *The Man Who Flew the Memphis Belle: Memoir of a World War II Bomber Pilot* (New York: Penguin Books, 2001), 310.

p. 270 "The darkest hour is just before dawn." Frank, *Downfall,* 3.

p. 270 Charlie Phillips interview courtesy of Mark Natola.

p. 270 "In this way, the bomb load of each bomber covered a strip 350 feet by 2,000 feet." Werrell, *Blankets of Fire,* 168.

p. 270 "he shifted his cigar and for the first time he smiled." Coffey, *Iron Eagle,* 164.

p. 270 . . . "Everyone there in the dugout said 'How beautiful!' " *Nihon no Kushu,* vol. 3, ed. Katsumoto Saotome (Tokyo: Sanseido, 1980).

p. 271 ". . . and where these silver streamers would touch the earth, red fires would spring up." Frank, *Downfall,* 7.

p. 271 ". . . One single bomb covered quite a big area, and what they covered they devoured." Ibid.

p. 271 ". . . Smoke and sparks were everywhere, and white-hot gusts came roaring down narrow streets." Miller, *The Story of World War II,* 450.

p. 271 "At one station, the fire left only a tangle of corpses around a melted fire engine." Frank, *Downfall,* 8.

p. 271 "The whole area was lighted as if it were broad daylight when we entered the drop zone." Wheeler, *Bombers Over Japan,* 166.

p. 272 ". . . panting 'huh, huh, huh' as they ran." Frank, *Downfall,* 10.

p. 273 "... killed or knocked unconscious its victims even before the flames reached them." Sherry, *The Rise of American Air Power,* 277.

p. 273 "Babies exploded on mothers' backs, and cars on streets were 'consumed like crumpled paper.'" Gavan Daws, *Prisoners of the Japanese War: POWs of World War II in the Pacific* (New York: William Morrow and Company, 1994), 319.

p. 273 ... "People on the outer edge of the group fell one by one, dead from inhalation." *Nihon no kushu,* vol. 3.

p. 273 "... I suddenly realized they were really burned bodies, still standing upright." Lewis and Steele, *Hell in the Pacific,* 195.

p. 273 "... No one stopped to help them." Frank, *Downfall,* 11.

p. 273 "... Now there wasn't a drop of water, only the bodies of the adults and children who had died." Ibid., 13.

p. 275 "... I started to hate America from the bottom of my heart." *Nihon no kushu,* vol. 3.

p. 275 "... 'That's flesh burning.'" *The World Today,* March 10, 2000.

p. 276 "swollen, contorted, blackened bodies that resembled 'enormous ginseng roots.'" Frank, *Downfall,* 14.

p. 276 ... "Probably she gave birth just before she was burnt to death." *Nihon no kushu,* vol. 3.

p. 277 "... He was dead and I screamed." Ibid.

p. 277 ... authorities came up with totals of 83,793 killed and 40,918 injured. Wheeler, *Bombers Over Japan,* 169.

p. 277 "... but even these immense totals are sometimes challenged as too low." Frank, *Downfall,* 18.

p. 277 "We scorched and boiled and baked to death more people in Tokyo on that night of March 9–10 than went up in vapor at Hiroshima and Nagasaki combined." LeMay, *Mission with LeMay,* 387.

Chapter 17: Enduring the Unendurable

p. 278 "... to knock out all of Japan's major industrial cities during the next ten days." LeMay, *Mission with LeMay,* 353.

p. 279 "... you should then have the ability to destroy whole industrial cities should that be required." Coffey, *Iron Eagle,* 166.

p. 279 "CENTER OF TOKYO DEVASTATED BY FIRE BOMBS ... City's Heart Gone." Sherry, *The Rise of American Air Power,* 287.

p. 279 "I not only saw Tokyo burning furiously in many sections, but I smelled it." Ibid., 288.

p. 279 "one of the most ruthless and barbaric killings of non-combatants in all history." Lewis and Steele, *Hell in the Pacific,* 200.

p. 279 "Guard against anyone stating this is area bombing." Werrell, *Blankets of Fire,* 157.

p. 279 "the economical method of destroying the small industries in these areas . . . of bringing about their liquidation." Sherry, *The Rise of American Air Power,* 292.

p. 279 ". . . the reduction of Japanese ability to produce war goods." Ibid., 287–90.

p. 280 ". . . drive inhabitants into the country and destroy their industrial utility." Ibid., 291.

p. 280 Radio Tokyo referred to the new U.S. policy as "slaughter bombing." Dower, *War Without Mercy,* 41.

p. 280 ". . . he and his men could do little to stop the fires." Werrell, *Blankets of Fire,* 166.

p. 280 ". . . but one could see the thought lurking behind the wooden faces." Robert Guillian, *I Saw Tokyo Burning: An Eyewitness Narrative from Pearl Harbor to Hiroshima* (Garden City, NY: Doubleday, 1981), 1–3.

p. 280 "set forth in a general's uniform and riding boots." Frank, *Downfall,* 18.

p. 281 "to shatter the enemy's ambitions." Quoted in Richard Wheeler, *Iwo* (New York: Lippincott and Crowell, 1980), 223.

p. 282 ". . . he insisted on rolling down his own collar for the execution." Robert L. Sherrod, *History of Marine Corps Aviation in World War II* (San Rafael, CA: Presido Press, 1980), footnote 15.

p. 283 ". . . he consoled my heart and gave me comfort more than anything else could do." Horie, *Ogasawara Sendan No Saigo,* 225.

p. 284 ". . . Battalion Commander: Major Matoba." Russell, *The Knights of Bushido,* 182.

p. 288 ". . . All the other officers agreed that liver was good medicine for the stomach." Ibid., 184.

p. 289 List ending "Nagoaka . . . Madison." United States Army Air Corps (USAAC), 1945.

p. 290 ". . . Skeletons of motor vehicles, including fire engines, dotted the landscape." Werrell, *Blankets of Fire,* 227.

p. 290 Curtis destroyed more than twice as much urban area in Japan: 178 square miles. Ibid.

p. 290 . . . damage in just two Japanese cities, Tokyo (56.3 square miles) and Osaka (16.4 square miles), nearly equaled all the damage done to all German cities put together. Ibid.

p. 290 "conventional bombing could easily end the war." Keith Wheeler and the Editors of Time-Life Books, *The Fall of Japan* (Alexandria, VA: Time-Life Books, 1983), 72.

p. 290 "We could bomb and burn them until they quit." Ibid., 17.

p. 290 "by October he would run out of cities to burn." Miller, *The Story of World War II*, 601.

p. 290 Thirty percent of the urban population — 9 million people — was homeless. "United States Strategic Bombing Survey Summary Report (Pacific War)."

p. 290 ". . . The fatality rate in the training program was higher than the rate in combat." LeMay, *Mission with LeMay*, 376.

p. 290 "The rice paddies might be sprayed with oil, defoliants, or biological agents, and the production of fertilizer further attacked." Sherry, *The Rise of American Air Power*, 312.

p. 290 "Workers had to barter for food in the countryside and absenteeism rose to 40% in the major cities." John W. Dower, *Embracing Defeat: Japan in the Wake of World War II* (New York: W. W. Norton and Company, 1999), 90.

p. 291 ". . . We looked dumbfounded at each other, amazed that someone was worse off than we." Gibney, *Senso,* 192.

p. 291 "Eat This Way — Endless Supplies of Materials by Ingenuity." Dower, *Embracing Defeat*, 91.

p. 291 ". . . important to avoid eating their bones since it had been demonstrated that this caused people to lose weight." Ibid.

p. 291 "How to Eat Acorns" and "Let's Catch Grasshoppers." Ibid., 94.

p. 291 "onion existence, with the clear implication of weeping as one peeled off layer upon layer of precious belongings." Ibid., 95.

p. 291 ". . . because the white man's heart was small." Daws, 275.

p. 292 ". . . they are resigned to all physical suffering and . . . [are] confident in their leaders." Frank, *Downfall,* 107.

p. 292 ". . . one never dies, never surrenders unconditionally." Herbert P. Bix, "Japan's Delayed Surrender: A Reinterpretation," *Diplomatic History* 19 (Spring 1995): 214.

p. 292 "proclaimed that Japan must fight to the finish and choose extinction before surrender." Frank, *Downfall,* 95.

p. 292 . . . These kamikaze tactics would "exchange" the life of a pilot for a military gain. Bix, *Hirohito and the Making of Modern Japan,* 480.

p. 293 . . . to throw themselves under the treads of tanks, were called "Sherman carpets." William Manchester, *American Caesar: Douglas MacArthur* (Boston: Little, Brown and Company, 1978), 436.

p. 293 Planes loaded with plague-infected fleas would take off from a submarine and contaminate San Diego. Nicholas D. Kristof, "Unlocking a Deadly Secret," *New York Times,* March 17, 1995.

p. 293 ". . . there would be room to produce a more advantageous international situation for Japan." Bix, *Hirohito and the Making of Modern Japan,* 492.

p. 293 ". . . We cannot allow Japan to perish because of them." Remarks by chief, Police Bureau, Osaka, in Hosokawa, *Joho tenno ni tassezu,* June 21, 1945.

p. 293 "If we are prepared to sacrifice 20 million Japanese lives in *kamikaze* effort, victory will be ours!" Lewis and Steele, *Hell in the Pacific,* 230.

p. 293 ". . . 32 million civilians who were being trained in the use of primitive weapons in order to make a heroic last stand." Wheeler, *The Fall of Japan,* 63.

pp. 293–94 "more than the combined armies of the United States, Great Britain and Nazi Germany." Manchester, *American Caesar,* 436.

p. 294 ". . . It was a recipe for extinction." Frank, *Downfall,* 190.

p. 294 "cost over a million casualties to American forces alone." Manchester, *American Caesar,* 438.

p. 294 ". . . between 1.7 and 4 million casualties, including 400,000 to 800,000 fatalities." Frank, *Downfall,* 340.

p. 294 ". . . a million soldiers on both sides would have been killed and a million more would have been maimed for life." Harold L. Buell, *Dauntless Helldivers: A Dive-Bomber Pilot's Epic Story of the Carrier Battles* (New York: Orion Books, 1991), 306.

p. 294 "exceeded the Navy's total losses from *all previous wars combined.*" Lewis and Steele, *Hell in the Pacific,* 202.

p. 294 . . . 200,000 British troops were scheduled to fight for *seven months* to retake Singapore. Paul Fussell, *Thank God for the Atom Bomb and Other Essays* (New York: Ballantine Books, 1990), 7.

p. 294 "for the heavy losses which undoubtedly would occur." Frank, *Downfall,* 127.

p. 295 ". . . It is the aim not to allow the escape of a single one, to annihilate them all, and not to leave any traces." Russell, *The Knights of Bushido,* 92.

p. 295 ". . . wanted to see what parts of the boy's body jumped and jerked with each turn of the knife." Ienaga, *Japan's Last War,* 189.

pp. 295–96 On August 1, American napalm burned out 80 percent of Hachioji near Tokyo. Frank, *Downfall,* 154.

p. 296 ". . . 'the primary's Hiroshima.'" Wheeler, *The Fall of Japan,* 90.

p. 296 ". . . the place was going to be (as the Potsdam Declaration had promised) obliterated." Fussell, *Thank God for the Atom Bomb,* 16.

p. 296 ". . . Without it, our mission would have been more difficult." Paul W. Tibbets, *Flight of the Enola Gay* (Columbus, OH: Mid Coast Marketing, 1989), 219.

p. 296 "a blinding pulse of light for perhaps only a tenth of a second." Frank, *Downfall,* 264.

p. 297 ". . . no order-of-magnitude increase in destructiveness over a conventional air raid." Frank, *Downfall,* 253.

p. 297 "... I suppose they believe also that a machine gun is a hundred times wickeder than a bow and arrow." LeMay, *Mission with LeMay,* 380.

p. 297 "... We have used it to shorten the agony of young Americans." Fussell, *Thank God for the Atom Bomb,* 22.

p. 297 "When you have to deal with a beast you have to treat him as a beast." Lewis and Steele, *Hell in the Pacific,* 215.

p. 297 "... extraordinary shame about the Hiroshima bomb correlates closely with lack of information about the Pacific war." Fussell, *Thank God for the Atom Bomb,* 12.

p. 297 "... you thank God for the atomic bomb." Ibid., 7.

p. 297 "no intention of proceeding to the Japanese front themselves." Ibid., 6–7.

pp. 297–298 "... The Japanese people know more about that than the American public will ever know." Richard Rougstad, "Pearl Harbor Pilot to Tibbets: 'You Did the Right Thing,'" *Sun Tzu's Newswire,* September 20, 1998.

p. 298 "... had our air force continued to drop incendiary bombs on Japan's cities." Sherry, *The Rise of American Air Power,* 321.

p. 298 Beginning in September, he was prepared to drop 115,000 tons a month. "United States Strategic Bombing Survey Summary Report (Pacific War)."

p. 298 "... Therefore it cannot be said that there are no countermeasures." Frank, *Downfall,* 270.

pp. 298–299 "... We kept on flying." LeMay, *Mission with LeMay,* 389.

p. 299 "With luck, we will repulse the invaders before they land." Wheeler, *The Fall of Japan,* 153.

p. 299 ... "There is no way left for us but to accept the Potsdam Proclamation." Ibid., 152.

p. 300 ... "We certainly can't swallow this proclamation." Ibid.

p. 300 "... That's the way the whole country felt." Cook and Cook, *Japan at War,* 78.

p. 300 "... Then the crews came home to the Marianas and were told that Japan had capitulated." LeMay, *Mission with LeMay,* 388.

p. 301 "... 'You bastards, I beat you.'" Miller, *The Story of World War II,* 643.

p. 301 Now the 31,617 American POWs were free. Dower, *Embracing Defeat,* 54.

p. 301 "... We were kids — seasoned by war, but kids." Hyams, *Flight of the Avenger,* 209.

p. 302 "... on the basis of the B-29 raids, felt that the cause was hopeless." Werrell, *Blankets of Fire,* 240.

p. 302 "Thinking of the people dying endlessly in the air raids I ended the war." Frank, *Downfall,* 18.

p. 302 "Fundamentally the thing that brought about the determination to make peace was the prolonged bombing by the B-29s." Werrell, *Blankets of Fire,* 240.

p. 302 "... The largest response for one category (over one-third) was 'air attack.'" Ibid., 234.

p. 302 "... even if Russia had not entered the war, and even if no invasion had been planned or contemplated." "United States Strategic Bombing Survey Summary Report (Pacific War)," 26.

p. 302 An astonishing 15 million people were homeless. Frank, *Downfall,* 334.

pp. 302–303 ... or about 19 percent of total losses during the Pacific war. Werrell, *Blankets of Fire,* 238.

p. 303 Another 334 Superfortress crew members were listed as captured or interned, of whom 262 survived. Frank, *Downfall,* 363.

p. 303 "propelled Japan onto its ultimately disastrous course of global competition with the Western powers." Dower, *Embracing Defeat,* 41.

p. 303 ... the USS *Missouri* lay just four and one half miles northeast of the spot where Commodore Perry had anchored his ship. Samuel Eliot Morison, *History of United States Naval Operations in World War II,* vol. XIV (Edison, NJ: Castle Books, 2001), 362.

p. 303 "Allied ships ringed the *Missouri* in concentric circles of power." Philadelphia, PA, *Evening Bulletin,* September 4, 1945.

p. 304 "Bill, where the hell are those airplanes?" Manchester, *American Caesar,* 453.

p. 304 "... I stood there and felt pretty tired." LeMay, *Mission with LeMay,* 390.

p. 305 Okinawa typhoon quotes and information from Morison, *History of United States Naval Operations in World War II,* supp., 15–17.

Chapter 18: Casualties of War

p. 308 The story of Colonel Rixey's discovering the Flyboys' fates is from Col. P. M. Rixey, *Japanese Camouflage: We Penetrate a Prepared Story in the Occupation of the Bonin Islands,* Private papers of P. M. Rixey.

p. 311 "Much of Japan's aggression was formulated outside the cabinet in conferences involving only the military and its commander in chief." Dower, *Embracing Defeat,* 325.

p. 311 "the major war criminal." Ibid., 326.

p. 312 "Hirohito will have to go." Ibid., 279.

p. 312 "argued that Hirohito should abdicate on moral grounds." Ibid., 321.

p. 312 "the notion that he should somehow assume responsibility for the war." Ibid., 320.

p. 312 "... absolving his faithful ministers, generals, and admirals of responsibility for the war." Ibid., 320.

p. 312 "had his officials brief him on the practice of abdication in the British monarchy." Ibid., 320.

p. 312 "met privately with his nephew and recommended that he step down." Ibid., 320.

p. 312 "urged the emperor to take responsibility for defeat." Ibid., 321.

p. 312 ". . . People are more concerned with food and housing problems than with the fate of the Emperor." Ibid., 305.

p. 312 "worry about Emperor, shame for Emperor, sorrow for him." Ibid., 305.

p. 312 ". . . in favor of Hirohito abdicating right away or at an opportune moment." Ibid., 327.

p. 312 ". . . 70 percent of Americans favored executing or harshly punishing the emperor." Ibid., 299.

pp. 312–13 ". . . Emperor Hirohito played a highly active role in supporting the actions carried out in his name." Bix, *Hirohito and the Making of Modern Japan*, 519.

p. 313 "found the war leaders all saying virtually the same thing." Ibid., 583.

p. 313 ". . . It is quite possible that a million troops would be required which would have to be maintained for an indefinite number of years." Foreign Relations of the United States, *Diplomatic Papers, 1946: The Far East,* vol. 8 (Washington, DC: U.S. Government Printing Office, 1946), 396.

p. 313 ". . . like worn-out garments after almost eight centuries of exalted existence." Dower, *Embracing Defeat,* 303.

p. 314 ". . . To try him as a war criminal would not only be blasphemous but a denial of spiritual freedom." Ibid., 298.

p. 314 "Hanging of the Emperor to them would be comparable to the crucifixion of Christ to us." Ibid., 282.

p. 314 ". . . any more than you remove the godhead of Jesus and have any Christianity left." Ibid., 284.

p. 314 "went to work to protect Hirohito from the role he had played during and at the end of the war." Bix, *Hirohito,* 582.

p. 314 ". . . 'I had already decided to push for war even if his majesty the emperor was against going to war with the United States.'" Takada Makiko, "Shinshutsu Shiryo kara mita 'Showa Tenno dokuhakuroku,'" *Seiji kiezai shigaku* 299 (March 1991): 41.

p. 314 ". . . connected Hirohito to political decisions during the past decade." Dower, *Embracing Defeat,* 324.

p. 314 "by all means go home immediately." Ibid., 326.

p. 314 "the prosecution functioned, in effect, as a defense team for the emperor." Ibid., 326.

p. 315 ". . . They made up the rules after the game was over." Ibid., 452.

p. 315 "We wanted blood and, by God, we had blood." Ibid., 452.

p. 315 ". . . or our generals and admirals would all be shot at sunrise without a hearing of any sort." Ibid., 627.

p. 315 "leader of the crime, though available for trial, had been granted immunity." Ibid., 460.

p. 315 "... the present Defendants could only be considered as accomplices." "Dissenting Judgement of the Member from France," in B. V. A. Röling and G. F. Rüter, eds., *The Tokyo Judgment: The International Military Tribunal for the Far East (I.M.T.F.E.), 29 April 1946–12 November 1948,* vol. 1 (Amsterdam: University Press Amsterdam, 1977), 496.

p. 315 "... on that point I am being comforted." Peter Maguire, *Law and War: An American Story* (New York: Columbia University Press, 2000), 193.

p. 315 ... a three-hour lunch with Emperor Hirohito at the palace. Ibid.

p. 316 "... a valuable property for post-war Japan; and one thus worth protecting." Ian Ward, *The Killer They Called a God* (Singapore: Media Masters, 1996), 295.

p. 317 "... never again will the like of these cases have to be presented." All quotes and information about the war crimes trials of Japanese officers, soldiers, and doctors stationed on Chichi Jima are from the Guam War Crimes trial transcripts, located in the National Archives, unless otherwise noted.

p. 318 "You are not Japanese," the general told him. Shepardson, *The Bonin Islands.*

p. 319 Japan had held 132,134 western POWs and 35,756 of them died in detention, a death rate of 27 percent. Tanaka, *Hidden Horrors,* 2.

p. 319 "Moreover, the postwar death rate among surviving POWs of the Japanese was also higher." Ibid., 2.

p. 319 More than 62,000 Japanese POWs — almost twice as many as Allied POW deaths — would die in the gulag. Cook and Cook, *Japan at War,* 403.

p. 322 ... 5,700 Japanese were indicted for war crimes. About 920 were executed, 525 received life sentences, 2,944 were sentenced to more limited prison terms, 1,018 were acquitted, and 279 were never brought to trial. Dower, *Embracing Defeat,* 447.

p. 326 "... and strips of their flesh used to flavor soup." Gilbert Cant, "Yankee Trader's Descendant Welcomes U.S. Flag," *Life,* June 24, 1946.

pp. 328–329 "... I want to shoot the person who killed my daughter." *Nihon no kushu,* vol. 4, ed. Seiichi Imai (Tokyo: Sanseido, 1981).

p. 329 "... 'Hiroko-chan, you must have been hot. Teruko-chan, you must have been hot.'" Cook and Cook, *Japan at War,* 349.

p. 329 "You had to live those years and walk that mile." Paul Tibbets, *Return of the Enola Gay* (Columbus, OH: Mid Coast Marketing, 1988), 8.

pp. 330–331 "... So I say I forgive them." Lewis and Steele, *Hell in the Pacific,* 251.

Bibliography

Ambrose, Stephen, *To America: Personal Reflections of an Historian.* New York: Simon and Schuster, 2002.

Alexander, Joseph H. *Storm Landings: Epic Amphibious Battles in the Central Pacific.* Annapolis, MD: Naval Institute Press, 1997.

Berg, A. Scott. *Lindbergh.* New York: Berkley Publishing Group, 1999.

Bergerud, Eric M. *Fire in the Sky: The Air War in the South Pacific.* Boulder, CO: Westview Press, 2001.

Bernard, Tom. "Japs Were Jumpy After Tokyo Raid." *Stars and Stripes,* April 27, 1943.

Bix, Herbert P. *Hirohito and the Making of Modern Japan.* New York: HarperCollins, 2000.

———. "Japan's Delayed Surrender: A Reinterpretation." *Diplomatic History* 19 (Spring 1995): 214.

Blumberg, Rhoda. *Commodore Perry in the Land of the Shogun.* New York: Lothrop, Lee and Shepard Books, 1985.

Brown, Dee. *Bury My Heart at Wounded Knee: An Indian History of the American West.* New York: Henry Holt and Company, 1970.

Bruce, Lt. Cdr. Roy W., USNR (Ret.), and Lt. Cdr. Charles R. Leonard, USN (Ret.). *Crommelin's Thunderbirds: Air Group 12 Strikes the Heart of Japan.* Annapolis, MD: Naval Institute Press, 1994.

Buell, Harold L. *Dauntless Helldivers: A Dive-Bomber Pilot's Epic Story of the Carrier Battles.* New York: Orion Books, 1991.

Bush, George, with Victor Gold. *Looking Forward.* Garden City, NY: Doubleday, 1987.

Butow, Robert J. *Tojo and the Coming of the War.* Princeton, NJ: Princeton University Press, 1961.

Cant, Gilbert. "Yankee Trader's Descendant Welcomes U.S. Flag." *Life,* June 24, 1946.

Center for Research on North America (CISAN), National Autonomous University of Mexico. *Voices of Mexico,* no. 41.

Clark, Frank. "The 36th Mission." *American Heritage* (May–June 1995): 46–48.

Coffey, Thomas M. *Iron Eagle: The Turbulent Life of General Curtis LeMay.* New York: Crown Publishers, 1986.

Cohen, Stan. *Destination: Tokyo.* Missoula, MT: Pictorial Histories Publishing Company, 1983.

Cook, Haruko T. "The Myth of the Saipan Suicides." *Military History Quarterly,* 7.3 (Spring 1995): 12–19.

Cook, Haruko Taya, and Theodore F. Cook. *Japan at War: An Oral History.* New York: The New Press, 1992.

Dallek, Robert. *Franklin D. Roosevelt and American Foreign Policy, 1932–1945.* New York: Oxford University Press, 1979.

Daws, Gavan. *Prisoners of the Japanese: POWs of World War II in the Pacific.* New York: William Morrow and Company, 1994.

DeHart, Greg. *One Hour Over Tokyo.* History Channel, May 26, 2001.

Doenitz, Karl, and R. H. Stevens, with David Woodward. *Memoirs: Ten Years and Twenty Days.* Cleveland: World, 1959.

Doolittle, Gen. James H. "Jimmy," with Carroll V. Glines. *I Could Never Be So Lucky Again: An Autobiography.* Atglen, PA: Schiffer Publishing, 1995.

Dower, John W. *Embracing Defeat: Japan in the Wake of World War II.* New York: W. W. Norton & Company, 1999.

———. *Japan in War and Peace: Selected Essays.* London: HarperCollins/Hammersmith, 1995.

————. *War Without Mercy: Race and Power in the Pacific War.* New York: Pantheon Books, 1996.

Drinnon, Richard. *Facing West: The Metaphysics of Indian-Hating and Empire Building.* Minneapolis: University of Minnesota Press, 1980.

Dyer, Gwynne, *War.* New York: Crown Publishers, 1995.

Dyer, Thomas G. *Theodore Roosevelt and the Idea of Race.* Baton Rouge, LA: Louisiana State University Press, 1980.

Elison, George. *Deus Destroyed: The Image of Christianity in Early Modern Japan.* Cambridge, MA: Council on East Asian Studies, Harvard University, 1988.

Esthus, Raymond A. *Theodore Roosevelt and Japan.* Seattle: University of Washington Press, 1966.

Foreign Relations of the United States. *Diplomatic Papers, 1946: The Far East.* Vol. 8. Washington, DC: U.S. Government Printing Office, 1946.

Frank, Richard B. *Downfall: The End of the Imperial Japanese Empire.* New York: Penguin Books, 2001.

Fussell, Paul. *Thank God for the Atom Bomb and Other Essays.* New York: Ballantine Books, 1990.

Gibney, Frank. *Senso: The Japanese Remember the Pacific War.* Translated by Beth Cary. Armonk, NY: M. E. Sharp, 1995.

Glines, Carroll V. *The Doolittle Raid: America's Daring First Strike Against Japan.* New York: Orion Books, 1988.

Grant, Ulysses S. *Personal Memoirs of U. S. Grant.* New York: Dover Publications, 1995.

Greene, Bob. *Duty: A Father, His Son, and the Man Who Won the War.* New York: William Morrow, 2000.

Greening, Col. C. Ross. *Not As Briefed.* St. Paul: Brown and Bigelow, 1945.

Grossman, Lt. Col. Dave. *On Killing: The Psychological Cost of Learning to Kill in War and Society.* New York: Little, Brown and Company, 1995.

Guillian, Robert. *I Saw Tokyo Burning: An Eyewitness Narrative from Pearl Harbor to Hiroshima.* Garden City, NY: Doubleday, 1981.

Hasdorff, Dr. James C. "Interview of Brig. Gen. Richard A. Knobloch." United States Air Force Oral History Program, July 13–14, 1987. Maxwell Air Force Base, AL: Air Force Historical Research Agency, 1987.

Haynes, Sam W. *James K. Polk and the Expansionist Impulse.* New York: Longman, 1997.

Hayostek, Cindy. "Exploits of a Doolittle Raider." *Military History,* March 1996.

Honda, Katsuichi. *The Nanjing Massacre: A Japanese Journalist Confronts Japan's National Shame.* Armonk, NY: M. E. Sharp, 1998.

Horie, Major Yoshitaka. *Ogasawara Sendan No Saigo (The Tragic End of the Soldiers Sent to Ogasawara).* Ogasawara Sen you kai, 1969.

Hyams, Joe. *Flight of the Avenger: George Bush at War.* New York: Berkley Publishing Group, 1992.

Ienaga, Sabura. *Japan's Last War: World War II and the Japanese, 1931–1945.* New York: Pantheon Books, 1978. (Originally published in Tokyo as *Taiheiyo Senso* by Iwanami Shoten Publishers, 1968.)

Keegan, John. "We Wanted Beady-Eyed Guys Just Absolutely Holding the Course." *Smithsonian* 14, no. 5 (1995): 34–35.

Kennedy, David. M. "Victory at Sea." *Atlantic Monthly,* March 1999.

Kernan, Alvin. *Crossing the Line: A Bluejacket's World War II Odyssey.* Annapolis, MD: Naval Institute Press, 1994.

LeMay, General Curtis E., USAF (Ret.) with MacKinlay Kantor. *Mission with LeMay: My Story.* Garden City, NY: Doubleday & Company, 1965.

Levine, Isaac Don. *Mitchell: Pioneer of Air Power.* New York: Duell, Sloan and Pearce, 1958.

Lewis, Jonathan, and Ben Steele. *Hell in the Pacific: From Pearl Harbor to Hiroshima.* London: Channel 4 Books, an imprint of Macmillan Publishers, 2001.

Lindbergh, Charles A. *The Wartime Journals of Charles A. Lindbergh.* New York: Harcourt Brace Jovanovich, 1970.

Maguire, Peter. *Law and War: An American Story.* New York: Columbia University Press, 2000.

Makiko, Takada. "Shinshutsu Shiryo kara mita 'Showa Tenno dokuhakuroku.'" *Seiji kiezai shigaku* 299 (March 1991): 41.

Manchester, William. *American Caesar: Douglas MacArthur.* Boston: Little, Brown and Company, 1978.

McClain, James L. *Japan: A Modern History.* New York: W. W. Norton and Company, 2002.

McManus, John C. *Deadly Sky: The American Combat Airman in World War II.* Novato, CA: Presidio Press, 2000.

Merrill, James. *Target Tokyo: The Halsey-Doolittle Raid.* Chicago: Rand McNally and Company, 1968.

Middlebrook, Martin. *The Battle of Hamburg: Allied Bomber Forces Against a German City in 1943.* London: Allen Lane, 1980.

Miller, Donald L. *The Story of World War II.* New York: Simon and Schuster, 2001.

Miller, Stuart Creighton. *Benevolent Assimilation: The American Conquest of the Philippines, 1899–1903.* New Haven, CT: Yale University Press, 1982.

Mitchell, Gen. William. "Building a Futile Navy." *Atlantic Monthly,* September 1928.

Morgan, Col. Robert, USAFR, Ret., with Ron Powers. *The Man Who Flew the Memphis Belle: Memoir of a World War II Bomber Pilot.* New York: Penguin Books, 2001.

Morison, Samuel Eliot. *History of United States Naval Operations in World War II.* Edison, NJ: Castle Books, 2001.

———. *Old Bruin: Commodore Matthew C. Perry, 1794–1858, the American Naval Officer Who Helped Found Liberia.* Boston: Little, Brown and Company, 1967.

Nelson, Craig. *The First Heroes: The Extraordinary Story of the Doolittle Raid — America's First World War II Victory.* New York: Viking, 2002.

Nielson, Chase. Testimony before U.S. Military Commission, Shanghai, China, February 27, 1946.

Nihon no kushu. Vol. 3. Edited by Katsumoto Saotome. Tokyo: Sanseido, 1980.

Nihon no kushu. Vol. 4. Edited by Seiichi Imai. Tokyo: Sanseido, 1981.

Nuland, Sherwin B. *How We Die: Reflections on Life's Final Chapter.* New York: Vintage Books, 1995.

Pasquarella, Helena. "Moorpark Man Recalls Fateful Flight Over Japan During World War II." *Los Angeles Times,* July 22, 1993.

Perry, Matthew C. *Narrative of the Expedition of an American Squadron to the China Seas and Japan Performed in the Years 1852, 1853, and 1854, Under the Command of Commodore M. C. Perry, United States Navy, by Order of the Government of the United States.* Compiled by Francis L. Hawks. New York: D. Appleton and Company, 1857.

Philbrick, Nathaniel. *In the Heart of the Sea: The Tragedy of the Whaleship Essex.* New York: Viking, 2000.

Pyle, Ernie. *Ernie's War: The Best of Ernie Pyle's World War II Dispatches.* Edited by David Nichols. New York: Simon and Schuster, 1987.

Rhodes, Richard. *Dark Sun: The Making of the Hydrogen Bomb.* New York: Simon and Schuster, 1995.

Rixey, Col. P. M. *Japanese Camouflage: We Penetrate a Prepared Story in the Occupation of the Bonin Islands.* Private Papers of P. M. Rixey.

Röling, B. V. A., and Rüter, G. F., eds. *The Tokyo Judgment: The International Military Tribunal for the Far East (I.M.T.F.E.), 29 April 1946–12 November 1948.* Vol. 1. Amsterdam: University Press Amsterdam, 1977.

Rooney, Andrew A. *The Fortunes of War: Four Great Battles of World War II.* Boston: Little, Brown and Company, 1962.

Rougstad, Richard. "Pearl Harbor Pilot to Tibbets: 'You Did the Right Thing.'" *Sun Tzu's Newswire,* September 20, 1998.

Russell, Lord of Liverpool. *The Knights of Bushido: A Short History of Japanese War Crimes.* New York: Berkley Publishing, 1958.

Sakai, Saburo, with Marin Caidin and Fred Saito. *Samurai.* New York: E. P. Dutton, 1958.

Sampson, Paul. "An Era Ends for the 'Yankee' Isles: The Bonins and Iwo Jima Go Back to Japan, Civilians." *National Geographic,* vol. 123, no. 1 (July 1968): 127.

Schaffer, Ronald. *Wings of Judgement: American Bombing in World War II.* New York: Oxford University Press, 1985.

Schultz, Duane. P. *The Doolittle Raid.* New York: St. Martin's Press, 1988.

Shepardson, Mary. *The Bonin Islands: Pawns of Power.* C. Barbara Shepardson and Beret E. Strong. Unpublished, 1998.

Sherrod, Robert. "The Nature of the Enemy." *Time,* August 7, 1944.

Sherrod, Robert L. *History of Marine Corps Aviation in World War II*. San Rafael, CA: Presidio Press, 1980.

Sherry, Michael S. *The Rise of American Air Power: The Creation of Armageddon*. New Haven, CT: Yale University Press, 1987.

Sledge, E. B. *With the Old Breed at Peleliu and Okinawa*. New York: Oxford University Press, 1991.

Smith, Holland M., and Percy Finch. *Coral and Brass*. Nashville, TN: The Battery Press, 1989.

Stinnett, Robert B. *George Bush: His World War II Years*. Washington, DC: Brassey's, 1991.

Tanaka, Yuki. *Hidden Horrors: Japanese War Crimes in World War II*. Boulder, CO: Westview Press, 1998.

Tenney, Lester I. *My Hitch in Hell: The Bataan Death March*. Washington, DC: Brassey's, 1995.

Tibbets, Paul W. *Flight of the Enola Gay*. Columbus, OH: Mid Coast Marketing, 1989.

———. *Return of the Enola Gay*. Columbus, OH: Mid Coast Marketing, 1988.

Tocqueville, Alexis de. *Democracy in America*. Vol. 2. Translated by George Lawrence. Edited by J. P. Mayer and Max Lerner. London: Collins/Fontana Library, 1968.

Tobin, James. *Ernie Pyle's War: America's Eyewitness to World War II*. New York: The Free Press, 1998.

Toland, John. *The Rising Sun: The Decline and Fall of the Japanese Empire, 1936–1945*. New York: Random House, 1970.

"United States Strategic Bombing Survey Summary Report (Pacific War)." Washington, DC: July 1, 1946.

U.S. Senate. *Official Documents Relative to the Empire of Japan,* 32nd Congress, 1st session. Executive Document #59, Message from the President. April 12, 1852.

Vonnegut, Kurt, Jr. *Slaughterhouse-Five or the Children's Crusade*. New York: Dell, 1969.

Ward, Ian. *The Killer They Called a God*. Media Masters, 1996.

Watson, C. Hoyt. *The Amazing Story of Sergeant Jacob DeShazer*. Winona Lake, IN: Life and Light Press, 1950.

Werrell, Kenneth P. *Blankets of Fire: U.S. Bombers Over Japan During World War II.* Washington, DC: Smithsonian Institution Press, 1996.

Wheeler, Keith, and the Editors of Time-Life Books, *Bombers Over Japan.* Alexandria, VA: Time-Life Books, 1982.

———. *The Fall of Japan.* Alexandria, VA: Time-Life Books, 1983.

Wheeler, Richard. *Iwo.* New York: Lippincott and Crowell, 1980.

Wiley, Peter Booth. *Yankees in the Land of the Gods: Commodore Perry and the Opening of Japan.* New York: Viking, 1990.

Wolfe, Tom. *The Right Stuff.* New York: Bantam Books, 1980.

Woodbury, David O. "Tokyo Calling Cards." *Collier's,* April 14, 1945.

Index

About the Author

James Bradley is the author of the #1 *New York Times* bestseller *Flags of Our Fathers* and the son of one of the men who raised the American flag on Iwo Jima. The story of the events on Chichi Jima was first brought to his attention after the publication of that book and involved several years of research, travel, and writing — including a return trip to Chichi Jima with President George H. W. Bush.